1980

THE FARMER'S LAST FRONTIER

Agriculture, 1860–1897

By FRED A. SHANNON

VOLUME V

The Economic History of the United States

❦

HARPER TORCHBOOKS
Harper & Row, Publishers
New York, Evanston, and London

Foreword

WHEN this series of nine volumes on the economic history of the United States was first conceived, the nation's economy had reached a critical stage in its development. Although the shock of the depression of 1929 had been partially absorbed, the sense of bewilderment which it produced had not yet vanished, and the suffering and the bitterness of its first years were being transformed into less substantial, though still anguished, memories. Reform measures, either in operation or proposed, were being actively debated, but with less sense of urgency than earlier.

To the Editors of this series a fresh consideration of America's economic history was justified by more than the experiences of the recent past or the obscurity of the future. Rich contributions to the literature of American history had been made through cooperative series dealing with the political, social, and cultural aspects of American life. Numerous single-volume surveys of the country's economic development had been written. But, as late as the end of the fourth decade of the twentieth century, the world's foremost economic power had not yet produced an integrated, full-length, and authoritative treatment of its own economic history.

Scholarly concern with American economic history has been constantly growing during the past half century, and chairs of economic history have been established in leading universities. A more profound understanding of the role of economic forces in the nation's history has not only been developed by historians and economists, but has also won some measure of popular acceptance. The earlier thin trickle of monographs has broadened in recent years into a flood of publications. At present, such specialized studies, the many collections of documentary materials, and the mountains of government reports on different facets of American economic life, are staggering in their richness and scope.

This series has been planned to utilize these available sources in the preparation of a full-scale, balanced, cooperative, and readable survey of the growth of American economy and of its transformation from one of primitive character to world pre-eminence in industry, trade, and finance. Clearly, in nine volumes all aspects of the nation's economic life cannot be treated fully. But such a series can point the way to new fields of study and treat authoritatively, if not definitively, the main lines of economic development. Further, the series is intended to fill a present need of those professionally concerned with American economic history, to supplement the economic materials now available in general school and college histories of the United States, and finally to provide the lay reader with the fruits of American scholarship. If these objectives are attained, then the efforts which have gone into the creation of this economic history of the United States will have been amply repaid.

Contributors to the series have been chosen who have already established their competence in the particular periods they are to survey here; and they are, of course, solely responsible for the points of view or points of departure they employ. It is not intended that the series represent a school of thought or any one philosophical or theoretical position.

Professor Shannon's THE FARMER'S LAST FRONTIER, Volume V in the series, offers in a single book the most comprehensive account available of agricultural developments during the years between the outbreak of the Civil War and the close of the nineteenth century. As the title suggests, his volume stresses the rounding out of the agricultural domain and the effect of this process not only upon the farmers in the new frontier areas and agriculture elsewhere in the country, but also upon the whole economy. More than other students of agricultural history, Professor Shannon emphasizes the significant role played by soils, climate, and other natural forces in the development of American farming. At no time, however, does he forget the people who farmed America's land during this period, and the question of their welfare is in the forefront of his treatment. To this problem he relates major issues of transportation, markets, credit, and finance. Agricultural settlement, immigration, and internal migration, public land policies, advances in technology, science and agricultural education, and the part played by government, also receive full consideration. The special problems of farming in each of the country's geographic divisions are developed, and the place of agriculture in the national economy is suggestively indicated. Professor Shannon's stimulating appraisal of agrarian protest and reform and the farmers' independent ventures into politics is particularly concerned with the economic aspects of these movements. Professor Shannon is no champion of traditional views, and some of them receive challenging treatment at his hands. Particularly noteworthy are his vigorous analyses and discussions of the "safety-valve" and "agricultural ladder" theories. This volume reveals not only extensive research and freshness of viewpoint but also the author's fundamental sympathy with farm folk and his understanding of their life and problems.

THE EDITORS.

Preface

IN this volume I have not written a history of the technical advances in agriculture, though such a work for the years since 1860 is badly needed. Instead, I have tried to view the scene as the farmer saw it and to picture the farmer himself as he affected and was influenced by the world in which he worked and lived.

Before 1860 farming, for the most part, had passed beyond the subsistence phase and had become commercial. In the next forty years agriculture reached out to its last frontier within the limits of the ultimate forty-eight states. The effects of this movement, and the reactions of farmers and herdsmen to their restricted migrations when there were no longer any large new areas to occupy with any reasonable hope of success, had their influence on agriculture, and on the whole economy, throughout the nation. Without denying that other approaches to the subject have ample justification, I have chosen to leave their pursuit to other writers, in the conviction that the rounding out of the agricultural limits was fundamental to all other changes.

The bibliography contains only such items as I found most useful in my studies, and I have no further apologies for anything I included or omitted, save this one point: of the publications that have appeared since the completion of the first draft of the manuscript, I have listed only such ones as I found of service in the revision.

Much of the credit for such virtues as the book may contain must go to my coeditors, for their diligence, suggestions, and criticisms. If I have sometimes insisted on being myself, and have clung to pet crotchets, it is not for lack of abundant advice to the contrary, and I alone am to blame. Though a large number of students have assisted me in combing for facts through tons of material, not one word of their discoveries was used until I had examined it at its source and noted its context. Any errors in the book are solely my own. Of all the assistance I have received none is more appreciated than that of my wife, Edna Jones, who for thirty years has been sympathetic with the erratic time schedule and house littering of a confirmed researcher, and who in this case, as previously, has done more than her share of the work of proofreading and indexing.

FRED ALBERT SHANNON.

Champaign, Illinois
January 25, 1945

Contents

List of Illustrations

List of Figures, Graphs, and Tables

CHAPTER I

Nature and the Farmer

THE TRADITION OF INDIVIDUALISM

THE American farmer has rarely been prosperous, as his experiences in the later decades of the nineteenth century amply illustrate. Fortuitous circumstances brought occasional periods of seeming profit, or just enough of the real thing to give courage for renewed efforts. Periods of inflation, generally an accompaniment of war, stimulated the prices of agricultural products so as to induce the farmer to expand his holdings and operations. Then came the inevitable deflation of everything but mortgages. Depression and hopelessness generally settled on the farmer before they reached other economic groups, and remained there longest.

If producing for the market, the farmer was utterly dependent on many forces outside his single effort to control, yet he remained an incurable individualist. He might band with his neighbors in a log rolling, husking bee, or threshing crew, but only when this form of cooperation had proved indispensable to himself. He formed squatters' rights associations to curb the grasping activities of land speculators. He engaged in rent riots, Shaysite revolts for monetary reform, and vigilante groups to suppress horse stealing. He joined local or national parties for free land, greenbacks, free silver, railroad legislation, restrictions on bankers, brokers, and middlemen, and for myriad other minor objectives all calculated to bring back lost prosperity or create it where it never before existed. But each time an end was gained or definitely lost he slipped back into his wonted habit of dependence on himself and nature. Even the farmers' clubs, the Grange, and the Alliances, with their goals of cooperative marketing, buying, and production and their united front against political and business evils, gained relatively few consistent adherents before 1900. The organizations rose and declined with the fate of a single issue or of a very few issues of immediate economic importance.

There were varied reasons for this traditional individualism, and none was more potent than the farmer's bafflement when confronted by natural forces. He was in perpetual conflict with a climate he could not conquer and soils that he seldom understood. A local agricultural society, made up of individuals who were more prosperous, might declare that a given crop or specialty was best suited to the region. The less fortunate neighbor tried the same crop in an identical way; it failed, and he began to doubt. The most successful gentleman farmer of the area tried out a new fertilizer or method of tillage and declared it a success. Another followed his procedure and got worse crops than before. The spontaneous conclusion of the disappointed one was that book farming should be indulged in only by such persons as could afford the luxury. The most erudite agriculturist of the region tried extensive and costly methods of building up his worst fields and could not conceal his inadequate results. The jeering onlookers decided that "grandpap's" methods were as good as any. The old man never got rich, but he subsisted and he never lost his meager accumulation by newfangled experimentation.

The roll of learned pioneers who failed in their efforts at soil building is a long one. Some soils are infertile because of "a lack of normal erosion." Many Eastern fields have been called worn out that never were or could be of much account. George Washington failed in some of his experiments because he was working with soils containing properties that should have been washed out but were not.[1] No amount of muck, marl, or manure on such acres could add as much as the cost to their value. Results like these could not jar the common run of farmers from their complacent faith in providence and in their own ability to manage somehow.

[1] Charles E[dwin] Kellogg, "Development and Significance of the Great Soil Groups of the United States," U.S. Department of Agriculture, *Miscellaneous Publication* No. 229 (Washington: Government Printing Office, April, 1936), p. 15, referred to hereafter as Kellogg, "Great Soil Groups."

SOIL VARIATIONS AS AN EXPLANATION

Though individualism of this sort ran deeper than was good for its devotees, only the researches of soil scientists in recent years have shown to what a degree the infinite variety of soils, even in the same neighborhood, justified their possessors' faith in their own will to succeed regardless of the practices of others. Before 1899 even the federal agencies had learned very little about soils except for chemical and geologic data. The fact that climate and plants make soil as much as soil and climate make plants was but dimly realized, and there was no classified body of knowledge on the subject to guide either established farmers or homeseekers. A long generation later, huge portions of the Far West had not yet been mapped, and certain areas to the eastward had been no more than sampled.[2]

A federal Department of Agriculture bulletin of 1913 is eloquent testimony as to the causes of many of the perplexities, failures, and heartaches of generations of earlier farmers on many frontiers. Nearly 800 pages are devoted to an analysis of 44 land provinces, comprising 290 groups with 192 subphases and 535 series, and including 1,750 different soil types, each needing special understanding if it were to produce at its best.[3] Even this was only a very incomplete study of many areas that had been occupied by farmers before 1900. With no scientific guidance at all on so important a matter, it is small wonder that the pioneers so often sought a region topographically and climatically similar to that from which they came. Whether or not the individual had an inner feeling that there only could he succeed, the chances were badly against him when he tried something radically new to his experience. But seldom had the pioneer become thoroughly familiar with his old farm before he left it, and never did he find one that was more than superficially similar to anything in his earlier experience. Even in one small locality he might encounter a score or

[2] C[urtis] F[letcher] Marbut, *Soils of the United States* (Washington: Government Printing Office, 1935), p. 2. This is a separately paged section of O[liver] E[dwin] Baker, comp., *Atlas of American Agriculture* (Washington: Government Printing Office, 1936), referred to hereafter as Marbut, *Atlas*.

[3] Curtis F[letcher] Marbut and others, *Soils of the United States* (U.S. Department of Agriculture, Bureau of Soils, *Bulletin* No. 96, Washington: Government Printing Office, 1913), 791 pp., *passim*.

more of types of soils that were intricate mixtures of stone, gravel, sand of many qualities, loam, clay, muck, or other substance, each requiring a different treatment for successful farming.[4] More years than he generally stayed in one place were needed to try out, by empiric methods, the best crops for each portion of his farm and the best ways of producing them.

When the farmer had any expert guidance at all as to the peculiarities of his land, he received it from chemists, botanists, and especially geologists, who considered only the materials from which the soil was made. The land was looked upon as a somewhat stationary reservoir of plant food, and it was thought that a knowledge of the soil's chemical elements, and the demands made on it by a given crop, would determine what the yield would be, as well as how long this yield might be maintained. Forecasts made on such a basis generally failed, because the scientists gave no consideration to constant changes made in the soil by microorganisms, higher plant and animal life, and climate. It was in Russia, about 1870, that the study of soils began to develop into a real science,[5] but not till 1914 were the findings of the Russians printed in a language—German—that many scholars of Western Europe and America could read. In 1927 an American translation of this book [6] had a revolutionary effect on investigation in the United States.

These Russian scientists found a sound justification for the backwoodsmen's almost intuitive seeking of similarities in new locations. The new studies revealed the fact that the chemical properties of a given type of weathered rock were of less importance than climatic and biologic factors in the making of soils. Even the visible and palpable physical characteristics were largely determined by climate and plant and animal life.[7] Thus, the migrating farmer of the nineteenth century, when he sought a climate, vegetation, and soil that reminded him of the most successful experiences of his youth, was following the safest course for him. But he could not find identical conditions, and even slight deviations often left him

[4] For examples see *ibid.*, pp. 184–219; Kellogg, "Great Soil Groups," p. 9; Marbut, *Atlas,* p. 11; See also, map between pages 10 and 11, herein.

[5] Kellogg, "Great Soil Groups," p. 2.

[6] K[onstantin] D[mitrievich] Glinka, *The Great Soil Groups of the World and Their Development* (tr. from the German by C. F. Marbut, Ann Arbor: Edwards Bros., 1927), see preface by Marbut. Referred to hereafter as Glinka, *Soil Groups of the World.*

[7] Kellogg, "Great Soil Groups," pp. 2–3.

totally at a loss in his efforts at adaptation to the new land. An adequate comprehension of the problem came to the soil scientists only after they began applying the Russian methods of study. They were aided in this by the striking but not precise similarity between the Russian and the American soil belts. But the American problem became more complex as it was realized that the United States has about all kinds of soils found anywhere in the world except the Tundra of the frozen North and certain tropical varieties. This situation made necessary a special American classification.[8] Long before this was accomplished the moving agricultural frontier had come to rest. No great proportion of farmers could give up in disgust and move on to new areas when they failed to solve the problems of the old. Agricultural specialization had become fairly stabilized, and this had been accomplished mainly by lessons learned in the university of hard knocks.

SOIL CHARACTERISTICS

An adequate understanding of the difficulties of the pioneer farmers, especially in the Western areas where agricultural Indians as preceptors were rare or nonexistent, must be preceded by some knowledge of soil characteristics beyond that possessed by the pioneers themselves. Too often the homeseeker judged the soil largely by its color, but this alone is a faulty basis for selection and often is no criterion at all. Darkness of soil may suggest the presence of abundant, well-weathered humus, or it may merely be the result of inadequate drainage, unimportant mineral content, or the type of oxidation that has taken place. In an effort to simplify the complex data on soil structure and behavior, Milton Whitney has likened the soil to an animal. He attributes to it not only color, but a skeleton, tendons and muscles, colloidal linings, and systems for digestion, respiration, and circulation.

The skeleton refers to the basic material of the soil, ranging from gravel or sand, down through loam, to clay, and all the various mixtures found in most soils. Almost any wide-awake farmer could ascertain this feature. But more important, and less easily noticed,

[8] Glinka, *Soil Groups of the World*, p. ii; Gilbert Woodring Robinson, *Soils: Their Origin, Constitution, and Classification* (London: Thomas Murby & Co., 2d ed., 1936), p. 379, referred to hereafter as Robinson, *Soils;* Marbut, *Atlas*, pp. 2, 11; Kellogg, "Great Soil Groups," pp. 7, 8, 14, 22.

is the articulation of this skeleton—that is, the manner in which the grains of soil are arranged.[9] The farmers' lack of understanding of this fact caused the deterioration or ruin of many a field by preventable erosion. On sloping land, if the lower layer of the true soil is hard-packed and resists the penetration of water, there is a greater run-off during rainfall and a consequently more serious loss of the topsoil than would occur if the structure were of the crumb or nut variety, easily penetrable by the water. Terracing, contour plowing, and subsoil tiling might easily have saved these farms had their soils been understood in time. On the other hand, in the dry regions of the Great Plains, soil grouped in grains or fine crumbs has blown [10] to such an extent as to constitute a major national problem. Such soil should always have been kept under sod, but pioneers settling on it in wet-weather cycles had no way of knowing this. The colloids—protoplasm of the soil—absorb and regulate the use of the chemical plant foods and prevent them from being washed away.[11] Nineteenth-century chemists knew these attributes, but soil surveys had not made the practical adaptations for the needs of farmers. Thus, fertility was wasted where it might have been preserved or strengthened.

The digestive processes in the soil are of prime importance in the feeding of plants. Here temperature, moisture, drainage, plants, chemicals, worms, and especially microorganisms play their part. All soils contain living organisms, which assist in breaking down plant refuse into humus and also produce plant food. A careful study of soil "population" is necessary for the best utilization of each type of farm land, but this was another matter in which the nineteenth-century farmer had no guidance.[12] Depending on the soil's texture and structure, air may penetrate sometimes fifty feet or more. This air helps in the decay of vegetable refuse, in the digestion of plant food, and in the elimination of gases. In the farmers' institutes before 1900 some of the farmers learned to help this aeration by deep tiling and other forms of drainage. The cir-

[9] Milton Whitney, *Soil and Civilization* (New York: D. Van Nostrand Company, 1925), pp. 24–27; Kellogg, "Great Soil Groups," pp. 5–6.

[10] Kellogg, "Great Soil Groups," p. 6.

[11] Whitney, *Soil and Civilization*, pp. 28–29; Kellogg, "Great Soil Groups," pp. 6–7.

[12] E[dward] John Russell, *Soil Conditions and Plant Growth* (London: Longmans, Green and Co., 6th ed., 1932), pp. 376–379; Whitney, *Soil and Civilization*, pp. 30–32.

culation of water in the soil was also aided by proper drainage, but other physical conditions determine the depth to which the water capillaries will go—ranging from a few inches apparently to miles. The success of well digging depends on horizontal veins of water also.[13]

If the nineteenth-century farmer had little scientific guidance in the choice and management of his land, it is equally true that he seldom lived on it long enough to fathom its mysteries by empiric methods. The Thirteenth Census (1910) revealed 54 per cent of the farm population living on tracts they had occupied for not more than five years. There was not the remotest chance of their getting acquainted with the soil in that interval. A lifetime was hardly enough to explore the possibilities of any new type. For example, only in recent years was it found that, with heavy fertilization, pineapples could be grown in Florida; that after a few years soil parasites caused "red wilt"; and that a crop or two of Natal grass or an iron variety of cowpeas would starve out the nematodes so that pineapples could be grown anew. In the best farming regions of Europe the tendency is to cherish old soils because the family, through generations, has learned to understand them. This also helps to account for the greater acreage production of those areas.[14]

In the earlier periods, the short span of family tenure in one place could largely be explained by the existence of a vast frontier and the lure of new prospects to persons doing poorly where they were. Yet there is more truth than fancy in the hoary legend of the family that became hereditary poor mountaineers because of a broken wagon axle in a region of thin soil, while another member of the expedition lost a wheel farther on and became a rich planter because he chanced to be stopped in the black belt. Efforts have been made to explain the prosperous farmers on the basis of greater native intelligence. This may have been true in some cases, but the majority of pioneers were enterprising, though ignorant. The man who stumbled on a good farm that would yield to the methods he knew best got wealthy enough to have leisure to develop his mind, and hence he got the reputation of being originally more intelligent.

In later decades the impermanency of tenure has been more

[13] Whitney, *Soil and Civilization*, pp. 32–33.
[14] *Ibid.*, pp. 4, 6, 24, 36, 38.

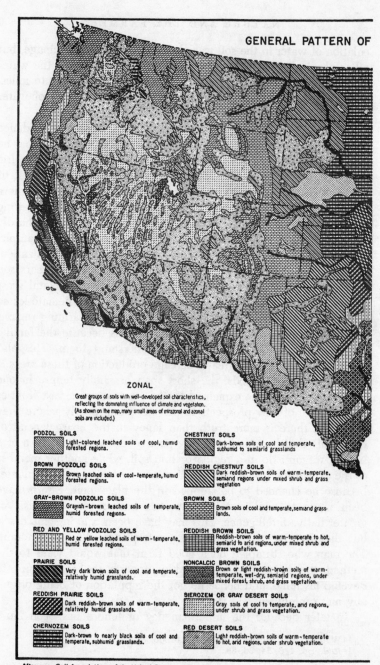

GENERAL PATTERN OF

ZONAL

Great groups of soils with well-developed soil characteristics,
reflecting the dominating influence of climate and vegetation.
(As shown on the map, many small areas of intrazonal and azonal
soils are included.)

PODZOL SOILS
Light-colored leached soils of cool, humid
forested regions.

BROWN PODZOLIC SOILS
Brown leached soils of cool-temperate, humid
forested regions.

GRAY-BROWN PODZOLIC SOILS
Grayish-brown leached soils of temperate,
humid forested regions.

RED AND YELLOW PODZOLIC SOILS
Red or yellow leached soils of warm-temperate,
humid forested regions.

PRAIRIE SOILS
Very dark brown soils of cool and temperate,
relatively humid grasslands.

REDDISH PRAIRIE SOILS
Dark reddish-brown soils of warm-temperate,
relatively humid grasslands.

CHERNOZEM SOILS
Dark-brown to nearly black soils of cool and
temperate, subhumid grasslands.

CHESTNUT SOILS
Dark-brown soils of cool and temperate,
subhumid to semiarid grasslands

REDDISH CHESTNUT SOILS
Dark reddish-brown soils of warm-temperate,
semiarid regions under mixed shrub and grass
vegetation

BROWN SOILS
Brown soils of cool and temperate, semiarid grasslands.

REDDISH BROWN SOILS
Reddish-brown soils of warm-temperate to hot,
semiarid to arid regions, under mixed shrub and
grass vegetation.

NONCALCIC BROWN SOILS
Brown or light reddish-brown soils of warm-
temperate, wet-dry, semiarid regions, under
mixed forest, shrub, and grass vegetation.

SIEROZEM OR GRAY DESERT SOILS
Gray soils of cool to temperate, arid regions,
under shrub and grass vegetation.

RED DESERT SOILS
Light reddish-brown soils of warm-temperate
to hot, arid regions, under shrub vegetation.

After map, *Soil Associations of the United States*, published in *Soils and Men*, Yearbook of Agriculture for 1938

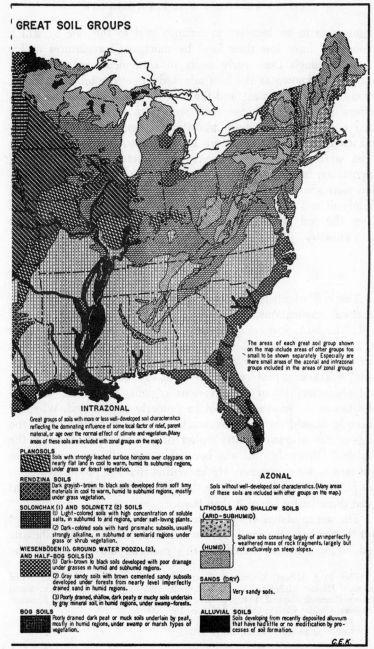

GREAT SOIL GROUPS

The areas of each great soil group shown on the map include areas of other groups too small to be shown separately. Especially are there small areas of the azonal and intrazonal groups included in the areas of zonal groups.

INTRAZONAL

Great groups of soils with more or less well-developed soil characteristics reflecting the dominating influence of some local factor of relief, parent material, or age over the normal effect of climate and vegetation. (Many areas of these soils are included with zonal groups on the map.)

PLANOSOLS
Soils with strongly leached surface horizons over claypans on nearly flat land in cool to warm, humid to subhumid regions, under grass or forest vegetation.

RENDZINA SOILS
Dark grayish-brown to black soils developed from soft limy materials in cool to warm, humid to subhumid regions, mostly under grass vegetation.

SOLONCHAK (1) AND SOLONETZ (2) SOILS
(1) Light-colored soils with high concentration of soluble salts, in subhumid to arid regions, under salt-loving plants.
(2) Dark-colored soils with hard prismatic subsoils, usually strongly alkaline, in subhumid or semiarid regions under grass or shrub vegetation.

WIESENBÖDEN (1), GROUND WATER PODZOL (2), AND HALF-BOG SOILS (3)
(1) Dark-brown to black soils developed with poor drainage under grasses in humid and subhumid regions.
(2) Gray sandy soils with brown cemented sandy subsoils developed under forests from nearly level imperfectly drained sand in humid regions.
(3) Poorly drained, shallow, dark peaty or mucky soils underlain by gray mineral soil, in humid regions, under swamp-forests.

BOG SOILS
Poorly drained dark peat or muck soils underlain by peat, mostly in humid regions, under swamp or marsh types of vegetation.

AZONAL

Soils without well-developed soil characteristics. (Many areas of these soils are included with other groups on the map.)

LITHOSOLS AND SHALLOW SOILS (ARID-SUBHUMID)

(HUMID)
Shallow soils consisting largely of an imperfectly weathered mass of rock fragments, largely but not exclusively on steep slopes.

SANDS (DRY)
Very sandy soils.

ALLUVIAL SOILS
Soils developing from recently deposited alluvium that have had little or no modification by processes of soil formation.

C.E.K.

Division of Soil Survey, Bureau of Plant Industry, U. S. D. A.

largely due to an increase in tenancy and to the rate at which freeholders have lost their land by mortgage foreclosures or for taxes. Although from early years of settlement certain regions came to be known as the best adapted to cotton, tobacco, wheat, general farming, grazing, and the like, the great majority of enterprisers in each region have done well to make a bare living, and their tenure has often been transitory. Unsolved problems of the soil itself, in the pioneering era before the subhumid lands of the West were occupied by farmers, were factors of overwhelming importance in producing this situation. The problems of the settlers were always different on each new frontier. They were puzzles mainly of soil in the East and of climate and soil in the West.[15] Even the soil perplexities of the East were inextricably linked with climate.

THE GREAT SOIL GROUPS: EASTERN

The soil scientists do not exaggerate when they connect "the practical implications of a knowledge of the great soil regions" with "the biological complex, and . . . human institutions." [16] Nor is it a strained concept to suppose that the "prairie region" or any other is "one of the areas that has stimulated changes in culture." [17] The next problem, therefore, is to note some of the origins and characteristics of these various regions. Otherwise, the perplexities of the pioneers cannot be properly appreciated. Why, for example, should the frontiersman take up an inferior farm at the edge of the wooded country rather than risk crop failures on the Prairies? Obviously, this was because a naturally treeless expanse was new to his experience. He knew that rich soil produced luxuriant plants, but could not realize that plants also made soil, and that grass did a better job of it than trees.

The accumulated stone particles produced by erosion are not soil, but merely the stuff from which true soil is made. Climatic and biologic factors transform this material into something the

[15] See Fred A[lbert] Shannon and others, *Critiques of Research in the Social Sciences: III* (Social Science Research Council, *Bulletin* No. 46, New York: Social Science Research Council, 1940), p. 37 *et circa*, referred to hereafter as Shannon, *Critiques;* Charles Carlyle Colby, *ibid.,* pp. 158–160.

[16] Kellogg, "Great Soil Groups," p. 1.

[17] Colby, in Shannon, *Critiques,* p. 159.

farmer can use. Yet, actual soil is not necessary to the fostering of all kinds of plant life; otherwise, soil could not have been created. For that matter, many alluvial deposits are only mixtures of various raw materials, yet are more productive than neighboring mature soils.[18] But it is quickly noted that undeveloped alluvium is only a very small part of the earth's surface that supports a human population of more than two billion.

Climate plays the most important role in the making of soil: first, because different kinds of weathering produce varying sorts of source material; and second, because climate determines the biologic processes that create true soil. The natural vegetation in the more humid regions is likely to be trees, in the less watered places tall grass, in subhumid areas short grass, and in arid localities a varying assortment of tenacious vegetation, each performing a special function in soil building, different from all others. Deciduous trees may put more organic material on top of the ground than do some grasses, but this happens in a climate where decomposition takes place so rapidly that less humus is left in the soil than is to be found in the grassy Prairies. On the other hand, grasses feed more on the calcium of the lower strata and transfer more of it into the soil than do the trees. Grasses also produce sodium colloids, thus affecting soil structure. Such organisms as fungi, bacteria, and the higher forms of animals that decompose vegetable matter are also regulated by the climate. Furthermore, the leaching process, so important in soil maturing, is affected by the relationship of rainfall to temperature. If the bulk of the annual precipitation comes in the hottest season, less leaching takes place than occurs when the heavy rainfall is at temperatures closer to the freezing point.[19]

On the basis of climate the specialists have divided the soils of the United States into two large groups—humid and subhumid to arid. The dividing line runs through western Minnesota, a small corner of northwestern Iowa, eastern Nebraska, central-eastern Kansas, central Oklahoma, and down through central-eastern Texas, approximately to the mouth of the Nueces River, or Corpus Christi.[20] This line approximates the ninety-sixth meridian, though

[18] Kellogg, "Great Soil Groups," pp. 16, 29; Marbut, *Atlas*, pp. 1, 11.
[19] Glinka, *Soil Groups of the World*, pp. 7, 36–39; Kellogg, "Great Soil Groups," pp. 10–13.
[20] Robinson, *Soils*, p. 380. See, also, the line between Prairie soils and Chernozem in map on page 12, herein.

no such fine discrimination between humid and subhumid areas could be made with any degree of seriousness. This division causes some confusion or uncertainty, because it places the Prairie soils in the eastern group, though in various important ways they have more resemblance to their nearest neighbor to the westward. Because of this interzonal difficulty, it seems best for the time being to refer to three groups—humid, Prairie, and subhumid to arid. Most persons will no doubt be satisfied with the terms Eastern, Prairie, and Western soils.

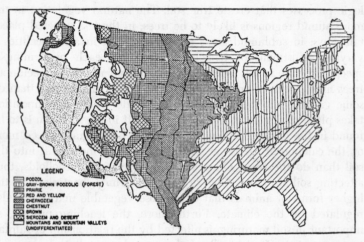

General Distribution of the Important Zonal Groups of Soils in the United States. (U.S. Dept. of Agriculture, *Misc. Pub.* 229.)

The Eastern ones are divided into three distinct zones. Much of northern Minnesota, Wisconsin, Michigan, Vermont, and New Hampshire, most of Maine, and an area in northern New York comprise the Podzol (grayish, ashlike) group. These soils developed with plentiful rainfall and mainly under coniferous forests—conditions that caused most of the plant-food chemicals to be leached out, deteriorated the colloids, and left the soil acid. This region has been useful mainly to the lumberman, and he has left it mostly denuded.

The next belt, extending from the Podzols down to southern Virginia, western North Carolina, southern Tennessee except the western end, and northern Arkansas, is the Gray-Brown Podzolic region, which is the most heavily populated portion of the Western Hemisphere and contains most of the centers of its culture. The soils, having sufficient rainfall and a moderate climate and having developed under deciduous forests, are much better adapted to general farming than are the Podzols, though they are much poorer in fertility than some of the regions to their west. The hardwood forests have returned more bases to the soil than have the conifers to the northward, though less than the grasses of the Prairies and

COLD DRY						COLD WET
TUNDRA						
NORTHERN DESERT	NORTHERN SIEROZEM	NORTHERN BROWN	NORTHERN CHESTNUT	NORTHERN CHERNOZEM	NORTHERN PRAIRIE	PODZOL
MIDDLE DESERT	MIDDLE SIEROZEM	MIDDLE BROWN	MIDDLE CHESTNUT	MIDDLE CHERNOZEM	MIDDLE PRAIRIE	GRAY-BROWN PODZOLIC / RED AND YELLOW
RED DESERT	SOUTHERN SIEROZEM	SOUTHERN BROWN	SOUTHERN CHESTNUT	SOUTHERN CHERNOZEM	SOUTHERN PRAIRIE	LATERITE
HOT DRY						HOT WET

Relative Positions of the Important Zonal Groups of Soils. Of these, Tundra and Laterite are not found in the United States. By comparing this sketch with the map on page 12 showing the distribution of the zonal groups in the United States it will be noted that the progression from right to left is interrupted by the mountains. (U.S. Dept. of Agriculture, *Misc. Pub.* 229.)

the Great Plains. The soils are slightly acid, but, because of their more plentiful rainfall, with some lime and fertilizer and other features of good farming, they can be made to produce better than some of the richer but subhumid soils.

The Southern group of the Eastern soils, with exceptions, some of which are shown on the map, are of the Red and Yellow variety. Like the Gray-Brown class, they have undergone leaching and acidulation, but under a different kind of original weathering of the parent rock, like that of the tropical Laterites.[21] This is the great region of Southern staple farming, though sugar cane has been

[21] Kellogg, "Great Soil Groups," pp. 19–22.

grown almost exclusively on alluvium. Since most of these Eastern soils were farmed and their possibilities noted in an empiric way before 1860, they will not be considered further in this treatment.

THE GREAT SOIL GROUPS: WESTERN

The richest of all the great soil zones, lying roughly between the ninety-sixth and one hundredth meridians, is the black soil (Chernozem)—the ideal of comparison for all other groups. Even the rare and unrelated patches of unusually rich soils in the East are rated by the same standard. But in between the leached Eastern soils and the Chernozems are the Prairie soils which, though not quite so fertile as the Chernozems, are, because of their greater rainfall, even more productive. As Van Hise has said, this "is the garden of the United States; it is the very heart of the country . . . . [with] by far the largest percentage of improved lands of any states in the Union . . . ."[22] It was this region into which the pioneers were flocking in the years before the Civil War, but which they had by no means fully occupied by 1860. It was from and through this same region that restless land seekers were to push, after all the desirable portions of the Prairies were engrossed, for the remainder of the century and until the last agricultural frontiers of the nation had been peopled.

Recent soil maps and descriptions have stressed the north-south direction of the Prairie and Great Plains zones and, in general, of the areas west of the Rocky Mountains as well, as compared with the east-west arrangement in the East. But dissatisfaction with this view has already been expressed,[23] and some investigators have begun to distinguish between northern, middle, and southern phases of every great soil group from the Prairies to the Pacific.[24] Perhaps it was an oversimplification in the first place to divide the whole country into only two great rainfall sections. It would be just as feasible and much more intelligible to mark out several humidity belts: abundant to excessive in the East; ample for all

[22] Charles Richard Van Hise, *The Conservation of Natural Resources in the United States* (New York: The Macmillan Company, printing of 1917), p. 272.

[23] For example, Colby, in Shannon, *Critiques*, p. 149.

[24] This is well brought out in "Soils of the United States," *Soils & Men* (U.S. Department of Agriculture, *Yearbook of Agriculture*, 1938, Washington: Government Printing Office, 1938?), pp. 1019–1161, and especially pp. 1052–1057, 1075–1101.

ordinary purposes in the Prairies; scanty but sufficient for spring or very hardy crops in the Chernozems of the eastern part of the Great Plains; insufficient except for grazing or occasional dry farming in the Chestnut soils of the western portions of the Plains; too scanty for any but large-scale dry farming, unless irrigated, but generally suited only to large ranching operations in the Brown soils of the Great Basin; too arid for anything but huge ranches and occasional irrigation in the Sierozem and Desert soils from Idaho to western Arizona and southeastern Arizona.

Just as in the humid East the soil zones show varying degrees of leaching and acidulation from extreme northern to extreme southern latitudes, so in each of the soil belts to the westward there is a difference between northern, middle, and southern phases. These latitudinal distinctions seem to be based on different temperature ranges in the soil-building processes, just as the longitudinal categories are founded on precipitation. Thus it would seem that a combined moisture and temperature approach will have to be employed in the study of any region, and the contrast between horizontal zones in the East and vertical zones in the West might just as well be abandoned. The only difference is that the longitudinal extent of the abundant-to-excessive-rainfall area is somewhat greater than that of any one of the successive Western regions, thus giving a verisimilitude rather than a reality to the contrast.

The Prairie soils, starting from an apex in extreme northwestern Indiana, extend in a wide, rough V till the legs reach the Chernozems in northwestern Minnesota and southern Texas. There are also some detached portions in southern Texas and Louisiana, and a similar crescent-shaped black belt (actually a different soil) in Alabama and Mississippi.[25] These Prairie soils, still somewhat of a mystery to the experts, are apparently not to be found outside the United States, though some rather small spots of similar features exist in Russia and elsewhere under the name of degraded Chernozems. The Prairie soils, like the Chernozems, were developed under grass but, apparently, with rainfall adequate for a more luxuriant vegetation. The grass has brought enough calcium to the top layer to sustain the colloids and prevent noticeable acidity, but there is

[25] E[ugene] W. Hilgard, *Soils: Their Formation, Properties, Composition, and Relations to Climate and Plant Growth in the Humid and Arid Regions* (New York: The Macmillan Company, 1906), p. 53, referred to hereafter as Hilgard, *Soils;* Marbut, *Atlas,* Plate II, between pp. 14, 15.

no accumulation of calcium carbonate in the subsoil as in the
Chernozems. Therefore the leaching process of the Eastern areas
seems to have been operating. There is some evidence to support
the theory that the soil is in process of becoming more leached,
that acid will accumulate, and that if it had been untilled the forests
would ultimately creep over the region, creating the same sort of
Gray-Brown podzolic soil found to the eastward. In Europe there
are some areas that have undergone this change, and some of the
forest soils of Wisconsin seem once to have been Prairie. On the
other hand, it is contended, natural erosion could make the grass
roots continually reach down to the lower calcium substratum, thus
continuing the Prairies indefinitely in their old status.

The break between forested and grass land is usually rather
abrupt, though there is no noticeable difference on either side of
the line in any of t'.e physical factors that usually determine the
type of vegetation.[26] It may well be that Prairie soils abound only
in the United States because the change from humid to dry regions
is more gradual than it is in other countries that have been studied
intensively. Perhaps the sudden break between tree land and Prairie
is merely the forest front gradually encroaching on the grass. Certainly man has made many kinds of trees grow abundantly on the
Prairies, and even farther west. Furthermore, farmers have so thoroughly cleared the once-forested land that what might have been
detected as an encroachment on the grassland has long since been
removed from observance. The mystery of the sudden break is even
easier than this. The tall grass of the Prairies, with its heavy mat of
fallen material and its thick tangle of roots, is an effective shield
against the sprouting of fallen seeds of trees, and the first deep
ravine would cut expansion by root sprouts. Again, frequent Prairie
fires could act as a check against the slightly inflammable deciduous
forests that bordered the grasslands. The autumn fires would kill
off the sprouts, but the grass would spring up again from its roots.
On the other hand, trees grow along the banks of streams clear out
into the Great Plains. There the soils are alluvial, in contrast with
their dominant neighbors, and are less adapted to grass ascendancy.

But, all mysteries aside, this dark, humus-filled, base-saturated
Prairie soil kept prudent farmers solvent even during the period

[26] Robinson, Soils, pp. 251–252, 254; Kellogg, "Great Soil Groups," pp. 14, 17–18
21; Marbut, Atlas, p. 62; Glinka, Soil Groups of the World, p. 121.

of agricultural distress following 1920, and that is saying a great deal. It has been shown by experimentation that the mere acts of breaking and cultivating Prairie soils tend to exhaust them of nitrogen, altogether independent of the amount removed by the crops,[27] but this matter is easily remedied by the raising of occasional crops of soybeans, clover, or other legumes. The various types of the soil generally retain moisture well, will grow any of a great variety of crops, and are unexcelled for corn.[28]

The Chernozems of the lower Great Plains, extending across the United States from North Dakota to Texas, were developed under slightly less than medium rainfall.[29] Their formation requires dry, hot summers and cold winters, a sufficiency of tall grass, such as the blue-stem, to produce humus and tap the subsoil for calcium, and an absence of trees or other covering that would protect the soil from extreme climatic conditions. Such soils are found in various other parts of the globe, and everywhere they are adapted to wheat growing, furnishing the bulk of the world's supply of bread. The rich layer of calcium and magnesium carbonates, brought up and fixed by the grasses, in turn produces still more abundant coverage to continue the process. The humus from herbage remains in the soil, as do the minerals, and the result is the richest soil the world can show. But even here there is some difference between the northern, middle, and southern varieties. Under the more protracted heat of the southern areas, the Chernozem is not as black as that of the North.[30] Ironically enough, the same climatic conditions that produce this soil also limit its use. Farms of less than a full section (a square mile) are hardly profitable, but with modern machinery a man and a good-sized boy can manage that much—a little extra help being needed in the harvest and threshing season where combines are not used. Social cooperation and community life among the farmers are probably not as well developed as in the Prairies, but the greater distances between homes add to the degree of sociability shown to the less frequent visitors.

The next region, extending out to the Rocky Mountains and, with some interruption, even into parts of Arizona, is that of the

[27] Russell, *Soil Conditions and Plant Growth*, p. 360.
[28] Marbut and others, *Soils of the United States*, pp. 158–159.
[29] Glinka, *Soil Groups of the World*, pp. 109–121.
[30] *Ibid.*; Russell, *Soil Conditions and Plant Growth*, p. 274; Kellogg, "Great Soil Groups," p. 18

Chestnut soils. As the High Plains approach, even the black Cherno-zem begins to fade and, as the higher and drier levels are reached, it merges into the Chestnut zone. This is the short-grass country, grama and the low, curling buffalo grass predominating.[31] This herbage furnishes less of humus and minerals than the tall grasses of the lower Plains, but a still lower rate of water erosion leaves a soil comparing in fertility with that of the Prairies. The rainfall, however, is so scanty and the evaporation rate so high that the major part of the region is suitable only for grazing. Wheat farming is carried on extensively in the wetter cycles of years, but even under dry-farming methods the experiment is often hazardous. Cultivation and excessive pasturing have subjected the area to frightful wind erosion, thus creating the notorious "dust bowl," though this term should be applied only to a minor portion of the whole region. Even on the Brown soils of the Great Basin some wheat is grown, but, except in especially favored spots, it has been found best merely to utilize the excellent, short, native grasses for grazing on a range basis. The Sierozems, still less fertile, are also useful for pasture if not more than one animal is allowed for each fifty or a hundred acres.

Last come the Desert soils, which even in the more fertile spots are so arid that thinly scattered grazing is hazardous.[32] In general the white man has relegated the poorest of Great Basin soils, that will support human life at all, to the Indians for reservations. How a sheep can pick a living off a hundred acres in the Navajo reserva-tion is a mystery to tourists. Perhaps this stimulates the buying of blankets and turquoise-studded silver ornaments from the post trader, in the hope that the Indian craftsmen will get a fair share of the proceeds.

This discussion of the great soil groups, of course, simplifies the whole problem, but it is justified by the dominance of the given classification in its region. For one thing, the whole mountain and mountain valley areas of the West, as well as the Pacific coast, have such diversified soils that no large grouping has seemed possible. In any of the other plateau or excessively hilly places the effects of erosion leave a succession of thin and rich spots, the less fertile

[31] Kellogg, "Great Soil Groups," p. 19; H[omer] L. Shantz and Raphael Zon, *Natural Vegetation* (Washington: Government Printing Office, 1924, in *Atlas of American Agriculture*), map on pp. 4–5.
[32] Kellogg, "Great Soil Groups," p. 19.

being the larger. Various glaciated areas, for example eastern
Massachusetts, present large tracts so scoured free of soil that a
goat would prefer to pass them up in search of pasturage, interspersed with smaller filled-in spots of high fertility. The flood plains
of all rivers differ from the neighboring higher ground. The swampy
lands and pine barrens, so unescapable in the South Atlantic coastal
plain, might as well be said to have no soil at all. Then there are
various intrazonal soils which are determined more largely on the
basis of relief and drainage than by the climatic factors that built
the dominant soils of the surrounding regions.[33] Finally, the multi-
tudinous types, based on texture, within a large classification must
not be neglected. The farmer who did ignore them was likely to
come to grief.

NATURAL FORCES OTHER THAN SOIL

Though it would be difficult to overemphasize the soil factor
from place to place, the migrant farmer was often more immediately aware of other phenomena. These included topographic relief, rainfall and other precipitation; temperature, the length of the
growing season, the abundance or scarcity of building materials and
natural shelter for livestock; the native food supply, the amount of
time and toil needed to get enough land in shape to produce subsistence, the problem of an adequate water supply for the family
and the livestock; the topography as it might affect transportation;
and the chance of survival in the struggle with strange Indian
tribes, wild animals, and endemic diseases. Only gradually did he,
if ever, become conscious of other natural differences like evaporation rates, or understand new blights, parasites, and other obscure
pests afflicting plants and animals. Certain of these factors gave
little worry to the pioneer, with his resistless urge to seek new experiences. His was not the nature of the "cracker" who shook with
ague for eighty years in the swamps of Florida but would not move
out for fear of encountering unhealthful surroundings. His judg-
ment of topography rested on that which pleased the farm-seeking
eye. He knew some Indian herbs that were a specific for every
calamity from shingles to a broken leg. If accompanied by a sufficient number of other settlers, he was willing to match his wits

[33] *Ibid.*, pp. 23–29; Hilgard, *Soils*, pp. 422–484.

against the Indians. He regarded dangerous animals highly. They
were usually sources of food or of skins for clothing and trade.

Whether his new home was in the forests or on the Prairies and
Plains, a vital consideration was the matter of a native vegetable
and meat supply for subsistence till adequate crops could be raised.
There was likely to be sufficient game in either environment, though
the varieties on the relatively treeless areas might be a little more
difficult to procure. The woodsman needed a longer time for clearing land than the Prairie farmer did for eradicating sod, but the
forests rendered this fact tolerable with a greater assortment of
edible vegetation, and thus something like a balance was maintained.

In either environment the matters of temperature and the length
of the growing season often had but a casual relationship to lati-
tude—a fact that might well mystify the pioneer. For instance, the
line that separates the region where the last killing frost is likely
to occur in April from that in which this happens in May is anything but a straight east-to-west affair. Instead, it runs in a south-
westerly direction from eastern Massachusetts to the western part
of North Carolina, then bends northward again into southern Ohio
and on to northern Illinois, after which it drops southwestward to
central New Mexico. On the other hand, much of the Great Lakes
shore line from Milwaukee to South Bend and in Ohio and New
York enjoys an equal freedom from late frost, though a wide belt
may separate those areas from the larger zone to the south. The
same sort of immunity extends in a narrow strip along the Mississippi River well up toward Minneapolis.[34] Great bodies of water
tend to ameliorate temperature along their shores far more than
they regulate rainfall. Thus, Columbus, Ohio, is likely to have later
spring frosts than Cleveland, and Chicago has the advantage over
points many miles to its southward. A line of first killing frosts in
the fall favors the same regions in about the same way, thus fixing
a division between the number of frostless days, or the growing
season.[35]

As to rainfall, evaporation, building materials, water supply,
and transportation perplexities, the problems tended to become

[34] William Gardner Reed, *Climate: Frost and the Growing Season* (Washington:
Government Printing Office, 1918, in *Atlas of American Agriculture*), map on
pp. 30–31.
[35] *Ibid.*, maps on pp. 34–35, 38–39.

more complex the farther west the farmer went, but there was no line of sudden break between the East and the West. The river bottoms, all through the Prairies, had timber enough for all ordinary building needs in the earlier years, but it had to be hauled to the place of use. In most of that region there was wood enough even for fences. Furthermore, barbed wire had been invented and had become attractively cheap before farmers had so filled the Prairies that many—in the late 1880's—were tempted out to the still less-wooded Great Plains.[36] As the agricultural frontier moved westward, the settler had the opportunity to adjust himself to the new situation, unless he moved an exceedingly long distance, without any sudden departure from old customs and methods.

Transportation, too, became increasingly difficult. Although the East was better supplied with rivers than the West, not many of them, even in the East, were navigable to any distance by steamboats. Among the greatest of them all, for transportation, were the Mississippi and the Missouri, which ran right through the Prairies. In fact, the Missouri was for decades navigated by steamboats out to the western limits of the Great Plains. For example, the town of Manhattan, Kansas, on one of the tributaries, was founded by persons headed farther west whose steamboat burned at that spot. On the other hand, in the wooded region of northern Ohio and Indiana agriculture could not be put on a commercial basis, in spite of rivers flowing into the Great Lakes, until in 1825 an artificial outlet, the Erie Canal, made Eastern markets accessible. Even then the local rivers were so inadequate that they had to be further supplemented by canals, and finally by railroads, before farming could be fully developed. A similar condition prevailed in the Prairies of Illinois. As the grasslands of that region were made more useful by the Illinois Central railroad following 1850, so were many areas farther to the East, as well as to the West. Even in those parts of the Great Plains where water transportation could be only incidental and occasional, numerous railroads were being built by the time a moving agricultural population found the Plains to be the next probable frontier. Without doubt, this lure of facile transportation induced thousands to take their plows to land that should have been left an open range. Certainly, agricultural settlement

[36] Shannon, *Critiques*, pp. 81, 86–87.

was not deterred more than was for the best by the scantiness of transportation agencies.

The story of water supply is about the same. In the East the people did not dig wells when they could carry water from springs, and this natural source was also found in many parts of the Prairies, as well as occasionally in the Plains. The greatest artesian basins in the United States are in restricted localities of the Great Plains.[37] Still, as in the East, most Prairie farmers had to depend on wells for the family water supply. In general the farther west one went the deeper the wells had to be dug or drilled. But the supply, when found, was usually constant unless abnormal demands were made on it. Here, as in other matters, the problem became intensified gradually with western longitude, and the pioneers had no violent adjustments to make unless they took unusually long jumps to their new homes. Migration, however, was generally within the state or merely over the line into the next state or territory.[38] The occasional family that came from afar could either rely on the advice of its neighbors, in this as well as in other things, or suffer violent change, or abandon the struggle. Even on the major part of the Great Plains there were plenty of through-flowing and constant streams for the water needs of the range-grazing economy to which the region was in all respects best adapted, and not till the later 1890's did the plow farmer, as a dynamic force in the region, begin to depend on windmills.[39] Still farther west, in the Mountain valleys and arid Great Basin, the water puzzle could be solved either by irrigation or, in the vastly greater areas where this was not possible, by an open-range grazing economy on an attenuated scale. Where irrigation was feasible, intensive farming could be practiced. Elsewhere the herbage was so sparse that the occasional water holes were sufficient, and they could often be supplemented, at considerable expense, by deep wells, windmills, and tanks.[40]

The problem of rainfall and evaporation, which both underlay and overshadowed so many other factors, again was one of increasing intensity as the agricultural frontier pushed westward.

[37] *Ibid.*, pp. 92–93.

[38] Fred A[lbert] Shannon, "'The Homestead Act and the Labor Surplus," *American Historical Review*, XLI, No. 4 (July, 1936), 645–646.

[39] Shannon, *Critiques*, p. 89.

[40] For example, see Will[iam] C[roft] Barnes, *The Story of the Range* (Washington: Government Printing Office, 1926), pp. 29–30.

Nowhere was there an abrupt break except where mountains intervened to give additional precipitation to small areas detached from the greater surrounding region. Quite often, even these tracts were of such difficult access as to delay for many years their utilization. For the major part of the West even a few inches' difference in average annual rainfall has a pronounced effect on the kind of crop that can be grown or the type of grazing that can be followed, but these belts shade gradually into each other, allowing opportunity for adjustment of farming practices. It is well enough for a rainfall map of the United States to show gradations by ten-inch steps for the eastern part, but this will not satisfy for the West.[41] Even in portions of the East there are regions where occasional protracted drouth disturbs the ordinary routine of agricultural economy, and in the Middle West, even before the Prairies are reached, adjustments have had to be made in crop specialization because of frequently recurrent drouth. And thus the problem becomes more acute until the difference in precipitation must be reckoned in stages of 5 inches or less. "Dry farming can flourish where the rainfall approaches 20 inches, but it is hopeless where the 10–inch limit is approximated. Even the kind and quality of grass varies greatly in the 10–20–inch limits." [42]

If Western rainfall came mainly in the colder seasons, agriculture would be much more rigorously limited than is actually the case. But, since most of it occurs in the spring and summer, when it can penetrate more deeply and be ready for immediate use, scanty enough as the rainfall is even then, it is still enough to keep the major part of the western half of the United States from being actually desert. But rainfall, even that of the planting and growing season, is not a full criterion of needs. Loose, deep, gravelly soils, where water quickly sinks below the roots of plants, and hard-packed, impervious soils, where most of the water runs off immediately, need a heavier precipitation throughout the year than do friable, loamy soils, rich in humus and mineral colloids. The twelve-inch cloudburst at Burlington, Kansas, late in May, 1941,

[41] The best maps are in J[oseph] B[urton] Kincer, *Climate: Precipitation and Humidity* (Washington: Government Printing Office, 1922, in *Atlas of American Agriculture*), pp. 6–7, 10–11, 18–19, 22–23, 26–27, 30–31, referred to hereafter as Kincer, *Precipitation and Humidity*.

[42] Shannon, *Critiques*, p. 21.

for example, was a large fraction of the year's total, but it was disastrous in its effects.

Also, elevation and longitude affect the thinness and dryness of the air, and this, in connection with variations in temperature, sunshine, and wind,[43] determines the evaporation rate, which is also influenced by the nature of vegetable growth, whether native or cultivated. Since the actual amount of evaporation from any piece of land is almost impossible to determine, all maps are based on evaporation from an open vat.[44] On this reckoning, evaporation, especially in the more arid, hot Southwest, is often much higher than the total amount of precipitation, which is clearly absurd except for purposes of comparison with other regions. Recent studies of rainfall and evaporation, involving atmospheric pressure, vapor tension, and temperature, have resulted in the creation of a mathematical formula for precipitation divided by evaporation, known as the P-E (precipitation-evaporation) quotient—more useful than previous calculations.[45] No information of this sort was available for the pioneers of the West. In fact, almost always in the past the specialists in geography, ecology, and soil science have carried on their researches ignorant or careless of what the others were discovering, and unaware of the causal relationship that exists between climate, soil, and vegetation.[46] Moreover, the historian has generally insulated himself from all the scientists.

FARMERS' ADJUSTMENTS TO NEW SURROUNDINGS

With all these differences between the sections, it cannot be imagined that pioneering was always the same in the East, and that no lessons learned there had any applicability to the West. It is true that the farmer who made the long jump from humid to arid surroundings found that much of his previous experience was of little use, but he was the exception in the generality of his

[43] The best temperature maps are in Joseph B[urton] Kincer, Climate: Temperature, Sunshine, and Wind (Washington: Government Printing Office, 1928, in Atlas of American Agriculture), 34 pp.

[44] Kincer, Precipitation and Humidity, p. 48.

[45] C[harles] Warren Thornthwaite, "The Climates of North America according to a New Classification," The Geographical Review, XXI, No. 4 (October, 1931), 635–637, map p. 642.

[46] Ibid., p. 655. Climate and Man, the Department of Agriculture Yearbook for 1941, devotes 1,248 pages to this subject.

neighbors. Nor is it to be supposed that drouth, plagues, devastating hailstorms, and overproduction in good years to provide for the bad were wholly peculiar to the West. Agricultural history is full of instances to the contrary.[47] From frontier to frontier, from the tidewater to the piedmont, on into the Appalachian valleys and plateaus, out in the Ohio Valley, on into the Prairies, venturing ever westward over the Great Plains, in the Rocky Mountain valleys and parks, and finally into actual desert conditions in the Great Basin, the frontiersman's experiences were always new and always different. He had to make adjustments of old knowledge to new surroundings. His institutions and his ways of life had to undergo alterations. Inasmuch as the West was occupied much more rapidly than the East, these changes came about more suddenly and with greater violence. But this was the last great rush of a population that had been growing by geometric ratio, to occupy what was left and usable of the government domain. Herein lies the explanation for any abrupt institutional break that may be found when the Far West is reached. At a time when population was clambering to its zenith of growth, when free enterprise and rugged individualism were rushing on toward maturity and eclipse, when the horizon of free land was already in view, it was only to be expected that institutions would have to make more sudden changes in the wild scramble for the occupation of the farmer's last frontier.

[47] See references in Shannon, *Critiques*, pp. 38–39.

CHAPTER II

Agricultural Settlement in
New Areas

OUTLYING SETTLED REGIONS IN 1860

THE movement of population to new lands after 1860 was largely
along lines drawn before that time, and to a great degree was
merely a further spreading out over already partially settled areas.
Even to the 1940's there was a comparatively small number of
persons tilling soil in regions wholly untouched by the hoe or plow
eighty years earlier. Yet, although there were dotted settlements in
the Spanish borderlands, around the Great Salt Lake, and in the
mining regions of the Rocky Mountains and the Great Basin, in
1860 an area which was half of the United States, and which lay
between the Pacific coast settlements and the Western frontier of
the Prairie farms, contained only 1 per cent of the nation's population. Roughly speaking, the ninety-fifth meridian separated the
regions containing from two to six persons to the square mile from
the territory occupied mainly by unenumerated Indians. In Texas
the settled portion reached about to the ninety-eighth meridian,
and in northeastern Kansas and southeastern Nebraska the ninety-
seventh was touched, but on the other hand there was an almost
total lack of population north of the forty-fifth parallel in Minnesota and Wisconsin, and north of the forty-fourth in Michigan.[1]
Down to 1900 the population frontier of two or more to the square

[1] Fred Albert Shannon, *America's Economic Growth* (New York: The Macmillan Company, 1940), p. 356, and map p. 139.

mile had reached only slightly on to the Great Plains from Texas to North Dakota, leaving much of the western portions of that tier of states relatively unoccupied. Westward of this line the map was blotched and speckled with isolated areas of two or more persons to the square mile, but even as late as 1930 there were large spots on the Plains and vast areas in the Western mountains and Great Basin that were almost as devoid of population as in 1860.[2]

Although, following 1860, an increasing percentage of the total population of the United States moved out into the hitherto almost uninhabited half of the nation, a good proportion of the number was engaged in livestock herding, mining, or commerce or labor in the towns and cities mainly dependent on and serving the herdsmen and miners. The expansion of soil tillage was slow before 1900, and has never become great, except for the wheat belt, as compared with the growing density of farming population in the older sections. Maps showing six or more persons to the square mile are more likely to reveal the frontier of plow farming than those ranging downward to two. On the basis of greater density, the maps already cited will show that to 1900 (or even 1930) much larger portions of the great West than previously indicated were still but slightly touched by the plow.

Yet, even before 1860 there was some farming in isolated spots in this wide expanse. Some Indians, under the influence of federal agencies, had turned to agriculture, sometimes to the disgust of their "blanket" neighbors. In 1862 and following, some of these became innocent victims of the reprisals of white farmers who were infuriated at attacks of altogether different roving tribes of hunters.[3] The Five Civilized Tribes of the later state of Oklahoma had been noted as agriculturists before Andrew Jackson removed them from their old cotton fields of the South, and they renewed their pursuits in their new location.[4] Even along the arid Southwestern border the Spanish missionaries had been training Indians in farm-

[2] C[harles] Warren Thornthwaite, "The Great Plains," in Carter [Lyman] Goodrich and others, *Migration and Economic Opportunity* (Philadelphia: University of Pennsylvania Press, 1936), maps pp. 212–213.

[3] Frederic Logan Paxson, *The Last American Frontier* (New York: The Macmillan Company, 1910), p. 235.

[4] See Angie Debo, *The Rise and Fall of the Choctaw Republic* (Norman: University of Oklahoma Press, 1934), *passim*.

ing and had taught them irrigation generations before the coming of the Anglo-American settlers.[5]

As to the more significant, remote and detached, early white settlements, the story of the Oregon pilgrims of the 1840's has been told so often that it is not necessary to stress here the fact that this was a purely agricultural migration. The even more colorful, if less heroic, California gold rush is less likely to be remembered as a stimulus to the rise of a permanent agricultural system. In fact, the new state of California had long been partially occupied by a leisurely, pastoral, Spanish group of the grandee type, who by 1850 were already grazing cattle herds numbering probably a little over a quarter of a million head. The food demands of the gold diggings stimulated this industry, so that by 1860 the herds totaled over two million and were greatly improved over the prevailing long-horn stock of 1849. But bad drouths in 1862–1864 brought that open range to a close as far as cattle were concerned, and there-after sheep began to take their place. Also, some of the newly arrived immigrants turned to farming, when luck went against them in the gold fields. And why should they not? The price of green vegetables was fabulous. When the bill of fare in a gold-mining settlement listed bean soup at a dollar, or a "square" meal at three dollars, payable in advance, the stranded miner might easily discern that more wealth for him could be dug from the ground with a hoe than by pick and shovel and pan. The soil was good and irrigation water available.

In 1850 the product of an acre and a half of tomatoes was rated at $18,000, though the purchasing value of this sum was to be discounted according to the prevailing high prices in nearly every other line. The student may well discount "tall tales" of from three- to seven-pound potatoes, "three-pound onions, fifty-pound cabbages, and three-hundred-pound squashes," but impressive enough is the fact that, though California imported 740,000 bags of grain in 1853, it needed no outside supply two years later, and in 1856 it had a surplus of about 70,000 sacks and barrels of grain and flour to export to Peru. Before the later date the state government was offering bounties and prizes in various agricultural lines. In-

[5] Herbert E[ugene] Bolton, "Defensive Spanish Expansion and the Significance of the Borderlands," in James F. Willard and Colin B. Goodykoontz, eds., *The Trans-Mississippi West* (Boulder: University of Colorado, 1930), p. 38.

deed, efforts at silk growing were under way, as on many another frontier since early colonial days in the East—and with about the same result.[6] The polyglot population of California continued in gold-rush style through succeeding decades, and various peoples left their agricultural imprint on the state. The orchard industry came from New York and middle Europe, the vineyards from Italy, truck growing from the Orient, the Mediterranean countries, and Portugal, and grain from Mexico and the American Middle West.[7]

Still earlier than the California gold rush came the first Mormon settlements in Utah, in surroundings seemingly less fitted by nature for agriculture and certainly far more inaccessible even than California. But segregation from the rest of mankind was highly desired by this persecuted sect, although it could not be maintained for long. When Brigham Young escorted his first party to the banks of the Great Salt Lake in 1846, the whole vast area belonged to Mexico, but two years later it became territory of the United States. While the desired escape from an unfriendly government had not been achieved, the remoteness from older frontiers and the small chance of early interference from the outside continued to stimulate migration. The converts came from numerous parts of the United States and Europe, and most of them were desperately poor. The first trains had crossed the Plains and mountains with their goods loaded on ox carts, but later comers could not afford this luxury. So from 1856 to 1860 ten companies dismounted from railroad cars at the end of the line in Iowa City, and went the rest of the way with their small store of absolute necessities thrown into hand carts. With four or five persons to the cart, each able-bodied individual taking his turn as a draft animal, they set out on foot. For about every one hundred emigrants there was a wagon with three yoke of oxen to haul the round tents, accommodating twenty persons each, and such other heavy equipment as was indispensable. The fourth and fifth companies underwent frightful experiences, culminating in mountain blizzards that took the lives of about two hundred. But further trains came, undaunted by these terrors, till a total of nearly three thousand persons with 662 hand

[6] E[dward] Douglas Branch, *Westward: The Romance of the American Frontier* (New York: D. Appleton and Company, 1930), pp. 439, 486–488.

[7] Carl Sauer, "Historical Geography and the Western Frontier," *The Trans-Mississippi West*, pp. 287–288.

carts reached Utah, many of the flimsy vehicles patched and re-
paired almost beyond recognition.[8]

Though many of the hand-cart pilgrims were aliens, the earlier
settlements were largely composed of New Englanders who gave
their communities a distinctly Yankee cohesive character. By dint
of Young's unusual managerial ability, and a vast amount of toil
stimulated by religious fervor, the Mormons, as they proclaim in
one of their songs, literally made "the desert bloom as the rose."
This was done by irrigation projects that suggest an origin in the
missions of New Mexico,[9] though divine inspiration has also been
credited with this achievement. Whatever its origin, the system
worked, and the population grew from 11,354 in 1850 to an estimated 25,000 in the next three years. Most of these people were
in the Salt Lake Valley and many of them were in Salt Lake City.[10]
Down to 1875 settlers in Colorado and western Texas continued to
wonder how Utah did so much with an irrigation system that they
could not imitate.

The mining frontier did not always leave behind it settled
agricultural communities, but, wherever soil and climate permitted, some farmers remained when the lodes ran thin. In spite
of the glory, extravagance, and glitter of Virginia City, the desert
lands around the Comstock Lode in Nevada did not entice farmers.
But in 1861, two years after the Comstock strike, rumors were
spreading of a new Golconda in the Salmon River region of Idaho,
and another gold rush was under way. With miners occasionally
panning out forty dollars worth of gold in one dip, and many
averaging a hundred dollars a day, within three years the valley
claimed a population of 16,000, half of them, as usual, miners, and
the rest, from preachers to gamblers, accumulating the spendings.
The same might be said for several other parts of the mountain
regions of Oregon, Idaho, and Montana.[11] But after each boom
and exodus there was left behind "a remnant of farmers to be
pestered by grasshoppers and Indians."[12]

The story was somewhat different in Colorado. The Pike's Peak

[8] LeRoy R. Hafen, "Handcart Migration Across the Plains," *The Trans-Mississippi West*, pp. 103–121; Branch, *Westward*, pp. 416–419.

[9] Sauer, "Historical Geography and the Western Frontier," p. 286.

[10] Branch, *Westward*, p. 422.

[11] *Ibid.*, pp. 493–495, 510–520.

[12] Shannon, *America's Economic Growth*, p. 357.

rush attracted from 12,000 to 15,000 persons in 1859, but only the loose surface rock could be mined with the slender equipment of the ordinary prospector. The impervious quartz of the substructure could be reduced only by heavy machinery. Within a few months many of the seekers for wealth who had crossed the Plains, their wagons carrying the sign "Pike's Peak or Bust," were on their way back, dilapidated and disillusioned, but still retaining enough spirit to change their inscriptions to "Busted, by Gosh!" [13] The difference here was that a somewhat larger number remained to take up farming. In 1859 corn around Denver and Pike's Peak was selling at from five to fifteen cents a pound, and several farmers planted crops of it in the river bottoms. The climate on the Plains just at the foot of the mountains is somewhat more humid than a few miles farther east, so even the crude irrigation methods used were sufficient to insure a crop. But some disappointed Missourians, returning eastward, pastured their draft stock on the half-grown plants. In the ensuing fight, in which there were several casualties on both sides, the outnumbered farmers were victorious. [14] Such agricultural beginnings were continued, and by 1866 Colorado was self-supporting in grain, potatoes, and most other crops. In 1867 the farmers began shipping food to army posts and the Montana mining camps. In 1870 the state's output of gold and silver was $4,000,000 and the value of agricultural products was $3,500,000. At that time a Denver convention was calling on the federal government for aid in irrigation. [15]

Along the divers wagon trails crossing the Great Plains were also numerous trading posts and stops for the changing of horses. Around most of these stations there was likely to be at least a small garden plot, though this might be a far cry from a settled agricultural community. Freight hauling across the Plains had come to be a big business before 1860, the markets being the mines, the Mormon groups, army posts, Indian agencies, and the Pacific coast. One of the biggest of the freight companies—Russell, Majors, and Waddell—was using 6,250 wagons and about 75,000 oxen. This firm sold out to Ben Holladay in 1862, who in turn disposed of his 5,000 miles of wagon routes to Wells and Fargo four years later.

[13] *Ibid.;* Branch, *Westward,* p. 490.
[14] Randall Parrish, *The Great Plains* (Chicago: A. C. McClurg & Co., 1907), pp. 297–298.
[15] Branch, *Westward,* p. 558.

In 1865 the Quartermaster General of the United States reported
that between Denver and Fort Leavenworth, 683 miles, the traveler
was "never out of sight of wagon trains" either of emigrants or
merchants.[16] Many of the towns in the western Prairies, such as
Council Grove and Topeka in Kansas, had sprung up as accessories
to this wagon trade. But way out on the Great Plains there were
stage posts, such as Julesburg in the northeast corner of Colorado,
that were peopled largely by riffraff. Such places were as violent [17]
as the later "hell on wheels" of the railroad construction camps or
the cow towns, but some also had their agricultural fringe as a
harbinger of later developments.

THE POPULATION FRONTIER IN 1860

Even within the Prairie frontier of two to the square mile the
population was sparser than the census designation would indicate.
There were not two persons to every section of land, but merely an
average of that number over the larger area. A family of six on one
quarter section might be miles distant from a cluster of twenty-five
or thirty on all quarters of a whole section. Or there might be an
emigrant outfitting station surrounded by a village of a few hundred that gave the hypothetical average for miles on every side.
Even in the next zone to the eastward, that of from six to eighteen
to the section, when one considers the greater number of villages
and the larger towns that helped create the mean, he will see that
even the upper limit represented hardly more than one family to
each 640 acres. This was scarcely a fourth as much as the land
would support. In other words, it was still a farmers' frontier only
partially settled. West of the Mississippi River, only easternmost
Iowa, a portion of northeastern Missouri, a narrow strip along the
Missouri River out to the northeast corner of Kansas, and the
Mississippi River delta in Louisiana had more than this six-to-
eighteen density.[18] Thus, in 1860, virtually all of the presumably
settled region west of the Mississippi River, or from the ninetieth

---

[16] Louis Pelzer, "Trails of the Trans-Mississippi Cattle Frontier," *The Trans-
Mississippi West*, pp. 139–145, referred to hereafter as Pelzer, "The Cattle Frontier";
Robert E[dgar] Riegel, *America Moves West* (New York: Henry Holt and Company,
c.1930), p. 418.

[17] Parrish, *The Great Plains*, pp. 289–296.

[18] Shannon, *America's Economic Growth*, map p. 139.

to the ninety-fifth meridian, was ready to be occupied by four or five times as many as the existing number of farming families. For, in contrast to much of the land east of the Mississippi, nearly all of this was suited to intensive agriculture. The larger part of the Prairies, then, and the woodlands of northern Wisconsin and Michigan, could absorb the bulk of farming expansion for many a year to come. Only the enticement of cheaper farms or free homesteads tempted the migrant to the westernmost Prairies or the margin of the Plains. Nevertheless, settlement went on in both directions.

The thin Podzol lands of northern Michigan and Wisconsin never proved attractive as farm sites, even after the lumber barons had stripped them of their timber. But southern, and particularly southeastern, Wisconsin had been desirable from a relatively early date. Many farmers from Vermont and western New York were moving to that spot in the late 1830's, selecting farms on the margin of woodland and Prairie, where they could clear fields for crops and have immediate pasturage and meadow for their livestock. The old fallacy still prevailed that Prairie land was too poor to support trees and therefore would not grow crops. Just before 1840 the Germans began arriving and settled the Lake region around Milwaukee. By 1860 the Yankees' farms were well developed and the Germans were getting a good start. Along with the Germans had come some Irish, who did not tend to stay long in one spot. Later there was a considerable number of Italian, Polish, and other alien arrivals who drifted generally into the towns and cities. Scandinavians and Bohemians also came, and they, with the native Americans, Irish, Germans, Welsh, and English, made up the bulk of the farm population.[19]

West of the Mississippi there was a great influx of homeseekers following a bad drouth in the Ohio Valley in 1854. The fertile soil of Iowa and southeastern Minnesota was already known, and there was still ample room for expansion in Missouri. During that decade the population of Minnesota was multiplied by twenty-nine, and yet only a corner of the state was settled. Iowa grew threefold and a half, reaching 675,000. Missouri almost doubled to approximately 1,200,000. Kansas, Nebraska, and Dakota Territory increased from almost nothing to 107,000, 29,000, and nearly 5,000 respectively.

[19] Joseph Schafer, "A Rural Life Survey of a Western State," The Trans-Mississippi West, pp. 300–306.

And yet the filling up had only begun, even in Missouri. Throughout the period, as later, people came in wagons, on trains to the rail ends, and by steamboat. In 1854 the roads across Illinois were crowded with wagons headed for Iowa. Twenty thousand persons were said to have crossed the Mississippi at Burlington in a month, and six or seven thousand a day were entering the territory by all routes. This movement continued for another two years without abatement. At the same time seventy-four trains left Chicago each day for points westward. Illinois was giving up some of her population to the newer territories, yet the state more than doubled during the decade.[20]

Though Thomas Hart Benton had declared the waters of the Missouri River too thick to swim in and too thin to walk on,[21] the "Big Muddy" itself was a great artery of emigrant traffic into western Missouri and Iowa and eastern Kansas and Nebraska until late in the 1860's. Its upper stretches were less used after the completion of the Union Pacific railroad in 1869.[22] Eastern Kansas and Nebraska were the outposts of the agricultural frontier of the North in 1860, as east Texas was in the South. The earlier settlers in Kansas did not pursue agriculture with any great vigor, though they spent far less time murdering and robbing each other than the "Bleeding Kansas" campaign of 1856 may have led many people to think. However, they did depend too much on the roadside industries attending the wagon trade of the Far West, and for the rest they relied largely on hunting, herding cattle, pasturing hogs, and raising a little corn. If one takes into account Senator John J. Ingalls's occasional tendency to overstate his case, there was still some truth in his assertion that the exports of the territory before 1860 were not enough to pay for all the whiskey the settlers drank each month.[23]

The situation in Nebraska, except for the smaller population, was about the same. Government contracts for corn to supply Fort Kearny kept a few farmers busy. Others sold cabbages at half a dollar and watermelons at a dollar each to prospective miners headed for Colorado. Also, they started herds with disabled cattle

[20] Branch, *Westward*, pp. 467–470.
[21] Everett [Newfon] Dick, *The Sod-House Frontier, 1854–1893* (New York: D. Appleton-Century Company, 1937), p. 6.
[22] Branch, *Westward*, p. 509.
[23] Dick, *The Sod-House Frontier*, p. 76.

bought cheap from the emigrants. There was less than eighteen acres under the plow for each resident of the territory in 1860, yet six charters for universities had already been issued.[24] Meanwhile, a considerable part of the population was living in sod houses costing less than $3 for materials such as a window, lumber for a door, latch fittings, a length of stovepipe, and a few nails. The cost of a more pretentious frame dwelling has been given as $250. The plowing of forty acres took $120 more, while the fencing of the field with walnut posts and rough lumber boards raised the whole cost of the improved farm to a little over $525.[25] The only other frontier state showing remarkable growth in the 1850's was Texas, which rose in population from 213,000 to 604,000 as a result of the rapid westward extension of cotton growing and the rise of a flourishing cattle business.

INTERNAL EXPANSION AND MIGRATION

Within the bounds of the frontier of 1860 there was a degree of internal expansion in every way commensurate with the possibilities. In any new area attractive to settlers the influx of homeseekers was followed by a rapid natural increase. Couples married young, and there was no economic urge to keep down the size of the family. In fact, a large number of stalwart sons who could clear more land or break more Prairie sod was a positive asset. Several daughters could be accepted with tolerance, for in time they would be replaced by wives of the sons, who would thus contribute to the biological processes necessary to the accumulation of a plentiful amount of land in the family. As long as unoccupied fields were still available in the neighborhood, this growth by internal expansion became an increasing factor in the total of mounting population. Then, as the better unused acres became scarcer, the incentive to immigration abated, and the tendency of surplus sons to move out on the next frontier noticeably increased. Ultimately the saturation point was reached, after which the influx of new blood did not keep pace with the exodus of the discontented. It has been noted that the increase of immigration over emigration reached its peak after about thirty years; then there occurred a

[24] Branch, *Westward*, pp. 477, 581–582.
[25] Dick, *The Sod-House Frontier*, pp. 78, 112.

state of balance between the two forces for a like period, when natural increase was the sole factor of growth; and finally, a net emigration set in.[26]

Excepting Kentucky and Tennessee, the states immediately east of the Mississippi had all been settled after the year 1800, and by 1860 the period of noticeable exodus was in full swing. Yet, until the end of the century there were second-choice lands available in the older states, and these were occupied by the less venturesome surplus farmers as well as by others who were tied to the locality by sentiment. Thus, despite the rise of industrialism and urbanization in the East Central states, particularly the northern group,[27] a portion of the remarkable increase in population in the four decades found homes on farms. This tendency may be explained by the new agricultural practices, which were more intensive and thus made smaller farm units imperative.

The major part of the agricultural frontier of 1860, west of the Mississippi, was still in the very early stage of growth, where immigration was all-important and emigration was so slight as to be negligible. What, then, inspired migration to the new lands, and what was its source? As good a definition of migration as any is the phrase, "leaving a spot and not returning to it."[28] The direction taken by migrating people is the one of "least resistance" ahead; of "greatest pressure behind"; of highest "desire within"; of the most intensive "pull, or attraction, or supply from without"; and of the will of the individual concerned.[29] In other words, migration is caused by conditions in the locality of the old habitation, and its direction is determined by relative circumstances in the new regions considered as future homes. Most peoples have a certain attachment to their familiar neighborhoods, and are not inclined to leave, regardless of any ordinary greater attractiveness elsewhere, unless hard times, real or prospective, drive them to move.

[26] C[harles] Warren Thornthwaite, assisted by Helen I. Slentz, *Internal Migration in the United States* (Philadelphia: University of Pennsylvania Press, 1934), pp. 1–2, 10, referred to hereafter as Thornthwaite, *Internal Migration.*

[27] Arthur Meier Schlesinger, *The Rise of the City, 1878–1898* (Vol. X of *A History of American Life*, A. M. Schlesinger and D. R. Fox, eds., New York: The Macmillan Company, 1933), pp. 53–77.

[28] Otis Tufton Mason, "Migration and the Food Quest: A Study in the Peopling of America," Smithsonian Institution, *Annual Report of the Board of Regents,* 1894 (Washington: Government Printing Office, 1896), p. 523.

[29] *Ibid.,* pp. 524–525.

But in America there was no fast adherence to this rule. There was a tradition of pioneering. From the time of the first settlements on the Atlantic coast, each generation had succumbed to the urge to try new experiences in changed surroundings. The frontiersman, nurtured in the cradle with the idea of something better beyond, did not need the existence of actual want, the desire of quick wealth (except for the gold rushes), or even land hunger to induce him to load the family and a few necessities and heirlooms on the wagon and start out into the wilderness.[30] Perhaps the colonial quitrent collector was getting too insistent. Maybe neighbors were living less than a mile distant, and the country seemed too crowded. In later periods it might be that the school officials were demanding regular attendance of the children, even in rush seasons or bad weather. It was time to move on. What the women thought made little difference. They were trained to obey and permitted to grumble.

The Americans of the period had hearty appetites, and the country afforded the opportunity to gratify them. Two fifths of the food of the United States, it was reckoned in 1930, was at that time of animal origin—meat, eggs, and dairy products. For this reason more land must be used for each person than in countries subsisting almost wholly on a vegetable and fish diet. Two and a half acres of crops and ten acres of pasture were needed to supply each inhabitant, and if all got what they needed an even greater amount of land could be utilized. But, to take the opposite extreme, in Japan, where no meat or milk was consumed by the mass of the people, a quarter of an acre of crops of high yield, and no pasture, sufficed. The situation in earlier years seems not to have been noticeably different. From the Civil War till shortly after the end of the century, agricultural production in the United States remained on a par with the increase of population,[31] and this relationship was maintained—with only occasional gluts in a few commodities caused by actual overproduction—by a people spreading out over all the first-choice lands of the nation.

Till after 1900 the rule did not fail that, at least in agricultural

[30] A[lfred] C[ort] Haddon, *The Wanderings of Peoples* (Cambridge, Eng.: University Press, 1911), pp. 1–4.

[31] Oliver E[dwin] Baker, "The Trend of Agricultural Production in North America and Its Relation to Europe and Asia," in Corrado Gini and others, *Population* (Chicago: University of Chicago Press, 1930), pp. 218–220, 244–246.

population, the greatest growth was in the newest lands, and generally those closest to the older regions. From 1860 to 1900 the West North Central states (Missouri to Minnesota and Kansas to North Dakota) grew, with an astonishing degree of regularity, from a population of 2,170,000 to 10,347,000; the West South Central states (Louisiana, Arkansas, Texas, and Oklahoma) from 1,748,000 to 6,532,000; the Mountain states and territories (all to the westward except those fronting on the Pacific Ocean) from 175,000 to 1,675,000; and the Pacific states from 444,000 to 2,417,000. Only one section of the East (the East North Central, comprising Ohio, Indiana, Illinois, Michigan, and Wisconsin) exceeded the growth in actual numbers of the West North Central states,[32] and this was mainly due to urbanization.

As to the sources of migration to the trans-Mississippi West, the same rule held as on previous frontiers. That is, the people were coming, except for newly arrived aliens, largely from states that had been settled in the forty or fifty years preceding.[33] Even with all the efforts of the Emigrant Aid societies of New England, Kansas was occupied mainly by persons from Missouri, Illinois, and Iowa.[34] By 1860 only 4,208 of the residents of Kansas were of New England birth. New York and Pennsylvania accounted for 12,794. The contribution of Iowa alone equaled New England's, but about 11,000 had come from Missouri and 31,000 from Illinois, Indiana, and Ohio.[35] Persons from the near-by states were the ones who stayed. Their experiences in their earlier homes had better equipped them for the new environment.

Since 1850, the United States Bureau of the Census has recorded migration on a state-of-birth basis, and, since 1870, native Negroes have been listed separately from the whites. Such data, useful as they are, take no account of various steps in migration between birth and the census. On this basis, many a Kansas settler of 1860, who had become acclimated to the West in Missouri or Iowa, may have been credited to a more easterly state. But even these inadequate returns are useful in showing the amount and

[32] Warren S[impson] Thompson and P[ascal] K[idder] Whelpton, *Population Trends in the United States* (New York: McGraw-Hill Book Company, Inc., 1933), pp. 14–15; or see any number of the *Statistical Abstract of the United States*, under the heading of "Population by States."

[33] Thornthwaite, *Internal Migration*, p. 10.

[34] Shannon, "Homestead Act and Labor Surplus," pp. 645–646.

[35] Branch, *Westward*, pp. 474–475.

direction, westward to farms and eastward to cities, of interstate migration.

From 1860 to 1870 the states of net loss by emigration (more moved out than in) were northern New England, New York, Pennsylvania, the East North Central group except Michigan, the Gulf states except Texas, and Arkansas and Georgia. The greatest losers were Ohio, 269,000, and New York, 231,000, and the total loss for all was 928,000. The gainers were mainly Michigan, Minnesota, Iowa, Missouri, Kansas, Texas, California, and Oregon, with a total gain of 548,000. Kansas, Iowa, and Missouri, the highest and in that order, received 382,000 among them, while most of the rest in the West were in Minnesota and Michigan. Between 1870 and 1880, every state east of the Mississippi (except for slight gains along the Atlantic coast), as well as Louisiana, Missouri, Iowa, and (again slight) Utah and Nevada, showed a net loss by migration, totaling about 1,300,000. Illinois was now the great loser, with 320,000, but Ohio, Indiana, and Wisconsin together had a somewhat larger total. Gains in Minnesota and Arkansas were small, showing that the frontier of settlement was moving out of the first tier of trans-Mississippi states. The huge losses in the East North Central states, considering the almost static condition of the Atlantic coast, also indicate the source of Western growth, which amounted to 1,127,000. Kansas was far and away the big winner, with 347,000, while Texas with two thirds and Iowa with half as many ranked next. Dakota Territory joined the list and took 56,000, but Colorado far outstripped her with 96,000. The whole Pacific coast barely exceeded Colorado, while the High Plains and Great Basin showed only a slight increase.

In the decade of 1880–1890, the losses of the East and the Old South were relatively small. But the Old Northwest (East North Central), with Iowa and Missouri, accounted for 1,087,000 out of the 1,363,000 for the whole country. Again, Illinois contributed the largest number, but Iowa was a close second with 228,000. Except for a slight growth, indicating a coming reversal, in Arkansas, all of the Western states and territories profiting numerically from the exchange were west of the Louisiana-to-Minnesota tier. Including Arkansas they had acquired slightly over a million from the other states. Kansas was slipping badly, surrendering the palm to Nebraska with 240,000. But the Dakotas also had acquired 126,-

000 between them and achieved statehood. Washington was the prodigy of the Pacific, with 153,000. The states of the higher Great Plains and Rocky Mountains, along with Idaho, were now coming to be the agricultural frontier. Colorado claimed 100,000, Montana 40,000, Idaho 27,000, and Wyoming 22,000, while Texas slipped back to 64,000, and New Mexico, Arizona, and Utah were slightly more than static. With the Comstock Lode worked out, Nevada had a net loss by emigration of 12,000, a considerable number for so small a state. The livestock and mining businesses were having their effect in the northern Plains and mountains, but homesteaders were also venturing out on the Great Plains.

In the 1890's the industrial Northeast gained considerably, and the region east of the Mississippi, as a whole, had drawn slightly from the states to the west of the river. The greatest net emigration was from Kansas, which lost 220,000. But some of Nebraska's loss of 202,000, Iowa's 134,000, Missouri's 114,000, and Arkansas's 108,-000 went to the mushroom territory of Oklahoma, which acquired altogether 432,000 in the decade. The Great Plains, mountains, and Pacific coast were also slipping back toward a static condition. Idaho and Arizona gained a little over the 1880's. New Mexico, as during the preceding decades, was depending almost solely on natural increase, while Nevada and Utah again declined. A still "booming" Oklahoma gave the Great Plains and Mountain states most of their migration growth of 1900–1910. But that area lost 423,000 in the next decade and 935,000 in the 1920's. In fact, in the 1920's there was a net loss for every state west of the Mississippi, except for an almost stationary Oregon, Nevada, Arizona, and New Mexico, and an enormous expansion in California that had been accelerating ever since 1900.[36] By 1900, as far as emigration was concerned, the farmer's last frontier had already been reached. Population growth from that time in the Great Plains and Mountain states was dependent on natural increase and some immigration, mainly from Mexico.

Not only had migration done its work for the Great Plains, mountains, and Great Basin by 1900, but there had already been a series of advances and retreats, particularly on the Plains. Extra-heavy rainfall in the early 1880's had attracted farmers to parts of Montana, Wyoming, Kansas, Colorado, New Mexico, and Ari-

[36] Thornthwaite, *Internal Migration*, pp. 5–6, and Plate II.

zona that were normally too arid. Then in the later years of the decade the precipitation grew scanty and remained low through the greater part of the nineties. The settlers suffered, mortgaged their land to hold on, and finally many had to leave anyway. Some areas had fewer people, even after biological increase, in 1900 than in 1890. This situation had something to do with the vigor of the Populist movement.[37] As recovery set in, on the Prairies and Plains after 1895, the price of land rose by degrees to a level that ordinary farm laborers could not pay, and it was even beyond the reach of the type of farmers' sons who in earlier generations had furnished so large a proportion of the migrants. Some of these were ready to take the ultimate venture of farming in the arid regions,[38] but they proved little more than a balance for the disillusioned homesteaders who were moving out.

ORGANIZED INDUCEMENTS TO SETTLEMENT

Both in internal migration and in the settlement of aliens, the railroads and other transportation agencies played an early and important part. In Indiana the builders of the Wabash and Lake Erie Canal had paid for part of the digging in farm tracts. The Illinois Central railroad company also had often paid the construction gangs partly in land scrip, of which the Irish got a good share.[39] In these and other ways the transcontinental railroads enticed settlers after 1865. These companies were recipients of land grants and had a twofold stake in the business. First, they wanted to dispose of their gift lands at as high a price as possible; and second, they needed a large population along their right of ways as a constant source of freight revenue. Nearly two years before the rails of the Union Pacific reached Wyoming, the land agent of the company established the town of Cheyenne. This later capital of the territory and state was well located to serve a number of military posts, and was soon to be a junction point with the railroad

[37] Riegel, *America Moves West*, pp. 551–552.

[38] Marcus Lee Hansen, *The Mingling of the Canadian and American Peoples* (completed by John Bartlett Brebner, New Haven: Yale University Press, 1940), p. 17.

[39] Carl [Frederick] Wittke, *We Who Built America: The Saga of the Immigrant* (New York: Prentice-Hall, Inc., 1939), p. 150. Best on the Illinois Central is Paul Wallace Gates, *The Illinois Central Railroad and Its Colonization Work* (Cambridge: Harvard University Press, 1934).

from Denver. By 1866 the Union Pacific in eastern Nebraska was flanked with settlements extending several townships back from the rails. In 1878 and 1879 the company was selling land in the same region at from $6 to $8 an acre, on terms. In 1892 this same land, if improved and good, was bringing $25 an acre, but times were so hard that in one township, for example, 67 per cent of the farms were mortgaged at the average rate of $8.78 an acre, or over $1,500 for each owner.[40]

On the purchase of land the usual terms of credit were a tenth down and eleven years for the rest at 6 or 7 per cent interest, but for the first three years the only payment required after the first installment was the interest. A tenth off the purchase price was given for a six-year contract; a fourth off was allowed for all-cash sales—terms which showed that the credit buyer was paying much more than the stipulated interest rate. But even the cash price was sufficiently padded. Santa Fé railroad bonds were selling at 65 in the 1870's, but were accepted at face value for land, and the Union Pacific followed a similar policy. Another evidence of padding was the practice of the Northern Pacific of crediting railroad fares of migrants to the price of any land bought within the ensuing two months, and the further free transportation of purchasers' families to the new homes. Prices ranged from $2.50 to $8.00 an acre, depending on the distance from the railroad. The terms were seven years at 7 per cent.[41]

Sometimes the railroads established colonies, particularly of immigrants. For example, a considerable number of German Mennonites left Russia in 1874 at a time when the Kansas legislature had just released conscientious objectors from militia service. Some 1,900 of these Mennonites came into Kansas, bringing $250,000 in gold. The Santa Fé took them in charge and exchanged 60,000 acres of land for their money. It gave to each of the larger colonies four sections of land and built huge barracks to house the immigrants until they could erect their own homes. The gift land was sold

[40] Branch, *Westward*, pp. 559, 582, 584–585.
[41] *Ibid.*, p. 553; Dick, *The Sod-House Frontier*, pp. 188–189. The standard treatment of the Northern Pacific practices is James B[laine] Hedges, *Henry Villard and the Railways of the Northwest* (New Haven: Yale University Press, 1930). The most recent work on the subject is Richard C[leghorn] Overton, *Burlington West: A Colonization History of the Burlington Railroad* (Cambridge: Harvard University Press, 1941).

and the proceeds put in the community's poor fund.[42] This was all good business for the railroad, and the largess of a few extra sections of land that had cost nothing was, after all, covered in the price of the rest.

Like the state governments, land companies, and steamship lines, the railroads sent agents to European countries, as well as to the ports of entry of the United States, to offer their wares for sale. There was keen competition among the railroads for the immigrants' business, some of their handbills reading almost like a modern soap advertisement. The customer, because of his wisdom in trying the right brand, would become little short of perfect. A pamphlet of the Northern Pacific, for circulation in foreign countries, insisted that the people of Montana never became ill except from overeating. The same company had emigration offices in New York and St. Paul, and sent agents to many countries of Europe, each supplied with maps and descriptive pamphlets of the railroad's lands, printed in the language of the country being canvassed. The foreign agents of the railroads fraternized with steamship officials and maintained an effective press-agent service with the newspapers of the various countries. Preachers were preferred as agents to distribute circulars and posters and to appeal personally to prospective immigrants in their native countries. By 1872, the railroads' representatives were particularly numerous in the farming communities of England, Norway, and Sweden, and every ship that landed in New York was besieged by agents from all points from the Far West.

Other speculative groups, like the National Land Company, leagued with the railroads in this work. It was joined by the German Colonization Company of Chicago, in 1869, in trying to get settlers for Colorado at a time when the Kansas Pacific was the only railroad leading to that territory. In the next two years the National Land Company set up sixteen colonies in Colorado and Kansas, half of the pioneers coming from Europe and the rest from various parts of the United States.[43] Steamship companies were active in the game, and in the 1860's Sweden was fairly overrun by their agents

[42] Dick, The Sod-House Frontier, pp. 189–191.
[43] Branch, Westward, pp. 551–552, 557–558; Dick, The Sod-House Frontier, pp. 187, 189–191.

and those of others. America was pictured as a land of milk and honey. Some homesick Swedish-Americans were given their steamship fares back to the old country in return for coaxing their former neighbors to cross the Atlantic on ships of the donor. The fine American clothing of these visitors added to the lure of 160 acres of free land in Minnesota, and the appeals were fruitful.[44]

Western state governments also contributed generously to the horde of agents. In 1852 and 1853 Wisconsin appointed a commissioner of immigration, to reside in New York, and also a publicity man, who soon had articles on Wisconsin in over nine hundred newspapers. Pamphleteering in Germany, Ireland, and Norway was another device. Minnesota established a board of immigration in 1867. It also sent Swedish-, Norwegian-, and German-speaking agents to meet immigrants in Eastern ports of the United States and Canada and to act as interpreters and guides. Iowa had a similar board in 1870 and began sending representatives to Europe. All the little states that wanted to become big were soon competing for their share, and many localities had their own organizations.[45] Before long the bait offered the immigrants was being snapped up also by native Americans, who hitherto had neglected some of the more frigid regions. Hamlin Garland was one of those who left Iowa in the 1880's for Dakota. The land boom of that territory was the big topic of conversation on the Prairies. When speakers in the farmers' institutes urged diversification as a means of competition with cheaper wheat lands to the northwest, the farmers insisted that they would stick to their specialty and follow the wheat belt. Also, they argued, by staying where they were they would waste their "rights" to free government land. The soil farther away looked better even than the rich Iowa dirt, and some of it really was, regardless of what might be learned later about a less dependable climate. They were told that even the deep winter freezes of five or six feet were a blessing, because as the land slowly thawed in the spring it would hold water all the longer, allowing grass roots to penetrate to a permanent supply.[46]

[44] George M[alcolm] Stephenson, *A History of American Immigration, 1820–1924* (Boston: Ginn and Company, c.1926), pp. 33, 39–40.
[45] Branch, *Westward*, pp. 551, 555–556; Dick, *The Sod-House Frontier*, p. 187.
[46] Dick, *The Sod-House Frontier*, p. 186.

IMMIGRATION AND SETTLEMENT

There are voluminous public documents recording American immigration before the Civil War, many of them faulty. Until 1868 the government merely enumerated the lists of passengers on incoming ships, thus failing to distinguish between immigrants and traveling Americans and visitors.[47] Thereafter the differentiations were more carefully made, and the destination and occupations of the immigrants were better noted in the census data. By 1880, when the "new immigration" from Eastern and Southern Europe began to become noticeable, there were in the United States about a million each of German and Irish birth, 717,000 Canadians, 664,000 English, and 440,000 Scandinavians, out of a total of some 7,000,000 foreign born. Many other nationalities of smaller numbers were represented, and some of these will be considered here. But many of the newer type of arrivals, like the Chinese, went largely to the manual labor of the cities, and the Japanese truck-gardener type was not yet a cause of serious alarm even in California.

No special problems arose regarding the English immigrants. Their kind was everywhere in America, and they scattered out in equally ubiquitous fashion. Seldom did they seek the areas of scanty population. Elsewhere, when they took to farming, there were plenty of neighbors who spoke something sufficiently similar to the English language to welcome and initiate them into the agricultural mysteries of the locality. During this period Great Britain was trying to direct her emigrants toward Canada and Australia, but this did not prevent a larger contingent from coming to the United States. For that matter, even large numbers of those who were "assisted" to Canada soon drifted over the border.[48] Again, the Irish immigrants did not all remain in the cities. In 1860 more than 87,000 of them were in Illinois, and another 32,000 came to the same state before 1870, quite a number of them settling on farms in every county. An Irish farming community in McHenry County maintained three Catholic churches of respectable size. By 1860 there were also 50,000 Irish in Wisconsin and a great number of Irish farmers in Iowa. Though they may have come over under

[47] Robert R[ené] Kuczynski, *Population Movements* (Oxford, Eng.: The Clarendon Press, 1936), p. 21.
[48] Stephenson, *History of American Immigration*, p. 27.

contract for construction gangs, a fair proportion remained to farm.
At this work they were as good as any, but were less satisfied than
the Teutonic stocks to remain in one spot through bad times as
well as good.

There were even Irish colonies. Around 1869 a South Dakota
newspaper editor, a militant Anglophobe, planned an Irish settlement to strike at Canada when the time became ripe for the
establishment of the Irish Free State. O'Neill, Nebraska, was
founded for a like purpose. Farming colonies of Irishmen were to
be found in no less than six Nebraska counties before the close of
the 1880's, and there were others in Kansas and southward to
Arkansas, as well as in Virginia and Georgia. Western bishops fostered an Irish Catholic Colonization Association of the United
States. An Illinois corporation capitalized at $100,000 tried dili-
gently to get Irishmen out of Eastern cities and into the better
surroundings of Western farms. It established colonies in Minnesota and Nebraska, but went to pieces in 1891. Before this time
Bishop John Ireland of New York had placed eight hundred Irish
families in four settlements in Minnesota, and they ultimately
spread out over 300,000 acres. Their records show that the cost of
improving a quarter-section farm, including a house and the plowing of 30 acres, was $1,174 (in a sample case), the installments
being spread out over several years.[49] By the 1890's the opportunity
for cheap lands and for rapid expansion from outside was already
waning in the Prairies. There were never enough of these city
dwellers transplanted on Western farms to affect in any perceptible
degree the labor surplus or provide a safety valve for labor discontent.[50]

As far as the farm population is concerned, the influence of
Canadian immigration was more important than that of either the
English or the Irish. Some French Canadians drifted down into the
mill towns of New England, but the bulk of the movement was of
English or Scottish Canadians to farms in the Northwest. In 1860
about the only white population of the Dakota region was in the
extreme northeastern corner near Winnipeg, and apparently was
an overflow from Canada. During the Civil War some Canadians

---

[49] Wittke, *We Who Built America*, pp. 149–153.
[50] Shannon, "Homestead Act and Labor Surplus," p. 641. For further discussion
of this point, see pp. 55, 356–359, below.

settled in Kansas and Missouri, but far more went to Michigan, where swamp land given the commonwealth by the federal government was represented by scrip in the wallets of speculators. In this greenback period a Canadian dollar was worth two American ones, and slow settlement had caused the scrip to fall in value. Consequently, the Canadians could get as good land as that region contained for from twenty to thirty cents an acre in gold. The price of rosin, pitch, tar, and turpentine was so high that it was profitable to distill the stumps from cut-over land. Another industry was started by pumping steam from the sawmills down into deep wells and boiling down the salt brine that was brought up. During the same years Canadian loggers, and farmers in their wake, were tempted to the less-exploited Wisconsin timber lands. In those years also, as profits in the mines of British Columbia began to fall, miners—mostly from the United States in the first place—wandered back into Washington, Oregon, and California. The population of the Canadian province soon dropped from 15,000 to 6,000.

Immediately after the war, Northern draft dodgers and Confederate refugees began their return trips, some of them lingering on Western farms. Then, between 1865 and 1890, came the great surge of Canadians into Iowa, Minnesota, Kansas, Nebraska, and the Dakotas. In Canada, as well as in the eastern United States, "the West" in those years meant the area of those states. When the Canadian referred to his own territory from Manitoba to the Pacific he said "our West." Then, after the end of the eighties, as hard times became pronounced in the West, the movement of immigration was checked for many years. From 1860 to 1900 the Canadian-born population of the United States rose from about a quarter of a million to 1,180,000.[51]

The heaviest waves of German immigration in the nineteenth century were from 1840 to 1860 and in the 1880's, but there was no total cessation in the interim. The Republican homestead planks of 1856 and 1860 were a bait for German support, and the Homestead Act of 1862 was a new temptation for immigration. Social legislation in Germany did not get a start till after 1883, and even then America still looked better to many Germans. The climate and soil of Wisconsin were recognizable to them, and the state welcomed

[51] Hansen, *Mingling of Canadian and American Peoples,* pp. 159–218 *passim.*

them. From Milwaukee, where their fellow nationals had settled in large numbers, they were directed to the most likely farm sites. But many Germans went to other states. By 1900 almost a third of the people of Texas were either German or of German extraction,[52] though immigrants in the rest of the South after 1865 were a smaller percentage of the total population than before the war. It has been estimated that Germans have developed 672,000 American farms, including 100,000,000 acres, but after 1870 the newcomers included more of artisans and day laborers, and fewer farmers. The German on the land often reflected very little of the cultural sympathies of his city relative, paying far more attention to the condition of his barn than to that of his house.[53]

Of the Scandinavian countries, Denmark has furnished fewer immigrants than either Sweden or Norway, largely because of greater opportunities at home. But beginning about 1825 in Norway and 1841 in Sweden, those countries began to catch what was called the "American fever." After the migration was well under way it was hard for neighbors left behind to believe the vast size of American farms, but letters from trusted friends began to carry conviction. Hence, the largest number of immigrants came from localities in Scandinavia where the subdivision of landholdings had gone furthest. Then, in the thirty years following 1850, there were bad economic conditions, including crop failures, in the homeland. Money was tight and loans were hard to get. Many townsmen were unemployed and the rest were paid little, at a time when there seemed a great demand for industrial and domestic workers in America. Then, too, the constant propaganda of paid emigration agents was supported by the arguments of one-time neighbors who had already made the venture. And, finally, there was fretting against the restraints of a social system that was as yet far from attaining the degree of democracy to be found in the next century. And connected with all this, particularly in Sweden, was the fact that the established church was so rigid in its discipline as to cause widespread unrest. Though there was no downright persecution in the worst sense, many Swedes who came to America joined other churches, and some later immigrants were positively embittered

[52] Stephenson, *History of American Immigration*, pp. 51–52; Wittke, *We Who Built America*, pp. 201–203, 207.
[53] Wittke, *We Who Built America*, pp. 208–210.

toward Christianity. Immigration from the three countries reached 10,000 a year by 1865, and attained a peak of 105,326 in 1882. By 1900 there were over 1,000,000 American people of Scandinavian birth, and 2,000,000 of their children.[54]

The first colony of Swedes was in Wisconsin, but by 1860 they were plentiful in Iowa, Illinois, and Michigan; it was not until the big rush after 1860 that Minnesota became extensively populated. At least four hundred Swedish names are attached to places in that state. The Dakotas became thickly dotted with Swedes in the 1880's, but they were also numerous in the rest of the western Prairies. Lindsborg and the Smoky Hill Valley in Kansas were receiving their quotas by 1868. There were forty thousand even in Texas by 1906. About a quarter of all the Swedes in America have remained farmers, this being a larger percentage than that of the native Americans or Germans, and three times the ratio for the Irish.[55]

Norway lost a larger proportion of her population to the United States in the nineteenth century than any other country except Ireland. By 1900 over half a million Norwegians had arrived. In 1870 the great bulk of them were to be found in Wisconsin, northern Illinois, Minnesota, and Iowa. But by 1880 their big belt was from Lake Michigan out to the Missouri River in the Dakotas, and north of a line from Chicago to Sioux City. Some also went west into Utah and the state of Washington. During the "great Dakota boom" of the 1880's they looked over and took up much of the eastern two-thirds of North Dakota. About half the Scandinavian immigration to 1890 was Norwegian, most of the settlers being farmers or laborers.[56] Danish settlement was widely scattered, but more Danes came to Iowa and Minnesota than to any other state. By 1920 there were 190,000 Americans of Danish birth and 277,000 of their descendants. Many of the Scandinavians had gone to the frontier in covered wagons and lived for years in log cabins, dugouts, or sod houses. There was nothing very brilliant about their activities, but they were doggedly persevering, and successful farmers.[57]

Russian-Germans—or Mennonites—in Kansas have already been

[54] Stephenson, *History of American Immigration*, pp. 30–37; Wittke, *We Who Built America*, p. 262.
[55] Wittke, *We Who Built America*, pp. 269–271.
[56] *Ibid.*, pp. 286–287, 289.
[57] *Ibid.*, pp. 293–296.

mentioned. They also went to other places throughout the West, as did some of the Swiss, Dutch, Welsh, French, and East European Jews. Before 1900 there were numerous Bohemians in central-eastern Iowa, and they were strong in northern Illinois.[58] It was customary for these foreign-language groups—like the Mennonites —to congregate in communities of their own kind. In Kansas there was a colony, established by Ned Turnley, which was supposed to rehabilitate drunken sons of the British nobility. Its agricultural potentialities were never discovered, for the lords withdrew their support when the desired reforms were not achieved, and the group broke up. A like fate befell a vegetarian colony near Humboldt, Kansas. The inhabitants opposed the use of meat, tea, coffee, to-bacco, and a number of other things, and insisted on substituting hydrotherapy for medicine. But, failing to make a living on ab-stinence and hope, this colony also expired, leaving behind only the name of Vegetarian Creek. In the late 1870's a colony of some fifteen or twenty thousand wretchedly poverty-stricken Southern Negroes was assisted to a start in Graham County, Kansas, where they founded the town of Nicodemus. This group worked hard and succeeded,[59] though Nicodemus remained small and unimportant.

In summary, it may be said that immigrants did far more than their share in the making of the agricultural West, as their prede-cessors had also built up the East. Further inferences to be drawn regarding the combined effect of migration and immigration on the growth of the West are reserved for a later discussion (pages 356–359).

[58] *Ibid.*, pp. 300–338, 405–418.
[59] Dick, *The Sod-House Frontier*, pp. 191–198.

CHAPTER III

Disposing of the Public Domain

FACT AND FANCY ABOUT THE NUMBER OF HOMESTEADS

IT is easy to assume that those pioneers moving on to earlier un-cultivated land in the cotton states, the Prairies, the timbered regions of the upper Lake district, and out into the only partially charted Great West, generally took up free homesteads in areas where they could make a living. But history must sometimes be prosaic—even painfully so. It is true that the number of farms in the United States grew from about 2,000,000 in 1860 to 5,737,000 in 1900, and that the total land in farms rose from 407,213,000 to 838,592,000 acres.[1] It is equally true that not quite 600,000 patents for 80,000,000 acres of homesteads were issued in those same years.[2] In other words, even if all the homesteaders had kept and lived on their holdings, less than a sixth of the new homes and a little over a sixth of the acreage would have been on land that came as a gift from the government. Eighty-four out of each hundred new farms had to be achieved either by the subdivision of older holdings or by purchase. Furthermore, as will be demonstrated later, an astonishing number of homesteaders were merely the hired pawns of land monopolists who took over the land as soon as the final patents were received, thus reducing free farms more nearly to an eighth, or possibly a tenth, of the increase for the forty-year period. Again, the bona fide homesteaders usually got only the

[1] *Statistical Abstract of the United States,* 1910 (Washington: Government Printing Office, 1911), p. 121.
[2] Public Lands Commission, *Report,* 1905 (*Senate Document* No. 189, 58 Cong., 3 Sess., Washington: Government Printing Office, 1905), p. 175.

least desirable tracts, on poorer lands, far from transportation and society, while the ubiquitous monopolist and speculator held the better tracts for resale at a price too high for the class of persons the Homestead Act had presumably been intended to benefit.

THE IDEALS AND HOPES OF HOMESTEAD ADVOCATES

The land reformers of the 1840's—George Henry Evans and his followers in the labor movement, Andrew Johnson and other friends of Southern and Western tenant farmers (as well as industrial laborers) in Congress—had hopes of devising a measure that would forever end land speculation and monopoly and that would dispose of government land by gift only—and to persons who would have inalienable title. They wanted the remainder of the public domain to be held as a reservoir to furnish relief to wage laborers and release for servile tenants for ages to come. Until the matter became a political issue in 1856, support for the measure was about equally divided between the Northern and Southern inhabitants of the region lying west of the Appalachian Highlands. The opposition came from the Atlantic seaboard states where it also was divided about equally between the Northern and Southern sections. In the hot debates over a homestead bill in the early 1850's the strongest support came from members of Congress from the Southwest—from men who championed the cause of the underdogs, whether they were industrial workers in the overcrowded cities or renters and hired workers on the farms. Only the Negro slave was exempted from their benevolence. Few indeed there were among the advocates, like Orlando B. Ficklin of Illinois, who saw that there would be only a moderate rush of settlers to free farms; that the class most needing the boon was "too poor to find means to pay the expense of emigrating from the older to the new States, and of settling on these lands. . . ." The real beneficiaries, he saw, would "be generally of the middle, or rather not of the very poorest class, and . . . the number will not be so large by a great deal as is anticipated by some gentlemen." [3] Presumably, even Ficklin did not suspect that land monopolization would proceed with an increased tempo after the Homestead Act was adopted.

[3] Shannon, "Homestead Act and Labor Surplus," pp. 640–644; Ficklin's speech in *Congressional Globe*, 32 Cong., 1 Sess., Pt. 2, p. 1183, and *ibid.*, App., p. 523.

TERMS AND SHORTCOMINGS OF THE HOMESTEAD ACT

Under the Homestead law, as finally enacted on May 20, 1862, any American citizen or alien who had filed his or her intention papers, if twenty-one years of age or over, or if the head of a family, or if he had served as many as fourteen days in the army or navy of the United States, and if he or she had never fought against the United States or given aid and comfort to an enemy of the United States in time of war, was permitted for a ten dollar fee (later there were several additional commissions) to file claim to as many as 160 acres of hitherto unappropriated public land. After having "resided upon or cultivated the same for the term of five years immediately succeeding the time of filing the . . . [claim], if at that time a citizen of the United States . . . .," the settler, on payment of other commissions, could get a final patent, and his homestead was not to be seized for any debts contracted before the issuance of his deed.[4]

The amendments and interpretations of this law, down to the end of the century, and afterward as well, were so many and complicated that any attempt at their enumeration would be worse than "a weariness of the flesh," but a few must be mentioned. Before long, it was decided that both husband and wife could not take out separate homesteads—an excellent excuse for postponing legal marriage for a few years, until incontestable patents were obtained. (Houses could easily be built on dividing lines between quarter sections.) The choice between residence or cultivation for five years came to include both, but the ban against ex-Confederates was dropped in 1866. Until 1879, most persons could homestead only 80 acres in the reserved government sections within the grants made to railroads; thereafter, they might increase this to 160 acres. Union veterans of the Civil War were granted this privilege in 1870. No person who already owned as much as a quarter section could take out a claim, but possessors of smaller amounts might round out their holdings by a sufficient number of acres to make 160 in all. Commissions of $12, in addition to the original $10, were assessed in the Mountain and Pacific divisions, or $24 on the strips reserved for railroad land grants—$8 or $16 in the Central states.

<hr>

[4] 12 U.S. *Statutes at Large*, pp. 392–393.

Elaborate oaths and proofs of residence, cultivation, and intention to keep the land were required before receipt of the final patent.[5]

In its operation the Homestead Act could hardly have defeated the hopes of the enthusiasts of 1840–1860 more completely if the makers had actually drafted it with that purpose uppermost in mind. In fact, most of the consequent abuses were a direct outgrowth of shortcomings, weaknesses, omissions, and direct provisions of the act itself. In the first place, the avowed intention—to provide homes in the West for needy people from the more congested parts of the country—was defeated by the shortcomings of the law. There were no provisions at all for getting day laborers and tenants to the places where the lands were to be had. The public domain of 1862 was confined to the states and territories (Texas not included) west of the Mississippi, except for Michigan and Wisconsin and three of the Gulf states. However, penniless laborers of the cities and farms of the crowded East would scarcely be attracted to the Gulf states. Men working for $250 a year, or less—and this was the great toiling mass to be helped—could not even keep their families from hunger without the additional wages of their wives or children or of both. Where then were they to procure fourteen or sixteen dollars in initial fees and commissions, transportation for five hundred or a thousand miles, the price of draft animals and the most essential of implements, and sustenance for the first two or three years of grubbing or "sodbusting" until sufficient food could be grown to feed the family and pay expenses? Transportation alone for a family of five would be the equivalent of half a year's wages.

For that matter, what was the industrial worker going to substitute for experience when he turned to farming? It was hard enough for the Missouri farmer to get along in Kansas, or the Iowa farmer in Nebraska. Two thirds of all homestead claimants before 1890 failed at the venture, and the great majority of all these were persons who had spent all their earlier lives on the land.[6] Of course,

---

[5] John W. Keener, comp., *Public Land Statutes of the United States*, 1916 (*Senate Document* No. 547, 64 Cong., 1 Sess., Washington: Government Printing Office, 1916), pp. 76–79, 100–101, 106–107, 110, 238–239, 393–396; Roy M[arvin] Robbins, *Our Landed Heritage: The Public Domain, 1776–1936* (Princeton: Princeton University Press, c.1942), pp. 213, 214.

[6] Shannon, "Homestead Act and Labor Surplus," pp. 644–645; cf. Clarence H. Danhof, "Farm-Making Costs and the 'Safety Valve': 1850–1860," *The Journal of Political Economy*, XLIX, No. 3 (June, 1941), 317–359.

there were members of construction gangs who got stranded in the West, drifted about for a while, worked on others' farms, habituated themselves, and finally took up homesteads. There were other Eastern laborers who managed in some way to acquire funds and emigrate. But these were a very small percentage of all the homesteaders, and they were a still smaller fraction of the wage victims of the cities. From 1860 to 1900, while the population of the nation was increasing by nearly 45,000,000, possibly 400,000 families, totaling 2,000,000 people, got free land from the government and kept it for themselves. In the same period (see page 351) about 7,000,000 had bought farms or had become wage laborers or tenants and their families on the land, and 36,000,000 were left to swell the population of the towns and cities.

Undoubtedly more immigrant families were enticed to America in the expectation of free farms than the number of homesteads patented to natives and the foreign-born combined. The surplus of land-seeking aliens, together with the far greater number who were originally looking for industrial occupations, furnished many applicants for each job vacated by any city worker who proved up on a homestead. It is a fair estimate that for every industrial toiler who made good on the land there were twenty farmers' sons who moved hopefully, and a few successfully, into the cities. The failure of the Homestead Act to provide means to get poor families to the farms, extend them long credit for all the rest of their needs for at least the first year, and give them guidance in farming was the first and one of the greatest defects of the measure.

Almost, if not entirely, as bad was the failure to provide for the cancellation of patents if the homesteads were ever sold, transferred, or mortgaged to anyone but the government. Free farms were intended for the sole use of the patentees and their heirs forever. But, by prearrangement, too many of them were acquired by hirelings, merely to build up huge estates for others. Private mortgages annihilated the holdings of a great number, for the benefit of land-loan companies, whereas government loans, if foreclosed, would have brought the land back into use for other homeseekers. Again, the Homestead Act failed to stop the public auctioning of lands and other cash sales (in certain areas), railroad grants, or gifts to states which could be held for cash sales or, worse yet, turned over to private speculators. Indian lands reverting to the government and soldiers' pension scrip also helped speculators to monopolize immense tracts after 1862, with as great ease as at any earlier period. The continuation down to 1891 of the Pre-emption Act of 1841, and the partial substitution therefor of the new Commutation Clause of 1891, also tended to defeat the purpose of a free farm for any who needed it, and to add to the bulk of speculative holdings. It would be difficult to overemphasize the fact that the Homestead Act was far from being a substitute for preceding legislation. In fact, as Paul W. Gates has amply demonstrated, the new law was merely superimposed on an accretion of heterogeneous measures of earlier generations, so as to make even more confusing an already "incongruous land system." [7]

The original act permitted filers on claims who did not wish to remain the full five years to buy the land (the "commutation clause") at the legal minimum of $1.25 an acre ($2.50 on reserved sections in the zones of the railroad land grants), after proving settlement or cultivation. This fact was openly advertised by the Commissioner of the General Land Office in 1873.[8] By interpretation, this meant that six months' residence on the land, including small improvements, was sufficient before commutation could be made.[9] As long as it was easy for speculators to grab up huge blocks of land by other than piecemeal methods, this commutation privilege, though abused, caused less harm than it did later. In time, however, it appeared to need clarification. So in 1891, when the cattle ranchers of the West and the timber men of the western Great Lakes areas were convinced of the necessity of engrossing all land in sight, Congress came to their rescue. The result was the Commutation Clause of March 3 of that year, which allowed purchases at the minimum price after fourteen months' residence and cultivation.[10] In actual practice this amendment also suffered be-

[7] Paul Wallace Gates, "The Homestead Law in an Incongruous Land System," *American Historical Review*, XLI, No. 4 (July, 1936), 654–656, referred to hereafter as Gates, "Incongruous Land System." For the labor "safety valve," see pages 356–359, herein.

[8] Willis Drummond, *Brief Description of the Public Lands of the United States of America, Prepared by the Commissioner of the General Land-Office for the Information of Foreigners Seeking a Home in the United States* (Washington: Government Printing Office, 1873), p. 11, referred to hereafter as Drummond, *Brief Description of Public Lands.*

[9] J[ames] D[avenport] Whelpley, "The Nation as a Land Owner," *Senate Document* No. 183, 57 Cong., 1 Sess. (1902, reprinted from *Harper's Weekly*), p. 10.

[10] 26 *Statutes at Large*, p. 1098.

yond its original wording for since a "constructive residence" (theoretical) of six months was deductible, the settler was required to occupy his land only during the eight more pleasant months of one year.[11] The purpose to which this clause was devoted is eloquently exposed by the Public Lands Commission of 1905 in the following words:

The appearance of commuted homestead entries within the "timber" and "prospective mineral" belts one year after proof is that of a neglected and abandoned claim. The log house shows evidence of decay, and the clearing surrounding same has grown a healthy crop of brush and weeds. In two years after proof the house has fallen down and only very dim signs of a clearing are visible. It begins to look as though the pioneer had retraced his steps and once more sought civilization. In three years after proof almost every sign or resemblance of habitation and cultivation has disappeared and the claim has once more taken on its virgin appearance. In townships where commutation has been heaviest, within these two belts, now no trace of habitation is to be found save an occasional trapper or hunter. In fact one can travel over this area for days without even finding a settler to stop over night with, while the Government plat shows that dozens of homes were once established there.[12]

From 1881 to 1900 patents to the number of 95,144, for a total of nearly 13,939,000 acres, were granted on commutation, and the tendency was becoming accelerated. In the next four years nearly half as many commutations for half as much land were allowed as in the preceding twenty years.[13] In fact, as though to hasten further the process of monopolization, on June 5, 1900, Congress authorized any person who had already commuted a homestead to file on a second one.[14]

An additional serious deficiency of the Homestead Act was that, while positively encouraging monopolization in the more valuable farming and lumbering regions, it tempted settlers out to the arid stretches where a quarter section was barely enough for the grazing of two or three cattle. Even where dry farming was possible, no family could exist on the product of 160 acres. Before 1890 one person could acquire 1,280 acres direct from the government, but

---

[11] Public Lands Commission, *Report*, 1905, p. 66.

[12] *Ibid.*, p. 69; see also, Binger Hermann and E[than] A[llen] Hitchcock, "Commuted Homestead, etc., Entries Attacked on Grounds of Fraudulent Intent," *Senate Document* No. 130, 57 Cong., 2 Sess., p. 5.

[13] Public Lands Commission, *Report*, 1905, p. 180.

[14] 31 *Statutes at Large*, pp. 269–270

even this amount was too small in many parts of the Far West, where from 10,000 to 25,000 acres of grazing rights were the best economic unit.[15] Persons who tried to accumulate the necessary area had to resort to subterfuges and evasions of the laws. Others, unable to accomplish this feat, overgrazed the land to its ultimate destruction, or plowed it up only to see it blow away.

Sweeping and serious as this indictment of the Homestead policy may seem to be, it fails to tell more than a minor fraction of the whole story. Further demonstration of the faults before mentioned is necessary, but it is best first to enumerate the other principal land acts and policies of the federal government in the later years of the nineteenth century, so that the consequences of the system can be considered as a whole rather than piecemeal.

SUBSEQUENT LAND ACTS

Of all the land laws passed after 1860 the Timber Culture Act of March 3, 1873, perhaps contributed least to the growth of speculation and monopoly. It too, however, fell rather short of the hopes of its authors. Painfully aware of the frequent shortage of rainfall in the West, and realizing that trees tend to retain moisture in the soil, Senator Phineas W. Hitchcock of Nebraska introduced the measure that was vainly expected to change weather conditions on the Great Plains. The law, applying to the same classes of persons as did the Homestead Act, permitted any of them, even if they already had a homestead and a pre-emption claim of a quarter section each, to take out papers on another 160 acres of relatively treeless land. The original law required the planting of one fourth of the area in trees within ten years. This proving too much, an amendment of June 14, 1878, limited the amount to one sixteenth and reduced the time to eight years. But for every year that the young seedlings or sprouts were destroyed by grasshoppers, drouth, or other calamity, a year's extension of time was allowed. In not less than eight years, when proof was given that at least 2,700 seeds or slips had been planted for each required acre and

[15] Paul Wallace Gates, "Recent Land Policies of the Federal Government," *Certain Aspects of Land Problems and Government Land Policies* (Part VII of the *Supplementary Report of the Land Planning Committee to the National Resources Board,* Washington: Government Printing Office, 1935), pp. 68–71, referred to hereafter as Gates, "Recent Land Policies."

that 675 or more trees to the acre were still living and thriving, the settler could get a deed to the tract.[16]

Under this law, until its repeal eighteen years later, more than 245,000 original entries were made for nearly 37,000,000 acres. But, after repeated extensions of time, to 1904 only 65,292 final patents were issued for a little more than 9,745,000 acres. About nine tenths of these deeds went to persons who did not comply with "the letter of the law, to say nothing of the spirit." [17] Almost eight million of the proved-up acres were in Nebraska, South Dakota, Kansas, and North Dakota, in that order. The only other state that approximated half a million acres was Colorado.[18] Most of the claimants were too far east to interest or greatly bother the cattle barons, and the regular speculators found easier methods than fooling around with tracts they might have to wait a decade or more for. The "tree claims" were generally in locations that the speculators had first passed up anyway. Thus the law operated mainly to add to the farms of persons who needed half or three quarters of a section to make a living, and was, in consequence, an exception to the rule that the land laws never fitted the actual needs of the settlers. Contrary to many notions, where serious effort was actually made, these tree claimers had a fair degree of success. A forest service bulletin of 1905, covering 47,000 square miles in Nebraska, 34,000 in Kansas, and 28,000 in Colorado, is quite revealing on this point. One of the illustrations is of "White Elm and Hackberry" in "Rooks County, Kans.," and another is of "A Clump of Bur Oak which has Taken Possession of a Prairie Within Twenty-five Years, Buffalo County, Nebr." [19] The shelter-belt idea of the federal government in the early 1930's was not as ridiculous as it was reported.

Unlike the Timber Culture Act, the Desert Land Act of March 3, 1877,[20] evidently had as its primary object the granting of special privileges to great cattle companies. In the first place, a California

[16] 17 *Statutes at Large*, pp. 605–606; 20 *ibid.*, pp. 113–115; *Senate Journal*, 42 Cong., 2 Sess., p. 262 (February 20, 1872); Henry N[orris] Copp, *The American Settler's Guide* (Washington: published by the editor, 2d ed., 1882), pp. 69, 71–72.

[17] Whelpley, "The Nation as a Land Owner," p. 9; Public Lands Commission, *Report*, 1905, p. 183.

[18] Public Lands Commission, *Report*, 1905, p. 183.

[19] Royal S[haw] Kellogg, "Forest Belts of Western Kansas and Nebraska," U.S. Department of Agriculture, Forest Service, *Bulletin* No. 66 (Washington: Government Printing Office, 1905), frontispiece and illustration facing p. 32.

[20] 19 *Statutes at Large*, p. 377.

ranching company wanted title to a large amount of pasture land, and succeeded in getting a special act of Congress granting its request, provided it would irrigate a portion of the tract. This success led to demands from others, and finally the general law was passed,[21] for the Pacific coast and Great Basin states and territories as well as for Montana, Wyoming, New Mexico, and Dakota territories. Under this act the claimant paid twenty-five cents down on each acre and swore to try to irrigate any amount up to one section within three years. When he gave satisfactory proof that the area had been sufficiently watered, the payment of an additional dollar an acre completed the deal. The purpose of the act—to encourage monopolization while throwing dust in the public's eyes—appeared in the fact that assignment of any tract to another person could be made at any time after filing the entry and before final proof. There was nothing illegal in the transfer unless an agreement to that purpose preceded the taking out of the claim. Such an evasion was almost impossible to prove, and for years at a time no effort was made at cancellation of grants for fraud.[22]

A clause in a miscellaneous appropriation act of August 30, 1890, limited to 320 acres the total amount of land any person could enter upon under any or all of the laws,[23] and a further amendment to the Desert Land Act in 1891 ordered the spending of three dollars in improvements on each acre before title would be granted.[24] Even then the law was a foolish mistake as far as its presumed purpose went. No one person could cultivate even 320 acres of irrigated land, and three dollars an acre would not be enough even to make a beginning at irrigation. Consequently, no effort was made to get water, all exertion instead being centered on getting witnesses to make the required oaths at the land office. Some individuals made a practice of giving testimony for hire. For the benefit of those who had tender consciences about perjury, a bucket of water would be poured on the ground, thus giving reality to their declaration that they had "seen water upon the claim." Hundreds of cases were known where water enough for forty acres was used to get title to thousands. One little stream

[21] Whelpley, "The Nation as a Land Owner," p. 9.
[22] Hermann and Hitchcock, "Commuted Homestead Entries Attacked," pp. 4, 7.
[23] 26 *Statutes at Large*, p. 391.
[24] *Ibid.*, pp. 1096–1097.

would be turned from claim to claim just as the time came to prove that water was there.

But from the point of view of its originators and advocates the law was a huge success. The land acquired did not have to be actual desert, but merely such as would not grow crops without irrigation. It was good grazing land, and was wanted for that purpose only. So the cattle or sheep company with ample funds would merely advertise that they would pay a given sum an acre for as many acres as needed. Then any persons of legal age, not otherwise disqualified, could make the entries, pay the down installments with money received from the company, swear to lies for each other, make the transfers, receive their bonuses, and move on. Between 1877 and 1901 filings were made for 36,951 claims covering 9,140,517 acres, but only 10,912 patents were issued, for 2,674,695 acres. These figures tell their own story. About three out of four entrants really tried to make good and failed. The rest were merely the pawns of land monopolists. It was conservatively estimated that at least 95 per cent of the final proofs were fraudulent.[25]

The Timber and Stone Act of June 3, 1878, differed from its predecessors, just described, in several respects. It was supposed to apply only to lands "unfit for cultivation" and "valuable chiefly for timber" or stone. Any citizen or alien who had filed his intention papers, after swearing that he believed the tract contained no valuable minerals and that he had made no agreement to transfer his holding to anybody else, could buy as much as a quarter section for $2.50 an acre. Originally the law applied only to California, Nevada, Oregon, and Washington Territory, but in 1892 its provisions were extended to all "public-land states."[26] If the act was intended for any other purpose than rapid monopolization of all the valuable timber as yet not patented in the United States, then Congress was very remiss in the phraseology. In the first place, an acre cost less than the value of one log from one tree where it stood as yet unfelled. Again, the officials took no care to reserve valuable minerals to the government or to see that the land was unfit for cultivation. Finally, by failure to provide that the transfer of the property or timber rights to others, after purchase, would result

---

[25] Whelpley, "The Nation as a Land Owner," pp. 11–13. See also Public Lands Commission, *Report*, 1905, pp. 79–81.

[26] 20 *Statutes at Large*, pp. 89–91; 27 *ibid.*, p. 348.

in the cancellation of the grants, the land office positively encouraged the engrossment of the forests. The extension of the privilege after fourteen years of wholesale graft, and without any further safeguards, is surely convincing evidence of a brazen disregard for the general welfare.

In 1901 the Commissioner of the General Land Office stated: *"Immense tracts of the most valuable timber land, which every consideration of public interest demanded should be preserved for public use, have become the property of a few individuals and corporations. In many instances whole townships have been entered under this law in the interest of one person or firm, to whom the lands have been conveyed as soon as receipts for the purchase price were issued."* The whole process was fraudulent, yet it was almost impossible to prove that the claim filers had perjured themselves as to their innocence of motive. In fact, a Supreme Court decision of 1892 virtually made a farce of the prior agreement.[27] Before 1900, nearly 27,000 entries had been made for 3,600,000 acres. Then, as timber lands grew scarce, in the next four years, in Theodore Roosevelt's administration, the amount was more than doubled. In 1903 alone nearly half as much timber land was monopolized as in the whole period from 1878 to 1900.[28]

But in this last grand rush, several of the speculators overstepped themselves and landed in prison as a consequence. Among those who were sentenced were Senator John H. Mitchell and Representative John N. Williamson of Oregon. Williamson got a new trial and Mitchell died pending his appeal. Binger Hermann lost his position as Commissioner of the Land Office in consequence of his laxity. Then he secured election to Congress by managing, through a trick, to get himself photographed with Roosevelt. Nevertheless, the courts subsequently convicted him of frauds, but he managed to secure leniency, while a number of the lesser criminals were required to serve sentence. The most illuminating account of the details of the whole disgraceful business was told by S. A. D. Puter, one of the convicted looters. His testimony might be impeached on the basis of his criminal record, were it not that it tallies so closely throughout with the official records, that it is so care-

[27] Hermann and Hitchcock, "Commuted Homestead Entries Attacked," pp. 2–3, italics in the original.
[28] Public Lands Commission, *Report*, 1905, p. 186.

fully and voluminously supplied with reprints and facsimiles, and that the collaborator of the book was himself a land-office official who was not implicated.[29]

The California Redwood Company, Puter says, ran "men into the land office by the hundreds." Twenty-five alien sailors at a time were marched from their boardinghouses to the courthouse to file their first citizenship papers; then to the local land office to take out claims; next to a notary public to "execute an acknowledgment of a blank deed"; thence to the paymasters for their fifty dollars each; and finally back to their ships or boardinghouses. At a later time, Willard N. Jones, before conviction for his activities, was buying the services of applicants for ten dollars each. Then he found he could get plenty of them for a quarter as much. Ultimately they became so numerous that he was credited with procuring some at the cost of a glass of beer.[30]

Perhaps the greatest timber raid of all was the series of events culminating in the setting aside of the Mt. Rainier National Park reserve. James J. Hill arranged this for the Northern Pacific railroad. The company had huge land grants in the Rainier district, much of which was useless for farming and not high grade for timber. So on March 2, 1899, Congress authorized the national park for that area, and allowed the Northern Pacific, in its place, to trade 450,000 acres for an equivalent of richer timber lands elsewhere, from which it proceeded to drive out prospective homesteaders. But this was all legal, and therefore above reproach. The whole transaction was only one of a series following upon the Forest Lieu Act of June 4, 1897, allowing monopolies general rights to make such transfers. The Secretary of the Interior, C. N. Bliss, a McKinley-Hanna henchman, ruled that the timber barons could even strip their lands of trees and then exchange them for a like amount elsewhere.[31]

---

[29] S[tephen] A[rnold] D[ouglas] Puter and Horace Stevens, *Looters of the Public Domain* (Portland, Ore.: The Portland Printing House, 1908), pp. 59–66, 142–145, 220, 227, 339, 341–342, 387, 433, 445–452, 454; John Ise, *The United States Forest Policy* (New Haven: Yale University Press, 1920), pp. 185–190.

[30] Puter and Stevens, *Looters of the Public Domain*, pp. 16–25, 32, quotation p. 18.

[31] *Ibid.*, pp. 368–385; 30 *Statutes at Large*, pp. 36, 993–995; Ise, *United States Forest Policy*, pp. 176–185.

RAILROAD LAND GRANTS

Under the four basic acts just described, barely 96,000,000 acres were disposed of, and possibly half of this was retained by the original claimants. In 1860 the unreserved and unappropriated government domain covered approximately a billion acres. In 1900 about half of this remained (aside from Alaska, acquired in 1867), but much of it was nonarable, and most of the rest of it had been reserved by one means or another.[32] Over 183,000,000 acres had been given to or reserved for railroad companies (including some grants made before 1860). Nearly 3,000,000 acres had been granted for wagon roads and canals; 140,000,000 acres were donated to the states; and, in addition, 100,000,000 acres, procured from the Indians, and another 100,000,000 acres held for cash sales, were open for disposal after the passage of the Homestead Act.[33] The homesteaders, even including those who acted as tools of speculators, got just about one acre out of every six or seven that the government gave up. Those who took free farms to keep received about one acre in ten. This was the actual fulfillment of the hopes of 1862 that all the remainder of the public domain would be used to ease the load of economic pressure in the nation.

In the second half of the nineteenth century, by far the greatest single method of withdrawing land from homestead entry was by grants to railroad companies to encourage the construction of new lines between 1850 and 1871. The gifts were made direct to the companies in the territories, and through the medium of the state governments elsewhere. Not till 1938 was an authoritative estimate of these grants available.[34] But the main purpose here is to show not only how much land was finally patented, but also how much was withheld from settlement during the remainder of the century,

[32] Public Lands Commission, *Report*, 1905, p. 360.

[33] Gates, "Incongruous Land System," pp. 657–662; Thomas Donaldson, *The Public Domain* (Washington: Government Printing Office, 1884), p. 273; Public Lands Commission, *Report*, 1905, p. 361; "Aids to Railroads," Federal Coordinator of Transportation, Section of Research, *Public Aids to Transportation* (Washington: Government Printing Office, 1938), II, Pt. 1, 33.

[34] *Ibid.;* John Bell Sanborn, *Congressional Grants of Land in Aid of Railways* (University of Wisconsin, *Bulletin* No. 30, *Economics, Political Science and History Series*, Vol. III, No. 2, Madison: 1899), is mainly a legislative history; Lewis Henry Haney, *A Congressional History of Railways in the United States, 1850–1887* (University of Wisconsin, *Bulletin* No. 342, *Economics and Political Science Series*, Vol. VI, No. 1, Madison: 1910), is much more informative on background.

how much the pioneers had to pay for farms that cost the corporations nothing, and how the system affected the homesteader.

The railroads got over 134,000,000 acres directly from the federal government, in addition to nearly 49,000,000 acres through the intermediary of the states or, as in Texas, from the state itself. By a very conservative estimate, this constituted a gift of a net value of $516,000,000, while one somewhat prejudiced calculation set the sum at $2,480,000,000. In addition, the railroads were given some 840,000 acres by local governments, individuals, and the like, its valuation being figured at $232,000,000, but this was not an item affecting the homesteader. If to this there be added the $48,000,000 permanently accruing to the Union Pacific and its affiliates from federal loans, the large but incalculable value of stone, timber, and other building materials from government lands, all the bonuses voted by local governments to encourage railroad building, and all the other governmental favors received, the magnitude of public charity to the corporations begins to become apparent. Of all the federal grants of railroad land, only about 22,000,000 acres were patented before the administration of President Lincoln,[35] thus making the problem one of concern mainly after the adoption of the Homestead Act. Many of the railroads did not live up to the terms of their charters, and after delays of several years their grants were canceled or made smaller. Otherwise, the gifts would have been far larger than the 183,000,000 acres already mentioned. But, stating the figure in a more comprehensible way, the 286,000 square miles actually donated was an area larger than the state of Texas, or nearly a tenth that of all the United States.

The grants to the Union and Central Pacific lines and their subsidiaries were twenty square miles for each mile of track in the territories, and ten in the states. Most of the later Pacific railroads got forty and twenty. These gifts came not in solid strips, but in alternate sections like the squares of one color on a checkerboard. The other squares may represent the sections reserved by the government for sale at $2.50 an acre or limited homesteading. None of the government-reserved areas might be occupied until the railroads received their full shares. This meant that for many years

[35] Donaldson, *The Public Domain,* pp. 269–273; "Aids to Railroads," pp. 32–33, 52–55.

strips from forty to eighty miles wide (half on each side of the railroad) were closed to settlement, except for such lands as the railroads themselves held for sale at from four to ten dollars an acre, or more.

But this was not all. The government widened the closed belts to 60 and 120 miles, in order to make sure that the corporations got adequate compensation for tracts already held by settlers within the railroad zones. Thus, at one time or another, something like three tenths of the area of the United States (and a much larger fraction of the West) had to remain unused, while prospective homesteaders took the lean pickings, from 30 to 60 miles remote from a projected railroad line. For example, in 1870, Congress extended the time of a company to build the first 20 miles of a line that had got its land grant in 1853 (cf. page 107, below). For a long time, the Northern Pacific held in escrow a 120-mile strip all the way from the western border of Minnesota to Puget Sound, and the Southern Pacific did likewise for a 60-mile band through California and 100 miles in the territories, until Grover Cleveland abated this nuisance in 1887. Meanwhile, the Northern Pacific was cutting timber off government lands while saving that on its own. The directors of the same line revealed that if they could get only two dollars an acre from their gift lands they could build the road from the proceeds alone, and have $20,000,000 left over for pin money.[36] As a matter of fact, the average price received for railroad land as early as 1880 was $4.76 an acre, or more than twice the Northern Pacific's conservative estimate. The lowest average for any line was $2.14. Though much Western land would not bring that price, even in the twentieth century, it must be kept in mind that the railroads selected routes across the country over the very best lands discoverable in any area. Also, the Northern Pacific's big seizures of timber might be remembered. The profits from this alone should have been enough to construct the whole line from Duluth to Tacoma.

Cleveland's action in 1887 was to throw open to settlement most of the land within the railroad-indemnity limits, and this was a great aid to the homeseeker. It is also noteworthy that when the

[36] Henry George, *Our Land and Land Policy* (New York: Doubleday and Mc-Clure Company, 1901, 1st ed., 1871), pp. 20–21, 24, 33; Gates, "Incongruous Land System," p. 657.

companies came into final possession of their grants they seldom tried to hold a permanent monopoly. They wanted cash, and they needed settlers to add to their freight and passenger revenues.[37] In many cases, however, they encouraged speculative buying by others. Thus were the huge bonanza farms of the 1880's built up.[38] The argument is often advanced that the Western railroads could not have been built without federal aid. Perhaps private enterprise would have failed, if left to its own devices. But government construction and operation would have been less costly to the public had not such a solution been unthinkable to the rulers of that generation. As it was, the companies were not only given their railroads—they were given a bonus to accept them.[39]

CASH SALES BY FEDERAL AND STATE GOVERNMENTS

Cash sales of government land included the transactions under the Desert Land and the Timber and Stone acts as well as the Pre-emption Act, and commutation under the Homestead Act. But the entire amount disposed of under those measures was only a small part of what was open for cash sales or to be had for scrip issued by the federal and state governments. Down to 1889, as well as at any time before 1862, the financial status of the speculator alone limited the amount of land he could buy from the federal government. In the Dakotas and parts of other states, entries by cash and scrip were not allowed, but in portions of Kansas, Nebraska, and the Lake, Gulf, and Pacific states more than a hundred million acres could be had. Purchases of from 100,000 to 600,000 acres were common in Eastern timbered areas as well as on the Prairies, but after 1889 the 320-acre limit was applied to all.[40]

From 1784 to 1880 the government had sold 197,000,000 acres for $209,000,000, about a seventh being after the passage of the Homestead Act. In only eight years before 1862 did the receipts from cash sales exceed those of 1869. Between 1862 and 1904 some 108,000,000 acres were sold at auction, or by other methods, this being almost exactly 39 per cent of all land (277,000,000 acres)

[37] Sanborn, *Congressional Grants of Land in Aid of Railways,* pp. 82–83; "Aids to Railroads," p. 32.
[38] Gates, "Incongruous Land System," p. 658.
[39] Shannon, *Critiques,* pp. 43–44.
[40] Gates, "Recent Land Policies," pp. 62, 69.

sold from the public domain since 1784.[41] Since the later period was just 35 per cent of the entire life of the public domain, it is clear that the average rate of sales per annum after 1862 was a little greater than before that date. This reservoir the speculators so drained that the best farming portions of Kansas, Nebraska, Missouri, California, Oregon, Washington, and elsewhere were monopolized ahead of the truly pioneering homesteader. One of the engrossers, the American Emigrant Company, advertised Iowa lands before 1870 as "Better than a Free Homestead," and then listed all the disadvantages of free farms. The worst of it was that the representations were mainly true. In Kansas between 1868 and 1872, settlers were offered over 8,000,000 acres of huge holdings, in the hands of railroad companies and other monopolists and including the state's own 90,000 acres of agricultural college grants. In less than nine years before 1880 the Santa Fé railroad sold well over 1,000,000 acres in Kansas at an average price of a little above $5.00 an acre, and the state itself sold over 500,000 acres of school and college lands at prices ranging from $2.88 to $4.72; and this was all in addition to what was sold by other private agencies and the federal government.[42]

A favorite tool of the speculators was negotiable federal scrip, issued at various intervals almost from the birth of the republic. As late as 1882 there was yet in circulation, unredeemed, a little of the Revolutionary War bounty scrip originally emitted to satisfy the claims of Virginia soldiers. This could still be presented at the rate of $1.25 an acre for the purchase of land.[43] Then, under a series of acts from 1849 to 1857, "swamp lands" to the amount of over 65,000,000 acres were conveyed to the states in which they were located, this being the amount reached by 1904. Again, in 1862, the Morrill Land Grant Act for agricultural colleges authorized the distribution of scrip for 7,672,800 acres to be located wherever the states chose, and, as the Confederate states were restored and other states were admitted to the Union, this donation was increased. This scrip soon fell in value, and some of it was sold to speculators for less than fifty cents an acre, though generally for more. Through its use, other valuable portions of the Western

[41] Calculated from tables in Donaldson, *The Public Domain*, p. 17, and Public Lands Commission, *Report*, 1905, pp. 199, 361.
[42] Gates, "Incongruous Land System," pp. 660–664.
[43] Copp, *American Settler's Guide*, p. 11.

states were engrossed.[44] The states also often handled the swamp-land grants in a suspicious manner. Speculators would get the county surveyor to declare a desirable tract to be swamp, buy a few affidavits as to the swampy character, and take out a patent from the state. Then, in many cases, the purchase price would be returned to the buyer. Probably half the land obtained was not swamp at all, and by 1870 some of the farms thus procured were worth twenty dollars an acre.[45]

While Congress was feeling so generous about the disposal of the poor man's heritage, it surrendered millions of other acres under the "mineral land law, to build wagon roads, in salt claims, and under the timber and stone act" at minimum prices. Yet, several thousand bills were defeated to give land for the petty schemes of private individuals, such as "to aid them in arctic explorations, to start dairies, private schools, to pay the expenses of trips abroad . . . . ," and myriad other worthy causes. Apparently it took a big transaction to get an act of Congress in authorization. Persons with strong political connections did not indulge in petty seizures. Some $200,000,000 were paid to Indian tribes to quiet their claims, and then the land was turned over to speculators at less than cost.[46]

An example of the Indian-land deals is the treaty with the Cherokee tribe, July 19, 1866, to permit them to sell 800,000 acres of their lands in southeastern Kansas, to any individual or corporation, at a dollar an acre. The lack of consideration for squatters already in the area led to public indignation that caused an amendment to the treaty. But in the meanwhile the Secretary of the Interior sold the lands, at the stipulated price, to the American Emigrant Company. By 1867 something like 12,000 squatters had arrived, and their number soon reached 20,000. Several railroad companies were interested in the tract, and land values were rising. Before this time the Attorney General had found irregularities in the transaction, and the transfer was forbidden. A sale was finally arranged with an agent of the Kansas City, Fort Scott, and Gulf

[44] Public Lands Commission, *Report*, 1905, pp. 156, 361; Gates, "Incongruous Land System," pp. 664–665. For further information on swamp-land warrants, see Paul Wallace Gates's volume in this series.

[45] George, *Our Land and Land Policy*, pp. 59–61; Whelpley, "The Nation as a Land Owner," p. 4.

[46] Whelpley, "The Nation as a Land Owner," pp. 4–5.

railroad. Then the company was allowed to trade its contract for the earlier and more lenient—and illegal—one that had first been offered to the American Emigrant Company. This sale was ratified by the Senate in 1866, and the railroad got its lands at a dollar an acre, but squatters in the tract had to pay $1.92 or get out.

The Indian lands were often partly improved and choice for settlement. Therefore they became an easy prey for speculators. The stipulation in some cases was that the land must be sold, not homesteaded. There were possibly 175,000,000 acres of Indian reservations in 1862, and much of this amount was exchanged for less desirable locations, the surrendered areas being offered at private sale in huge blocks to monopolists. Later they were auctioned off, but not always in small, farm-size tracts. Finally, the Dawes Severalty Act of 1887 required the sale of all future Indian lands in quarter-section lots. Since 1862 the General Land Office has disposed of between 100,000,000 and 125,000,000 acres of Indian lands.[47]

The states, in the disposal of their school lands, agricultural college scrip, and other donations from the federal government, were almost as lax as the federal government, if not more so. Texas, Tennessee, Kentucky, and the original area of the Atlantic seaboard states were outside the public domain, and Texas after 1860 had the bulk of her area still to sell or give away. But the rest of the extradomain states, as well as Texas, got their agricultural college grants in the West, often engrossing the best tracts in the states and territories that had not as yet received the gifts of their own lands. Wisconsin got 210,000 acres, but by 1870 other scrip for Wisconsin land amounted to over 1,000,000 acres. Nebraska got 90,000 acres and other states took nearly a million within her borders. California was given 150,000 acres, but Eastern states located claims on 750,000 more. None of the 140,000,000 acres of donations of one kind or another to the states could be given away to homesteaders. So speculators seized the land and regrated it to farmers at several times the cost to themselves. Scrip land bought at fifty cents an acre was often resold, without improvements, for five or ten dollars.[48]

[47] Gates, "Incongruous Land System," pp. 660–662, 672–674. For the Cherokee Treaty see U.S. *Session Laws*, 39 Cong., 1 Sess., "Treaties," pp. 115–125.
[48] Gates, "Incongruous Land System," p. 659; George, *Our Land and Land Policy*, pp. 18–19.

The result was that school funds in the states were low, while the children of the people victimized by unwise governments and by speculators got poor educational facilities. Down to 1906 Kansas was not receiving a tenth of her due in revenue from her lands. One of the state treasurers of Nebraska stole $300,000 of school-land funds, and sundry officials in the territories of New Mexico and Arizona followed his example. Kansas lost hundreds of thousands of dollars through fraudulent sales, and the proceeds from her common school lands were just about enough to buy each school child a second reader. Toward the end of the century the price of what lands the states had left was rising, and in 1889 Congress ordered that no more agricultural college land should be sold for less than ten dollars an acre. Since the worst of the tracts would not bring this amount, they had to be leased. A rental policy from the start would have brought far more returns to the treasuries, and would have injured the homestead cause no more than the plan actually followed.[49]

GREATER AND LESSER LAND MONOPOLISTS

The impression must not be left that land monopolization occurred only after 1860. It dated back to early colonial days of English, Dutch, and Spanish rule in America. The list of great land-holders, exclusive of the railroad companies, is a long and, in spots, an illustrious one, both before and after 1860. In the earlier period Henry L. Ellsworth, Commissioner of the Patent Office and progenitor of the federal Department of Agriculture, held 110,000 acres in Indiana and Illinois, which he let out to tenants. Michael L. Sullivant had 80,000 acres in three counties of Illinois alone (see page 155, below). Before 1870 William Scully, an Irish-American, accumulated some 250,000 acres in Illinois, Missouri, Kansas, and Nebraska. By 1935 there were 1,167 tenants on lands still held by his descendants. In 1866 Amos Lawrence, of "Bleeding Kansas" fame, bought 58,360 acres of agricultural college land in the state he helped to build. Two years later Senator John Sherman of Ohio made a more modest venture for 2,560 acres in Missouri. Ezra

[49] D. M. Richards, "Management of Our School Lands," University of New Mexico, *Bulletin* No. 42, *Educational Series*, Vol. I, Art. 2 (Albuquerque: The University, 1906), pp. 1–8.

Cornell procured 512,000 acres for Cornell University, which also ultimately took over about 350,000 acres from speculators in the scrip—all in the better parts of the West. Between 1868 and 1871 William S. Chapman bought for cash at the land office 650,000 acres in California and Nevada. Then he added "swamp" lands in California till his total was above 1,000,000 acres. All sorts of charges of fraud, bribery, perjury, and other corruption were leveled at him, but he had too much influence with the governments of the United States and California for any prosecution to affect him. His failing as a baronial landlord was bad management. His lands were of the best in the state, but he lost the bulk of them to Henry Miller, who devoted them to cattle raising. In 1886 there were twenty-nine foreign syndicates and individuals who held 20,747,000 American acres. Eleven timber firms in later years got hold of over 12,000,000 acres. This list is merely representative, and could be extended indefinitely. Among the consequences of the practice was widespread tenancy. The ratio of tenants to total farms for Iowa, Kansas, and Missouri in 1890 averaged 24.7 per cent. In some of the Southern public land states it ranged upward to 48 per cent, but largely for a different reason (see next chapter).[50]

No worse conditions of engrossment could be found in the nation than in California. Despite its large proportion of mountains and deserts, that state had more arable land than Ohio, but by 1870 a person had to approach a speculator to get an acre of it. Farming was done mainly by tenants or on estates of a thousand acres and upward. Henry George declared that a strong man on a good horse could not gallop across one of the larger holdings in a day. By 1870, the greater landlords, particularly the Southern Pacific railroad, ran the state government to suit themselves. The larger individual units of immense size were the outgrowth of vague Mexican grants, liberally interpreted by federal officials. The maximum Mexican gift was eleven "leagues" of 4,438 acres each. But, despite an adverse United States Supreme Court decision, these were stretched out so that eleven leagues could be patented in place of one.

A big attempt failed (as told by Henry George) when a certain

[50] Gates, "Recent Land Policies," pp. 64–66; Gates, "Incongruous Land System," pp. 665–669. See also pp. 154–156, herein, for additional data on large land holdings.

José Dominguez sold his rights to the Big Grape-Vine Rancho for one dollar. This consisted of about 7,000 acres, but the purchaser tried to stretch it into 208,472 acres, including "many valuable farms and vineyards" belonging to others. The public outcry in this instance resulted in the ordering of a new survey. Another holder named San Luis Obispo owned 43,266 acres in the one county of San Luis Obispo, but paid taxes on only a tenth of that area. An ex-surveyor general of the United States (identified in the *Official Register* as Edwin F. Beale), who knew how to "pull the wires" as well as the surveyor's chain, laid hold on 300,000 acres, a tract 75 miles wide. The butcher's firm of Miller and Lux owned 450,000 acres, and around one of their tracts was 160 miles of fence. These instances are representative of a large number of great holdings, fraudulently procured. [51] It was this situation in California that inspired Henry George to evolve his single-tax theory.

EFFORTS AT LAND-LAW REFORMS

From early days, powerful voices were raised in protest against the looting of the public domain, but they were drowned out by still more potent interests. Representative George W. Julian of Indiana spoke and wrote incessantly on the issue. Henry George, as early as 1870, was exposing with incisive accuracy the multitude of abuses. In 1885 William A. J. Sparks, Commissioner of the General Land Office under Grover Cleveland, had good reason for accusing many of his predecessors of being stupid or venal in most of their activities. In 1886 he ordered a cessation of all grants under the Timber Culture and the Desert Land laws, but had to bow to the storm of protest and rescind the action. Foreseeing an end to wide-open opportunity, the monopolists then did their worst, so that entries under the different laws rose in 1886 to the highest point since 1856. But the ultimate victory was with Sparks, when in 1889 Congress was stampeded into ending most forms of cash sales, and in 1890 when the limit of 320 acres to one individual was adopted. Then in 1891 the repeal of the Pre-emption and the Timber Culture acts, and the limitation of the Desert Land Act,

[51] George, *Our Land and Land Policy*, pp. 38–44, 71–73; *Register of Officers and Agents, Civil, Military, and Naval, in the Service of the United States*, 1863 (Washington: Government Printing Office, 1864), p. 102.

locked other stables after the horses were stolen.[52] But nothing
was done to stop further engrossment of land by the use of fraudulent entry and transfer. The legitimate needs of the farmer in arid
regions were denied, but some of the most brazen of big appropriations were yet to come.

Throughout the period, Congress took a thoroughly unrealistic
attitude toward the whole question. In 1870 the House of Representatives passed a resolution that railroad grants should cease,
but in the following year 20,000,000 more acres were donated before the hostility of the West brought a permanent cessation.
Congress, under the influence of the pressure groups of that day,
passed laws with convenient loopholes which the Land Office at
Washington utilized. Even the Congressional resolution of 1866 to
end cash sales in the conquered South was intended to punish
Confederate leaders rather than to provide forty acres for each
Negro, with or without a mule. In the same year Thaddeus Stevens
and Ben Wade pushed through Congress a bill giving a Montana
mining company 12,800 acres of mineral and timber land for $1.25
an acre. This bill was vetoed by Andrew Johnson in savage terms.
True friends of homesteaders, in Congress, had constantly to be on
guard against the slipping through of such measures when few
members were present, or in special night sessions, ostensibly called
for last-minute routine. The ban on Southern sales was lifted in
1876, after the real objectives of the extreme reconstructionists had
been won, and thereafter, till 1888, the chicanery of the West was
duplicated viciously in the South.[53]

Though the forces of reform continued to demand a surgical
cure of the land-fraud cancer, Congress was satisfied with pallia-
tives and salves. A number of acts in the late 1860's showed how
little Congress cared for bona fide homesteaders. In 1875-1877 the
Commissioner of the Land Office agitated for the opening of all
lands to public sale. In 1879 a representative in Congress from
California could not get even a respectful hearing for a Constitutional amendment to prevent all sales. Yet, in 1873 a government
publication blandly informed newcomers to American shores that
the Homestead Act "has prevented large capitalists from absorbing

[52] Gates, "Incongruous Land System," pp. 656, 680-681.
[53] Ibid., pp. 655, 658, 670-672, 678; Paul Wallace Gates, "Federal Land Policy
in the South, 1866-1888." The Journal of Southern History, VI, No. 3 (August,
1940), 303-330.

great tracts of the public domain. . . ." For twenty-five years before 1900 each Secretary of the Interior demanded the repeal of all laws providing for land entry, except the Homestead Act with an inviolable five-year residence clause. Henry M. Teller said, "Not another acre should be sold for scrip." Another writer declared in 1901:

There is not a land law in effect which applies intelligently to the public agricultural domain as it is now to be found, and each and every law which is in force is used daily as a means for the fraudulent segregation of land from the public domain by those whom the law did not contemplate as possible beneficiaries.

The same writer had a realistic understanding of Western needs, and would adjust the size of the homestead to geographic conditions.[54]

In 1880 a Public Lands Commission proposed a model land bill of 52 pages, in 27 chapters and 282 sections, to take the place of all preceding legislation. It was not ideal, but would have been a remarkable improvement. It was merely buried away in the documents. Twenty-two years later the Secretary of the Interior, Ethan Allen Hitchcock, was recommending repeal of the Desert Land Act, the Commutation Clause, and other land-grabbing measures, on "the avowed policy of the Government of preserving the remaining public lands for homes for actual settlers." At the same time his coauthor and Commissioner in the Land Office, Binger Hermann, was belittling the extensiveness of fraud. As yet, Hermann's own malfeasance was undiscovered. The Hermann-Hitchcock document also revealed that during the depression of 1893–1897 there was no great activity under the Timber and Stone Act, but that, with the return of good times, the raids were renewed with greater vigor than ever before.[55] In other words, in depression times, when labor needed a safety valve, workers not only could not go west to take up farms; they could not even go west and profit from spurious entries. Now the last of the farmer's frontiers was essentially closed, except for internal expansion.

[54] Drummond, *Brief Description of Public Lands,* p. 11, first quotation; Whelpley, "The Nation as a Land Owner," pp. 13–14, inset quotation; Gates, "Incongruous Land System," pp. 677, 679.
[55] Public Lands Commission, *Report,* 1880, *House Executive Document* No. 46, 46 Cong., 2 Sess., pp. xlix–c; Hermann and Hitchcock, "Commuted Homestead Entries Attacked," pp. 3–5, 13–17, quotation p. 5.

CHAPTER IV

Land and Labor in the New South

THE WAR AND ITS EFFECTS

BEFORE the close of the nineteenth century, the portion of the country perhaps least affected of all by intersectional migration, immigration, and federal land policy was the conquered South. Even the process of monopolization of Southern public lands, following the close of political reconstruction, did not essentially alter the previous system of huge estates operated by servile labor, interspersed with numerous holdings of yeoman farmers and with the run-down or never valuable tracts of small freeholders and tenants. The principal difference was that a larger proportion of the new monopolistic holdings, than of the old, was in the hands of Northern individuals and companies.[1] This, however, was nothing peculiar to the new Southern scene alone.

The Civil War itself was far more than a mere struggle between different labor and social systems. It was, in part, a contest for supremacy between Southern agricultural capitalists and Northern industrial capitalists.[2] Perhaps it would be more accurate to say that it was an effort on the part of the Southerners to maintain their system, unimpaired and unsubjugated, alongside the younger and

[1] Gates, "Federal Land Policy in the South," pp. 319–323.
[2] See Louis M[orton] Hacker, *The Triumph of American Capitalism* (New York: Simon and Schuster, 1940), pp. 322–373; Charles A[ustin] Beard and Mary R[itter] Beard, *The Rise of American Civilization* (New York: The Macmillan Company, 1927), II, 52–121.

more virile rival. But the Southern institution was not only archaic; it was weak; and it fell. This did not signify that the Southern agricultural system was to be materially altered in a technical way. It was simply to become more subservient to the business needs and interests of Eastern manufacturers, merchants, and bankers. If before the war the South depended too much on a one-crop basis, after the war this trend was accentuated. The victors needed more cotton, more tobacco, more sugar, and they wanted them at as low a cost as possible. They would extend credit the more readily to the landlord who would specialize most in what was wanted. Therefore, the landlord would retail the credit to the worker who would grow nothing but the one crop. The half-bankrupt landlord took it out of the slender income of the hungry share cropper, and both suffered in consequence. As Vance has quoted a Southern governor: "The Negro skins the land and the landlord skins the Negro." [3] Then the Southern politician voted to perpetuate the system, and ultimately contrived (though the race issue was used as a screen) to disfranchise the mass of the people, black and white, who might otherwise bring about a peaceful revolution.

During the Civil War there was a temporary shift to Southern national self-sufficiency in agriculture, as there was an effort in other economic lines as well. This was largely made imperative by the Northern blockade, but it was also an outgrowth of the effort to realize the aims of Southern nationalism. Some Confederates tried to solace themselves with the delusion that a decisive victory would be followed by such high prices in a cotton-starved world that the cost of the war could be paid from the first few years' receipts. But, as the months drew out into years, even the most optimistic planter saw the futility of piling up surplus bales of cotton to mildew or be seized by advancing federal armies. Furthermore, since the customary outside supplies of food were cut off, self-preservation itself demanded the growing of more cereals, meat, and vegetables.

On the other hand, there was no inducement to produce these crops for large-scale internal trade. One region would yield corn about as well as another; the transportation system was breaking down, both because of the shortage of factories to build repair

[3] Rupert B[ayless] Vance, *Human Factors in Cotton Culture* (Chapel Hill: The University of North Carolina Press, 1929), p. 65.

materials and because of the purposeful destruction by invading armies; and surplus foodstuffs were drained off by the Confederate government, wherever they could be had, by means of forced produce loans and taxes on products in kind. Wheat farmers, in particular, preferred to hoard their surpluses, or else produce only for their own needs, in order to prevent the authorities at Richmond from seizing their stores at confiscatory prices. It was good military policy for the North to sanction the destruction of all crops and caches of food or cotton that the armies could uncover. The faithfulness of Generals William T. Sherman and Philip H. Sheridan to this trust is well known. Though Sherman executed the policy more consistently and over a wider area, it was Sheridan who boasted that a crow could not fly across the Shenandoah Valley, after his expedition of destruction, without carrying its own provisions.[4]

Regardless of these discouraging conditions, habitual cotton planters could not refrain from producing more of the staple than could be marketed, even though the combined crops of 1862–1865 totaled no more than three quarters of the four million bales of 1861. Very little of this, except for the crop of 1865, was of any pecuniary benefit to the South. Countless bales were thrown up on the lines of fortifications to impede cannon balls; much went to waste for lack of adequate storage; great quantities were burned by the Confederates to prevent its capture by the invaders. But the victors found other stores, where there was no facility for shipment, and in passing by they also contributed to the conflagration. Other quantities were confiscated or bought by Northern agents and shipped to the mills of New England. Many citizens of the South willingly sold their cotton to these buyers, preferring the relative security of Northern greenbacks to the almost worthless currency of the South or to the prospect of confiscation by their own armies.[5]

At the close of the war, agriculture was almost prostrate. Many slaves had remained on the plantations, for Northern armies had passed through only relatively narrow strips of the South. But even where the labor force had not been disrupted—for example, on the

---

[4] Some of the unannotated passages here, and in later pages, are adapted from the author's *America's Economic Growth*.

[5] See Edgar L. Erickson, ed., "Hunting for Cotton in Dixie: From the Civil War Diary of Captain Charles E. Wilcox," *The Journal of Southern History*, IV, No. 4 (November, 1938) 493–513.

small farms operated solely by white labor, which outnumbered plantations five or more to one—the landowner was without money, credit, adequate transportation, or marketing agencies. In the chaotic financial situation, land values were often down to a tenth or less of their earlier rating. Farm buildings and implements were in bad repair, where not gone entirely, and in Georgia, Louisiana, and elsewhere less than half as many livestock existed as in 1860. All the bonds for the loans to the Confederate government and all the currency on hand were worthless. Until May, 1865, the proceeds of anything sold were taxed 25 per cent by the federal government, and even later any cotton stored over from earlier slave production was taxed a like amount. Though the North boasted of its charity to stricken Southern families in the early days of the Freedmen's Bureau, the truth is that the South sent northward in taxes and confiscated property far more than was returned. Though the news that the federal government got only 114,000 of the 3,000,000 bales of cotton confiscated or burned by Northern agents may have brought a sardonic grin to Southern faces, this was scant consolation for the loss. The Secretary of the Treasury, Hugh McCulloch, himself doubted the honesty of most of his department's representatives, and it is known that one of them sold a subordinate position for $25,000.[6]

Drouth and crop failures in 1865 and 1867, without even the relief of extraordinary prices for the salvage, completed the ruin. Before the end of 1865 hundreds of thousands of white people, in addition to unknown numbers of wandering blacks, were totally destitute, many of them starving to death. Stories were told of men and women pulling their own plows. Undoubtedly, a more foreseeing reconstruction system, giving a farm to every family, black or white, would have been of far greater worth to the section, then and forever afterward. The outright confiscation of large parts of estates created by slave labor, to make farms for freedmen, would in the long run have created more prosperity for the section than the growth of land monopolization that took place instead, and the simultaneous establishment of a system of quasi serfdom that left

[6] Walter Lynwood Fleming, *The Sequel of Appomattox* (Vol. XXXII of *Chronicles of America Series*, Allen Johnson, ed., New Haven: Yale University Press, 1919), pp. 4–10.

the toilers without ambition and the landlords with ruined soils and finances.

CHANGES IN LANDOWNERSHIP

The conditions mentioned above represent the worst effects of the war. But even the reconstruction that followed the war did not cause a wholesale disruption of great landed estates. Regardless of the sale of large areas in 1865, and later numerous losses of title through tax and mortgage foreclosures, the main result was a change in ownership. Many a planter had to compromise with a carpetbagger, selling one plantation to get money to operate another, or taking the newcomer in as a partner. The former holders of mortgages, the speculators, and sometimes, but not often, the more energetic of the Negroes became the new owners. Disturbed political conditions and abundant sales kept land values down for a considerable time. Yet, by 1870, all farming lands, with improvements, in the ten cotton states were rated at 52 per cent of their prewar value, the decline being from $1,479,000,000 to $764,000,000. In general, the states specializing most in cotton, and having the largest black population, suffered worst, the decline in Louisiana being 67 per cent. Throughout the latter part of the decade, and until the close of reconstruction, mortgage sales were a monthly event at nearly every courthouse in the South.[7]

A first glance at the statistics would indicate a far greater breakup in big estates than actually happened. In this same decade the average holding declined from 536 acres to 247 in Louisiana, and from 316 to 212 in North Carolina. In the entire cotton belt it was from 402 to 230. At the same time there was an even greater relative increase in the number of farms. Between 1860 and 1870 the number of holdings of less than a hundred acres in Mississippi grew from 23,250 to nearly an even 58,000. In the entire area of the Confederacy during the decade the number of all agricultural holdings advanced from a little over 549,000 to nearly 732,000, or approximately a third. Bruce, considering only the period from 1870 to 1900 and excluding Texas from his calculations, saw a

---

[7] M[atthew] B[rown] Hammond, *The Cotton Industry* (New York: The Macmillan Company, 1897), p. 127; Emory Q[uinter] Hawk, *Economic History of the South* (New York: Prentice-Hall, Inc., 1934), p. 429.

doubling in the number of farms (holdings were actually multiplied by 2¾), and a tripling and quadrupling in some of the states. Because in this area the acreage increase was only a seventh during the thirty years, he assumed that the subdivision of estates was the main explanation.[8]

This is a most unconvincing supposition. Florida, Alabama, Mississippi, Louisiana, and Arkansas were all public-land states, and in these many new farms were started. Much of the rest of the South was relatively undeveloped, though the unpatented land was generally of an inferior grade. Even if the increase in acreage in the given area were only a seventh (but the census figures reveal 22.7 per cent), most of the new holdings there were of the less-than-one-hundred-acre variety. It would take ten or a dozen of these to balance one moderate-sized, say a thousand-acre, plantation. A doubling in the number of holdings might well have been accounted for by this factor alone, without any subdivision. But there was a growth in the number of large estates as well as of small tracts, thus offsetting any hasty conclusion. There is, in addition, another explanation. It is easy to confuse "holdings" with "ownerships." From 1865 to 1900 tenancy and share cropping had mounted alarmingly, and each servile holding was included in the count of farms. The inadequacy of the census reports, as well as the fact that the plantations as such did not break up, explains in large part both the decrease in average size and the growth in total number of holdings.[9] The census did not show that share croppers' patches were parts of larger proprietorships. Furthermore, when one person owned numerous plantations, each was listed as a separate unit instead as a part of a vastly larger total acreage. For example, in 1890 the census accounted for 171 farms of less than 20 acres each in Catahoula Parish, Louisiana, but the tax assessor could account for only 19. Such officials are not in the habit of overlooking the small owner. Though the figures are not

    [8] Philip Alexander Bruce, *The Rise of the New South* (Vol. XVII of *The History of North America*, Guy Carleton Lee, ed., Philadelphia: George Barrie & Sons, ¢.1905), p. 19; Hammond, *Cotton Industry*, p. 129; Hawk, *Economic History of the South*, p. 430; *Ninth Census: Industry and Wealth*, pp. 340–341; *Twelfth Census: Agriculture*, I, 142.

    [9] See Robert Preston Brooks, *The Agrarian Revolution in Georgia, 1865–1912* (University of Wisconsin, *History Series, Bulletin*, Vol. III, No. 3, Madison: University of Wisconsin, 1914), p. 45; *Ninth Census: Industry and Wealth*, pp. 340–341; *Twelfth Census: Agriculture*, I, 142.

strictly comparable, the census estimate of 95 acres for the average Louisiana farm of 1900 is not as revealing as the data for 1910, showing 904 acres as the average size of holdings subdivided among tenants and sharecroppers in 29 of the 61 parishes.

The tendency was for the average freehold to increase in size. The assessment rolls of five parishes in the plantation areas of Louisiana showed freeholds of 50 acres and less, declining from 78 per cent of the total in 1860 to 48 in 1873, and standing at 53 in 1880. For the same years the ownerships of a hundred acres and upward increased from 34 per cent of all freeholds to 74 per cent, and in 1880 they were 70 per cent. In nine parishes where small farms had predominated in 1860, there was found a great increase of cropping and tenancy between 1873 and 1880. About the same percentage of shifting size of freeholds prevailed as in the planting parishes, but the ratio of proprietors to croppers and tenants changed from 60:40 in 1873 to 55:45 in 1880. Between 1860 and 1880 the number of plantations of a hundred acres and upward in the state showed nearly a threefold increase, while the number of smaller farms diminished. This resulted in a growth in share cropping and tenancy and in absentee landlordship. By 1900, plantations of over a hundred acres enclosed half the cultivated land in the state, and over half the farmers were not proprietors.[10] There is no reason to suppose that the situation was widely different in the Southern states for which detailed studies based on tax rolls have not been made.

Most of the farms on new lands were bought by yeoman whites. Some of the blacks also succeeded, but their slave training had cramped their initiative to such an extent that most of the new owners were incapable of retaining their farms. Later, when broken in to the share-cropper system, few ever got enough money ahead to make a down payment, and those who moved to industrial jobs in the cities lost their interest in farming, even if they succeeded in accumulating a few dollars. Since most Southern states took no account of color of owners in compiling data on freeholders, the record of Negro landownership is rather incomplete. In Georgia,

[10] Roger W[allace] Shugg, *Origins of Class Struggle in Louisiana: A Social History of White Farmers and Laborers during Slavery and After, 1840–1875* (University, La.: Louisiana State University Press, 1939), pp. 235–237, 239–241; *Twelfth Census: Agriculture*, I, 88; *Thirteenth Census: Agriculture, General Report and Analysis*, p. 887.

for example, in 1900 46.7 per cent of the population was colored, but Negroes had title to only 4 per cent of the land. The situation was comparable in Virginia. At about the same time the average wealth of the Negro in Virginia was estimated at eighteen dollars, in Georgia at thirteen dollars.[11]

THE RISE OF SHARE CROPPING

Since there was no intention on the part of the new reconstruction leaders in Congress (after 1870) to make freedom a reality to the Negro—to equip him with land, implements, necessary livestock, and training in management and self-reliance—it was not difficult for the planters who retained their old estates, and the newcomers who acquired the rest, to devise a new labor system giving the black man no more economic security than he had had in slavery: that is, a bare living. Roger Shugg, referring to the new proletariat of black and white after 1880, says that their condition "clearly demonstrate[s] the failure of the majority of people to improve their social and economic position after the war." The old leaders of the Congressional "radicals" were primarily concerned in the establishment of Republicanism in the South and the continuance in power of the newly triumphant industrial capitalism. They used the Negroes to help them achieve the purpose, and then a new group of leaders left the pawns to the mercy of their former owners.[12] There was no studied cruelty in the process, but it was a grievous blow to the hopes of those of the black race who really knew what was going on and cared about the outcome. This number was far greater than many contemporary Southern observers cared to admit.

The Negro had a reasonable hope for a division of the land after the war, a hope based both on the assurances of Northern soldiers and on the dire prophecies of Southern orators trying to stiffen Confederate resistance to invasion. The last declaration of the Confederate Congress in March, 1865, was a warning of the impending breakup of plantations into farms for Negroes. But sundry confiscation acts and decrees of Union generals during the war consti-

---

[11] Hammond, *Cotton Industry*, pp. 130–131; Brooks, *Agrarian Revolution in Georgia*, p. 44; Bruce, *Rise of the New South*, pp. 21–22.

[12] Shugg, *Origins of Class Struggle in Louisiana*, pp. 290–291; Hacker, *Triumph of American Capitalism*, pp. 374, 380–381.

tuted an even more definite promise. Under the act of 1862 all of St. Helena Island and much of Port Royal Island were confiscated and sold to Negroes on easy terms. Under the act of March 3, 1863, more plantations were subdivided in the same manner. Freedmen's colonies were established pursuant to an act of July 2, 1864, and still more were set aside under the Freedmen's Bureau Act of March 3, 1865, forty-acre tracts being especially stipulated. For a time in 1863 various Mississippi plantations, including ten thousand acres of Jefferson Davis's lands, were farmed by black aspirants to ownership. Then, in January, 1865, General Sherman reserved a strip thirty miles wide along the coast and the islands off the coast southward from Charleston and along the St. Johns River in Florida, for Negro settlement on forty-acre tracts, and the federal government virtually indorsed the procedure till late in the year. But by October, President Johnson had recovered from his early determination for a general confiscation. Sherman's order was revoked, and in a short time it became clear that general divisions under the confiscation acts would not be confirmed. But the Negroes were not easily to be dispossessed from the sea islands. In a short time they had made improvements on the land exceeding the previous valuation accumulating over two centuries of plantation improvement. The second Freedmen's Bureau Act (1866) furnished little relief to the freedmen threatened with dispossessment. Sometimes the Negroes used armed force to prevent eviction by the military. But the consequence was that down to 1910 nearly 60 per cent of the Negro farmers of Beaufort and Charleston counties in South Carolina owned their own land. This was a situation rare in the South. There were sporadic efforts, elsewhere, to procure a division of land by force, but with untrained leadership there was no success. No land was given away, and none was actually confiscated.[13]

The reaction to this situation was double-barreled in its effects. Landowners, fearful of confiscation, sometimes turned the freedmen off their plantations and dispersed them with violence. Before the close of 1865, as a result of such actions, hundreds of the blacks were said to be wandering throughout the country west of Savan-

[13] Oscar Zeichner, "The Transition from Slave to Free Agricultural Labor in the Southern States," *Agricultural History*, XIII, No. 1 (January, 1939), 23–24; for Sherman's orders see Sidney Andrews, *The South since the War* (Boston: Ticknor and Fields, 1866), pp. 208–211; James S[tewart] Allen, *Reconstruction: The Battle for Democracy, 1865–1876* (New York: International Publishers, c.1937), pp. 43–72.

nah, with pilfering and thieving as their only recourse.[14] During
that winter, according to a Freedmen's Bureau official, no less than
seventy thousand Negroes were without homes in eastern Virginia
alone. At the same time, the blacks, returning from the Union army
or from refugee camps, refused to give up their prospects of
homesteads or to return to the old labor gangs. Some would work
for reasonable wages, but far more wanted to buy or rent land, and
to this the owners would not agree. There resulted an impasse
during which the roving bands congregated "in camps, towns, and
cities." [15]

The first resort of the ex-Confederates, in this stalemate, was
the law. The bulk of the Negroes had remained on the old plantations, but the existence of camps in the neighborhood was always
an inducement to further dispersal of farm hands, and was also a
menace to the preservation of white supremacy. Consequently, the
Black Codes of 1865 and 1866 were adopted. These were cleverly
worded, apparently applying, as in the Georgia law, to "all persons
wandering or strolling about in idleness, who are able to work and
who have no property to support them. . . ." But it was thoroughly
understood, in the North as well as in the South, that these words
applied almost exclusively to Negroes. Such persons were to be
tried, convicted, and imprisoned or put to work on the roads, or,
preferably, turned over for a year to some planter to work out
their sentences.[16] Such acts or clauses as were not soon repealed
were quickly negated by an aroused Congress, but they are eloquent testimony to the determination of the planters to restore as
much as possible of the *status quo*. The Negro must be kept in
the status of a second-class citizen.

Meanwhile, the codes had been of some effect while they were
in force. Many freedmen wandered back to the old home, without
compulsion, and tried working for hypothetical wages. Most of the
features of the slave-gang system of labor continued, but the living
costs of the workers were deducted, at the employer's estimate,
from the stipend. Growing dissatisfaction with this arrangement led
many workers to break their contracts, and sometimes the whole
plantation force would leave in the night. An official report for

[14] Andrews, *South since the War*, p. 368.
[15] Zeichner, "Transition from Slave to Free Labor," pp. 24–25.
[16] Brooks, *Agrarian Revolution in Georgia*, pp. 13–14.

1866 in Georgia mentioned the loss of a hundred thousand workers in three years' time, it being supposed that they had drifted westward in search of higher wages. A Mississippi planter declared that he had recruited hands in Georgia, and could have had all he wanted, had not the "despicable" Georgians frightened the Negroes into believing they were to be sold in Cuba. This westward migration continued unabated at least till 1868, the Freedmen's Bureau being particularly active in securing locations where the best pay was to be had. In general, the persons who returned from roving to work for wages found it difficult to settle down again.[17]

In violating their agreements the Negroes were only following the examples set by their employers. Rations were not furnished according to the contracts, either in quality or in amount. Plantation disciplinary methods of slavery days were frequently restored. Even the pathetically small wages agreed on were not always paid. Many Georgia planters turned their workers away at the end of the season with little if any money. The Freedmen's Bureau officials often used their influence to quiet the Negroes' fears of contracts and to dispel their hopes of free farms, but discontent accumulated. Accordingly, some planters spoke about driving off all the Negroes and importing Chinese coolies in their place, thus to relieve themselves of "this cursed nigger impudence." Nevertheless, bombast did not solve the problem, and by 1867 it was coming to be realized that for many years to come the Negro was to be the planters' almost sole reliance for labor.[18]

In justice to the planter it must be said that the payment of wages in those troublous times was a most difficult contract to live up to, but those who adhered to their agreements, and dealt fairly with the workers, not only were able to get all the help they needed, but also prospered more than the shrewd neighbor whose policy drove the hands from the field before the crop was ready to harvest. Some of the wages from 1865 to 1867 would compare favorably with the general level elsewhere, and even at a later period except for the fact that the legal tender of the 1860's and early 1870's was greatly depreciated in value. Also, theoretical wages and actual payments were likely to show a wide divergence, and in some cases even the contractual stipend was astonishingly

[17] *Ibid.*, pp. 17–18, 28, 30.
[18] Zeichner, "Transition from Slave to Free Labor," pp. 25–27.

low. Thus, in 1865, wages in the cotton belt ranged from $2 to $18 a month with additional board. In 1867 the average varied from $100 a year in South Carolina to $158 in Arkansas. In the following year the payments for the same states were $93 and $115, while Georgia dropped as low as $83 and Texas maintained a level of $130. These figures, also, were in addition to food.[19]

On the more fertile Western lands it was possible to pay higher wages than in the old Piedmont, and as late as 1873 Georgia was still losing her Negroes, probably 20,000 leaving that year. Consequently, it was in the older region that the first reaction set in against wage payments. But elsewhere, as well, there was discontent with the inability to maintain or restore the old plantation system of absolute control over the workers. There had to be assurance that the field hands would be present when wanted, and this the wage system did not supply.[20] But more than this was involved. Poor whites, so long as they could refrain, would not work in the fields with Negroes, so they expanded on hitherto unused lands, or else went to town. In the heart of the cotton belt they were never numerous enough, anyway, to substitute for any considerable fraction of the blacks. Immigrants could not be lured into the section, with its servile wage scale. The Negro had to be utilized somehow, and the landlords thought they knew how to get the tasks well done and still keep the worker properly meek and docile. The spirit of the whole procedure was revealed in the slogan of "work nigger work" as a substitute for the earlier "forty acres and a mule." By 1869 the gang-labor system was on the verge of collapse in the Eastern cotton belt, and, as if by common consent, the wage system was dropped, by many of the planters, in favor of share cropping.[21]

This, however, was no suddenly derived formula. It has been said that share cropping came about on the demand of the Negroes, who could live throughout the year under no other system. Even if this were true, no such sophistry will explain the ultimately almost universal trend to the new idea. It was the outcome of years of experimentation to find what method would produce the most constant supply of submissive labor at the lowest cost. Several de-

[19] *Ibid.*, p. 29.
[20] *Ibid.*, pp. 29–30.
[21] Brooks, *Agrarian Revolution in Georgia*, pp. 25–26.

vices besides wage payments were tried out from the earliest days of disruption of the slave gangs by invading armies. Frequently, the workers were merely promised their keep, to be charged against them, and a share of the crop at the end of the season, from which their expenses were to be deducted. Then they worked in gangs, as in the old days, and frequently at the end of the year found themselves in debt, instead of having a few coins to jingle together. On the other hand, one such laborer in 1866 is said to have accumulated a fortune of thirty dollars.[22] Another experiment was a modification of serfdom, where the worker got a few acres with a hut, and wood to burn, then worked in the owner's fields four or five days out of the week for the privilege of raising his own food on the plot reserved for him. Occasionally there was to be found the regular form of tenancy; but sooner or later most of the owners adopted the share-cropping system.[23]

Share cropping and tenancy are altogether different things, even to the legal relationships. The tenant has a lease on the land, can generally have some choice in what he grows, and is a free agent in the commercial world. He buys where he wishes to, and at the end of the season or at some other stipulated time pays the landlord the prearranged rental, whether in cash or a share of the produce. The cropper, on the other hand, is hired just before the spring plowing season to grow a crop of cotton or tobacco on a number of acres corresponding to the size of his family. That is, the more prospective pickers there are in the family, the larger the number of acres. The owner gives close supervision to everything that is done, and he wants nothing grown except what he can sell. If the tenant takes time to keep a garden he does so at the neglect of the major interest, and, furthermore, he deprives the owner of the privilege of selling him additional groceries. At the end of the season the whole crop is taken by the landlord, who assesses its value, deducts what the cropper owes from his share, and pays for the remainder, if any. The shares in general are in thirds, one for labor, another for land, and the last for draft animals, implements, seed, fertilizer, and other farming necessities. If the worker supplies all but the land he gets two thirds, if he

    [22] Zeichner, "Transition from Slave to Free Labor," pp. 28–29.
    [23] Holland Thompson, *The New South* (Vol. XLII of *Chronicles of American Series*, New Haven: Yale University Press, 1919), pp. 65–67.

furnishes only his labor he gets one third, and in between he gets in proportion to what he contributes—that is, at least in theory. There are many modifications of this system, but in each the cropper has no legal claim to a renewal of the contract. He may even be deprived of the use of the house during the inactive winter months.[24] By 1868 it was estimated, no doubt in exaggeration, that most of that year's contracts were on the share-cropper basis. But in 1880 the census reports showed that over 31 per cent of the landholdings in Georgia were farmed under that arrangement.[25]

THE CROP-LIEN CREDIT SYSTEM

Had the cropper system always been fairly administered and the workers encouraged to do their best—if the tendency toward small landownership had not been positively discouraged—a larger number of the more energetic Negroes could have become possessors of their own soil. Some did, in spite of the system. Share cropping flourished most in the very richest agricultural regions of the South, where intelligent farming methods should have yielded bountiful results. But the new practice fell far short of getting the most from the land while building up the soil itself. The main reason for this, aside from the crushing of individual initiative through slaveowner tactics of management, was the credit system that grew up alongside of and merged with the structure of labor control.

For a few years after the war, the old-time factors continued to be the principal marketing agents for the growers of staples. But as cropping took the place of slavery, the landlord no longer could mortgage his labor supply for credit, and the uncertainties of crops in the period of transition made necessary some other means of financing the croppers during the season. So the workers, and sometimes the owners as well, turned to the local country storekeepers with whom they were acquainted. At the same time, the postwar extension of railroad and telegraph lines enabled the neighborhood merchant to market the staples directly, thereby taking the business away from the factors in the port towns. Thus, it was a safe investment for the storekeeper to advance groceries, seed, fertilizer, im-

[24] For variations, see Zeichner, "Transition from Slave to Free Labor," pp. 31–32; Hammond, *Cotton Industry*, p. 133.
[25] Brooks, *Agrarian Revolution in Georgia*, p. 47.

plements, or other needs to the croppers or independent farmers, in
return for a lien on their crops. It is said that some merchants were
so generous as to advance as much money for funeral expenses
as they thought could be recovered, with ample interest.[26]

Thus there arose the crop-lien system, under which the farmer
pledged his crop, to be handled by the merchant when it was
harvested. The lien has been officially defined as "a bond for the
payment of a specified amount—usually about $100—given to the
storekeeper by the farmer, and pledging the growing crop as collateral security." [27] To make sure of their rights in this regard, the
lien holders got them well defined in laws, of which the North
Carolina acts of 1868 and following are a fair example. Inasmuch
as this legal relationship ot cropper and creditor is not sufficiently
well understood, the following essential part of the code is quoted.

If any person shall make any advance either in money or supplies to
any person who is engaged in or about to engage in the cultivation of the
soil, the person so making such advance shall be entitled to a lien on
the crops which may be made during the year upon the land in the
cultivation of which the advance so made has been expended, in preference to all other liens existing or otherwise, except the laborer's and
landlord's liens, to the extent of such advance: Provided, an agreement
in writing shall be entered into before any such advance is made to this
effect, in which shall be specified the amount to be advanced, or in
which a limit shall be fixed beyond which the advance, if made from
time to time during the year, shall not go; which agreement shall be
registered in the office of the register of the county in which the person
to whom the advance is made resides, within thirty days after its date.[28]

In South Carolina, for example, this lien, in the form of an
inflexible chattel mortgage, was duly attested and recorded with the
clerk of the county court, for a small fee. This bond not only compelled the farmer to give the storekeeper enough of the current
crop, at prevailing prices, to insure payment in full, but also mortgaged future crops if one was not enough, and sometimes even

[26] Hammond, *Cotton Industry,* pp. 144–145; George K[irby] Holmes, "Peons of
the South," American Academy of Political and Social Science, *Annals,* IV, No. 2
(September, 1893), 266, 271; M[atthew] B[rown] Hammond, "The Southern Farmer
and the Cotton Question," *Political Science Quarterly,* XII, No. 3 (September, 1897),
461.

[27] *Tenth Census: Cotton Production,* II, 520.

[28] George P[ierce] Pell, ed., *Revisal of 1908 of North Carolina* (Charleston, S. C.:
Walker, Evans & Cogswell Co. Publishers, 1908), ¶ 2052, referred to hereafter
as *North Carolina Code,* 1908.

required additional security.[29] Loans were for an indeterminate period, but installments had to be paid from each portion of the crops as they were gathered. In South Carolina, which may be considered as typical, "from one-third to three-fifths of the crop" was taken to satisfy these obligations.[30]

Though the croppers generally made their deliveries "to the best of their ability"—it was dangerous not to—the merchant took a considerable risk on a crop that might mature and might not, so even the more honest of them charged enormous rates of interest. This interest was clumsily, but often sufficiently, concealed by weighting the price of the goods furnished during the season, to the extent of from 10 to 200 per cent above normal prices where competition prevailed. As a rule, the difference between cash and credit prices amounted to an interest charge on the loan of from 40 to 110 per cent, but the cropper had no other recourse. In South Carolina, around 1880, "when the cash price of corn" was 75¢ a bushel, the credit customer paid $1.25 or more.[31] But was it *credit* for which such interest was extorted? Each day's provisions were earned before they were procured.

Most of the storekeepers, doing nearly all their business on credit, never even set a cash price on many goods, particularly fertilizer and implements. In general, the amount of price weighting depended on the length of term of the loan. Staples marketed as much as three months before the end of the season—some cotton was ready to pick by the middle of August—might lower the credit charges to the extent of a fourth, for all they would cover. Purchases during the last month before final settlement were frequently listed as cash. Such terms seem better in print than they generally were in practice. Low prices for cotton, and high costs of all provisions, got the farmer into a perpetual state of indebtedness, so year after year he merely struggled to clean the slate for a new start. Until this could be done, he was wholly at the mercy of the merchant as to what he might buy and how much, what he should grow and the acreage of it, and how he should manage each detail of his work. If the cropper was a Negro, and in the earlier years he usually was, the restrictions were all the more rigorous. No other

[29] For a sample lien see Hammond, *Cotton Industry,* pp. 147–149; see also *ibid.,* p. 146, and Hammond, "Southern Farmer and Cotton Question," p. 462.

[30] *Tenth Census: Cotton Production,* II, 521.

[31] *Ibid.,* pp. 518, 520; Hammond, *Cotton Industry,* pp. 146, 151–154.

merchant except the one holding the lien would give him a cent's worth of credit, and he seldom had any cash.[32]

In the greater part of the South the merchant demanded that cotton, more cotton, and almost cotton alone should be grown, because this was something he could always market and the growers could neither eat it up behind his back nor slip it out for surreptitious sale. Cotton must be raised regardless of how the crop impoverished the soil or the farmer. Thus there was a constant tendency toward overproduction and low prices which continued the book records of indebtedness. If the worker grew corn and hogs (the staples of diet except for the occasional luxury of molasses) the storekeeper could sell less pork and meal at his bloated prices. So the cropper who dared to till a truck patch was quickly warned that he was lowering his credit.[33]

From August until the end of the year, and sometimes into early January, the family went over the fields time and again, picking the bolls as they opened and hauling the product to the gin, which again was owned by the merchant. The value of the net lint was then credited on the worker's account. Any attempt to sequester any of the cotton for sale elsewhere, even if beyond the amount due the storekeeper, was visited with quick retribution. In South Carolina, if the lien holder even suspected such intent, he could get an order from the clerk of the court to have the sheriff confiscate the whole crop for sale, the costs of the procedure being levied on the producer. The practice in North Carolina was somewhat similiar,[34] and these are typical states.

The abuses to which this system could lead were plentiful and sometimes ingenious. It grew worse as landlord and merchant ultimately and almost universally became the same individual. The weighting of prices, coupled with intricate bookkeeping, could show a debt to the store at the close of each year, if the laborer were industrious enough that a continuation of his services was desired. Again, the books could be made to balance exactly for the more shiftless cropper who was to be asked to move on. The workers were often perplexed at this magic, but were generally not sufficiently quick at ciphering to keep pace with the nimble-tongued

[32] *Tenth Census: Cotton Production,* II, 520; Hammond, *Cotton Industry,* pp. 149–151, 155.

[33] Holmes, "Peons of the South," p. 267.

[34] *Tenth Census: Cotton Production,* II, 520; *North Carolina Code,* 1908, ¶ 2054.

bookkeeper. Besides this, the person who persisted in demanding too close a check could easily be branded a troublemaker and neighborhood nuisance, and run out of the county by an obliging deputy sheriff. The casually inquisitive cropper might obligingly be shown the accounts, with sound accompaniment. "Here's-a-side-of-white-meat-you-bought-April-thirteenth.-Here's-a-side-you-didn't-buy-May-twenty-sixth.-Fifteen-cents-a-pound,-total-four-dollars-eighty-cents." Fifteen minutes of this, in one rumble of the tongue, was enough to throw even the more than ordinarily well versed cropper into a stupor. Furthermore, were not his admiring neighbors peeping through the screen door to see their educated companion show the bookkeeper "what's what"? The cropper's own dignity and the respect of his fellows for him must be maintained. "Yassuh, yassuh, reckon that must be 'bout right. Sorry I troubled you Capt'n. So long!" and he was gone, still perplexed but not daring to admit it.

The still shrewder debtor was at an equal loss at the final reckoning. Told that the books exactly balanced, shown the accounts, given the customary screed of explanation, a look of comprehension lighted his face. "Then I don't owe you nothin', Capt'n?" "No, you don't owe me a cent." "An' you don't owe me nothin'?" "You saw the books." "Then what's I gonna do with them two bales I ain't done hauled in yet?" "Tut, tut! Just look at that! Here's two pages stuck together. I'll have to add this whole account up again." So run the stories, and they are not entirely as apocryphal as is often asserted. The bookkeepers themselves, in their more confidential moods, have been the most versatile informants. T. S. Stribling's novelized accounts [35] are those of a person native to the community he described, who was not thanked by the gentry for his frankness.

Exploitative as it was, the system was not one calculated to enrich many of the planter-merchants. Crop failures or absconding laborers left the managers in a predicament, though the runaway was in a worse one when caught. Repeated cotton crops, without intermission, left the soil barren and all but a dead loss. The planter himself was usually in debt, directly or indirectly, to Northern banks or merchants. Not all landlords, perhaps no major portion of them, consciously robbed their underlings, and the perennially un-

[35] T[homas] S[igismund] Stribling, *The Store* (London: William Heinemann, Ltd., 1932).

settled accounts of the more scrupulous planters show that the bed of the patriarch was not always an easy one.[36]

Perhaps the worst effect, even on the lien holder, was the degradation of the croppers—white and black. A constant diet on "the three M's" (meat, meal, and molasses) did not produce alert, sturdy workers. The word "meat" itself was a euphemism. In elegant terms the product was (and is) salt side pork, bereft of the slightest streak of lean. In common parlance it is "white meat," "fat back," or "sow bosom," with "buttons" protruding on the rind. The meal for the hoe cake or pone was made from white corn, almost devoid of vitamins. Even the molasses furnished nothing to the human system except fuel. The victims of such food became lank, potbellied, and pellagrous. As late as the 1940's malnutrition and starvation (usually disguised under a more pleasing name) were all too common among share croppers. Hookworm and malaria, as well as pellagra, syphilis, and other ailments, took their toll of life and energy. In the springtime, poke greens and pot liquor might liven up the diet and put new spirit into the workers, but the effect was not lasting. As the poor whites have been worst pictured,[37] they were not innately depraved, subhuman beings. More often they were primarily the victims of circumstances. The landlord himself could not prosper when his labor force was reduced to such conditions. It is small wonder that the South remains poverty-stricken.

Before 1900 the crop-lien practice was strongest in the older states of the Southeast, but was quite widespread throughout the South. Also, for a considerable time, it operated mainly with Negroes, and in the greatest intensity where they were most numerous. It was only in the later years of the century that white tenants and croppers outnumbered the black, and that the system began to sweep through eastern Texas and Oklahoma and southeastern Missouri. By the 1890's it included about three quarters of the cotton-field workers, and in Alabama 90 per cent of them. In eleven counties of South Carolina in 1880 merchants had liens totaling well over $2,300,000. Yet, this averaged only $77 to the operating unit,[38] which sum represents the total living cost of a family. The interest on the

[36] See Hammond, *Cotton Industry*, p. 156.

[37] As in Erskine Caldwell, *Tobacco Road* (New York: Charles Scribner's Sons, 1932).

[38] *Tenth Census: Cotton Production*, II, 521; Hammond, "Southern Farmer and Cotton Question," p. 462.

value of a slave in the 1850's, not counting the cost of his keep, amounted to as much as that.

A Senate committee in 1893 was told that over nine tenths of the cotton farmers of some areas were insolvent. Some of the planter witnesses testified that under the lien system they also were bound to merchants to raise too much cotton and were not permitted to grow necessities for their own use.[39] Peonage was creeping up on many an independent farmer as well as the share cropper.[40] As forced overproduction increased, the price of cotton declined. This brought demands for still larger crops, until the returns got so low that credits had to be reduced, thus holding the ruinous cycle partially in check at starvation's verge. Land values remained so low and the soil was getting so poor that merchants would not take mortgages on the farms unless the owners' chattels were insufficient to be desired as security. This explains why Southern farm mortgages in 1890 were so few as compared with more prosperous parts of the country. Only 3.38 per cent of all farms cultivated by the owners were mortgaged in Georgia, and 8 per cent in South Carolina, while the percentage was 53.29 in Iowa, 30.46 in Massachusetts, and 48.91 in New Jersey.[41]

WHITE AND BLACK FARM LABOR

The system just described was not conducive to the development of a large class of small freeholders, whether white or black, as the low cost of land might have seemed to warrant. The supposed breakup of the plantation system was in part a transference from gang labor to tenancy.[42] Not all the landless farmers were croppers at any time during the era. South of the Potomac and Ohio rivers and in Texas, by 1900, there were over 150,000 whites and 233,000 Negroes classed as cash tenants, in addition to 402,000 white and 229,000 black share croppers.[43] As far as income is concerned, they might as well all be lumped together, for the supposed cash of the first group was actually store credit, and the crop-lien

---

[39] *Senate Report* No. 986, 53 Cong., 3 Sess., Pt. 1, p. 400 *et circa*.

[40] Holmes, "Peons of the South," *passim*.

[41] *Ibid.*, pp. 267–268; Hammond, *Cotton Industry*, p. 158.

[42] Paul H[erman] Buck, *The Road to Reunion, 1865–1900* (Boston: Little, Brown and Company, 1937), p. 145.

[43] Bruce, *Rise of the New South*, p. 33.

system predominated. In general, in the black belt and other regions where share cropping and tenancy prevailed, there was a lack of prosperity, whereas the yeoman farmers of the less attractive areas, largely because of their greater economic freedom, flourished in comparison.[44]

That agricultural labor, under such conditions, should have been inefficient is only to be expected, and the testimony to that fact is overwhelming. Also, it is usually said that the white workers were generally superior to the black. If so, then race discrimination, leading the Negro to feel that whatever effort he exerted would avail him nothing, might well be advanced as a potent cause. Sometimes the Southern white man's point of view, often also absorbed by Northern visitors, is quite apparent. As one commentator put it: "I have seen cotton-fields still white with their creamy fleeces late in December, because the negroes were either too lazy or too busily engaged in their annual merry-making to gather the harvest." The same author gave credence to the Negro's greater propensity to stealing.[45] Another felt that the great amount of supervision required justified the rates of interest charged, on the basis of "wages of superintendence." The Negroes, he declared, would burn their fences because they were too lazy to cut wood; they did not care for vegetables and did not know how to cook them; even their chickens were of the dunghill variety; and hunting and fishing were entirely too diverting to them.[46] Still others commented on the like and similar traits, and Hammond even tries to fix the blame for the one-crop economy on the Negro's preference for it.[47]

Yet, another author, a Southerner not given to praise of the black race, says that ". . . the negro is preferred to the native or foreign white hand by a large number of the Southern landowners, especially by those engaged in raising cotton. This class declares that he gives less trouble than a white man because content with

[44] [Joseph] Allan Nevins, *The Emergence of Modern America, 1865–1878* (Vol. VIII of *A History of American Life,* New York: The Macmillan Company, 1927), pp. 358–359.

[45] Edward King, *The Great South* (Hartford: American Publishing Company, 1875), pp. 299, 301.

[46] Carl Kelsey, *The Negro Farmer* (Chicago: Jennings & Pye, 1903), pp. 30–31.

[47] Brooks, *Agrarian Revolution In Georgia,* p. 101; Matthew Brown Hammond, "Cotton Production in the South," *Economic History, 1865–1909* (Vol. VI of *The South in the Building of the Nation,* James Curtis Ballagh, ed., Richmond: The Southern Publication Society, 1909), pp. 96–97; Hammond, *Cotton Industry,* pp. 181, 184–185.

less comfortable lodgings, with coarser food, and with smaller wages."[48] This confession of exploitation needs no further comment. It seems in itself enough to explain even the less credible charges against the black worker. Before 1900 the poor of both races were deprived of political recourse, through poll-tax disfranchisement. The troublemaker who paid the tax could be made to move out of the precinct before the next election.

SOUTHERN CLASS STRUCTURE

From the foregoing discussion it appears that the South did not possess a classless society, but the North had nothing to boast of in this regard, either. In the North there was a small class of industrial capitalists, a class diminishing relatively in numbers but growing in power and dominating a larger class of wage laborers, a class increasing in numbers and comparatively powerless. In the South there was a large class of landlords and merchants, ruling a still larger number of tenants, croppers, and day laborers. Till the end of the century the Southern economy was still predominantly agrarian, while the North was passing into the phase of industrial and financial supremacy, where class distinctions might readily lead to conflict. This is no denial of the fact that industrialism was growing in the South also, but even the Southern industrial leadership was largely agrarian in its mode of thought. The company store and the truck system of wage payment in the mill, factory, or mine were so similar to the crop lien that the share cropper who moved to town found no difficulty at all in adjusting himself to the situation.

The explanation of agrarian methods in Southern industry is not far to seek. The more usual urban capitalist before 1900 was, in fact, a former planter or planter's son. Many a rural patriarch of the slave era grew so disgusted with his inability to adjust himself to a wage or tenant basis that he sold out and moved to town, to seek another sort of livelihood. Others became absentee landlords, a type that was known, but was not so common, in ante-bellum days, even among free Negroes.[49] Some Northerners—first carpetbaggers and, later, others—came to the South and remained to

[48] Bruce, *Rise of the New South*, p. 27.
[49] See Carter G[odwin] Woodson, *Free Negro Owners of Slaves in the United States in 1830* (Washington: The Association for the Study of Negro Life and History, Inc., c.1924).

participate in the industrial development, but the bulk of the persons at the head of the mills and factories were former slaveowners, or their sons, who had spent their earlier lives on farms or plantations.[50]

This movement went on gradually throughout the period. Some planters absorbed the country stores and ruled in feudal squalor; others gave up the contest, let the merchants take over the land for what could be got for it, and invested their slender proceeds in cotton mills. The new promoter knew exactly where to sell stock for expansion purposes. Some of his old neighbors were still on the land, and when they had some money ahead they were willing to speculate or to hedge against the uncertainties of future crops by putting a nest egg in the industrial coop. Appeals were made to the North for investments.[51] There was some response in the 1880's and again in the late 1890's, but it was not till the beginning of the next century that the flow of capital into the South, except as credit to the country merchants, was widespread. Even this latter was not in the form of long-term investment. As the cropper was bound to the merchant, so the merchant was dependent on the Northern commission men or the local banks, which themselves were obligated to Northern creditors. Often the country storekeeper had to pay 18 per cent interest,[52] and this as well as the principal flowed back to its home in New York. As long as this neighborhood ex-planter-capitalist and planter-investor combination existed, fairly cordial relations continued between the two classes, and they have never ceased their joint efforts to suppress lower-class unrest and protest at its fountainhead. Some exception to this description of Southern capitalism may be taken in regard to the Birmingham iron region, some of the railroads, lumbering, coal mining, and the furniture industry, but in general the picture is accurate.

That a yeoman-farmer class, in between the landlord-capitalist and landless-farmer groups, continued after the war is indisputable. It is also quite apparent that this petty freeholder was generally not a cotton grower. Even before the war, though more white people than Negroes worked in the fields, the cotton laborers were black by a ratio of eight to one, while the white yeoman farmers were

[50] Bruce, *Rise of the New South*, pp. 152–154.
[51] Buck, *Road to Reunion*, pp. 150–151.
[52] William B[est] Hesseltine, *A History of the South, 1607–1936* (New York: Prentice-Hall, Inc., 1936), pp. 648–651.

largely confined to subsistence crops on the less fertile acres. In 1876 nearly four tenths of the cotton was grown by white people, and by 1899 a little over six tenths of the approximately 24,000,000 acres were operated by white people. The 849,000 cotton farms of the whites included 14,616,000 acres, while the 569,000 holdings of black men comprised 9,650,000 acres. Oddly enough, it may seem, there was less than half an acre difference between the average size of the patches farmed by the two races, each being in the neighborhood of seventeen.

On the other hand, though it may have been noted that by 1900 white croppers outnumbered the black by about five to four, at the same time about five out of every six Negro farmers were croppers or tenants, while the rest were either freeholders or wage laborers and mainly concerned with cotton growing. But little over half of the whites farmed cotton, five eighths of their number being croppers or tenants. This left nearly 300,000 white freeholders or wage laborers in the cotton fields, while some 800,000, a considerable proportion of them yeoman farmers, were engaged in other agricultural pursuits.[53] This arithmetical consideration must not obscure the fact that, as far as income is concerned, in the cotton belt there was little difference between croppers, tenants, and small freeholders. All were victim to the crop-lien system wherever it prevailed. Hence there were essentially two classes: on the one hand, the landlord-merchant-banker-capitalist group, numbering approximately a sixth of the total population and having all the political power; on the other, the great bulk of field workers, living from enfeebled hand to empty mouth. Yeoman farmers outside the crop-specialization belts enjoyed a higher status.[54]

As has already been shown, Southern public policy was all on the side of the crop-lien credit system. This was maintained to the almost total neglect of banking and the building of a sound financial structure. As long as the merchant could make more by squeezing the farmer than he could by legitimate banking, he stuck to the practice he knew best, and his was the class that shaped public

[53] Charles William Burkett and Clarence Hamilton Poe, *Cotton, Its Cultivation, Marketing, Manufacture, and the Problems of the Cotton World* (New York: Doubleday, Page & Company, c.1906), pp. 36–37, referred to hereafter as *Cotton;* Hawk, *Economic History of the South,* p. 457; Hammond, *Cotton Industry,* p. 129. For agricultural wage laborers, see Chapter XV, below.

[54] The account of this stratification is well developed in Shugg, *Origins of Class Struggle in Louisiana,* pp. 274–313.

policy. Even if 18 or 20 per cent of his extortionate interest rates went to Northeastern banking houses, that which was left was more than he could make in any other way, but only if considered from the point of view of immediate advantage. In the long run, the continued impoverishment of the masses retarded the whole economic improvement of the section, so that ever afterward its problems have been a drag on the entire nation. If there is validity in the argument that the South was a mere colony of the Northeast,[55] it can be accepted only with rigid qualifications. Certainly, the masses of the Northeast made no profit from any other section of the country; instead, they were exploited by the same groups that profited from the marketing and processing of Southern staples. The part of the country in which the business leaders lived is largely immaterial. The important fact is that certain conditions in the South made the effects of exploitation more severe and general than in most of the rest of the nation.

The plantation and slavery system of the prewar era definitely retarded a well-rounded economic development and the accumulation of a mass of capital for future development of the section. The Civil War left the Southern propertied people in a status verging on general bankruptcy, and thus more dependent than ever before on credit from outside sources, and the risks of Southern investments made the terms of this credit unusually hard. Rich soil was rare, and the constant demands for large immediate crops led to the practice of "skinning" much of the remaining fertility from the soil, this process being cumulative. The available labor force, to handle this situation, was composed largely of former slaves in whom initiative and foresight had not been developed; of poor whites whose way of living was conditioned by competition with the underpaid Negroes; and of yeoman white farmers who operated largely on the periphery of staple-specializing regions, where their contributions were mainly supplementary to, rather than a part of, the main developments. The economic and political leadership of the South in this period proved inadequate to cope effectively with this combination of circumstances.

[55] See Walter Prescott Webb, *Divided We Stand* (New York: Farrar & Rinehart, Inc., c.1937); Benjamin B. Kendrick, "The Colonial Status of the South," *The Journal of Southern History*, VIII, No. 1 (February, 1942), 3–22.

CHAPTER V

Southern Crops and Special Problems

TRANSPORTATION FACILITIES IN 1861

IN transportation facilities, during the greater part of the period from 1860 to 1900, the South was less at a disadvantage as compared with other sections than it was in some other things. For that matter, even in 1860 the slave states were better equipped than is sometimes realized. Too much is made of the fact that the seceding states had only 9,000 miles of railroads out of 30,626 in the entire country. Indeed, this was a fair amount in proportion to population. But it must be remembered that all except about 2,000 of the national mileage was east of the Mississippi River. Missouri, Iowa, Louisiana, and Texas were only making beginnings, California and Arkansas had hardly started, and for the rest of the trans-Mississippi West there was not a mile listed in the Census of 1860. Inasmuch, then, as a comparison is made of railroad transportation according to needs, it must be confined to the states east of the Mississippi River. On this basis the seceding states (not counting West Virginia) had 7,969 miles out of a total of 28,451, or 28 per cent. But the same group had just about 7,000,000 people out of a total of 26,900,000, or 26 per cent. On the population-mileage basis, then, the South was slightly ahead of the North. If all the border slave states be included in the South, the ratio would favor the North a little, for the border group was not as well supplied as the cotton belt.

On the basis of area, the South did not rate so well. The same seceding states east of the Mississippi had 372,411 out of 856,122 square miles in all the states east of the same river,[1] or 43.5 per cent of the area as compared with 28 per cent of the railroad mileage. This, again, may easily be exaggerated as to significance, for the South was much the more bountifully supplied with navigable rivers. But, even with this advantage, the South Atlantic states had a larger mileage of railroads than the East North Central group, and more than the Middle Atlantic and New England states combined. It was only in the East South Central states that the comparison on any basis was bad, but there the river facilities were best of all; and yet those states were making a good start, with a mileage almost equal to that of New England.[2]

Likewise, there is little to the contention that the South lacked networks like those of the North. Most of the lines of both sections were of mixed gauges, preventing the use of the same rolling stock on railroads that met. Although the North had three connections between the Eastern and Western networks, one of these was through slave territory all the way from Baltimore to the Ohio River opposite Cincinnati. But, for that matter, the South also had a through route from Richmond to Memphis and another from the leading Atlantic coast towns (from Richmond to Savannah), reaching to Mobile, Vicksburg, Memphis, and New Orleans. Even the points of contact between the South and the North were as numerous as those between the Northeast and the Northwest.[3] If some of the Southern construction was looser than the best in the North, the financing was sounder. Only for military purposes were the Southern lines less effective, and even this would not have been disastrous except for the lack of adequate rolling mills and machine shops to construct repair materials, and the ravages and confiscation practiced by the Northern armies and government. The effect of the war on Southern railroads has already been briefly mentioned,[4] but the postwar recovery must follow a discussion of other forms of transportation.

[1] Computed from the *Statistical Abstract of the United States,* 1931, pp. 2, 8, 412.
[2] *Ibid.,* p. 412.
[3] Caroline E[lizabeth] MacGill, *History of Transportation in the United States before 1860* (Balthasar Henry Meyer, ed., Washington: Carnegie Institution of Washington, 1917), see maps in back of book.
[4] See pages 77–78, above.

WAGON ROADS AND WATERWAYS

Though nothing very favorable could be said about the common run of wagon roads anywhere in the country in 1860, and while improvements down to 1900 were nowhere phenomenal, the conditions in the South were probably a little worse than in any of the older settled regions of the North. An exception should be made for Kentucky, which was noted for its fine roads. Yet, the highways to steamboat landings, railroad stations, and the port towns, poor as they were, were of primary importance in the marketing of produce. Cotton might be hauled long distances on carts or wagons at twenty cents a ton mile, without eating greatly into the value of the load. But the writer in 1873 who opined that this freight would consume only one nineteenth of the value on a hundred-mile trip, was thinking of cotton values no longer in existence. The price in 1873 was fourteen cents, had been near that for several years, and was to go lower.[5]

It was twenty years after the war before the South began to realize the importance of the wagon road in its transportation system. An English traveler of 1870 noted a brief stretch of shell road near New Orleans, used mainly for the training of race horses, but he had little to say about other improved highways.[6] A "Better Roads Movement" was under way, and agitation for government aid was begun about 1885. Magazine articles were starting to bemoan the long neglect of the highways, and pointed out that toll roads were taking more money from the people than would good systems of state roads. In 1891 Congress received guidance from the consular service on foreign experiences, and shortly afterward conventions met in a number of Southern cities to discuss the problem of improving the roads. Poverty and unprogressiveness in the rural areas impeded the movement, personal service on the roads being used instead of a tax for real improvements. Before the end of the century some progress was noticeable, and hope was being

[5] W[illiam] M[ason] Grosvenor, "The Railroads and the Farms," *Atlantic Monthly*, XXXII, No. 193 (November, 1873), 592; United States Department of Agriculture, *Yearbook*, 1899 (Washington: Government Printing Office, 1900), pp. 377, 764, this and other numbers will be referred to hereafter as *Agricultural Yearbook*, with date.

[6] Robert Somers, *The Southern States since the War, 1870–1* (London: Macmillan and Co., 1871), see p. 193, *et passim*.

expressed that the "horseless carriage" and the bicyclists would soon force worthy improvements within the states. Convict labor was the mainstay of ordinary work (and not a pretty sight either), but heavy machines, iron bridges, and stone roadbeds required more civilized forms of labor control for the more important developments. By the end of the century, the Illinois Central railroad was doing missionary work, and the state of Tennessee was building a modernized state highway system.[7] Though the farmers had to wallow through mud for the rest of the period, now they were beginning to get an inkling of easier traveling in the future.

Southern canals were of relatively little importance in agricultural marketing. Even before the Civil War, they were of only local significance. The Chesapeake and Ohio Canal never paid interest on its bonds after 1864, and following 1870 it was mainly used for moving coal. The James River and Kanawha Canal got no federal aid after 1874, and was taken over by a railroad company in 1880, for abandonment.[8] If there was any other new construction, it was too little for mention. For some years after the war, Southern rivers got much smaller attention from Congress than ever before, and the South, before the war, had always been discriminated against in this regard. In 1866, a river-and-harbor appropriation of the usual pork-barrel variety, aside from some snag pulling, allowed $75,000 to the chastized states, out of a total of $3,500,000 for the nation. Thereafter, for several years, the mouth of the Mississippi was dredged at an annual cost of about $200,000 until, under an act of March 3, 1875, James B. Eads was permitted to build his truly effective jetties. By that time, the whole lower river was littered with snags and sandbars. In Cleveland's administration, the South got more consideration, so that by the middle of July, 1888, over $1,000,000 had been appropriated for the rivers of Arkansas alone.[9]

The most significant development in river craft was the substitution of tugs and barges for the palatial packet steamboats of

---

[7] N[athaniel] S[outhgate] Shaler, "The Common Roads," *Scribner's Magazine*, VI, No. 4 (October, 1889), 475–478; *House Miscellaneous Document* No. 20, 52 Cong., 1 Sess.; Hawk, *Economic History of the South*, p. 491; *Agricultural Yearbook*, 1899, pp. 380, 749–750; Bruce, *Rise of the New South*, pp. 303–305; Martin Dodge, "The Government and Good Roads," *The Forum*, XXXII, No. 3 (November, 1901), pp. 294–297.

[8] MacGill, *History of Transportation*, pp. 269, 272–273.

[9] *House Executive Document* No. 56, 39 Cong., 2 Sess., I, 28–37; *ibid.*, No. 46, 44 Cong., 2 Sess., II, 40; *ibid.*, No. 6, 51 Cong., 1 Sess., II, 32.

earlier years. Between 1870 and 1891, steamboats registered at New Orleans dropped in number from 455 to 128, and their tonnage from 46,000 to 20,000. In the later year, on the whole lower Mississippi, there were 308 steamboats with a tonnage of 70,000, and 272 "unrigged craft" (barges) of 178,000 tons. At the same time, the entire Mississippi River system had 1,114 steamboats (211,000 tons) and 6,339 barges (3,183,000 tons). Much of the lower Mississippi River trade was entering and leaving railheads on the river. During the 1880's the barge business gained steadily till almost a third of approximately 6,500,000 tons of freight carried on the lower Mississippi was in barges. This resulted in great freight savings, the charge on a bag of one hundred pounds of grain from St. Louis to New Orleans dropping from twenty cents to ten between 1877 and 1899. As late as 1899, water rates were only half as much as those charged by railroads where there was competition.[10] Because the freight cost, both coming and going, is paid by the farmer, this saving often made the difference between ruin and success.

Rivermen, however, could not hope to compete with railroads, which could be built to any place that had goods to ship. Passenger traffic soon began to slip, and freight followed. In the years from 1871 to 1875 the trade between St. Louis and scattered parts of the South changed from about 1,000,000 tons each by water and rail (the rivers slightly in the lead) to 781,000 tons by water and 1,-613,000 tons by rail. In the southward traffic the river was still ahead. By 1880, in the entire South the tonnage was 16,600,000 on railroads and 2,500,000 by river craft. The railroads not only paralleled the rivers—cutting rates till the steamboats gave up the contest and then raising them again—but also headed directly toward Eastern shipping points and centers of manufacturing. As early as 1855 a little cotton was shipped eastward by rail; in 1860 the amount was nearly 109,000 bales and by 1870 almost 381,000. Thereafter improved presses allowed forty-seven bales to occupy the car space of an earlier twenty-two, and in 1876 the northeastward shipments reached 695,600 bales, while Gulf ports received 2,-283,000 and South Atlantic ports 1,520,000. Nearly half of the Northeastern receipts went direct to domestic mills, whereas none

[10] *House Executive Document* No. 6, 52 Cong., 1 Sess., II, lix–lx; *Senate Report* No. 307, 43 Cong., 1 Sess., II, 618–620; *Eleventh Census: Transportation*, II, 435; *Agricultural Yearbook*, 1899, pp. 660–661.

had gone there except by circuitous routes before 1867.[11] Soon after 1900, packet steamboats were a rarity below Cairo.

THE RAILROADS AND THE FARMERS

The problem of the rebuilding and extension of railroads was a perplexing one, and not readily solved. Many lines were destroyed or run down to comparative uselessness; others were in the possession of the federal government, those useful for military purposes being run by the army. When these were returned to their former owners or to the state boards of public works, the federal government canceled all costs for the buildings, bridges, and tracks it had constructed or rebuilt for military purposes. But the prewar obligations of the railroad companies took precedence over dividends. Some of the lines indebted to the federal government got a partial remission ten years later. Still others, like the Central of Georgia, which had temporarily suffered so bad a fate at the hands of Sherman, were free of debt, and the Georgia line itself was in a prosperous condition by 1867. A few of the weaker roads were aided by the Southern Express Company. Then came the reconstruction orgy, in which carpetbag financier-legislators, according to the nation-wide practices of that time, voted themselves state bonds, covering about half the anticipated cost of construction (up to $16,000 a mile), for lines some of which were never built. In one issue of $4,720,000 in bonds, $1,300,000 were fraudulent. When the market for such bonds dropped about to zero during the Panic of 1873, this practice was checked.[12] "Home rule" had been restored in four of the states by that date anyway, and came to three more in the following year. Before prosperity returned, reconstruction had ended everywhere.

[11] *House Executive Document* No. 46, 44 Cong., 2 Sess., II, 106, 142–143; *Tenth Census: Transportation,* bottom folio, pp. 258, 703. For this whole subject Charles Henry Ambler, *History of Transportation in the Ohio Valley* (Glendale, Cal.: The Arthur H. Clark Company, 1932), is most useful.

[12] Ulrich B[onnell] Phillips, "Railway Transportation in the South," *South in the Building of the Nation,* VI, 305–307, referred to hereafter as Phillips, "Railways in the South"; Haney, *Congressional History of Railways in the United States, 1850–1887,* pp. 165–167; Somers, *Southern States since the War,* pp. 87–89; Walter L[ynwood] Fleming, *Civil War and Reconstruction in Alabama* (Cleveland: The Arthur H. Clark Company, 1911), pp. 589–592; *House Report* No. 34, 39 Cong., 2 Sess., pp. 70–314 *passim; House Executive Document* No. 155, 39 Cong., 1 Sess., pp. 417–427.

The railroad land grants of the same era hit the South as well as the West. In 1866 President Johnson asked for extensions of time for the building of roads to which grants had been made from 1850 to 1856, and in some instances succeeded (cf. page 66, above). Then the carpetbaggers appealed so often to their friends in Congress for land donations that Morrill of Vermont offered the following amendment to a resolution: "Provided, that anybody in any state may have power to build a railroad from one spot to another spot, and shall have all the lands adjoining, not claimed by any other railroad." [13] In spite of the forfeiture of grants for some defaulting lines, to 1886 over 9,215,000 acres were certified to the five Southern public-land states for railroad construction.[14] Regardless of all this activity, the railroad mileage of the entire South (south of Pennsylvania, the Ohio River, Missouri, and Kansas) grew only from 10,000 in 1860 to 13,400 in 1870, and to 21,200 in 1880. From nearly a third of the nation's total mileage in 1860, the section had declined relatively to 22.7 per cent of the 93,300 miles of the later period. Then, with Northern capitalists interested, the mileage more than doubled in the next decade and reached 55,000 miles by 1900, or 28.5 per cent of the total for the United States. Considering that Southern population at the end of the century was only 32.3 per cent of the national total, and the land area was merely 29.5 per cent, the showing of railroad building in the twenty years was quite remarkable. If one wishes to object to the areal concept, on the basis that the Mountain states were as yet little settled, it can be countered that the same was true of the bulk of Texas. By the omission of all this region, the South still had only about a third of the total area.[15]

In the first twenty years, despite the relatively small mileage of the South, the traffic was so light that rates were considerably higher than for the United States at large. About 1870, when the average ton-mile rate for a number of Northern and Western lines

[13] *Senate Executive Document* No. 37, 39 Cong., 1 Sess., pp. 1–3; *House Executive Document* No. 6, 51 Cong., 1 Sess., II, 46–47; C[lara] Mildred Thompson, "Carpet-Baggers in the United States Senate," in *Studies in Southern History and Politics; Inscribed to William Archibald Dunning* (New York: Columbia University Press, 1914), pp. 173–174, quotation p. 174.

[14] Haney, *Congressional History of Railways in the United States, 1850–1887,* p. 13.

[15] Data compiled from *Statistical Abstract of the United States, 1931,* pp. 2, 9, 412.

was about 1.9 cents and the mileage passenger fare was 2.4 cents, the corresponding charges on the Atlanta and Richmond line were from 3½ to 4 cents and from 4 to 5 cents, or just about double. So rapid was later progress that, before 1900, some Southern rates were among the lowest in the country (but see page 296, below).[16] The early rate wars, collapse in the Panic of 1873, subsequent pooling, and finally consolidation into big networks went on in the South as elsewhere in the United States. Further bankruptcy in the Panic of 1893 was partly the result of excessive bond issues and official speculation in stocks. Immediately afterward, the J. P. Morgan Company organized the Southern Railway system, and, thereafter, banker control was in full sway. Though this development was to bring other evils in its wake, at least some order was brought into the management. Rarely, if ever again, could it be said of a company that "they kept their books with a lead pencil and an eraser." [17]

The service of the railroads to the farmers was also hindered by tardy growth in technical improvements. Steel rails were not generally laid to replace wrought iron till after 1885. Double-tracking was the rare exception before 1900. The standard gauge was found on only a tenth of the mileage south of the Ohio River by 1880, and to the end of the century gauges of five feet and five and a half feet were frequent in many parts of the South. The main line of the Southern Railway, 800 miles in length, was described in 1897 as a mere aggregation of earlier railroads unified "without regard to systematic adjustment of gradients or alignment." Four million dollars for improvements would have cut transportation costs a fourth.[18] It needs no argument to show that agriculture was bearing the cost of transportation inefficiency.

[16] *Agricultural Yearbook*, 1899, pp. 648–649, 662; Bruce, *Rise of the New South*, p. 297.

[17] *Senate Report* No. 307, 43 Cong., 1 Sess., II, 793; *House Executive Document* No. 7, 48 Cong., 2 Sess., II, 11–18; Harry Turner Newcomb, "The Present Railway Situation," *North American Review*, CLXV, No. 492 (November, 1897), 595; John Moody, *The Railroad Builders* (Vol. XXXVIII of *Chronicles of America Series*, New Haven: Yale University Press, 1919), pp. 189–191; *The Nation*, LXVII, No. 1,724 (July 14, 1898), 26, quotation.

[18] Somers, *Southern States since the War*, pp. 90–91; Ulrich Bonnell Phillips, *History of Transportation in the Eastern Cotton Belt to 1860* (New York: Columbia University Press, 1908), p. 383; W[illiam] W[ilson] Finley, "Southern Railroads and Industrial Development," American Academy of Political and Social Science, *Annals*, XXXV, No. 1 (January, 1910), 101; *Tenth Census: Transportation*, bottom folio, pp.

Though the farmer apparently realized the poor service he was offered, he was slow in doing anything about it. If railroad rates were too high, the man who had the legal right to market his own cotton would simply hitch the mule to the cart and haul a couple of bales at a time to the nearest exchange or steamboat landing. Texas had had the foresight to put strict regulation clauses into her railroad charters. The Grange movement of the 1870's was too weak in the South to achieve important state railroad legislation. As depression on the farm deepened, and farmers' clubs merged into the Alliances of the 1880's, agitation became widespread, and a national Farmers' Alliance meeting in 1889, representing every Southern state except West Virginia, demanded government ownership of railroads. While this movement was unavailing, other forces were active. The growth of mining, lumbering, and manufacturing brought more freight to the railroads, thus making lower rates possible. Also the Panic of 1893 had the salubrious effect of wringing much surplus water out of the financial structure. Yet the public failed to benefit. Between 1890 and 1900 the freight charges on 105 commodities dropped 26 per cent, while 531 rates rose 30 per cent.[19]

The growth of the railroads had a marked influence in a shift in trade centers. Down to 1860, the dominance of port towns such as New Orleans, Mobile, Savannah, and Charleston was secure. But, as trade revived after the war, other cities began to tap the interior by means of rails. Wilmington, North Carolina, had high hopes of becoming a Southern New York, and did make some gains. Memphis multiplied her cotton receipts by ten, to achieve half a million bales in 1875. Most of this went by rail to the Atlantic coast instead of, as formerly, to New Orleans and Mobile. Though rates to Liverpool were lower for New Orleans than for New York, before 1880 much even of the old grain trade slipped away to the Eastern mart. This was the result of varied causes. Railroad connections as yet being inadequate, the Gulf port was not in a favorable position for the internal distribution of exchanged imports. Also, the new steam vessels were often too big to pass the bars at the river's

306–307; J. A. Latcha, "Cheap Transportation in the United States," *North American Review*, CLXIV, No. 486 (May, 1897), 606, quotation.
   [19] Grosvenor, "Railroads and the Farms," p. 592; *House Executive Document No. 6*, 51 Cong., 1 Sess., II, 648; Thompson, *The New South*, pp. 31–34; Bruce, *Rise of the New South*, p. 298.

mouths, and the Towboat Association was a monopoly that charged extortionate rates for pulling the ships over. After the federal government would dredge the channel the association would block it again artificially. As a result, the Texas trade, as late as 1877, was avoiding New Orleans in favor of St. Louis, whence it could be shipped eastward.[20]

With the more rapid railroad development after 1880, the Southern ports began to recover their losses. In the 1890's the exports from twenty-three of them grew from about $306,000,000 to $511,-000,000. Most of the expansion was for New Orleans, Galveston, and Mobile, while Norfolk, Richmond, and Charleston receded badly. Cities in the interior were also affected by the changes. In North Carolina, by 1900, Charlotte owed her prominence to cotton shipments, and Durham to tobacco. In South Carolina, Columbia arose as a rival to Charleston. Atlanta, with ten railroads, was a·distributing center hardly identifiable with the ruins of 1864. Birmingham, nonexistent till after the war, was important as an agricultural distributing center, altogether apart from her prominence in the iron industry. Nashville, Lexington, Shreveport, Houston, and Dallas, as other representatives of the trend, all were important trade marts by 1900. Each of the group rose on the basis of good rail connections, new manufactures, and a bountiful trade in farm goods and needs.[21]

SOUTHERN STAPLES IN FOREIGN TRADE

The dependence of Southern farmers on world markets, to a far greater extent than was the case for farmers of any other section of the country, is not hard to demonstrate. The exports of domestic products of the United States in the last year before the war blockade amounted to about $316,000,000 in value, of which three quarters were of Southern origin. Cotton alone was over six tenths of the United States' total, while tobacco, at 6 per cent, slightly exceeded Northern breadstuffs and nearly equaled the cured meats and other "provisions." Seven eighths of all American exports were agricultural, including a small amount of forest products, and the

[20] Somers, *Southern States since the War*, pp. 34, 58, 75–76; *House Executive Document* No. 46, 44 Cong., 2 Sess., II, 109, 143–146; *Senate Report* No. 307, 43 Cong., 1 Sess., I, 197–200.

[21] Bruce, *Rise of the New South*, pp. 231–249, 252, 477.

bulk of all such goods was from the South. During the war the North lost the handling, for use and export, of $400,000,000 worth of Southern wares, but the worst hardship was on the blockaded section, which needed this trade for its success in the struggle. There was also a danger that the remote parts of the world, trying to supply Europe with cotton during the conflict, would emerge in a strong position to contest the South's earlier supremacy. Yet, in all the domestic turmoil of the year 1867, the exports of the partially reunited nation were virtually up to the level of the prewar years, and again the South was supplying seven tenths of all. But less of the gains from such trade were retained by the Southerners during the carpetbag regime, and their imports lagged behind for lack of purchasing power.[22]

For the next thirty years, and into the next century, the cotton farmer still depended mainly on the foreign market. Of the 2,500,-000 bales picked in 1867, five eighths went abroad; in 1870, 1880, and 1890 almost exactly two thirds of constantly increasing crops were exported; and in 1897, out of a harvest over four times the weight of that of 1867, seven tenths went to foreign countries.[23] As yet there was nothing to fear in the competition from Egypt, Brazil, Peru, India, or elsewhere. Egyptian cotton was a specialty, of high price, and devoted to fine uses where the American short-staple product did not compete. The Peruvian fiber superficially resembled wool and was used as an adulterant with that textile, this being another item of unconcern to the domestic grower. India, with a lint more nearly resembling the American cotton, fought for a leading place in the Liverpool market till about 1870, and then turned to the manufacture of her stocks at home. This had an indirect effect on the American producer. India not only supplied much of her own market for cotton goods, but also cut into the British trade with other Oriental countries. This, in turn, tended to

[22] *DeBow's Review*, VII, n.s., Nos. 1 & 2 (January–February, 1862), 121; *Statistical Abstract of the United States*, 1931, pp. 522–523; *American Annual Cyclopaedia and Register of Important Events*, 1861 (New York: D. Appleton and Company, c.1862), p. 107; *ibid.*, 1867, pp. 127–128; Hammond, *Cotton Industry*, p. 345; Emory Richard Johnson, T. W. Van Metre, G. G. Huebner, and D. S. Hanchett, *History of Domestic and Foreign Commerce of the United States* (Washington: Carnegie Institution of Washington, 1915), II, 64, referred to hereafter as Johnson and others, *History of Commerce*.

[23] *Agricultural Yearbook*, 1899, pp. 764–765.

restrict the growth of British purchases from America.[24] Increased buying in other countries prevented this fact from checking the growth of American exports.

The South was largely responsible for the fact that, though it had pretty much of a monopoly on cotton raising, there was so little prosperity growing out of this trade. Overconfident of their ability to continue their leadership forever, the producers were careless in their ginning, baling, and storage, thus putting on the market a badly deteriorated product, which correspondingly had to be sold at lower-grade prices. The inability of the growers to regulate the supply was an even more serious fault. The American crop, dominating the world market, determined the price. The same was not true of exported foods. When a short American cotton crop was reported in Liverpool, the price advanced at once; but a scanty wheat crop had no such effect. There, the shortage had to be world-wide to cause a similar rise: there were too many other areas of large production. The failure of organized farmers to prorate and regulate their output, of course, allowed this situation to keep cotton prices down.[25]

But the diagnosis was easier than the cure. The tradition of individualism was too strong for great collective action on the part of any class of American producers before 1900. The North and the West had no such world monopoly on any product as did the South. Hence their destiny was less in their own hands. Though tobacco and some other Southern products also entered into foreign trade, the problems they presented were about like those of Northern and Western goods, and they need no special mention here.

CROPS AND THEIR MARKETING: COTTON

The previous discussion, and much that follows, can best be pointed up with a graph. The state of affairs in the years 1861–1865 was such that orderly tables cannot represent it. To the dispirited Southerners of April and May, 1865, the only ray of sunshine for

---

[24] Alfred B. Shepperson, *Cotton Facts* (New York: A. B. Shepperson, 1895), pp. viii, 95; Hammond, *Cotton Industry,* pp. 346–350.

[25] Hammond, *Cotton Industry,* pp. 351–352; Shepperson, *Cotton Facts,* p. iv; Samuel T. Hubbard, "The Cotton Situation," *Banker's Magazine* [U.S.], L. No. 2 (January, 1895), 176–179, 181; Hammond, "Southern Farmer and Cotton," p. 451.

Cotton Data, 1866–1898 [26]

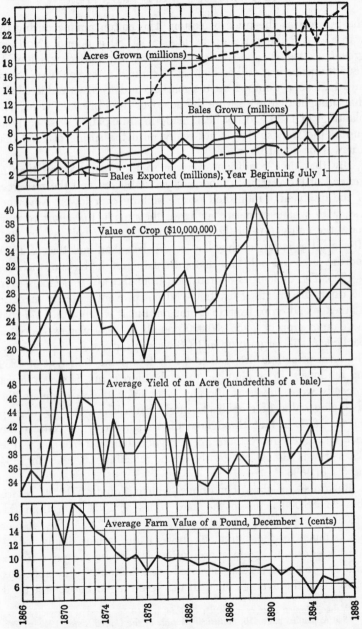

[26] From table in *Agricultural Yearbook*, 1899, pp. 764–765; for data see Appendix, page 415, herein.

the future was the price of cotton. The cotton famine during the war had run the price up as high as $1.80 a pound (Northern greenback values), and 70 cents at most any period was low. In 1865 the price was still as high as 30 cents,[27] after Southern hoardings had been dumped on the market, and the two million bales that brought that price were the holdover from previous years. The plantings of 1865 had not been made in anticipation of so early an end of the war, so it was not really until the spring of 1866 that a new start could be made.

By that time conditions were in some respects worse than at the end of the war, with labor not yet stabilized and the resources of the insolvent, vanquished people sinking ever lower. Nevertheless, with whatever means at hand, they made the effort to start anew the cultivation of the only crop they really believed in. But, after a bitter struggle, they had a crop less than half that of 1860, and the price was only half that anticipated on the basis of the sales of 1865. The difficulties of transition from slave to free labor—even the rigors of carpetbag taxation—did not prevent a steady increase in acreage and crops from that time on. But it was not till 1877 that the banner crop of 2,155,000,000 pounds in 1859 was exceeded or reached. A still larger crop in 1878 was no indication of prosperity. The farm price had dropped to a new low point—half that of 1869 and the lowest to be plumbed for eight more years. Hence, the net proceeds were the least for any year since the war, unless the advancing value of greenbacks might cause the value to overtop that for 1867. In fact, throughout the remainder of the century the price was rarely more than a cent higher than in 1878, and in the 1890's it was almost constantly lower, reaching 4.6 cents in 1894 and 5.7 in 1898.[28]

Regardless of these conditions, which brought a lower return from 23,688,000 acres in the hard times of 1894 than from the 9,350,000 acres of the panic year of 1873 (approximately 40 per cent as much for the individual grower), the farmer simply redoubled his efforts and grew more cotton as soon as the price rose a point or two again. As may be noted from the table in the appendix (page 415), the average yield to the acre ranged between a third

[27] Vance, *Human Factors in Cotton Culture*, p. 116.
[28] See Appendix, page 415; *Statistical Abstract of the United States*, 1909, p. 587.

of a bale and a half of a bale, the upper figure being only in 1870. Also, as previously noted, the average farmer's family tended only about seventeen acres of cotton. This means that a five-or-six-bale crop was all that could be expected. At the upper limit, and with the price at the rare ten cents, the three-hundred-dollar return allowed the worker's family a hundred dollars' credit for the year's living expenses, and this was spent at the weighted prices charged at the country store. On a cash basis the family, even when fairly large, probably got five dollars a month to spend for food, clothing, and incidental luxuries. When the price of cotton dropped to five cents, even the storekeeper could go broke.

The expanding acreage was mainly in Texas and, after 1890, in Oklahoma. The general maintenance of acreage yield down to 1880 and the increase of the nineties over the eighties must be partially attributed to this opening of new farms in the richer Western soils, and especially, in the later decade, in Oklahoma. Another reason is that the competition from better and cheaper soils enforced the use of additional fertilizer in the older Atlantic coast states. Reports for 1876 showed that 35 per cent of the cultivated acres of North Carolina were being fertilized, 60 per cent in South Carolina, and 42 in Georgia. Florida, Alabama, and Mississippi ranged between 10 and 15 per cent, while Tennessee and the states west of the Mississippi River used too little to be noted. By 1889, South Carolina was manufacturing more than half a million tons of rock phosphates annually. At about that time Florida also began producing and, later on, extensive deposits were mined in Tennessee. But such fertilizer as reached the Western fields was usually rotted cotton seed.[29] Toward the end of the period even the cotton seed was largely marketed. "The meats," said George K. Holmes, "are made into oil cake and oil meal for feeding stuff and for fertilizers; into crude oil, cotton-seed stearin, salad oil, cottolene [lard substitute], miners' oil, and soap, and the oil is exported to Europe and brought back again as olive oil. The hulls may be used for making paper; they are made into bran for cattle food; they are used for fuel, and are an important contribution to the list of fertilizers." The ten-million-bale cotton crop of 1897 brought the landowners about

[29] Hammond, *Cotton Industry*, pp. 135–136, 174–175; Bruce, *Rise of the New South*, p. 41; *Agricultural Yearbook*, 1899, p. 338.

$30,000,000 extra revenue from seeds [30] or about a tenth of the value of the fiber itself.

Little, if any, of this new source of income went to the actual growers. Had they received a share it would not have raised their average family income fifty cents a month. Yet, the landlords and merchants stuck to cotton growing. Leading agricultural authorities urged greater diversification, but hope sprang eternal and nobody wanted to trust his neighbor in a crop-reduction program. Before the war it had been found the most economical labor management to have as many acres planted in corn or other crops as in cotton. Any worker could plant and tend twice as much cotton as he could pick, so the spare time from the cotton field was clear gain in the corn. But the share-cropper-and-lien system changed all this, and by 1900 so little corn was grown on the cotton plantations that cattle did not recognize it as feed until gradually introduced to the mysterious object thrown on the pile of cotton-seed hulls. Since the South would not solve the problem by cooperative methods, there was probably as much irony as humor in Ambassador Wu T'ing-fang's remark, before a group of Southern manufacturers, that the surplus problem could be solved if each man in China would add just one inch to the length of his shirt.[31] Had the suggestion been heeded, the more likely result would have been a rush to increase the cotton acreage.

Other remedies were nearer at hand, and some of them were utilized. The possibilities of the market for cottonseed products were barely touched by the end of the century, but the rise of Southern cotton mills reduced the freight costs on a part of the cotton. These mills and other new industries created a larger urban population to be supplied with foods, thus encouraging greater diversification. The same development caused a somewhat freer circulation of money, thus enabling some farmers to change to a cash basis. Even the old practice of dumping all the cotton on the market at once, thus depressing the price, was being abated.[32] But, before 1900, few of the farmers were aware of any benefits from these nascent changes. The protracted marketing, for example,

[30] *Agricultural Yearbook,* 1899, pp. 329–330, quotation; James A[ugustin] B[rown] Scherer, *Cotton as a World Power* (New York: Frederick A. Stokes Company Publishers, c.1916), pp. 354–356.

[31] Vance, *Human Factors in Cotton Culture,* p. 114.

[32] *Twelfth Census: Agriculture,* II, 408.

was not so much the work of the growers as of the professional speculators, who by the 1890's had established numerous cotton exchanges in the Southern states, as well as in St. Louis and New York.[33] It would be difficult to show that their withholding of cotton from the general market was of any benefit to the farmers, who continued, because of their credit status, to haul each bale to the merchant as soon as it was ginned.

However complex the system of the cotton exchanges may have been, marketing was a simple process for the independent grower, landlord, or merchant. The procedure as described in 1929 was not essentially different from that of thirty and more years earlier. The crop was hauled, usually a bale or two for each load, to the cotton yard in the nearest cotton town. There the owner met the buyers, who were either local merchants, agents of firms in the larger exchanges, or occasionally representatives of Southern mills. Next, the cotton was graded into nine classes, ranging from "middling fair," down through "middling," to "good ordinary." Then it was sold at auction, the bids being affected by grade, location, freight costs to central exchanges, and the like. The seller could either accept a bid or haul the cotton back to be dumped in his front yard for exposure to the weather. If financially able, he might store it in a warehouse for a later sale. All this, it goes without argument, applied merely to the "owner." The ordinary share cropper or indebted freeholder had no part in the transactions. The further marketing system, through the exchanges, was one that the growers knew little about and could not control.[34]

TOBACCO: CULTIVATION, HANDLING, AND MARKETING

The next greatest Southern staple, after the war as before, was tobacco. Like cotton, during the war its growing diminished greatly and for some varieties stopped entirely. Though some 404,000,000 pounds were produced in 1860, the recovery till 1870 was only to 227,000,000 pounds. After that date the different states, North and South, advanced their output to an estimated 725,000,000

[33] Hammond, *Cotton Industry*, p. 302.
[34] Robert Hargrove Montgomery, *The Coöperative Pattern in Cotton* (New York: The Macmillan Company, 1929), pp. 1–8; Rupert B[ayless] Vance, *Human Geography of the South* (Chapel Hill: The University of North Carolina Press, 1932), p. 194.

pounds in 1898. The chewing and heavier smoking habits of the nation not having changed much during the generation, less than a third of the portion domestically consumed went into cigars and commercial cigarettes. The revived industry following 1865 showed a remarkable shift westward, especially into Kentucky, western North Carolina, and southern Ohio, and there was a noticeable growth also in Connecticut, New York, Pennsylvania, and Wisconsin. After a long period of dormancy, there was likewise a recovery in Missouri. In 1900, Kentucky alone sold tobacco worth $18,-500,000, or nearly as much as the combined lot of all the rest of the Southern states. Throughout the period the South grew about five sixths of the nation's crop, and half or more of the total was exported.[35]

During the century, Maryland never recovered her place in the industry. Though in 1878 the state came near to the record of 51,000 hogsheads (1,000 pounds) of 1860, by 1890, a particularly low year, it had dropped back to little more than a fourth of its peak, after which there was some recovery. Virginia, likewise, had to give precedence to other states. After 1865, the North Carolinian growers found their lemon-yellow leaf gaining in favor, and soon its production expanded beyond the state's limits into Virginia and eastern Tennessee. This was a superior cigarette tobacco, and so had to await the later popularity of cigarettes. In 1864 nearly twenty million cigarettes had been manufactured commercially. But the "tailor-made" product was not immediately popular, and there was almost an extinction of sales by 1869. Then came a gradual recovery, followed by a boom produced by the Panic of 1873. Cigarettes, not being heavily taxed at the time, were the poor man's smoke. The white burley, a sport from the red variety, was discovered in Ohio in 1864, and soon took over the limestone areas of that state and Kentucky. As a consequence of the blockade, Florida lost its market for the spotted-leaf cigar wrappers, known as "Old Florida," and when her industry revived after 1888 it was with domestic adaptations of Cuban and Sumatra leaf. The new wrappers, though not quite as flavorful as their progenitors, sold readily at from seventy-five cents to two dollars a pound.

[35] Meyer Jacobstein, "The Conditions of Tobacco Culture in the South," *South in the Building of the Nation*, VI, 66–67; *Agricultural Yearbook*, 1899, p. 771; Bruce, *Rise of the New South*, p. 51.

This did not add greatly to the cost of cigars, for a pound would wrap five hundred of them. The bulk of the Florida crop was for fillers and other use. The Acadian's perique continued, after the war, to be grown in its original three parishes of Louisiana. Cured under heavy pressure and in its own juice, it was highly coveted by fastidious pipe smokers, but was used in such small quantities that the greatest annual yield was only about 100,000 pounds. At a dollar a pound its culture was expanded, but after its production was increased the price was cut in half.[36]

Not much change was wrought in the methods of growing and curing. The air, wood, charcoal, and flue processes were all in use before 1860, and continued to be applied in the later period according to the kind of tobacco and the demands of the customers in all parts of the world. Great Britain, for instance, wanted an olive-green product, picked before quite ripe and cured with wood till the odor of the smoke was apparent. But she paid the best price of any foreign country,[37] and was entitled to be indulged in her idiosyncrasy. The planting in hotbeds, resetting, constant attention, and frequent shifting of fields to new or fallowed areas were time-tested procedures of culture that could not be improved upon. Tobacco was not overproduced to as great an extent as was cotton. It was grown on farms along with the other crops, and the quantities cultivated depended on the prevailing price. In Florida, the buyers, becoming interested in improving quality, started experiments with new seeds in the 1880's, and their example was soon widely followed. Choice soils, practical methods of fertilization, and thorough tilling practices also showed good results.[38]

These benefits were mainly for the tobacco trust and the consumers. The grower, often a cropper or tenant anyway, and bound by his debts, was wholly at the mercy of the buyers, who were few. The old method of auctioning in public warehouses prevailed, one of the marts being in a city or town in each district. There, on sale days, the product was piled loose in the "bright flue-cured" regions, or in open hogsheads in the burley country. The buyers, working in collusion, paid no attention to grades, but offered a flat price for the heap. When the numerous grades were selling at

[36] *Agricultural Yearbook,* 1899, pp. 429–433, 436, 437–438.
[37] *Ibid.,* pp. 429–436 *passim.*
[38] Bruce, *Rise of the New South,* pp. 52–53.

from a cent to a dollar a pound in the central markets, the farmers would get possibly eight cents for the mixture. Late in the century, the American Tobacco Company bought much burley at private sales. In the North each individual farmer was visited by an agent who bargained as to the price.[39]

Before the buyers resold the tobacco it was finely graded by experts into as many different varieties and qualities as there were separate demands at home or abroad. Each country had its own notions as to color, texture, and taste. Great Britain was the heaviest buyer, followed in order by Germany, Italy, Canada, Spain, and a score or more of other countries or areas throughout the world. After Great Britain, Austria was the most particular and paid the better price, followed by Italy, France, and Spain. An import duty of eighty-seven cents a pound in England made it necessary that the tobacco be stemmed and thoroughly dried before shipment. Agents from the foreign countries bought the product in the larger markets, Danville, Virginia, being the biggest in the world for the bright loose leaf. The average exports in the 1890's amounted to about 280,000,000 pounds and brought a little under $24,000,000.[40]

MINOR CROPS

The earlier discussion of the one-crop system in the cotton belt should not leave the impression that the system prevailed everywhere in the South. As rice had been grown on the same plantations with indigo, in the English colonial period, so again rice became a part of a two-crop system, with sugar, before 1900. Previous to the war about four fifths of the rice was grown in a narrow coastal strip of the Carolinas and Georgia. When the industry revived, several years after the war, it was mainly in Louisiana, though, to the end of the century, a little was produced in the older area. Between 1868 and 1895, the Louisiana crop increased from 14,-000,000 to 128,000,000 pounds, or over three quarters of the na-

---

[39] *Agricultural Yearbook,* 1899, pp. 435–436; Jacobstein, "Conditions of Tobacco Culture," pp. 70–71; Meyer Jacobstein, *The Tobacco Industry in the United States* (Vol. XXVI, No. 3 of Columbia University *Studies in History, Economics and Public Law,* New York: The Columbia University Press, 1907), p. 78; James E[rnest] Boyle, *Marketing of Agricultural Products* (New York: McGraw-Hill Book Company, Inc., 1925), p. 387.

[40] *Agricultural Yearbook,* 1899, pp. 433–434, 436, 440; Bruce, *Rise of the New South,* p. 50.

tion's total of 169,000,000 pounds in the later year. These records were not to be surpassed, or reached again, till 1899, when the crop was 250,000,000 pounds, and this figure was doubled in 1903.[41] The alluvial soil of the lower delta of the Mississippi was more suited to the cereal than was the old rice coast, and the lay of the land encouraged the growing of an additional crop on the sugar plantations. The river has built its bed higher than the level of the surrounding delta, so that all rainfall and overflow from the river run back from the banks into the swamps. Sugar was planted up next to the levee, while the newly cleared fields next to the swamp were devoted to rice. Another encouragement to rice growing in the new area was the introduction of heavy machinery, comparable to that of the Prairies. Rice insects and diseases retarded the crop on the Southern Atlantic seaboard, and the types of soil discouraged the use of the newer implements.[42]

The half-billion-pound sugar crop of 1854, extraordinary in that era, was somewhat exceeded in 1861, but was not equaled again till 1893. While other Gulf states and Georgia had participated lightly in the industry before the war, afterward they confined themselves to the making of a little molasses. Even in Louisiana there was not much recovery before 1877, when the Sugar Planters' Association was founded. Its research laboratory and experimental fields helped to bring about more economical production at a time when an expanding world output made competition difficult. By the end of the century, the association was aiding the state experiment station. In order to succeed, the planters had to adopt every new implement and process that would bring the greatest economy, and they spent large sums annually for machinery of Northern manufacture. Though great efforts were made in the 1890's to encourage sugar-beet growing in the North and West, the results were, as yet, negligible. The forty thousand long tons produced in 1897, mainly in California (but a little in Nebraska, Utah, New Mexico, and New York), were only about one eighth as much as the Louisiana product. Had the beet output been multiplied several times over, the effect on the market would have been

[41] Patrick Hues Mell, "The Conditions of Rice Culture in the South since 1865," *South in the Building of the Nation*, VI, 73–75; Bruce, *Rise of the New South*, pp. 55–56; *Agricultural Yearbook*, 1909, pp. 531–532.

[42] Mell, "Conditions of Rice Culture," pp. 74–75; Bruce, *Rise of the New South*, pp. 58–60.

imperceptible, for America grew only about 4 per cent of the world's sugar and had to import five sixths of the consumers' demand. Under the first arrangements for the marketing of sugar cane, with the local manufacturers, the grower got half the sugar made from his deliveries. This provision was changed later to a straight sale basis.[43]

In 1860, the South, with 42 per cent of the improved land of the United States, had grown 43 per cent of the corn, 26 per cent of the wheat, 54 per cent of the beef cattle, 36 per cent of the dairy cattle, 54 per cent of the hogs, 27 per cent of the sheep, and 43 per cent of the horses and mules, and smaller shares of other goods,[44] besides all the cotton, rice, and sugar, and nearly all the tobacco produced in the whole country. Since the South had only western Texas and Oklahoma into which to expand, after 1865, while the nation as a whole was occupying the Prairies, Plains, and the vast regions farther west, it was not to be expected that the section, becoming yearly a decreasing fraction of the total improved area, could maintain so remarkable a position in the later years. The only fair approach is to see how nearly the South's production of these general farm goods kept pace with her population.

Though corn growing was almost banished from the cotton belt by 1890, there were big regions where there were few changes made in crop procedure, and where cereal production continued, generally on a subsistence basis, just as in earlier generations. In 1860, the area comprising the sixteen Southern states of later years had a population of a little over 11,000,000; in 1900, the number was 24,500,000, or a little more than double. In the same period wheat production increased only from 46,000,000 to 72,000,000 bushels, which was over an eighth of the national crop. Corn growing had advanced almost a half, above the 364,000,000 bushels of 1860, to 515,000,000, and was a quarter of all grown in the United States.[45] When the expansion of cereal growing into Oklahoma and

[43] William C. Stubbs, "Sugar Products in the South," *South in the Building of the Nation*, VI, 79–84; *Twelfth Census: Agriculture*, II, 454–457, 465; *Agricultural Yearbook*, 1899, pp. 14–15, 57, 238, 544, 744, 781–782; Bruce, *Rise of the New South*, pp. 59–60.

[44] Percy Wells Bidwell and John I[ronside] Falconer, *History of Agriculture in the Northern United States, 1620–1860* (Washington: The Carnegie Institution of Washington, 1925), compiled from tables on pp. 341–453 *passim*.

[45] *Agricultural Yearbook*, 1899, pp. 765, 766; *Statistical Abstract of the United States*, 1931, pp. 8–9.

northern Texas is considered, in addition to the growth in the older
border states, it may be seen that even the agitation for diversification in the 1890's had scarcely got the lower South back to the level
of 1860, while the per capita amount could not have been as much
as half as great. But the boll weevil was already beginning to do
its work in the cotton fields, and the time was not far off when
further attacks were to be made on the one-crop system. A Southern
commentator of 1896 observed: "The planters who kept their corn
cribs in Cincinnati and smoke houses in Chicago have either failed
or learned better." [46] He was slightly overconfident in his estimate,
but a change actually was under way, even though it had not
gone far.

The livestock business, in general, was closely related to corn
production. Cattle growing, even in 1860, was coming to be largely
a Texan industry, but big herds were still to be found in Louisiana,
and the roaming of "piney woods" cattle over the public highways
has never ceased in large parts of the Gulf coast. Razorback hogs
also flourished in the oak forests, and continued to furnish the
choicest of American hams. Each cotton patch had to have its horse
or mule, but, as in earlier decades, the breeding of these animals
took place mainly in the border and Northern states. At the end
of the century, about a quarter of the horses, seven tenths of the
mules, a third of all cattle, two sevenths of the dairy cattle, one
eighth of the sheep, and three tenths of the hogs of the United
States were in the sixteen Southern states.[47] Since Southern cattle
growing on a large commercial scale was mainly confined to Texas,
and to that part of Texas that is primarily Western, rather than
Southern, the discussion of this subject will be postponed to a more
appropriate place.

Truck growing and fruits also found their place in the Southern
scheme, before 1900, being especially prominent along the South
Atlantic coast. The soil and climate were favorable; Northeastern
markets were within easy shipping distances; and there was a
bountiful supply of labor to be exploited cheaply in the picking
and packing season. Women, children, and migratory workers were
mainly employed. In 1866, Charleston began to attract notice for

[46] Quoted by Thomas F. Hunt, "Cereal Farming in the South," *South in the
Building of the Nation*, VI, 108.
[47] *Statistical Abstract of the United States*, 1926, pp. 608–609.

her northbound cargoes, and, about 1885, the first rail shipments were made from Norfolk. Refrigerator cars, rapid transit, and close markets encouraged the expansion of the business. In 1899, the South's truck crops were valued at $80,000,000. Peanuts from Virginia and North Carolina were also becoming an important addition to the states' income, while strawberries, potatoes, cabbage, and sweet potatoes yielded heavily. Georgia was the most noted for her orchards, the number of peach trees increasing from 2,788,-000 in 1890 to 7,669,000 in 1900. Cherry, apple, pear, and prune orchards expanded almost as rapidly. Alabama, Mississippi, Texas, Louisiana, Tennessee, Arkansas, and Kentucky also succeeded in numerous branches of the fruit industry. In a favorable year, Florida produced a million boxes of oranges, but frost killing of the trees caused smaller crops in the 1890's. In 1900 the South's income from her orchards was about $14,000,000. As another considerable item, there might be mentioned the 1900 income of $24,219,000 from poultry, and over $4,000,000 to the beekeepers.[48] If the future was not to bring to the South the prosperity its geographic conditions warranted, it was not because of a lack of examples of what might be done by greater diversification.

[48] Bruce, *Rise of the New South*, pp. 63–71; Andrew M. Soule, "Vegetables, Fruit and Nursery Products and Truck Farming in the South," *South in the Building of the Nation*, VI, 127–135.

CHAPTER VI

The Progress of Farm Mechanization

REASONS FOR NORTHWESTERN ASCENDANCY

WHILE, for the most part, the Southern farmer stuck to his one-mule plow of eight-inch bottom, his hoe, dump cart, and other like primitive equipment, the phenomenal expansion of Prairie-state agriculture was dependent on the latest improvements in farm implements. The large-scale methods, necessary for success in the subhumid parts of the Great Plains and farther to the west, would have been impossible without the new machines. The difference between the South and the West was not just a degree of progressiveness, unless the Southern insistence on excessive cotton growing could be so disparaged. The great degree of manual labor required by tobacco culture, and the bafflement of genius in all attempts to invent a cotton-picking machine, forced the individual farmer to grow the two outstanding Southern staples on an exceedingly small acreage. Even if plowing and cultivating with improved implements had been applied on an open-field, collective basis, the family could pick no more than formerly. The spring and early summer days of release from the cotton would have been wasted anyway because the lien system prohibited second crops.

But the Prairies and the eastern fringe of the northern Great Plains were eminently adapted to the growing of cereals, and the main problems of their once-tedious labor of harvesting and threshing had been solved before 1860. Only further refinements had to be added in the later period. Corn, and especially wheat, could be most economically grown on a large scale. Hence, as in earlier decades, it was primarily the North Central states that were to profit from the inventive skill of the scientists and mechanically minded farmers. Even into the 1940's the widely heralded mechanical cotton picker had not lived up to the early promises for it. Had a really effective picker been developed at the same time as the reaper, the propertyless surplus of Southern farmers would still have needed government aid for resettlement on new Western lands. Even then, the land monopoly would have been a discouraging hindrance. This speculation introduces quite an array of *if*'s. But, even without the cotton picker, a more wisely conceived homestead act than that of 1862 could have taken the tenants to free farms, thus forcing diversification and greater prosperity on the South.

Other factors, as well as those mentioned, drove the farmers of the Northwest to ever-greater mechanization. During the Civil War, the military-bounty system tempted a disproportionately large number of rural young men into the army. The bounties were highest in the great urban centers, from Chicago eastward, thus almost depopulating the Western farming communities of available recruits. Then, when the drafts came, the quotas of the large cities were already filled, while the rural communities were forced to give up about all the able-bodied men between twenty-one and forty-five years of age that were left. Furthermore, many of the lads from eighteen to twenty-one, or even younger when they could fool the officials, were drained off to the centers paying high bounties or to serve as substitutes for drafted men. By August, 1862, "some communities had only women, old men, and boys left," and an Iowa township reported "only two men between eighteen and forty-five remaining. . . ." These were exceptions for so early a period of the war, but the situation was to grow worse and more widespread as the months passed. Where the bounty system and the draft did not get the men, draft dodging often succeeded. Canada and the mining towns of the Far West got untold numbers of temporary residents before each draft. In 1864 alone, at least 150,000 men crossed the Missouri River into the territories, in addition to all who went by other routes. Some even escaped to the

South.[1] Of this group, however, a considerable proportion came from the towns and cities.

This man shortage on the farm came at a time when produce was bringing fancy prices. Crop failures in Great Britain from 1860 to 1863, and a general shortage of food in continental Europe part of the time, added to the demand for goods, while the wasteful methods of army supply nearly made up for the loss of Southern markets. After 1863, though Great Britain was buying less than formerly, greenback prices made easy the paying of farm mortgages and raised hopes for indefinite prosperity. Certainly, it seemed, this was the time to expand farming operations in spite of the labor shortage. Old men, boys, even women could operate cultivators, mowing machines, and reapers. The output of mowing machines in Northern factories rose from 20,000 in 1861 to 70,000 in 1864, and other implements became correspondingly popular.[2]

After the war, even when deflation came, disturbed conditions in Europe continued the demand for American surpluses for a number of years, and rural adversity did not become widespread till the Panic of 1873. But the opening of the Suez Canal in 1869, the long period of relative peace after 1871, and the railroad penetration of the Ukrainian wheat fields were pointing to a reversal of European buying habits. Yet, down to 1880 the exports of wheat increased fairly steadily, even in proportion to the expansion of acreage and yield. The average of exports in 1866 and 1867 was only about a tenth of the crops, whereas in 1880 it was three eighths. In the same years, the acreage had increased from 15,000,000 to 38,000,000, the yield from 152,000,000 to 499,000,000 bushels, and the farm value of the crop from $232,000,000 to $474,000,000. Thereafter, the price was low and, though the acreage did not increase till 1897, the movement of the wheat belt into richer lands caused an occasional increase in output of as much as a fifth. But only once again before 1897 was the proportion of exports so great. Also, after 1880, though the national average value of an acre of land showed little change, the rapid settlement of very cheap land in the Western wheat belt was balanced against rising prices in the

[1] Fred Albert Shannon, *The Organization and Administration of the Union Army, 1861–1865* (Cleveland: The Arthur H. Clark Company, 1928), I, 298; II, 24, 67–68, 109, 188–191, quotation p. 68.

[2] Emerson David Fite, *Social and Industrial Conditions in the North During the Civil War* (New York: The Macmillan Company, 1910), p. 7.

older areas. This compelled the owner of the dearer land to look to his efficiency, and better implements were a part of the solution.[3]

When hard times struck, even if the freeholder lost his farm, he had to hold on to his machinery if possible in order, as a tenant, to keep up competition with others. Moreover, when he was at all able to do so, it was feasible for him to scrap old implements for improved new ones, so that cheapened production costs might keep pace with lower prices. Cooperative control of output might also have had its virtues, but that form of wisdom prevailed little more in the North than in the South. At a first glance, the figures of $246,000,000 for the value of farm implements and machinery in 1860, as compared with $761,000,000 in 1900, would indicate very little per capita growth. It was only a little over threefold, while the total population had been multiplied by two and a half, the number of farms by almost three, and the amount of improved land by two and a half. In fact, the average value of implements to the farm had increased only from $120 to $133. But this is only a minor part of the story. The implements of the later date were vastly more efficient, and their cost was far lower in proportion. Also, the valuation of Southern farm equipment, in 1900, was less than half that of 1860, while in the rest of the country it was nearly doubled. It may also be noted that 48 per cent of the 1900 valuation was in the twelve North Central states, and 20 per cent was in the nine North Atlantic states, leaving less than 17 per cent for the South Central group, and a small remainder for the rest of the country.[4]

SOIL-WORKING IMPLEMENTS

In any consideration of this period, it must not be overlooked that, before 1860, patents had already been granted in the United States for the basic principles of most of the modern machines. These included steel and chilled-iron plows, disc harrows, grain drills and planters, reapers and other harvesters, a grain binder, threshing machines, straddle-row cultivators, and numerous minor

[3] *Agricultural Yearbook,* 1899, p. 760; *Statistical Abstract of the United States,* 1926, p. 577; B[everly] T[homas] Galloway, "Intensive Farming," *The Making of America* (Robert Marion LaFollette, ed. in chief, Philadelphia: John D. Morris and Company, c.1905), V, 322–342.

[4] *Agricultural Yearbook,* 1899, p. 323; *Twelfth Census: Agriculture,* I, xvii, xviii, xxix–xxx. Figures for machinery vary slightly in different sources.

implements.[5] In the majority of cases only refinements in efficiency, durability, and ease of handling could be added. It seems logical, in a discussion of the outstanding developments, to start with the breaking of the soil, and follow the farm implements through to the harvesting, storing, and marketing of the products.

As late as 1880, fields of grain that had been seeded by hand broadcasting, after the breaking of the soil with a wooden plow, were still common. Reaping with a sickle and threshing with a flail had not been entirely abandoned. But half a century before this, the movement was already well under way that was to mark such practices as the evidence of unprogressiveness as well as a cause for continued poverty. In 1837 John Deere of Illinois (though John Lane of Chicago preceded him in invention), began manufacturing plows with steel-faced moldboards that would scour even in the clinging humus of Prairie soil. Such plows were soon widely sold, but the high cost of steel stimulated further experimentation. In 1868, James Oliver of Indiana, who had been working on the idea for fifteen years, mastered the art of hardening the surface, and made his first actually successful chilled-iron plow. After several other improvements, he got further patents, till in 1877 he turned out the really modern plow that made him rich. During the same years William Morrison and John Lane devised a system of facing the wearing parts of the plow with steel, thus helping further in the conquest of the tough sod and sticky loam of the Prairies.[6]

The next step was to take the farmer out of the furrow and put him on a seat, where he could give full attention to the team and adjust the cut of the furrow by means of levers. A patent for a sulky plow had been granted as early as 1844, but it was twenty years later before F. S. Davenport and Robert Newton of Illinois made a completely successful one. In 1873, sixteen different models of sulky plows competed in a St. Louis farming exhibition, yet, in 1866, one firm had sold 36,000 of the Newton models alone. Vari-

[5] Eldridge M. Fowler, "Agricultural Machinery and Implements," *1795–1895: One Hundred Years of American Commerce* (Chauncey M[itchell] DePew, ed., New York: D. O. Haynes & Co., 1895), II, 352–355.

[6] Frank N. G. Kranich, "Growth of Farm Machinery," *The Field Illustrated,* XXVIII, No. 3 (March, 1918), 147; Neil M[cCullough] Clark, *John Deere: He Gave to the World the Steel Plow* (Moline, Ill.: privately printed, 1937?), p. 35; R[obert] L. Ardrey, *American Agricultural Implements* (Chicago: the author, c.1894), pp. 13–18; M. C. Horine, "Farming by Machine," *A Popular History of American Invention* (Waldemar [Bernhard] Kaempffert, ed., New York: Charles Scribner's Sons, 1924), II, 251–254.

ous other improvements followed, including a third wheel to replace the landside and thus lighten the draft. G. W. Hunt's three-
wheeled plow was introduced by the Moline Plow Company in
1884. Some of the earlier sulkies carried more than one share, and
in 1859 the Fawkes steam plow with six shares, though not a proved
success, indicated the future possibilities. Further experiments, in
the next decade, with gang plows drawn by steam tractors were
hailed with interest, but it was said that, as yet, steam did not take
"kindly to his new-found toil. . . ." Yet, so far did the innovation
proceed that, before 1900, fifty-horsepower steam tractors were
drawing sixteen ten-inch plows, four harrows, and a seed drill in the
great wheat fields of the Pacific coast, thus breaking and planting
a thirteen-foot strip at a single operation, or fifty acres in a day.
Such machines were not then found practicable elsewhere. Most
of the roseate prophecies for the future of this sort of plowing had
to await fulfillment till the further development of the gasoline
tractor in the next century.[7]

Clod crushers, harrows, and soil packers of one kind or another
are of about as ancient an origin as the plow itself. Though spike-
toothed harrows were used by the Romans, and forms of disc harrows were known long before 1860, the spring-tooth variety seems
to have been first invented in practical form by David L. Garver
of Michigan, and patented in 1869. This type had the special
advantage that the teeth would trip instead of catching on roots
and rocks, and would also automatically dislodge their accumula-
tions of debris. The disc, not recommended for stony soils, would
cut and turn under all ordinary stubble and other humus-forming
roughage. Before 1890, many improvements were made in both
types, including levers to adjust the pitch of the spring teeth and
the angle and depth of the disc. Litigations over numerous patents

[7] Ardrey, *American Agricultural Implements*, pp. 19–20; L[ynn] W[ebster] Ellis
and Edward A. Rumely, *Power and the Plow* (Garden City: Doubleday, Page &
Company, 1911), pp. 153–154; Bidwell and Falconer, *History of Agriculture in the
North*, p. 285; John C. Merriam, "Steam," *One Hundred Years' Progress of the
United States* (no ed. listed, Hartford: L. Stebbins, 1870), quotation from p. 263;
Edward W[right] Byrn, *The Progress of Invention in the Nineteenth Century* (New
York: Munn & Co., Publishers, 1900), p. 207; Leo Rogin, *The Introduction of Farm
Machinery in Its Relation to the Productivity of Labor in the Agriculture of the
United States during the Nineteenth Century* (Vol. IX of University of California
Publications in Economics, Berkeley: University of California Press, 1931), p. 44;
Charles L. Flint, "Agriculture in the United States," *One Hundred Years' Progress
of the United States*, pp. 30–32.

led the principal manufacturers to pool their holdings in the National Harrow Company, in 1890.[8] Till after the end of the century, some farmers continued to use limbs of trees or clod crushers made from sections of logs.

SEED PLANTERS AND CULTIVATORS

The numerous inventions of drills and other machines for sowing or planting seeds had not been widely adopted before the Civil War. Grain drills were used extensively in the level and well-cleared sections of Michigan by 1870, but shortly before this it was reported from Champaign County, Illinois, that they were almost unknown in the Prairies. For that matter, the early drills were of little use except in clean, well-pulverized earth, and the Prairie soils were so fertile that large crops could be grown without excessive care in their preparation. Again, an expert hand broadcaster could seed an amazingly large area in a day, and the harrowing or dragging in of the grain was accomplished quickly by a boy and a horse. The resulting stand of grain was likely not to be as even as that on the drilled acres, but it was satisfactory. Sometimes, even into the twentieth century, hand-operated mechanical broadcasters, carried by their users, were employed, especially in the reseeding of thin spots. Intermediate between this device and the drill were box seeders that merely dropped the grain to the ground from a cart—used in some wheat areas until the late eighties —and the endgate scatterer, which did the same sort of work as the hand broadcaster, except that it fed from a wagon instead of a bag. Introduced into the spring-wheat regions of the Mississippi Valley in the early 1870's, a generation later the endgate seeder was still extensively used for the sowing of grain in the Northwest and Pacific coast areas.[9]

As drills were improved in adaptability and design, their use spread rapidly through the Western wheat belt, and, by 1874, they were generally adopted. The Buckeye drill and the Farmer's Friend,

[8] Ardrey, *American Agricultural Implements*, pp. 21–22.
[9] *Ibid.*, pp. 27–28; Rogin, *Introduction of Farm Machinery*, pp. 196, 199–204; Horine, "Farming by Machine," p. 258; Edwin S. Holmes, "Wheat Growing and General Agricultural Conditions in the Pacific Coast Region of the United States," U.S. Department of Agriculture, Division of Statistics, *Miscellaneous Series, Bulletin No. 20* (Washington: Government Printing Office, 1901), pp. 24–25.

both made in Ohio, were early favorites. Although American drills were late in rivalry with the English, by 1876 the American supremacy was so assured that the British refrained from any exhibit at the Centennial Exposition in Philadelphia. Various forms of furrow openers, adapted to different types of soil, were tried until, after 1890, the disc was found best for most of the greater wheat belt. Improvements in the evenness of seeding, and increases in breadth, made the machines more economical than any of the more primitive devices, each of which had required a second going-over of the field to cover the grain.[10]

The development of corn planters, before 1860, left only a few major alterations to be made. The checkrower, planting the corn in hills equidistant horizontally and transversely, so that the field can be cultivated alternately lengthwise and crosswise, was a special need of the Western farmer. John Thompson and John Ramsey of Illinois further developed the Robins device of the 1850's, and, in 1864, patented a checkrower that proved to be a money-maker for the company that secured its control in 1875. In the westernmost tier of the North Central states, deeper planting was made necessary by the scantiness of rainfall. Here the lister, introduced about 1880, solved the problem. It was a double-moldboard plow, throwing furrows in opposite directions, away from each other, and leaving the field a series of ridges and trenches. A subsoiler, beneath the shares, left a seedbed into which the corn was dropped from an attached box, and there was a covering wheel, behind, to complete the process of corn planting with one operation of the plow. As the stalks grew, the ridge between the rows was merely dragged with a "sled," time after time, until a smooth field of deeply planted corn was ready to lay aside till the harvest. The lister has never been equaled for this work by any other device.[11]

The corn cultivator, useful also for other crops planted in widely spaced rows, was another implement highly developed before 1860, but down to that date the double-shovel walking plow was gener-

[10] Russell Howard Anderson, "Grain Drills through Thirty-Nine Centuries," *Agricultural History*, X, No. 4 (October, 1936), 177, 179, 187, 200–201; Edward H[enry] Knight, "Agricultural Implements," *House Executive Document* No. 42, 46 Cong., 3 Sess., V, 102–111; Rogin, *Introduction of Farm Machinery*, pp. 195–199.

[11] Horine, "Farming by Machine," pp. 261, 263–264; Fowler, "Agricultural Machinery and Implements," p. 355; for the lister, see illustration in *Webster's International Dictionary*.

ally used in the Prairies. In later years, the disc or spring-tooth varieties proved generally more efficacious. By the 1890's, millions of dollars were invested in the manufacture of "an almost endless variety of cultivators—hand and horse, single and double, walking and riding, shovel-bladed, spring-tooth, disk, etc." By that time also, many farmers, who did not insist on riding, found that the walking cultivators could be held nearer small corn, under perfect control, and that they needed less space for turning at the end of the row.[12]

HAYMAKING AND HARVESTING MACHINES

By 1860, the two-wheeled, hinged-cutting-bar mowing machine was developed to an approximately permanent form. This was followed, during the war, by the revolving horse-drawn hayrake, which was soon superseded by the spring-tooth rake that could be tripped at intervals, so as to leave the hay in windrows for easy loading. The sixty or seventy designs of this implement were essentially alike in principle. Then, in the 1890's, came the side-delivery rake, better adapted to the use of mechanical loaders. Experiments begun by the Keystone Manufacturing Company of Sterling, Illinois, around 1876, produced a machine that picked the hay from the windrow and placed it on an endless carrier, to be deposited on the moving wagon to which it was attached. By 1890, its use permitted the loading of a ton of hay in five minutes. In 1864, the first patent was issued for a harpoon hayfork. Thereafter, carrier tracks could be placed just under the ridgepole of the barn, and, by use of block and tackle attached to a harpoon fork and pulled by a horse, a whole load of hay could be dragged in two or three lifts into the portion of the loft where it was to be stored. Tedders, for the turning of the hay during the curing, were popular and of numerous makes all through the period, and before 1900 all-steel implements were replacing the earlier wooden ones. In 1866 George Ertel of Quincy, Illinois, perfected his continuous baling press, the power coming from a horse attached to a rotating sweep. He, like many other inventors, developed other people's ideas. Around 1880,

---

[12] Ardrey, *American Agricultural Implements*, p. 36; quotation from Fowler, "Agricultural Machinery and Implements," p. 354.

some steam-operated presses were in use, working with three times the speed of their predecessors.[13]

There was a far greater room for improvement of harvesting machinery. The harvester patented by the Marsh brothers (Charles Wesley and William Wallace) of DeKalb, Illinois, in 1858, was only beginning to prove its worth during the Civil War. Its distinctive characteristic over earlier reapers was that, instead of dumping the cut grain on the ground, it had a platform behind, on which men could ride and tie the bundles as fast as the grain came from the reel. The farmers and hired hands grumbled at the speed necessary for keeping up with the machine, until the Marsh brothers showed that deft-handed German girls and volunteer hoboes from the onlookers (their own men in disguise) could do the work easily. In 1864, W. W. Marsh himself bound an acre in 55 minutes, but the ordinary procedure was for two men to ride a larger machine, and work at a somewhat more leisurely rate. Three men could keep up on a seven-foot swath. Until 1871, there were no practical rivals to the Marsh harvester. Then several companies began manufacturing them under licenses from the inventors, Cyrus H. McCormick being added to the list in 1875. Down to and including 1879, a hundred thousand such machines had been sold.[14]

The trouble with them all was that, though speeded up, the labor of binding was very little less than in the days of Gideon. An automatic binding device would release two or three men from each harvester. As early as 1850, John E. Heath had invented a twine binder that proved unsuited to harvesters, and it was not till 1873 that wire binders came into use. One of these, invented by J. F. and J. H. Gordon of Rochester, New York, was sold to McCormick, and another, begun by Sylvanus D. Locke of Wisconsin and improved by Charles B. Withington, was acquired by the same company. Many others came on the market in the 1870's,

[13] Ardrey, *American Agricultural Implements*, pp. 90–102; W. B. Thornton, "The Revolution by Farm Machinery," *World's Work*, VI, No. 4 (August, 1903), 3771.

[14] Herbert N[ewton] Casson, *The Romance of the Reaper* (New York: Doubleday, Page & Company, 1908), pp. 50–51; Byrn, *Progress of Invention*, pp. 201–202; Ardrey, *American Agricultural Implements*, p. 60; Horine, "Farming by Machine," pp. 275–276; Deering Harvester Company, *Official Retrospective Exhibition of the Development of Harvesting Machinery for the Paris Exposition of 1900* (Paris: 1900?), pp. 84–85; exhaustive on McCormick is William T[homas] Hutchinson, *Cyrus Hall McCormick*, Vol. II (New York: D. Appleton-Century Company, 1935), *passim*.

all with the same defects: the wire had to be cut from the bundle before threshing, and, if a bundle slipped by without this precaution, it was likely to do damage to the threshing machine, to cattle eating the straw, or to milling machinery. Then John F. Appleby, continuing the work of Jacob Behel of Illinois, succeeded with a twine knotter, which, in 1878, he sold to the Deering company. McCormick then took over the rights to a similar device, patented by Marquis L. Gorham, and the rivalry between harvester companies continued. By 1880, the self-binder was a complete success, and as wire binders wore out they were replaced by the twine machines. Two men and a team of horses then could harvest and shock twenty acres of small grain in a day. Improvements on the binder since that time have been mainly to enhance its strength, capacity, and simplicity.[15]

As the wheat belt moved westward, where the air was drier, a simpler method of harvesting could be followed. There the header, invented before the war, was used effectively. Cutting a swath twice or more the width of that of the binder, it was pushed across the Plains by four-horse teams, taking only the heads of the grain and leaving the long stubble to be grazed or plowed under. The heads were carried up an endless apron to be dumped loose in a broad-bedded, hopper-shaped wagon with the side farthest from the header built high. This was known as a "barge." Then it was stacked loose in the open till the threshing crew came along. On the Pacific coast a still more complex machine was used. This was the combine, introduced into California about 1880. Cutting a swath of from twenty-six feet to twice as many, it was propelled across the fields by a steam tractor, threshing and bagging the grain as it went, and sometimes at the rate of three 150-pound bags a minute. The combine was not used east of the Rocky Mountains till 1910 and later, and then, in smaller sizes, it was pulled first by horses and afterward by gasoline tractors. By the use of these various harvesters, the task that has been described as "the most burdensome and exacting operation on the farm" was so lightened before the end of the century that one man, with ease, could

---

[15] Ardrey, *American Agricultural Implements*, p. 53; Horine, "Farming by Machine," pp. 279–281; Deering Harvester Company, *Harvesting Machinery*, p. 90; Byrn, *Progress of Invention*, p. 205; Reuben Gold Thwaites, "Cyrus Hall McCormick and the Reaper," State Historical Society of Wisconsin, *Proceedings*, 1908 (Madison: The Society, 1909), p. 256.

accomplish as much as the toil and sweat of twenty men two generations earlier. Yet the cradle never ceased to be used in some of the small Southeastern fields, and sometimes in other places where the terrain will not admit heavy machinery. The expert cradler, though worth traveling far to see, has become a rarity.[16]

Refinements in the threshing machine, after 1860, were in the way of greater capacity and cleanness of work, stronger construction, the application of steam power, self-feeders, automatic band cutters, weighers, and straw stackers. The thresher used in the wheat belt of the North Central states before 1870 was an eight-to-ten-horsepower affair, using nine men—or thirteen if the straw was stacked—and threshing 300 bushels a day. The two-horsepower machine, handling 135 bushels a day, was also in use. Some steam-driven threshers of that time had a capacity of 600 bushels, and, in the nineties, as much as 1,000 bushels were reached. The stacking of the straw was an old-time puzzle, solved in 1882 by "a radial stacker of the belt-conveyor type," that heaped the straw in a horseshoe arrangement. Invented earlier, but first proved out two years later, was the blower of a James Buchanan. At the Indiana State Fair, in 1884, Buchanan's men "laid ten-dollar bills in the shoe," or place where the grain was closest to the stacker, to prove that the suction would not pull the grain out with the chaff and straw. Many years later, the customers of traveling threshing crews mistrusted the "antics" of the blowing device when the yield of the shocks fell below expectations. But the same sort of stacker has since been used on most threshing machines, corn shredders, and silo fillers. In 1891, the McKain company bought Buchanan's patent, together with others, and created one of the most powerful agricultural-implement monopolies of the period before 1900.[17]

No corn-harvesting implements of the prewar years were of any great importance, and it was long afterward before any but the crudest of devices were in use. A combined shucking and fodder-

[16] Horine, "Farming by Machine," pp. 276–277; Byrn, *Progress of Invention*, pp. 206–207; *Agricultural Yearbook*, 1919, pp. 145–146; Rogin, *Introduction of Farm Machinery*, p. 120; C. C. Johnson, "Combines Long Known in Washington," *The American Thresherman*, XXXIII, No. 1 (May, 1930), 26; A. E. Starch and R. M. Merrill, "The Combined Harvester-Thresher in Montana," University of Montana, Agricultural Experiment Station, *Bulletin* No. 230 (Bozeman: 1930), p. 6; quotation from Ardrey, *American Agricultural Implements*, p. 40.

[17] Rogin, *Introduction of Farm Machinery*, pp. 185–191; Horine, "Farming by Machine," pp. 296–297.

shredding machine was patented by J. F. Hurd of Minnesota in 1890, and it was rapidly improved. The stalks were fed in at one end and the cleaned ears came out in one direction, while the fodder, cut to proper size for feeding, was blown in another. In 1892, A. S. Peck of Illinois got a patent on a corn binder that had most of the basic features used in later years. Several manufacturers took over the production of the machine, and others tried imitations. Corn shellers handling 2,500 bushels a day were known by the end of the century. One of the first American silos of record was built by Manly Miles of the University of Illinois in 1875. He copied the models in use in France. Other slightly earlier American experiments have been mentioned, but Miles is credited as being the pioneer of a successful movement. He was soon copied in New York and other Eastern states as well as in the Prairies. The first silos were built square or rectangular, and some were of the pit type, but soon the circular form prevailed, and by the 1890's they looked so much like those of forty years later that the difference is hardly distinguishable in the pictures. About all that was to be found out about the preparation and storage of silage was known before 1900, and the silo was taking the corn belt from Indiana to the Dakotas by storm. Ensilage-cutting and silo-filling machines awaited further development.[18]

MISCELLANEOUS IMPLEMENTS AND MACHINES

Two inventions did more than all others in revolutionizing the dairy industry in the later decades of the century. One was the centrifugal cream separator, first successfully used in America in 1879, and the other was the centrifugal cream tester. Inasmuch as the method of operation of the separator was essentially the same then as at any later time, it would be a work of supererogation to describe it. Before 1900, separators were run "by hand or power—a dog or a sheep, a bull or a horse, water, electricity, or steam." Not only did the new method save much labor over the old gravity system, but also it took all of the cream instead of three quarters, and produced it at any required degree of thickness. More than

[18] Horine, "Farming by Machine," pp. 285–287; Ardrey, *American Agricultural Implements*, p. 126; *Agricultural Yearbook*, 1899, pp. 616–620, Plate LIX facing p. 618.

40,000 centrifugal separators were in use in the United States before 1900.[19] In the earlier days, the separators were large machines located at commercial plants. The farmers, taking their milk to these stations, got their quota of skimmed milk back from a common tank, thus often carrying diseases from others' herds to their own. The cream tester was the invention of S. M. Babcock of the experiment station first of New York and then of Wisconsin. Again, the details of the testing process have been the same since the introduction of the machine. The use of the tester requires care, but not mechanical or chemical skill. The devices were manufactured, before 1900, in large commercial sizes and also in a hand-operated small design that no commercial milk producer could afford to do without. At last, the time had come when he could detect cheating on the part of the creamery without fail. Though numerous milking machines had been patented before 1900, not one of them was a practical success. As to churns, one of them had been patented on the average of every ten or twelve days for over seventy years.[20]

Except for the heavy steam tractors used with threshing machines and for large-scale Pacific coast farming, little advance was made with artificial power for farm work. Early tractors were capable of drawing the threshers from one place to another, as well as running them when set. About 1888, Jacob Price and Daniel Best produced improved engines for plowing and harvesting. These monsters so packed the soil that, a few years later, Benjamin Holt tried out an immense tractor with rear wheels each eighteen feet wide, for use in the wheat fields of California. When this proved to be only another steam roller, he began to develop the idea of the lag-bed or caterpillar-tread, but succeeded only after 1900. In order to keep such engines in operation, it was necessary to have two teams and drivers busy hauling coal and water, yet, for a time, it was felt that the huge wheat ranches of the Far West could not be run without them, and that for this purpose they were more economical than horses (but see page 144 below). By 1900, there were thirty-one firms in the United States manufacturing, all together, over six thousand traction engines, averaging in cost a little more

[19] *Agricultural Yearbook*, 1899, pp. 393–395, quotation p. 393.
[20] *Ibid.*, pp. 391, 395–398; "The Cream Separator: Its Development, Advantages and Unsolved Problems," *Scientific American*, CVII, No. 6 (August 10, 1912), pp. 112, 124; Alvin J. Reed, "Facts about the Cream Separator," *The Progressive Farmer and Southern Farm Gazette*, XXXI, No. 6 (February 5, 1916), 178, 180.

than a thousand dollars each. Gasoline tractors were also tried, without success, in the 1890's.[21]

No effort has been made here to mention anything but the outstanding inventions of the period. Some idea of the number of omissions can be gained from a summary of the Patent Office down to November 17, 1899. By that time, patents had been issued for the various agricultural pursuits as follows: "Vegetable cutters and crushers, 701; fertilizers, 822; bee culture, 1,038; trees, plants, and flowers, 1,102; care of live stock, 3,749; dairy, 4,632; thrashers, 5,319; harrows and diggers, 5,801; fences, 8,404; seeders and planters, 9,156; harvesters, 12,519; plows, 12,652." [22] This means an average of about two agricultural patents for each working day since the first patent law was passed in 1790. Between 1860 and 1900 the annual value of American manufactures of agricultural implements rose from $21,000,000 to $101,000,000, while the efficiency of each unit was immensely higher in the later years. Not all of this increase was for domestic use, but, by 1900, more money was invested in harvesters than in any other machine in the world except the steam engine. An estimate, made shortly after 1900, listed the machines necessary for a well-managed farm devoted to mixed agriculture and stock raising, and placed the value at $785.[23]

The decline in prices of farm machines over the span of years cannot well be presented in statistical form, mainly because of the vast improvement in the efficiency of newer models, and because the price does not adequately reflect the difference between very similar models in the matters of durability and workmanship. Some figures from a Department of Agriculture list will be given, however, to demonstrate something of the trend (see next page).

As significant as anything else in these figures is the tendency, after 1880, for prices to become stabilized and, after 1895, even to rise. This was the period when monopoly was creeping into the farm machinery business. During the 1880's, the number of manufacturing firms in the field diminished from 1,943 to 910, while the invested capital grew from $62,000,000 to $145,000,000. The num-

---

[21] Horine, "Farming by Machine," pp. 300–305; P. S. Rose, "Farm Motors," *Cyclopedia of American Agriculture* (L[iberty] H[yde] Bailey, ed., New York: The Macmillan Company, 1907), I, 222.

[22] *Agricultural Yearbook*, 1899, p. 319.

[23] *Twelfth Census: Manufactures*, IV, 344; C. J. Zintheo, "Machinery in Relation to Farming," *Cyclopedia of American Agriculture*, I, 216.

ber of employees increased from 39,600 to 42,500 and their total wages from $15,000,000 to $22,000,000. The cost of materials remained stationary, at $32,000,000, but the sale value of the output grew from $69,000,000 to $81,000,000.[25]

PRICES OF TYPICAL MACHINES, 1860–1900[24]

Kind of Machine	Date				
	1860	1880	1890	1895	1900
Walking plow (a)	$12.00	$ 14.00	$ 13.00	$ 13.00	$ 14.00
Walking plow (b)	11.50	7.35	5.94	5.70	4.75
Gang plow (a)	60.00	60.00	55.00	50.00	48.00
Gang plow (b)	18.00	25.00	14.00	12.50	12.00
Three disc plow	....	75.00	70.00	70.00	75.00
Cheapest solid disc plow	....	20.00	15.00	12.00	15.00
Best solid disc plow	....	100.00	75.00	60.00	75.00
Cultivator (a)	....	26.00	22.50	21.50	23.00
Cultivator (b)	7.00	6.50	5.00	4.00	6.00
Drill (a)	90.00	70.00	52.00	48.00	50.00
Drill (b)	65.00	75.00	60.00	50.00	50.00
Twine binder (a)	....	325.00	140.00	125.00	120.00
Twine binder (b)	....	300.00	150.00	125.00	125.00
Twine binder (c)	....	175.00	135.00	125.00	125.00
Twine binder (d)	....	175.00	160.00	150.00	140.00

ECONOMIC AND SOCIAL EFFECTS OF MECHANIZATION

Repeated estimates have been made of the saving in human labor and money required to produce a unit of each of numerous crops, as a result of mechanization. Leo Rogin has traced the savings in man power for wheat production by different sorts of implements. For example, with the sickle a good man could reap, bind, and shock from half to three quarters of an acre in a day. An expert cradler could cut three acres in a day, but it took three binders for each two cradlers to maintain the pace in good wheat country, and shocking consumed an additional quota of time. The result was that, for each man employed, an acre of good wheat could be cut, bound, and shocked in a day by use of the cradle. The early reaper equaled four or five cradlers, thus saving

[24] George K[irby] Holmes, "The Course of Prices of Farm Implements and Machinery for a Series of Years," U.S. Department of Agriculture, Division of Statistics, *Miscellaneous Series, Bulletin* No. 18 (Washington: Government Printing Office, 1901), pp. 15, 17, 19, 22–23.

[25] *Ibid.,* p. 8.

three men in the cutting of ten acres with a hand-rake reaper, or four men with a self-raking machine. Furthermore, two less men were needed for binding behind a reaper than for an equivalent area covered by cradlers. Five men were thus saved in a ten-to-twelve-acre cutting by a self-raking reaper, over the number needed in cradling the same field. With the Marsh harvester, two binders did the work of four or five working from the ground. Again, the self-binder released these two men from binding. Like savings of man power can be seen for the threshing machine, as compared with flailing and winnowing.[26] But an array of such details for a great number of farm operations soon becomes confusing.

Fortunately for all studies of this subject, in 1898 the United States Commissioner of Labor, Carroll D. Wright, published a report of some 1,600 pages on *Hand and Machine Labor*, the bulk of it in tabular form. The early part of this report is devoted to agricultural labor, and twenty-seven different farm crops are analyzed. It was impossible, even in so exhaustive a study, to get the same date for all the hand processes. Yet, nothing else can be substituted for these figures, for, as Wright says: "The report presents a body of information which it would be impossible to secure a few years later." In many cases, persons familiar with the old processes had to be interviewed in detail to procure the information, and their records have nowhere else been preserved.[27]

A close study of the tables (see sample for wheat in the Appendix, page 416) reveals not only the saving in man-hours of labor, but also the change in labor costs for the production of each unit; and this cost can be broken down into that part attributable to wages and the other part for the labor of draft animals. The table on page 142, adapted from Commissioner Wright's *Report*, shows the labor cost (both man and animal) for the production of each bushel, ton, or hundred pounds (as the case may be), both by the older and by the newer methods of production. The last column in each section shows what percentage of the worker's daily wage is represented by the cost of producing one unit. Thus, in 1830, the man and animal labor cost in the making of a bushel of wheat represented 38.34 per cent of a wheat-field worker's daily

---

[26] Rogin, *Introduction of Farm Machinery*, pp. 125–141, 176–191.
[27] U.S. Commissioner of Labor, *Thirteenth Annual Report* (1898): subtitle, *Hand and Machine Labor* (Washington: Government Printing Office, 1899), I, 6.

wage, while in 1896 the corresponding percentage was 6.75. The study of these last columns eliminates the necessity of adjusting monetary values for the distant dates. It may be noted that the savings by use of machinery were higher for Northern crops than for Southern, and higher for wheat and oats than for any of the rest in the list. In fact, in the tobacco fields the cost of production by the new methods was greater than by the old. This was largely

COSTS OF LABOR BY HAND AND BY MACHINE [28]

Comparison of labor costs (man and animal) for the production of different crops by hand methods (mainly) in early years, and by machine methods in the 1890's. Hours of labor virtually the same in every case (ten a day). In each comparison, the productivity and adaptability of the land is approximately the same (exception for cotton, as indicated).

Crop	Unit of measure	Hand Methods					Machine Methods			
		Date	Daily wage; man (Dollars)	Daily hire; horse, ox, or mule (Dollars)	Labor cost of one unit (Dollars)	Ratio of cost of one unit to daily pay of a man (%)	Date	Daily wage; man (Dollars)	Daily hire; horse, ox, or mule (Dollars)	Labor cost of one unit (Dollars)	Ratio of cost of one unit to daily pay of a man (%)
Wheat: 20 bu. to acre	1 bu.	1830	.50	.12½	.19 +	38.34	1896	1.50	.50	.10 +	6.75
Corn: 40 bu. to acre; un-shelled, fodder left in field	1 bu.	1855	1.00	.37½	.13 −	12.58	1894	1.00	.50	.08 +	8.27
Oats: 40 bu. to acre	1 bu.	1830	.50	.12½	.10 −	19.35	1893	1.50	.50	.04 −	2.67
Hay: loose in barn. 1 ton to acre	1 ton	1850	1.00	.50	1.92 −	191.68	1895	1.25	.50	.63 +	50.51
Hay: baled; 1 ton to acre	1 ton	1860	1.00	.37½	3.19 −	318.56	1894	1.25	.50	1.91	152.85
Potatoes: 220 bu. to acre	1 bu.	1866	1.00	.50	.07 −	6.59	1895	1.00	.50	.03 −	2.99
Cotton: 750 and 1,000 lb. in seed to acre	100 lb.	1841	.50	.25	1.23	246.06	1895	1.00	.50	.94	94.20
Rice: rough; 2,640 lb. to acre	100 lb.	1870	1.00	.50	.27 +	27.27	1895	.65	.50	.08 −	12.17
Sugar cane: at grinder; 20 tons to acre	1 ton	1855	1.00	.50	1.99 −	198.77	1895	.65	.50	.82 −	125.91
Tobacco: graded and packed; 1,500 lb. to acre	100 lb.	1853	.75	.37½	1.72 +	229.81	1895	1.00	.50	1.87 −	186.54

because of more care in grading and packing, while little improvement was made in machinery. The increase in daily pay, from seventy-five cents to a dollar, accounts for the slightly lowered ratio to a day's wage. One is led to wonder where in the South a dollar a day was paid for work in either the tobacco or the cotton fields in 1895. But, considering the items for rice and sugar cane, it is noted that the wage dropped from a dollar to sixty-five cents in the transition from hand to machine methods—a considerable factor in the labor-cost saving for the unit of production.

[28] Calculated from *ibid.*, II, 442–449, 452–455, 460–461, 466–473.

Another table is presented showing the man-hours of labor and the human-labor wage cost for the growing of each acre of the same ten crops under hand and machine methods. The totals for the twenty-seven units of the original study are included for comparison. A great disparity will be seen between the time and wage savings in the different items. For example, by the use of the disc gang plows, broadcast seeders, five-section harrows, and combines

HOURS AND WAGES BY HAND AND BY MACHINE [29]

Comparison of hours of human labor and wages for the production of one acre each of different crops by hand methods (mainly) and by machine methods (same acres and years as in preceding table).

Crop	Time Worked				Labor Cost	
	Hand		Machine		Hand	Machine
	Hours	Minutes	Hours	Minutes		
Wheat	61	5.0	3	19.2	$ 3.5542	$ .6605
Corn	38	45.0	15	7.8	3.6250	1.5130
Oats	66	15.0	7	5.8	3.7292	1.0732
Hay: loose	21	5.0	3	56.5	1.7501	.4230
Hay: baled	35	30.0	11	34.0	3.0606	1.2894
Potatoes	108	55.0	38	00.0	10.8916	3.8000
Cotton	167	48.0	78	42.0	7.8773	7.8700
Rice: rough	62	5.0	17	2.5	5.6440	1.0071
Sugar cane	351	21.0	191	33.0	31.9409	11.3189
Tobacco	311	23.0	252	54.6	23.3538	25.1160
TOTAL: 10 crops	1,194	12.0	619	15.4	$ 95.4267	$ 54.0711
TOTAL: 27 different crops	9,760	47.7	5,107	52.6	$1,037.7609	$598.1338

the work of a man in the wheat field was more than eighteen times as effective in 1896 as it had been with the crude implements of 1830. On the other hand, there was very little time saved in producing an acre of tobacco. In the growing of tobacco plants for transplanting (an item not included in the table), a unique situation is revealed. In 1844, this task for one acre required 199 hours and 12 minutes, but, in 1895, changed methods consumed 353 hours and 11 minutes. The experts of the Bureau of Labor devoted a long

[29] Selected from *ibid.*, I, 24–25.

paragraph to an attempted explanation of this paradox, and then admitted that the reasons were insufficient.[30]

Another item, omitted from the tables here presented, is the growing of wheat with the huge steam-propelled machinery of the Pacific coast. This was deleted because no accounting was made of the cost of operating the tractors, and, therefore, no comparison could be made with costs by horsepower. But, even with this omission, it is interesting to observe that the steam operations took only 21 fewer minutes for the making of 20 bushels of wheat to the acre than were required by the use of horses; and the man-labor cost was 5.75 cents higher. Perhaps this may help to explain why the use of the huge tractors was relatively temporary and why the experiment did not spread to other areas.

In the ten crops listed, the time saving by improved methods was 48.1 per cent; and in the twenty-seven crops of the *Report* it was 47.7 per cent. These low ratios are due to the fact that numerous farming operations, requiring many hours of labor, were only slightly affected by machinery even in the 1890's. These include the growing of orchard trees and vegetables, and most of the staple crops of the South. An exception from the vegetable group should be made for potatoes.

But cereals, hay, and cotton were the really great crops, and the ratio for cereals was far above the average. The harvest for small grains generally lasts about ten days, during which time the grain is ripe enough to cut and not so overripe as to thresh out on the ground in the cutting. Thus, in the day of the sickle and flail, the farmer was limited to the amount of the grain he could reap, or about 7½ acres for each mower. But, in the 1890's, he might well grow 135 acres, if he wanted to specialize to that extent. The same rule did not hold for cotton. It was foolish to grow more cotton than could be picked, and the time needed for picking in 1895 was not much less than in the earlier decades. The individual grower could raise very little more cotton, but he might devote the surplus time created by improved soil-working implements to the growing of additional amounts of other crops. As has already been seen, under the share-cropping and crop-lien system, not only was this discouraged, but even the introduction of improved machinery was retarded.

[30] *Ibid.*, I, 24–25, 91–93.

Some of the gains, above mentioned, came before 1860, but most of them were achieved afterward, the exact percentage being unascertainable. Moreover, many farmers in the 1890's were not utilizing the opportunity to work with the best implements. It was estimated, in 1899, that, if the most economical methods had been employed on all farms producing corn, wheat, oats, rye, barley, white potatoes, and hay, the saving in labor cost, over old methods, would have exceeded $681,000,000 a year, 77 per cent of this for corn alone. Though the actual economy was much less, the Census of 1900 showed a lowering in cost of all items of production of the leading crops, over a forty-five year period, amounting to 46.37 per cent.[31] No general data exist for the compiling of tables and graphs of the different sections of the nation, on such matters as total cost of production, and its relation to prices received or prices paid. The best that even the Bureau of Labor's study could do was to reveal labor costs on sample farm units as a result of changes in machinery.

The beneficial consequences of these changes need scant discussion. The most obvious result was the reduction in spirit-deadening toil. This helped the man who was fortunate in his selection of soil and wise in management—and if factors outside his control permitted—to acquire prosperity and leisure, and give his family added cultural advantages. Certainly, the academies, high schools, colleges, and universities springing up in all the predominantly agricultural states, after 1860, were created out of the wealth produced, directly or otherwise, primarily by the farmers. So were the churches, the small-town industries, and many of the cultural activities, in which the farmers participated only slightly, in the cities. The cheapened cost of production made more bearable the fall in prices accompanying rapid agricultural expansion. It also offered the possibility of a higher standard of living for the industrial laborer, but this was offset by employers' wage-cutting programs, notable in the 1880's and 1890's.

At the same time, it reduced the number of people needed to feed and clothe the population of the United States and to supply its agricultural exports. Between 1860 and 1900, the cities and other nonfarm areas gained about 18,000,000 in population over the national average of growth, while the farms lost an equal number

[31] *Agricultural Yearbook,* 1899, pp. 331–333; *Twelfth Census: Agriculture,* I, cxxi.

(see page 357, below). In other words, some 18,000,000 less people got their living directly from the soil than would have under the agricultural standards of 1860 projected forty years later. Apparently, that number of people (including descendants) had found it necessary or possible to drift into the towns and cities (partly through excess of urban over rural immigration), and the cities were finding it difficult to digest the mass.[32] As for those who remained behind, at least in some areas, too many were of the unenterprising sort, and the effect of this on rural life is a point that needs not be labored. If, as N. S. B. Gras says, "one of the greatest of all faults of farm life is its ugliness. . . . And worse than this is the blissful satisfaction with the unsightly," [33] then here is a possible explanation. Furthermore, the expense of machinery, along with other factors, reduced the percentage of owners, and added to the numbers of tenants and hired workers. Persons too poor or too unprogressive to acquire the new implements, and others who expanded operations too rapidly in the brief periods of prosperity, soon joined the ranks of the victims of the land monopolists, those remaining on the land no longer being free agents. Between 1880 and 1900, the North Central states, where the bulk of the machinery was used, had a remarkable growth in tenancy [34] (see table in the Appendix, page 418). For instance, in Kansas, which already had a large farming population, the percentage of tenants to all farmers grew from 16.3 to 35.2, a difference of 18.9. Though the South had a head start before 1880, the increase in Kansas in the following twenty years exceeded that of any state of the Old South except Louisiana, whose growth (share croppers being classed as tenants) was 22.8 per cent. The rise in Oklahoma Territory and South Dakota was from virtually nothing to 21 and 21.8 per cent, respectively. On the other hand, the land monopoly of the aborigines of Indian Territory, by 1900, had made tenants of almost an even three quarters of all farmers—by far the highest rate for any part of the United States.

Very few mechanical improvements of these years were for use

<hr>

[32] See Schlesinger, *The Rise of the City*, pp. 53–120, for urban conditions.

[33] Norman Scott Brien Gras, *A History of Agriculture in Europe and America* (New York: F. S. Crofts & Co., Publishers, 1925), p. 428.

[34] H[adley] W. Quaintance, "The Influence of Machinery on the Economic and Social Conditions of the Agricultural People," *Cyclopedia of American Agriculture*, IV, 108–113.

Fraudulent Land Entries

A House "Twelve by Fourteen"

A Bona Fide Residence

In the illustration to the left, the witness swore at the land office that the house on the claim was "twelve by fourteen," with the mental reservation that he meant "inches" and not "feet." The house above was "witnessed" on scores of claims in Nebraska—one day on each claim, for a rental of five dollars.

A Central Pacific Train Crossing the Humboldt River

In their race for federal gifts of land and money, the Union Pacific and the Central Pacific railroads laid the crossties far apart and they were not extravagant as to the weight of iron rails. (*The Bettmann Archive.*)

A First-Class Hotel on the Plains in 1867

A First-Class Hotel on the Plains in 1869

A new edition of Albert D. Richardson's *Beyond the Mississippi*, in 1869, provided excellent propaganda for the Union Pacific Railroad.

The Levee at New Orleans

Shortly after 1900, packet steamboats were rarely seen on the Mississippi below Cairo, Illinois. (*The Bettmann Archive.*)

Mississippi River Transportation in the Nineteenth Century
(*after Currier & Ives*)

Several decades passed before steamboats thoroughly replaced flatboats. An item missing in the picture is a huge fleet of barges pushed by a tugboat. (*The Bettmann Archive.*)

Cotton Trains at Houston, Texas

The style of the locomotives and the type of couplers indicate that this picture dates between 1880 and 1900. (*The Bettmann Archive.*)

Mowing Grain with a Cradle, and Binding by Hand

Still a common practice in the 1860's, thirty years after the introduction of practical reapers, this method of harvesting has never been abandoned in some parts of the eastern United States.

Harvesting with a Header and Barges

This method was followed only in subhumid areas. The equipment in this picture looks identical with the outfit the author helped operate on the Great Plains in 1911.

Front View of Combine Used in the San Joaquin Valley in the 1890's

This combine, pushed across the field by a steam tractor, cut a 52-foot swath. It harvested about 100 acres in a day, cutting, threshing, and sacking up to 1,800 sacks between dawn and dark.

(*By permission of Charles Scribner's Sons.*)

Rear View of Same Machine

A Nineteenth-Century Silo

A Threshing Crew in the Day of the Steam Tractor

A 24-Gang Steam Plow in California, before 1900

The "Bull" Plow

Before the introduction of the steel and chilled iron plows, farmers used huge, unwieldy plows, such as this one, which barely cut beneath the sod. (*The Bettmann Archive.*)

Planting Wheat on a Bonanza Farm

"Factory methods" of farming long preceded the corporation farms of the 1920's. (*From a drawing by W. R. Leigh, by permission of Charles Scribner's Sons.*)

in the farm homes. If the men removed the wear on their clothing from the shoes to the seats of their overalls, the women still plodded along at their ancient tasks in time-honored fashion. Before 1900, some of them had party-line telephones, whose batteries endured a terrific strain when fifteen neighbors took down their receivers on a single conversation. But there was no other electric equipment of any kind, save an occasional incandescent light in favored spots near the towns. (Therapeutic quackery may also have introduced a few "electric belts.") A rotary egg beater might gladden an ambitious matron, and a kitchen sink was enough to cause excited comments among the neighbors.

Other factors than machinery contributed to the changes in agricultural production, particularly the growing attention to scientific methods as advanced by state and federal governments, agricultural societies, and book farmers. But all such things were subordinate to the mechanical improvements. Although the farm could be run with fewer hands, and the output to the laborer was better than doubled in many cases, the yield to the acre was rarely increased, and the tendency was more to wear out the soil than to improve it. Early in the twentieth century, a government study appraised this phase of the agricultural situation thus: "The success and prosperity of the American farmer are due to the unbounded fertility of the soils, the cheapness of farm lands, and the privilege of utilizing modern inventions in machinery rather than to systematic organization and efficient farm management." [35]

[35] Willet M[artin] Hays and Edward C. Parker, "The Cost of Producing Farm Products," U.S. Department of Agriculture, Bureau of Statistics, *Bulletin* No. 48 (Washington: Government Printing Office, 1906), p. 9.

CHAPTER VII

The Expansion of Prairie Agriculture

FRONTIER CONDITIONS

TO a remarkable degree the major agricultural developments of 1861–1897 centered in or grew out of the Prairie states. Not only did those states become the most highly mechanized, but their citizens wrought most of the significant inventions, and Prairie-state factories manufactured the bulk of the machines. From the eastern apex of the Prairies, near Chicago, railroads radiated in fan-shaped formation out to the Mississippi, to the northward bend of the Missouri, then ran in a more parallel fashion westward to the Great Plains and beyond. The cities along the southwestern shore of Lake Michigan and on the middle stretches of the Mississippi River, particularly in Illinois, were excellently located for serving the demands of farmers farther west, and their supremacy in machine output was not the only feature of their trade.

The Chicago stockyards, meat-packing industry, and wheat pit were famous as well as infamous before 1900. Rock Island and Moline, in Illinois, and Davenport, just across the river in Iowa, comprised an industrial center second only to Chicago in the production of implements. Milwaukee was an early rival in the packing industry—later overshadowed by East St. Louis, Illinois, and by Kansas City, Kansas, and Omaha. Minneapolis achieved supremacy in the Western Hemisphere in the flour-milling industry. These and numerous intermediate centers helped build Prairie agriculture, and were nourished by it. While the Prairies did not include much east of the Mississippi River, and though a great deal even of Missouri and Minnesota were outside the limits, there was enough similarity in the problems of all twelve of the states of the North Central division to lump them together in this discussion. This does not mean that the lessons of pioneering learned in Ohio would apply accurately in eastern Iowa, or that the Iowa experiences would serve aptly in the more westerly Prairies of North Dakota or Kansas. In fact, the special annoyances of the western Prairies call for a preliminary, separate consideration.

Clear out to the ninety-eighth meridian, and well beyond, the early settlers sought river or creek bottoms for their new homes, and there they found sufficient timber for the building of log houses, barns, and fences, with enough trees still left standing to shelter the livestock. Later comers, less fortunately located, could build sod houses, sometimes half or more underground and called dugouts. Such dwellings, whatever else may be said as to their commodiousness or sightliness, could be kept dry and with little fuel heated comfortably warm through the bitterest winter. The banks of the streams could not supply firewood for many families, but buffalo chips were an acceptable substitute, and in the early years they were plentiful. As the buffalo was eliminated, and the ground became well picked over, persons going on any trip through less gleaned territory would carry a gunny sack along and pause for a moment at each spot where a buffalo had stopped. When the cattle drives were started north out of Texas, farmers were often glad to have the beasts bedded down for the night in their neighborhood for the fuel they would leave behind. Again, because of the fuel question, it is not by accident that Kansas has come to be known as the Sunflower State, as a substitute for the earlier Jayhawker. Sunflower stalks, when cut green and seasoned, made good firewood; so seeds were imported till the volunteer plants spread over all the roadsides and neglected fields. A salesman in Dakota Territory, in 1871, claimed that the seed he distributed would provide twelve cords to the acre, or enough for a year's supply. Special stoves, also, were devised for the burning of hay, the better ones having the forage compressed into large cylindrical magazines and fed in automatically. The product of a hay-fired brick kiln at

Ord, Nebraska, in 1881, was still doing service in the walls of a house more than fifty years later.[1]

Another perplexity was the household water supply. It might be collected in cisterns or ponds, or be hauled in barrels from the creek. But water witches plied a thriving business, and sometimes their divinations coincided with a vein of water. Most of the early wells were dug by hand with pick, shovel, windlass, and bucket, just as was done in the East. A Bohemian woman west of the ninety-eighth meridian in Kansas dug such a well while her ailing husband drew up the dirt. In thirty years Nels Christensen of Nebraska dug more than two miles of wells, and once narrowly escaped being killed by a falling bucket when at the bottom of a well that was 280 feet deep. Driven wells were practicable in some places where the water was in a quicksand layer close to the surface. Sometimes wells as much as fifty feet deep were dug with elongated post-hole augers.[2] Not till the late nineties did deep drilled wells, equipped with windmills, become common.[3]

Blizzards and floods—for the rivers of the Plains and western Prairies can become most treacherous—took their toll of livestock and human lives, but drouth and hot winds were the greater menace to crops. The person who has never traveled through the subhumid regions when the temperature is 118° in the shade, and the shade is "all in the next county," can neither understand nor believe the truth of the situation. He prefers to change the topic of conversation to humidity. In the West, when the temperature is above 110°, the arrival of a breeze is a calamity. Wheat in the milky stage shrivels in the husk and becomes worthless except for chicken feed. Corn wilts and the blades turn crisp on the stalks. The man in the open feels no perspiration, but wishes he could. To all appearances he sweats dry salt till his face becomes white and his eyebrows are encrusted.

At the higher temperatures, when the hot winds are blowing, those persons who are free to do so take to their houses, close all the doors and windows, and pull down the blinds. At night, in such seasons, the seeker for comfort strips off all clothing and goes to

[1] John Ise, *Sod and Stubble: The Story of a Kansas Homestead* (New York: Wilson-Erickson, Incorporated, 1936), pp. 17–31; Dick, *Sod-House Frontier*, pp. 257–260.

[2] Ise, *Sod and Stubble*, p. 83; Dick, *Sod-House Frontier*, pp. 261–266.

[3] Shannon, *Critiques*, p. 89.

bed with a wet sheet over him, getting up three or four times in the night to resprinkle the covering. An electric fan played over the sheet, if electricity is available, gives a fair substitute for air conditioning. It is a common saying in Kansas that when a particularly wicked native dies he is buried in an overcoat so that he can endure the changed temperature in the afterworld. It is in the same area that the mule is alleged to have stood in a field of popcorn until the corn all popped; then looking around, he thought he was being buried in snow, and froze to death. Farther west, on the High Plains, the temperatures are not so extreme, and the summer nights are generally pleasant, but even there a hot wind often shrivels a growing crop.[4]

Prairie fires were a menace in the early years, particularly in the fall after a long, hot, dry summer. The least spark could begin one, and, when it got a good start, the only thing a person out in the open could do was to make all possible speed diagonally with the wind and away from the fire. If he rode a good horse, sometimes he escaped. Houses and other buildings were protected by repeated backfiring. When the big fire was first sighted, bearing down on them, the family would light a small fire that could be kept under control till all combustible material close to the buildings was consumed. Then they would circle out for another fire at longer range until everything was safe except from stifling smoke, suffocating ashes, and blistering heat. Dust storms were also well known many decades before they became a national problem in the 1930's. Trampling buffalo herds sometimes wrought havoc on overly dry pasture land, and the black soil of many an early farm was blown in dunes over the hedge fence soon after plowing. These storms were most likely to come in the early spring, after a dry, open winter. Sometimes they blew for days at a time, the visibility often being so low that objects could not be seen ten feet away at midday. When a rain started during such a storm the drops came down as mud pellets. Even in tightly closed houses people went about with wet cloths tied over their noses and mouths, the mud being washed out of the cloths occasionally.[5]

[4] Drouth, hot winds, floods, and blizzards are discussed in Dick, *Sod-House Frontier*, pp. 212–216, 221–231.

[5] Dick, *Sod-House Frontier*, pp. 216–220; Ise, *Sod and Stubble*, pp. 112–117, 252–259.

But the direst visitations of the 1870's were of grasshoppers. There had been pestilences of them before, but the worst since the coming of the white man was in 1874, and this was repeated in 1875 and 1876. The scourge spread out over Dakota Territory, Nebraska, Kansas, down into northern Texas, and eastward to central Missouri. With the crops half grown, the grasshoppers, borne in by the wind, descended in a cloud that so darkened the sun as to cause the chickens to go to roost. The weight of the insects broke the limbs from trees. They started in on the wheat and corn, progressing across the fields and mowing it to the ground. They ate everything green except native grasses, castor beans, and the foliage of some kinds of trees. They so loved onions that they ate them clear down in the ground to the roots, and, as one observer declared, "till their breath was rank with the odor." They also had a fondness for tobacco and red peppers. They killed trees by denuding them of the tender bark of the twigs and limbs. They ate the mosquito bar off the windows, then entered the house, ate the curtains (if any), and started in on the bed covers. Relishing the taste of sweat and grease, they ate into the sideboards of the wagons, the plow handles, and even so roughened hickory pitchfork handles as to ruin them. They covered the railroad tracks so heavily that they stopped the trains, the locomotive wheels spinning with insufficient friction to draw the cars through the slithering mass. Turkeys and chickens ate themselves sick. The insects polluted the streams with their dead bodies till the cattle were loath to drink. The only exaggeration in any of the stories was that of hogs and fish fattening on the pests till their flesh had a grasshopper flavor, and even this may be true.

Numerous inventions appeared for the eradication of the locusts, but, even though the devices caught tons, they were futile. The state of Minnesota paid bounties of fifty cents a bushel, and burned the catch in huge bonfires, but the clouds of pests kept pouring in. The native saying was, "Two new grasshoppers arrived to attend each dead one's funeral." After suffering repeated invasions, Nebraska passed a law making grasshoppers a "public enemy," calling out all able-bodied men to fight the evil, and assessing fines of ten dollars for each refusal to serve in the posse. After the scourge of 1874, the settlers were destitute. The insects stayed only from two or three days to two weeks in one spot, leaving when there was nothing remaining for them to eat. After they departed, all surplus livestock had to be sold. The Kansas legislature voted a bond issue, and over $70,000 was given for relief. Nebraska also issued bonds, mainly to buy seed for the next crop. Dakota authorized $25,000 for relief, but the "boosters" for immigration hushed up the matter till they got so poor they had to accept the grant. The federal government gave $150,000, mainly in the form of food and of clothing and shoes from the army stores. In later decades the pest was not quite so bad, but sometimes the conditions of 1874–1876 were approximated.[6]

There were other troubles as well. Wet weather came in cycles of years, tempting settlers farther west, then a succession of dry years would starve the disillusioned throngs back again (see Chapter XIII). John Ise, in *Sod and Stubble*, the story of his mother, reveals how a much-persevering family could exist meagerly during the lean years, and then when the fat ones came would celebrate with a new house, a still better house, and a new barn. For several years there were troubles with marauding Indians and claim jumpers, but a courageous householder could generally outbluff the latter. Rattlesnakes were a menace to unwary children, while doctors with their futile remedies, and quacks with their snakestones, were remote. Babies crawled into ant heaps and got badly chewed and poisoned in consequence.[7] Authentic stories are told of a baby that was dragged from its crib in an unfinished house, by a lynx that was scared away before serious damage was gone. The troubles recorded above were all in the Prairies, and before the Great Plains were invaded by farmers. Many of these stories could be duplicated by equally dire incidents on all preceding and later frontiers. Violent adjustments of ways of living had to be made by families coming in from afar—again, as had happened before and was to occur again in other new communities.

[6] Dick, *Sod-House Frontier*, pp. 202–212; Ise, *Sod and Stubble*, pp. 49–53, 64–67; Arthur Fisher Bentley, "The Condition of the Western Farmer as Illustrated by the Economic History of a Nebraska Township," Johns Hopkins University *Studies in Historical and Political Science*, XI, Nos. 7–8 (Baltimore: The Johns Hopkins Press, 1893), pp. 307–308, 310.

[7] Ise, *Sod and Stubble*, pp. 83–91, and see chapter headings; Branch, *Westward*, p. 583.

BONANZA FARMS

It was in this region that the bonanza farms sprang up in the late 1870's, flourished through the early eighties, and disintegrated in the hard nineties. The romantic ideas regarding the western gold fields had entered the Prairies, and yellow bonanzas, far more lucrative than the new ore strikes of the Black Hills, were to be panned out with the plow and self-binder. The land monopolists, fostered by the federal land laws, imbibing the new spirit of bigness hubbling up in the great transportation and industrial corporations of the East, and inspired by the availability of the new machinery, decided that the practices of big business could be emulated successfully on the farm. A succession of wet years furnished all the additional incentive that was needed. Weather conditions, it was felt, were undergoing a permanent change; moreover the railroads had already come, to care for transportation needs. Hence by 1880, Eastern readers began to learn about the farm managed by Oliver Dalrymple in the Red River Valley of the present North Dakota, where thirteen thousand acres of wheat comprised a single field. "You are in a sea of wheat," one article declared. "The railroad train rolls through an ocean of grain. . . . We encounter a squadron of war chariots . . . doing the work of human hands. . . . There are twenty-five of them in this one brigade of the grand army of 115, under the marshalship of this Dakota farmer." [8] Such metaphorical description was suitable to this new development.

It was the type of organization and management, not the mere size of the holdings, that astounded the reporter. For years before the Civil War, the people had the opportunity of knowing about the huge landholdings of the Prairie cattle kings. Theirs was an enthralling story, too little emphasized in history,[9] but it was a tale of a different kind. Great landholdings, devoted to grazing, left idle, or sublet to tenants, had been known from time immemorial, and had been found in America since early colonial days. In 1860, there were 501 farms of more than a thousand acres each in nine of the North Central states and territories, ranging from 194 in Illinois and 112 in Ohio to one each in Kansas and Nebraska. But Georgia

---

[8] C. C. Coffin, "Dakota Wheat Fields," *Harper's New Monthly Magazine*, LX, No. 358 (March, 1880), 529–535, quotation from p. 534.

[9] But see Paul Wallace Gates, in Volume III of this series.

alone had 902 and California 262.[10] By 1870 the number in the Prairie group had grown to 635, nearly all the gain being in Illinois, but the California list had increased to 713.[11] The Census of 1880 showed the new trend. In the two preceding counts, only a fifth and a fourth of the thousand-and-more-acre holdings of the North Central states had been west of the Mississippi River. Now, of the 2,990, and in spite of the fact that there had been a striking growth in number in the eastern group, 1,621 were in the western section. Missouri led, with 685, followed by Illinois, Iowa, Ohio, and Kansas. But Minnesota had sprung from 2 to 145 and Dakota Territory from none to 74, and these represented the true bonanza farms of the period. Yet, it must be noted that Georgia had 3,491 and California 2,531 of the larger estates of the same year.[12]

Years before the celebrated bonanza farms of Dakota and Minnesota, some of the Prairie cattle kings had set a precedent for large-scale farming, in connection with their feeding of livestock. Shortly after the Civil War John T. Alexander bought the Broadlands estate of Michael L. Sullivant, located in Champaign County, Illinois. It covered 23,000 acres (as part of an 80,000-acre estate, see page 71, above), and at one time had 1,800 acres in corn alone. With livestock, grain, hay, and farm implements, it was said to have cost Alexander nearly half a million dollars. Before this purchase he already owned some 80,000 acres on which he fed 32,000 head of cattle and 15,000 hogs, besides devoting 16,000 acres to corn. In the next three years he added 26,500 acres for another stock farm. Sullivant, meanwhile, developed 40,000 acres in Ford and Livingston counties, and in "five years he had 18,000 acres in corn, and 5,000 in other crops." His corn yield alone in one year was 450,000 bushels. Most of the work on the farm was done with the newest types of implements, including 150 "steel plows, 75 breaking plows, 142 cultivators, 45 corn planters, 25 gang harrows, a ditching plow operated by 68 oxen and 8 men, an upright mower to clip the hedges. . . .", and a great number of power-driven corn shellers.[13] In Atchison County, Missouri, David Rankin, over a fifty-

[10] *Eighth Census: Agriculture*, p. 221.
[11] *Ninth Census: Industry and Wealth*, pp. 345–366.
[12] *Tenth Census: Agriculture*, bottom folio, pp. 68–100.
[13] Arthur Charles Cole, *The Era of the Civil War, 1848–1870* (Vol. III of *The Centennial History of Illinois*, Clarence Walworth Alvord, ed. in chief, Springfield: Illinois Centennial Commission, 1919), pp. 382–383; quotations from Paul Wallace

years period, built up a 23,000-acre estate so magnificent that it could be described only in superlatives.[14]

The number of these excessive holdings in the eastern Prairies was always small in proportion to all farms in the states. In 1880, when Illinois had 649 superfarms and Champaign County alone had 27, the average-sized holding (tenant- as well as owner-operated) for both state and county was 124 acres. From that time on, great estates in Ohio, Indiana, and Illinois decreased in number, while there were only slight gains in Michigan and Wisconsin. But the movement was only getting a good start in the western tier of the Prairie states. Minnesota showed a steady increase in large holdings, to 365 in 1900; Iowa remained relatively steady and Missouri declined somewhat. But North Dakota rose steadily to 1,346 in 1900, South Dakota to 2,041, Nebraska to 2,364, and Kansas to 3,559.[15] In 1890, the twelve states had 4,468 farms ranging upward from a thousand acres, about seven tenths of them west of the Mississippi.[16] By 1900, over eight tenths of the 11,560 such holdings were in the tier from Kansas to North Dakota. By the same date, the California total had risen to 4,753, while Georgia had dropped to 1,858, and New York had 248.[17] These figures illustrate the trend.

By 1880, the era of the cattle kings in the eastern Prairies was passing. As population became denser the rise in value of land compelled a change to more intensive farming practices. The cattle business was moving out on the Plains, and the big farms in the older region were gradually broken up or let to tenants. But the western Prairies had become the new farmers' frontier, and there ensued a renewal of grand-scale farming. When the Panic of 1873 halted the construction of the Northern Pacific railroad, Bismarck, Dakota Territory, which was west of the Prairies, had already been reached. The railroad company then took the leadership in the establishment of bonanza farms.

James B. Power, land agent of the reorganized company, induced George W. Cass and Benjamin P. Cheney, president and di-

Gates, "Large-Scale Farming in Illinois, 1850–1870," *Agricultural History*, VI, No. 1 (January, 1932), 18.

[14] Donald Angus, "Breaking up the Biggest Farm," *The Country Gentleman*, LXXXIV, No. 45 (November 8, 1919), 6–7, 49.

[15] *Tenth Census: Agriculture*, bottom folio, p. 78; *Twelfth Census: Agriculture*, I, 186–204 passim.

[16] *Eleventh Census: Agriculture*, p. 118.

[17] *Twelfth Census: Agriculture*, I, 186–204 passim.

rector of the corporation, to exchange some of their almost worthless railroad bonds for eighteen sections of Red River Valley land in (North) Dakota, the ultimate purpose being to encourage land sales by demonstrating the productivity of the region.[18] The partners then employed Oliver Dalrymple, an expert wheat grower from Minnesota, to manage the business. The proprietors furnished all the capital for the venture, and when the returns had repaid all this, with interest, Dalrymple was to get "half of each farm, with its stock and improvements."[19] This arrangement was made in 1875. In the first summer, two full sections of sod were broken, and the first season's crop yielded twenty-three bushels to the acre. These results were widely advertised, and the Dakota boom was on. Capitalists bought up the depreciated railroad bonds to trade for land, and independent farmers swarmed in to get what they could of the rest, and of the unmonopolized parts of the government land, in the same region.[20]

The Red River Valley wheat lands reached back from ten to twenty miles on both sides of the river, for a three-hundred-mile strip in Minnesota and Dakota, and up to Lake Winnipeg in Manitoba—but there was no bonanza farming north of the United States. As a Minnesota observer described the Red River Valley, "The surface of the land is nearly level, with but sufficient undulation to afford good drainage; the soil a rich, friable, black alluvial mold some thirty inches deep, resting upon a retentive clay subsoil. . . . and almost every acre can be put under the plow in unbroken furrows from one end to the other."[21] Early settlers had been discouraged from diversified farming by grasshopper plagues, destructively cold winters, and horse influenza, but specialization in wheat was less hazardous. Only the spring variety could be grown, and, before 1870, this yielded a dark, inferior flour. Then, in 1870, Edmund N. La Croix, a French miller settled at Minneapolis, developed the middlings purifier, which, with the new roller process

[18] Harold E. Briggs, "Early Bonanza Farming in the Red River Valley of the North," Agricultural History, VI, No. 1 (January, 1932), 26–27.

[19] "The Bonanza Farms of the West," Atlantic Monthly, XLV, No. 267 (January, 1880), 37–38.

[20] John Lee Coulter, "Industrial History of the Valley of the Red River of the North," State Historical Society of North Dakota, Collections, III (Bismarck: Tribune, State Printers and Binders, 1910), 570–571; George N. Lamphere, "History of Wheat Raising in the Red River Valley," Minnesota Historical Society, Collections, X, Pt. I (St. Paul: Published by the Society, 1905), 21.

[21] The Cultivator & Country Gentleman, XLII, No. 1,268 (May 17, 1877), 317.

of grinding, removed all previous objections to the product.[22] The Dalrymple experiment could not have been started at a better time.

In the second season, 1877, Dalrymple got a twenty-five bushel average from 4,500 acres, and imitators made a start. In the preceding year the Grandin brothers of Tidioute, Pennsylvania, exchanged Northern Pacific securities for nearly a hundred sections of land, and got Dalrymple to manage as much of that area as was in the Red River wheat region. The total cost of making a crop on the Grandin bonanza in 1878, including interest on the permanent investment, was $9.50 an acre, and the yield was from twenty to twenty-four bushels, while the price was about 90¢. It was estimated that the Grandin holdings, of 61,100 acres of wheat lands, were five times the area of Manhattan Island. The Dalrymple interests were about 100,000 acres. Other bonanzas of note in North Dakota included the Hillsboro Farm, 40,000 acres; the Cooper Farms, 34,000; the Amenia and Sharon Land Co., 28,350; the Spiritwood Farms, 19,700; the Mosher Farms, 19,000; and the Antelope Farm, 17,300. The average of all was probably 7,000 acres, and the smaller holdings of two or three sections were not classed as bonanzas at all. Some of the estates were so broad that crews working on one side did not see members occupied on another portion during the entire season. Quite often, the owners lived in the East, and seldom were they the actual managers. By 1885 nearly all of the greater establishments had begun operations, and the valley up to the Canadian border was pretty thoroughly dominated by absentee landlords.[23]

The form of organization on the Dalrymple units may be taken as fairly representative of the system. "They had in crop in 1880 about 25,000 acres, conducted in farms of about 6,000 acres each of plowed land. To each of these farms there is a superintendent. These farms are again divided into divisions of about 2,000 acres each of plowed land, and each subdivision has its own farm build-

[22] Edward Van Dyke Robinson, *Early Economic Conditions and the Development of Agriculture in Minnesota* (University of Minnesota *Studies in the Social Sciences*, No. 3, Minneapolis: *Bulletin* of the University of Minnesota, 1915), pp. 76–78; William Allen White, "The Business of a Wheat Farmer," *Scribner's Magazine*, XXII, No. 5 (November, 1897), 531–548 for farming details.

[23] Briggs, "Early Bonanza Farming," p. 29; Coulter, "Industrial History of the Valley of the Red River," pp. 574–575, 580–581; White, "Business of a Wheat Farmer," p. 534; William Godwin Moody, *Land and Labor in the United States* (New York: Charles Scribner's Sons, 1883), p. 52; Alva H. Benton, "Large Land Holdings in North Dakota," *The Journal of Land & Public Utility Economics*, I, No. 4 (October, 1925), 408,

ings, boarding-houses, stables, blacksmith-shop, and so on, this size being considered there the most convenient, and as large enough for systematic management, while, if larger, the men might have to travel too far to and from their work." [24]

Following the first cost of land and equipment, the largest expense on the bonanza farms was for labor. This was highly seasonal and done by migratory workers. Harvesting crews started out in Kansas and followed the ripening wheat northward till they wound up in North Dakota and Minnesota, some even going on into Canada. They paid no railroad fares, and the chambers of commerce and newspapers liked to refer to them as tramps. Nevertheless, the critics recognized that these migrants were a necessity. Many of the workers were farmers released by a slack season in other parts, and some were lumberjacks seeking employment during the off season in their camps.[25] Harvesting is hard work, as anyone who has tried it can attest, and many a blacksmith turning from the sledge hammer to the pitchfork, with heavily calloused hands, has returned from the first day in the harvest field his hands so blistered that he was almost unfit for work for the next day or two. The harvest crew worked thirteen hours a day for from nine to twelve dollars a week, plus bed and board. The meals cost the management about thirty cents a day for each man, and the bedding was often a shakedown in the haymow. A few laborers had to be kept on throughout the year, and these got from fifteen to eighteen dollars a month. The Grandin bonanza used 10 men during the five colder months; 150 for April plowing; about 20 from May 1 to July 15; 100 during the rest of July; 250 in August and the first half of September (the harvest season); then about 75 till the end of October. One account mentions 400 men during harvest.[26]

The breaking of the soil was done by two-plow, riding gangs with four horses each, from four to five acres being turned by a unit in a day. Number one Scotch Fife wheat was sowed, about eighty pounds to the acre, harrows preceding and following the seeders. Dalrymple used 200 pairs of harrows and 125 broadcast seeders. Next, the feed crops of oats and barley were sowed, and some of the smaller operators planted flax, buckwheat, and turnips.

24 *Tenth Census: Agriculture*, bottom folio, p. 454.
25 Coulter, "Industrial History of the Valley of the Red River," pp. 577–578.
26 *Ibid.*, p. 577; White, "Business of a Wheat Farmer," p. 545; "Bonanza Farms of the West," p. 39.

During the harvest, Dalrymple used 155 binders, each handling fourteen acres a day and operated in groups of twelve or more. Each squad had an overseer and shockers. As soon as the approximately ten-day harvest was over, threshing began, with 26 steam threshers turning out an average of nine hundred bushels a day each. It took about twenty-five men and twenty horses for each unit to haul from the shock, run the machine, and transport the grain to the railroad station a few miles away.[27]

Before 1883, the yield of wheat was good, and prices were high. Bonanza managers could supply nearly all of their material needs at wholesale prices, and, if doing a big business, got rebates from the railroads on their wheat shipments. But, from 1885 to 1890, the seasons became drier, crops declined, prices dropped, and taxes mounted. In the next decade, the large-scale grower found it hard to compete with the smaller farmers who diversified their crops and cultivated their land more intensively. Hence, many of the larger bonanzas disintegrated, including the Dalrymple interests in 1896. The corporation farms of the 1920's were largely a renewal of the idea on a new wheat frontier farther west.[28] Though the Dakota boom and the bonanza farms hastened the settlement of the region, the results were far from being uniformly good. Thousands of families were tempted to take up farms where, even if the land was fertile, there was no assurance of enough good seasons to offset the bad. The best farming lands were monopolized, and, when the system broke down, the holdings were let out to tenants instead of being subdivided into freeholdings. But when the movement was at its height, few words were heard except in praise. William Godwin Moody was the rare exception of the individual strong enough to brave the disapproval of the chambers of commerce and the newspapers they influenced.[29]

A long discussion of this subject would seem out of place, con-

[27] *Tenth Census: Agriculture,* bottom folio, p. 455; Coulter, "Industrial History of the Valley of the Red River," pp. 571–573.

[28] Charles B. Spahr, "America's Working People," *The Outlook,* LXIII, No. 10 (November 4, 1899), 565; *Tenth Census: Agriculture,* bottom folio, p. 455; Coulter, "Industrial History of the Valley of the Red River," pp. 576–577; Malcolm C. Cutting, "Big Doings in Montana," *Country Gentleman,* XCIV, No. 5 (May, 1929), 22–23, 130–131.

[29] Briggs, "Early Bonanza Farming," pp. 35–37; W. B. Hazen, "The Great Middle Region of the United States, and Its Limited Space of Arable Land," *The North American Review,* CXX, No. 246 (January, 1875), 24; Gates, "Recent Land Policies," pp. 64–65; Moody, *Land and Labor, passim.*

sidering the small number of bonanza farms in proportion to the total of all landholdings in the West, were it not that the movement so accurately exemplifies the spirit of the times. In hope of riches for themselves, farmers of sub-bonanza caliber emulated the bigger rivals and copied their methods as far as they were able. They tried the big commercial game, not realizing that their lack of rebates, and favors of a similar order, worked against them, and that something nearer to a subsistence basis was better suited to their need. Also, the bonanza farms called further attention to land monopolization and the growth of tenancy elsewhere in the West. There were big wheat operations in the Pacific states at the same time, and often more highly mechanized than in the Red River Valley. Also, attention should be called again to the great number of immense landholdings from Kansas to South Dakota, where states of tenant farmers were being created. In 1886, a Congressional committee provided data on the number of American land monopolies controlled from foreign countries, by listing twenty-nine that totaled 20,747,000 acres, and including an English holding of 3,000,000 acres in Texas, as well as the Holland Company's 4,500,000 acres in New Mexico.[30] In the same year, a magazine article condemned the monopolistic system as being detrimental to the political and economic structure.[31] As Gates has said, the bonanza farms were "an amazing commentary upon . . . [a] so-called democratic land system."[32] But, lastly, the bonanza farms also illustrate how farming was done on the western Prairies, even though it was generally followed on a lesser scale.

THE MOVEMENT OF CEREAL CROP PRODUCTION

The bonanza farms also exemplify the magnetic attraction of the cheaper and more fertile frontier soils for wheat growers. From early Colonial days, wherever there were rivers to transport the grain to the coast, wheat followed the frontier, and remained close to the unplowed cattle range. And so the practice continued till the aridity of the farther West repelled all efforts to keep up the

[30] "Ownership of Real Estate in the Territories," *House Report* No. 3,455, 49 Cong., 1 Sess., p. 2.
[31] A. J. Desmond, "America's Land Question," *The North American Review*, CXLII, No. 351 (February, 1886), 153–158.
[32] Gates, "Recent Land Policies," p. 65.

advance. Before 1860, the center of wheat production had pushed out into the North Central states, which in 1859 grew nearly 55 per cent of the nation's total, while 46 per cent was in the five states of the group that lie east of the Mississippi River. Some wheat was still grown in small patches, mainly for local consumption, but, in general, the industry was thoroughly commercialized. By 1869, the movement into the West North Central states had already become pronounced, that area yielding 23.4 per cent of the national crop, as compared with 44.3 per cent for the East North Central. In the next decade the shift was not great, the eastern subsection merely holding its own, while the western group increased the total for all by 4 per cent, thus giving the whole section 71.6 per cent of the crop of the United States. Then, in the 1880's, the western seven states achieved the ascendancy they were to make permanent, and by 1899 they alone grew 46.6 per cent of the total crop, while all twelve accounted for 67.1 per cent. By 1909 the West North Central states increased their lead by another 10 points, after which the competition of the Mountain and Pacific states became more telling.

Thus far, there is a misleading element in the figures. The westward movement of the production center does not mean that the older wheat-growing regions of the Atlantic seaboard were all declining in their total output, but merely that they were making no substantial gains. An exception might be made for the South Central states, which, in the 1890's, temporarily regained virtually their percentage standing of 1859. This was mainly on account of the opening of the wheat lands of Oklahoma and northern Texas; and, after all, this was just a southward extension of what was happening in the whole western tier of the Central states. On the other hand, there were some Eastern states that showed an actual decline in wheat growing. But what the westward movement essentially means is that the East, in terms of its rapidly growing population, was supplying a diminishing proportion of its own demand, and that the West was taking over this market as well as the export trade. For that matter, the Mountain and Pacific states increased their percentage of the nation's crop (over the forty years) from 4.4 per cent to 13.7, the volume for 1899 being over ninety million bushels, or nearly as much as the North Central states had grown in 1859. By 1909, the same Far Western states, though their crop had declined a little, barely exceeded all the rest of the Union except the North Central states. But this is a big exception, for the latter alone grew 73.9 per cent of all. The leadership by states can best be presented by a table. By the end of the century, Minnesota

THE SIX LEADING WHEAT STATES (AND PERCENTAGES)
BY DECADES, 1859–1899

1859 56.4%	1869 55.7%	1879 53.4%	1889 50.2%	1899 49%
Illinois	Illinois	Illinois	Minnesota	Minnesota
Indiana	Iowa	Indiana	California	North Dakota
Wisconsin	Ohio	Ohio	Illinois	Ohio
Ohio	Indiana	Michigan	Indiana	South Dakota
Virginia	Wisconsin	Minnesota	Ohio	Kansas
Pennsylvania	Pennsylvania	Iowa	Kansas	California

was already slipping, and, thirty years later, was to be fifteenth in rank, while Kansas, with a crop seven times as large, reached ascendancy in a rather permanently fixed wheat belt.[33] The sudden rise and almost equally rapid decline in some states, such as Iowa and California, are largely the result of unusually good crops in those states in years when the leaders were not far apart in the race.

THE TEN LEADING CORN STATES (AND PERCENTAGES)
BY DECADES, 1859–1899

1859 70.8%	1869 72%	1879 78.9%	1889 80.7%	1899 75.5%
Illinois	Illinois	Illinois	Iowa	Illinois
Ohio	Iowa	Iowa	Illinois	Iowa
Missouri	Ohio	Missouri	Kansas	Kansas
Indiana	Missouri	Indiana	Nebraska	Nebraska
Kentucky	Indiana	Ohio	Missouri	Missouri
Tennessee	Kentucky	Kansas	Ohio	Indiana
Iowa	Tennessee	Kentucky	Indiana	Ohio
Virginia	Pennsylvania	Nebraska	Kentucky	Texas
Alabama	Texas	Tennessee	Texas	Kentucky
Georgia	Alabama	Pennsylvania	Tennessee	Oklahoma

[33] The figures are collected from Louis Bernard Schmidt, "The Internal Grain Trade of the United States, 1860–1900," *The Iowa Journal of History and Politics,* XIX, No. 2 (April, 1921), 196–245, as revised and extended in Louis Bernard Schmidt and Earle Dudley Ross, eds., *Readings in the Economic History of American Agriculture* (New York: The Macmillan Company, 1925), pp. 370–380; supplementary data from Fred Albert Shannon, *Economic History of the People of the United States* (New York: The Macmillan Company, 1934), p. 450. All figures were checked with the Census reports.

While the geographic center of wheat production was shifting from central Indiana to west central Iowa, in these four decades, the center of corn growing moved only from the southern tip of Indiana to a point in Illinois about fifty miles north of St. Louis. There it had remained almost stationary for ten years, and was just about permanently established.[34] The slow and gradual nature of the movement can most conveniently be shown in parallel columns of the leading states in the order of their productiveness. The striking feature of the picture is the substitution of Kansas, Nebraska, Texas, and Oklahoma for the old Southern leaders: Tennessee, Virginia, Alabama, and Georgia (table on page 163).

This can partially be explained by the growth of the one-crop specialization in the cotton belt, but still more important were the special advantages of the North Central states. Corn needs at least a five-month season, with enough but not too much rainfall, and hot weather during the period of growth. But it also needs cooler weather toward the last, so as to check the development of fodder to the advantage of the maturing ear. This last advantage was not to be found in Alabama and Georgia, except in the plateau country. The five North Central states leading in the 1869 Census grew half of America's corn, and seven of the same group accounted for 68.5, 70.7, and 66 per cent in 1879, 1889, and 1899. By 1880, these seven states were the world's greatest corn belt. In some years, the four that were west of the Mississippi River grew nearly twice as much as the three to the east, but a Western drouth in the late nineties moderated this ratio as well as reduced the national percentage for the whole seven.[35]

This ascendancy in the leading cereals does not mean that the North Central states were lagging in other respects. In 1899, they produced 77 per cent of the oats, 57 per cent of the barley, 52 per cent of the rye, 58 per cent of the hay, and 53 per cent of the potatoes grown in the United States. Furthermore, they had 44 per cent of the beef cattle, 52 per cent of the milk cows, 26 per cent of the sheep, 52 per cent of the horses, 23 per cent of the mules, and 61 per cent of the hogs. Some states led any of the Prairie group for certain commodities, such as California in barley, Pennsylvania

[34] Schmidt and Ross, eds., *Economic History of American Agriculture*, pp. 378, 383, 387.
[35] *Ibid.*, pp. 381–387.

and New York in rye, New York in potatoes, Texas in horses, mules, and beef cattle, New York in dairy cows, Montana, Wyoming, and New Mexico in sheep. But, except for sheep and mules, no one other section, and in most cases not all the other sections combined, could equal the records for the North Central states. In a line not ordinarily to be expected, Iowa had more beef cattle than any of the Great Plains states and westward, except Texas; Missouri and Illinois each exceeded Colorado. Montana, New Mexico, and Wyoming were the only states that had more sheep each than Ohio, and Wyoming's margin was only five hundred in nearly three million.[36]

THE CORN-HOG CYCLE

The bulk of America's corn crop has always been fed to hogs, and most of the corn has been consumed locally, it being more economical to take the profit from both kinds of production on the same farm. Consequently, the Middle Western supremacy in pork was a natural result of the leadership in corn. Even cattle feeders preferred to keep a drove of swine, for it was found that four cattle would waste enough corn to feed one hog, and the pork secured in this way was all clear gain. In 1874, Joseph G. McCoy was chiding the Great Plains cattlemen for not emulating the feeders of central Illinois in this respect.[37] It was also noted that a bushel of corn would make ten or twelve pounds of pig,[38] hence it became an empiric rule that hogs at five dollars a hundred pounds could be grown profitably on corn at fifty cents a bushel, or eight-dollar hogs on eighty-cent corn, and so on. If the price of the animals rose much above this ratio, little corn would be thrown on the market and the farmers would do their utmost to increase the size of their droves. But this tended to enhance the price of corn, and, when the overproduction of pork brought its price down past the rising value of corn, the hogs would be sold, regardless of their state of maturity, till the conditions were reversed again. But this,

[36] Calculated from *Agricultural Yearbook*, 1899, pp. 767–770, 819–821; *Statistical Abstract of the United States*, 1926, pp. 608–609.

[37] Joseph G[eiting] McCoy, *Historic Sketches of the Cattle Trade of the West and Southwest* (new ed., Washington: The Rare Book Shop, 1932), pp. 167–168 *et circa*, paged as in edition of 1874.

[38] U.S. Commissioner of Agriculture, *Report*, 1863 (Washington: Government Printing Office, 1863), p. 203.

in turn, reacted unfavorably on the corn market, thus again hastening the movement to revive swine production. So the amount that the public was able and willing to pay for pork determined, in a large degree, the price both for corn and for hogs; and this affected the corn acreage of the following year, though not according to any scientific or mathematical formula.[39]

As may be noted on the graph (page 167), the corn-hog cycle—from peak to peak—was from four to six years' duration. This is explained on the basis of the corn-hog ratio of prices. In 1876, and for two years following, the price of corn was very low, and on the down grade. So the farmers began producing more hogs, and in 1879 was the peak of pork production. But too many hogs were raised, and the price reached bottom levels in the same year. An advance in corn prices from 1879 to 1881 was followed by diminished hog raising and by correspondingly higher prices. Corn prices began falling again in 1882, but hog prices trended upward for another year, as production diminished. Then, in 1883, hog prices started downward. After about two years, the corn-hog ratio began having its effect on the number slaughtered. The reason was that, in those days, slow-maturing swine were the rule, and it required about eighteen months or more to prepare them for the market. Before 1900, as will be seen, the trend was toward more rapidly developing breeds. The corn-hog ratio in 1887 was 13.5—which means that a hundred pounds of hog were worth 13.5 bushels of corn. Since 10 was the acceptable ratio, the price of hogs in that year was remarkably favorable.

The corn crop in 1860 was about 839,000,000 bushels, but it dropped as low as 398,000,000 in 1863, largely because the Confederacy was not included in the reckoning and was not buying. The old level was surpassed in 1866 and 1868, and always afterward. There were numerous fluctuations, sometimes hundreds of millions of bushels in a year, as between 1872 and 1875 and again in the late eighties and the nineties. But, with each recovery, new records were usually set, until the two-billion mark was exceeded five times between 1889 and 1899. The average farm price declined from 57 cents (greenbacks), in 1867, to 31.7 cents (on virtually a gold basis), in 1878. Then it advanced to 63.6 cents in the bad year

[39] Alva Wilfred Craver, "Factors Which Tend to Cause Fluctuations in the Price of Live Hogs and Pork Products" (manuscript thesis in University of Illinois Library).

of 1881, but dropped immediately afterward and got as low as 32.8 cents in 1885 and 28.3 in 1889. But the lowest of all was at the depth of the depression in 1896, when the price was 21.5 cents.[40] It should be borne in mind that average prices, even on the farm,

Average Price of Hogs, Compared with the Total Production of Hog Products Per Capita and with the Price of Corn [41]

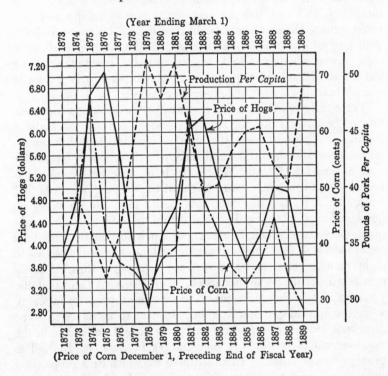

(Year Ending March 1)

(Price of Corn December 1, Preceding End of Fiscal Year)

mean that some producers got far less. Freight charges were so high in the western part of the corn belt that Kansas farmers, confronted with offers of seven or eight cents a bushel for their corn, found it

[40] *Agricultural Yearbook*, 1899, p. 759; Fred J. Guetter and Albert E. McKinley, *Statistical Tables Relating to the Economic Growth of the United States* (Philadelphia: McKinley Publishing Company, 1924), pp. 29–30.

[41] Adapted from U.S. Department of Agriculture, Bureau of Animal Industry, *Sixth and Seventh Annual Reports*, 1889–1890 (Washington: Government Printing Office, 1891), p. 88, with adjustments to show the relation between each dime in the price of corn and dollar in the price of hogs.

more profitable to burn it in their stoves, thus saving largely on the cost of fuel.

A scale of corn and hog prices for the years 1880–1899 shows more than a fair degree of correlation, with only three years (1881, 1890, and 1891) when the hog growers definitely lost on the basis of corn prices. But in some years the profit was quite handsome, particularly in 1893 when it amounted, on the customary basis of reckoning, to about 100 per cent. But quite often the only real profit went to the man who bought corn to feed his swine. In 1896, with hog prices at $2.90, such a buyer could make a gain, but the corn grower, whether he sold his grain or fed it, could take nothing but a loss. The relationship between the two prices over a term of years is best shown in graphic form (see page 167).

From early years, there was no lack of good advice on the selection of breeding stock for special purposes and the methods of feeding that would bring the quickest results. Berkshires were recommended for bacon, Poland-Chinas for lard, Duroc Jerseys for general purposes, Chester Whites for bulk, and the like. Agricultural journals constantly warned against the keeping of breeds that matured slowly, and the state and county fairs laid emphasis on quick and easy fattening. Practical demonstrations of results made quick converts of all alert farmers, so much so that the pigs they could market at two hundred pounds' weight at ages of from six to eight months came to be known as "mortgage lifters." [42] Some overly zealous raisers even insisted, with a straight face, that the young pigs' tails should be cut off to save the expense of fattening a useless appendage. But if enthusiasm ran to extremes in some directions, there was a positive and great benefit derived from the improvement of breeds. Yet, only the pig fanciers could afford to grow pedigreed animals. These required too much care, propagated lightly, and were subject to ailments that seldom bothered the old razorback or "hazel splitter." A little strain of the rangy woods animal eliminated much of this trouble, permitting litters of ten or a dozen instead of four or five, and yet producing pigs only slightly less worthy in a practical way than the delicately nurtured prize stock.[43] Between 1880 and 1899, the number of hogs in the United

[42] Joseph Schafer, *The Social History of American Agriculture* (New York: The Macmillan Company, 1936), pp. 127–130.
[43] Commissioner of Agriculture, *Report*, 1863, pp. 198–203.

States increased only from 34,000,000 to 39,000,000, and the valuation from $146,000,000 to $170,000,000; but 50,000,000 at $291,-000,000 in 1889, 52,000,000 at $241,000,000 in 1892, and 46,-000,000 at $295,000,000 in 1893 show what better prices could do for the industry. The number in 1892 and the value in 1893 were records for the period.[44]

THE CARE OF THE SOIL

If the Prairie farmers, while producing their "bumper" crops, did not wear out the soil as rapidly as did the early Virginia planters, it was only because of greater original fertility and the less exhausting qualities of the crops grown. Certainly, their attitude toward conservation in the early years was little, if any, different. This was a subject that just was not considered. Not much attention was paid to rotation, good plowing, or intensive cultivation. In every instance, the reports from new Western lands showed marvelous wheat crops for a few years, and then a decline as single-crop practices exhausted the soil to the point of unprofitability.[45]

When Oklahoma was opened to settlement, observers declared that they could tell the moment they crossed the state line from Kansas, because of the more luxuriant crops on the south side, but the difference did not remain long. The effects of land butchery were noticeable to some forward-looking individuals (eccentrics, to their neighbors), even in the 1850's. "It is true," one said, ". . . that us western farmers have been skimming God's heritage, taking the cream off, and leaving for parts unknown, until humanity has a heavy bill against us for wasting the vital energies of mother earth. . . ." [46] Another observed: "Could we be persuaded to practice the care and economy which are found indispensable to the farmer of the Atlantic and middle states, we might live as comfortably and grow rich as fast upon the cultivation of forty acres of land as we now do by the 'cut and cover' practice of skimming

[44] *Agricultural Yearbook*, 1899, p. 818.
[45] Edward Atkinson and L. G. Powers, "Farm Ownership and Tenancy in the United States," American Statistical Association, *Publications*, V, n.s., No. 40 (Boston: J. P. Shults, Printer, 1897), p. 335.
[46] Illinois State Agricultural Society, *Transactions*, III (1857–1858, Springfield: Bailhache & Baker, Printers, 1859), 149.

over a hundred." [47] But the attitude of the respectable conformists was expressed in these words: "To talk of manuring all our farms while they are so large is simply ridiculous. With the present scarcity and high price of labor, how is the farmer to find time and money or labor to manure his farm of from one hundred and sixty to fifteen thousand acres?" [48]

By 1867, the United States Commissioner of Agriculture was urging proper tilling and drainage, in order that the rain might soak down, instead of washing away the surface soil.[49] Yet, fifteen years later, the practices of the average farmer were still bringing down denunciations and dire prophecies from domestic and foreign experts alike. Hard "plow-sole[s]" were "formed by shallow tillage," and all above was run down the gullies.[50] English observers saw the same facts and expressed the doleful hope that "when no virgin land is left to exhaust" the despoilers of the soil would turn to the practices of more experienced countries, and save American agriculture before it was too late.[51] Another mentioned as a fact "plain to every one that the virgin soils of the western prairie are wasting under a false system of agriculture and would eventually give out. . . ." unless wheat specialization shifted to new areas.[52]

This situation was not universal, but the careful practices of the few spread slowly, and could not save the soil fertility of the many. As early as 1860, a Prairie farmer told of plowing from eight to twelve inches deep (probably overdoing it) for corn, deep planting, and careful cultivation.[53] At the same time, an agricultural scientist proposed rotating wheat with Hungarian grass and hemp. But the average farmer would dream at the plow handles, and then throw the stable manure into the ditches, or on the mud roads. Yet, the damage was not irreparable. Under careful handling, Prairie soil is remarkably recuperative, and agencies were multiplying for the

[47] *Ibid.*, I (1853–1854, Springfield: Lanphier & Walker, Printers for the State, 1855), 205.

[48] *Ibid.*, III, 431.

[49] Commissioner of Agriculture, *Report*, 1867, p. vii.

[50] Eugene W. Hilgard, "Progress in Agriculture by Education and Government Aid," *The Atlantic Monthly*, XLIX, No. 294 (April, 1882), 532.

[51] [Great Britain] Parliamentary *Reports: Commissioners, &c.*, 1880, XVIII, c.–2,678, p. 1.

[52] *Ibid.*, 1882, XV, c.–3,375–VI, p. 6; see also Harry J. Carman, "English Views of Middle Western Agriculture, 1850–1870," *Agricultural History*, VIII, No. 1 (January, 1934), 15.

[53] "Corn Items," *The Prairie Farmer*, XXI, o.s., No. 15 (April 12, 1860), 226–227.

dissemination of needed information. The agricultural colleges and experiment stations (see Chapter XII) slowly made impressions on the farmers. In 1874, the Grangers (Chapter XIV) gave ample stress to diversified and systematic farming.[54] Farm journals also instructed their readers in the ancient art of restoring nitrogen, a special need of Prairie soil, by the growing of legumes, which also, like the native grasses, loosened the subsoil and brought up calcium. Those who needed to know were told that feeding the crops on the farm, and returning the manure to the soil, restored four fifths of the fertility, and that the plowing under of certain crops renewed the humus.[55] By 1880, the agriculturists of the North Central states were spending nearly $2,000,000 yearly for commercial fertilizers, which was increased to $7,274,000 by 1900. Even the larger sum allowed only eleven cents to the average acre in Ohio, and one cent in most of the Prairie country.[56]

Before the end of the century, scientific rotation was being adopted by many farmers, but haphazard methods characterized others. One series, recommended by *The Prairie Farmer*, was to use a well-manured pasture for corn; then came a crop of oats, followed by wheat; and the final stage, before corn again, was to pasture the field for another two years and dress it with manure before plowing. For the more southerly Prairies, the recommendation was for pastured cowpeas, followed in turn by oats and wheat. Methods somewhat similar to these were followed in the corn belt, while, in the wheat states, legumes such as cowpeas or soybeans were succeeded in series by corn, oats, and wheat, in a four-year cycle.[57] As early as 1860, a corn-growers' club was stressing deep plowing, thorough harrowing, and careful cultivation.[58] Other farmers learned this through many years of experience. In truth, in later years, the soil became drier, and improved methods got to be a necessity instead of a fad. Not only was there less rainfall in the 1890's, but the old method of leaving the fields bare and hard

[54] John B. Turner, "Rotation—Wheat Culture," *ibid.*, No. 11 (March 15, 1860), 162–163; *Eighth Census: Agriculture*, xxxiii; *Tenth Census: Agriculture*, xxxix; Solon Justus Buck, *The Agrarian Crusade* (Vol. XLV of *Chronicles of America Series*, New Haven: Yale University Press, 1921), p. 28.

[55] D. A. Lillie, "Manure," *The Prairie Farmer*, XX, n.s., No. 2 (July 13, 1867), 20; *Agricultural Yearbook*, 1897, pp. 490–491.

[56] *Twelfth Census: Agriculture*, I, cxl–cxli.

[57] Geo[rge] J. Whiton, "Planning the Season's Work," *The Prairie Farmer*, LXXII, No. 3 (January 20, 1900), 1.

[58] "Corn Items," p. 227.

in the fall had caused the rain to run off and cut gullies instead of replenishing the water level of the subsoil. The deep plowing and frequent cultivation that this condition made imperative resulted in a conservation of the moisture as well as a saving of soil that otherwise would be washed away.[59]

Another lesson, even more slowly learned, was that subsurface drainage, by tile or other means, prevented the soil from packing, allowed the plant roots to grow deeper, permitted the land to be plowed earlier, and made possible a longer growth in the dry fall season. Deep tiling was better than shallow, both because the rows of tile need not be laid so close together and because more of the surface water was removed in this way. Soil long tiled became so penetrable that there was a minimum of surface runoff and, therefore, little erosion.[60] This was a lesson that was less needed on the westernmost Prairies. Erosion there was not so often the result of excessive rain. Sometimes the zeal for drainage had unfortunate results, because misapplied. In 1894, work was begun toward the draining of the Great Swamp in Wisconsin. The sum of $5,482,000 was spent reclaiming 800,000 acres, and, when it was all done, a peat bed, almost useless for crops, was the salvage. Sometimes, fires started in it that burned for years. Forty years later, the federal government was spending additional money to restore the land to its normally swampy condition.[61]

[59] G. W. Dean, "Corn-Growing in Illinois," *Prairie Farmer*, LXXII, No. 3 (January 20, 1900), 4; *Agricultural Yearbook*, 1895, pp. 123–128.

[60] Charles William Burkett, *Soils: Their Properties, Improvement, Management, and the Problems of Crop Growing and Crop Feeding* (New York: Orange Judd Company, 1907), pp. 152–159.

[61] Stuart Chase, *Rich Land, Poor Land* (New York: McGraw-Hill Book Company, Inc., c.1936), p. 144.

CHAPTER VIII

Special Problems of Prairie Farmers

TRANSPORTATION

EXCEPT for the continuation, in most districts, of wretchedly poor country roads, the transportation problems of the Middle Western farmers, after 1860, were of quite a different nature from those of farmers in most of the earlier history of the country. Canals, as in the South (see page 104, above), were no longer of much use, except perhaps in parts of Ohio and for the competition with rail rates afforded by the Erie Canal from April to December. Steamboats continued to serve localities that they could reach. But the advance of railroads was usually ahead of extensive settlement along the whole frontier line, and the squatters who found unmonopolized lands beyond the railheads, in the earlier years, did not have to wait long till transportation agencies overtook them. The problems that arose were partly, but not mainly, the old ones of the paucity of facilities. Rather, they were the monopolistic practices of the railroads, which often took the last cent of profit out of a crop, thus retarding commercial agricultural ventures and forcing self-sufficing practices, such as the burning of corn in the western Prairies.

The ordinary homesteader, forced by the railroad land grants to locate many miles remote from the right of way, had the special disadvantage of long hauls over roads that generally were no better than a series of ruts, and that often were so muddy that they were called "loblollies." Points even closer to the railroads were generally a few miles from a freight station, and, during certain periods of the year, one mile of road was about as impassable as a hundred. The old "National Road" through Ohio and Indiana, and out into Illinois, was of crushed-rock or gravel construction, and there were some other main highways of equal merit. In general, the care of the roads was a county or township responsibility. Side drainage ditches, culverts, and the grading or dragging of mud roads were matters usually under the control of a township supervisor, who called out farmers between twenty-one and fifty years of age, or their substitutes, with teams, to work out their road tax. Not till 1891 did any state make any radical move to pull out of the mud, and this was New Jersey. There a state system of improvement and maintenance was worked out so successfully that it was copied in New York, New England, and California. Before 1900, Indiana reported "58,000 miles of graded, graveled, and piked highways, over 8,000 miles of which are comparable with the best roads of France," [1] which apparently means that the other 50,000 miles were graded dirt, quite passable when dry and freshly dragged.

Laws were enforced regarding the width of wagon tires and the weight of loads that could be hauled over the graveled roads, especially during the spring thaws, but most of this improvement was east of the Mississippi River. So slow was progress west of the river that, as late as 1926, the Iowa farmer consulted the weather almanac as to whether it would be safe to go to town. In November of that year, thousands of automobiles mired down to the running boards on the way from a football game at Iowa City. That night came a hard freeze, which so endured that some of the cars were not chopped out till the following spring. It was said, with some degree of seriousness, that one could hop from running board to running board all the way to Cedar Rapids in the next county.

The story of railway construction is not for these pages, but the dealings of the companies with rural patrons is a matter of vital importance. Many complaints were heard from the holders of securities that the lines were paying inadequate dividends, and this was generally true. Various explanations of this fact, some of them quite ingenious, were offered, but the main reasons were over-

---

[1] Maurice O. Eldridge, "Progress of Road Building in the United States," *Agricultural Yearbook*, 1899, pp. 376–380, quotation p. 380.

capitalization and prohibitively excessive rates. One system, typical of many (see page 301, below), had stocks and bonds three and a quarter times the actual valuation of the property, and apparently four times the original cost. The net earnings of all railroads in 1883 were nearly $337,000,000 on an actual valuation of $3,787,000,000, or almost 9 per cent.[2] The Western average was, no doubt, less than this, but the accepted rule of charging all the traffic would bear was not always best even for the railroads.

The high hopes of Western farmers as to what the railroads were going to do for them were not long in fading. At one time it was prophesied that Burlington, Iowa, would soon exceed Chicago in commerce, and it was while spirits were in this empyrean that farmers, flush with Civil War profits, put their savings into railroad stocks and bonds and voted bonds on their townships and counties to induce the companies to send the lines their way. Then came the era of stock juggling, exemplified in the Erie war of 1868, and afterward there was the Panic of 1873, during which the small holders were cheated of their "securities" at the same time that they were paying ruinous charges on their shipments—rates that were imposed by the railroads to compensate for cutthroat competition elsewhere. Often, the companies collected the bonds donated by the local governments, sold them, pocketed the proceeds, dissolved, and were never heard of again. On February 4, 1938, the Treasurer of St. Clair county, Missouri, finished paying off $585,000 in bonds issued in 1871 to the Tebo & Neosho Railway, Inc. (later a part of the Missouri, Kansas, and Texas lines), for a railroad that never was built.

Though the average of freight rates declined considerably between 1870 and 1900 (see Chapter XIII), this does not mean that the Western farmer was reaping a proportional advantage. Railroad regulation was still in its infancy and, while average rates were less because of rebates to great industrial shippers, the rule for the little fellow, and for noncompetitive points, was still that of Drew, Fisk, Gould, and Vanderbilt. In 1869, it was noted in Congress that while wheat sold at $1.25 a bushel in New York the price in the West

[2] James F[airchild] Hudson, *The Railways and the Republic* (New York: Harper & Brothers, 3d ed., 1889), pp. 267, 282; Arthur Twining Hadley, *Railroad Transportation, Its History and Its Laws* (New York: G. P. Putnam's Sons, c.1885), p. 53; William Larrabee, *The Railroad Question* (Chicago: The Schulte Publishing Company, 1893), pp. 173, 175.

was 50 cents, on which basis the Minnesota surplus of sixteen million bushels would bring the farmers $8,000,000 and the railroads $12,000,000. At a later date, when Iowa farmers were burning their 15-cent corn (cf. page 168, above), the price in the East was $1.00 a bushel.[3] Producers of surplus crops, the prices of which are fixed by world market conditions, cannot pass freight costs on to the consumers.

The American Cheap Transportation Association, meeting in Washington, D. C., in 1874, denounced the small group of men that dominated the railroads as being as despotic as an ancient Caesar, and demanded federal competition as the remedy. The railroad magnates, taking their cue from Cornelius Vanderbilt, retorted that the lines were their own private property to do with as they saw fit. If the people did not like the policies let them grease their wagons and take to the highways. The companies gave annual free passes to public officials, including judges, who were friendly to their cause, and also to the clergy. They contributed to the campaign funds of their friends. They placed their own men, like William B. Allison of Iowa and Stephen B. Elkins of West Virginia, in the Senate. They bribed legislators and subsidized the press, whenever and wherever it seemed desirable. When the farmers of the upper Mississippi River states got control of the legislatures in the 1870's and began adopting the Granger laws that fixed rates and prohibited certain other abuses, the railroads started campaigns of "education" to make the acts unpopular. The incorruptible and opinionated Edwin L. Godkin, who scarcely realized the existence of the trans-Hudson West, joined in the crusade by denouncing the Illinois laws and declaring it would be ruinous to let railroad rates be fixed by "our Murphys and Caseys." Godkin was seemingly trying to live down his own Irish connections. The final upholding of the Granger legislation by the United States Supreme Court in 1876 ended the agitation for a time.[4]

[3] Robert Edgar Riegel, *The Story of the Western Railroads* (New York: The Macmillan Company, 1926), p. 281; Haney, *Congressional History of Railways, 1850–1887*, p. 245; D[avid] Philip Locklin, *Economics of Transportation* (Chicago: Business Publications, Inc., 1935), p. 12; *Kansas City Times*, February 5, 1938, p. 1, col. 7.

[4] *The National Convention of the American Cheap Transportation Association* (Troy: Whig Publishing Company, 1874), pp. 97–98; Larrabee, *Railroad Question*, pp. 205–230; [Edwin Lawrence Godkin], "The Latest Device for Fixing Rates of Transportation," *The Nation*, XVII, No. 420 (July 17, 1873), 36; further information on the Grangers in Chapter XIV, herein.

During the period, there was an intermittent agitation in Congress for federal control. It was argued in 1869 that, as the Eastern manufacturing interests were protected by a tariff, so ought the Western farmers be assisted by laws limiting the rates on the goods they sent to market. The Granger members of Congress wanted federal competition as a yardstick for rates. A Senate committee, headed by William Windom of Minnesota, reported in 1874 in favor of more internal waterways and one or more government-operated railroads, as competitors and rate standards for the independent lines. It also recommended a bureau of commerce to end such evils as greater charges for short than for long hauls, stock watering and secret rebates. Wherever water competed with rails, it was pointed out, the railroad rates were lowered to get the traffic, which was evidence enough that higher charges elsewhere were not necessary. The right of federal regulation anywhere was further strengthened as regards the land-grant railroads. In each case their charters contained restrictions on the issuance of bonds, and fixed prices for the stocks. Later on the use of American-manufactured iron and steel was made obligatory. Congress also reserved the right to regulate rates, and the Texas and Pacific charter forbade discriminations of any sort.[5]

The Senate made an investigation of the comparative costs of water and rail shipments, and, in 1886, showed great differences. In 1868, it had cost an average of 25.3 cents a bushel to ship wheat from Chicago to New York by the Great Lakes and the Erie Canal, while the railroads charged 42.6 cents. There were considerable variations in succeeding years, the waterways always being far the cheaper, till in 1877 a low point was reached of 7.5 cents by water and 20.3 cents by rail. The figures for 1882 were 8.7 and 14.6. Sometimes (as in the South, see page 105, above), just that 6 cents difference could change a farmer's loss into a gain, or the reverse. It should also be noted that the railroad averages were as low as stated only because of the existence of water competition during part of the year. It was customary to raise the rates much higher as soon as ice blocked the competing channel.[6]

[5] Haney, *Congressional History of Railways, 1850–1887*, p. 243; Riegel, *Western Railroads*, pp. 141–142; Windom's recommendations in *Senate Report* No. 307, 43 Cong., 1 Sess., I, 240–247.

[6] *Senate Report* No. 46, 49 Cong., 1 Sess., I, 171. For a different, but more complete set of estimates, see graph on p. 299, below.

During the late 1870's and early eighties, Representative John
H. Reagan of Texas and Senator Shelby M. Cullom of Illinois presented a number of bills for railroad regulation, Reagan's being the
more rigorous. But neither legislator could get his measure through
the other's house of Congress, and a deadlock ensued till after
the Wabash decision of the Supreme Court in 1886. In this case the
court declared that the privilege of a state, admitted in the Granger
decisions of 1876, to fix interstate rates on a railroad chartered by
the state, was unconstitutional. This reversal of opinion left no
legislative regulation of interstate commerce, thereby forcing the
hand of Congress. The result was the Interstate Commerce Act of
1887. This law forbade most of the earlier abuses, such as rebating,
unreasonable rates, the long-and-short-haul evil, pooling, and traffic
agreements. An Interstate Commerce Commission was created to
administer the law, no member to be connected in a financial or
official way with any railroad. The commission was given fact-
finding powers and the authority to examine the books of the carriers. All rates and fares were to be printed, published, and placed
on file with the commission, but a ten days' notice was sufficient
for any rate change. Fines and (two years later) prison sentences
were fixed for violation of any of the provisions, but the law was
full of defects. Chief of these was the lack of rate-making powers
for the commission, and the placing of the burden of proof on the
injured shipper.

From time to time some of the loopholes were stopped, but the
courts favored the railroads and found new means of evasion. Not
until 1894 did the courts admit the right of the commission to
compel witnesses to appear for testimony. Even then, the fear of
self-incrimination retarded the effectiveness of the law, until, in
1896, Congress granted full immunity. But even this had little
effect. In 1897, pooling was outlawed, and traffic associations arose
instead. Cases dragged through the courts and were reopened years
after they were thought to be settled. Rebates were hidden by
clever devices, and the Supreme Court itself virtually annulled the
long-and-short-haul clause, in 1897. By that time, as Associate Justice John M. Harlan said in dissent, the commission was made "a
useless body for all practical purposes . . . . shorn, by judicial interpretation, of authority to do anything of an effective character."
Really effective railroad regulation remained to be worked out in

Results of Tree Planting on the Plains and of Irrigation Farther West in the Nineteenth Century

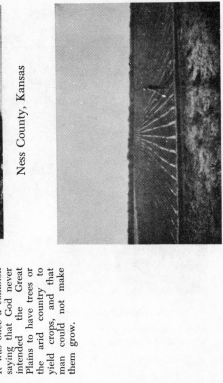

Ness County, Kansas

It was once a common saying that God never intended the Great Plains to have trees or the arid country to yield crops, and that man could not make them grow.

Buffalo County, Kansas

An Arid-Country Field at First Irrigation

The Same Field a Few Years Later

Dining-Sleeping Car on the Union Pacific

This is another of Richardson's "plugs" for the Union Pacific in 1869. He was critical about the financing of the line.

The Burton Stock Car

The stock car was one of several types introduced in the 1880's to reduce shrinkage of animals in transit. (*The Bettmann Archive.*)

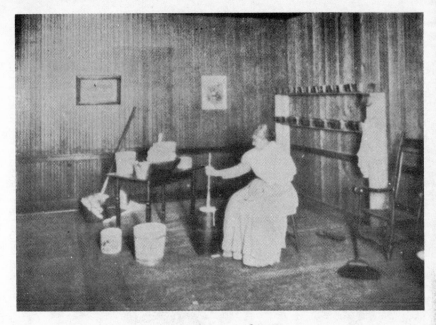

Butter Making in the Home
This type of churn has never gone out of use.

Butter Making de Luxe in the 1890's
This type of churn, also, has continued in use.

A Country Fair of about 1880 (*after Currier & Ives*)

The fountain behind the judges' stand and the diminutive stature of the man holding the horse are not vouched for. (*The Bettmann Archive.*)

A Junior Naturalists' Club in Rural New York

The boy in the central foreground was apparently not impressed with the gaiety of the nineties.

A Traveling Agricultural Library

Such exhibits were star features at many farmers' institutes in the late nineteenth century.

A Massachusetts Road of the 1890's, before Improvement

The Same Road after Improvement (and in a more favorable season)

Types of Farm Homes, 1861–1897

A suggestion of "American Gothic" is seen in this survival of the 1880's near Kenney, Illinois.

An example of the farm architecture of the 1870's, this home near Lodge, Illinois, is also typical of many in the Great Plains area.

The "Greek Revival" is exemplified in many of the features of this farm home close to Pleasant Plains, Illinois.

The builder of this home, at De Land, Illinois, about 1870, must have been a devout reader of Nathaniel Hawthorne

[All photographs on this and the reverse page, except those otherwise accredited, were taken at the author's request by his student Donn Hayes of Springfield, Illinois.]

Types of Farm Homes, 1861–1897

This Iowa sod house, because of the number of its windows and the sawed planks supporting the roof sods, can be classified as an "aristocrat" of its kind. (*Photograph by courtesy of the Iowa State Historical Society.*)

This house near Bloomfield, Iowa, suggests an original owner of unusual piety.

Though austere in external form, this home in the Mendota, Missouri, neighborhood has a walnut staircase which is a fine piece of craftsmanship.

The farm laborer's cabin was photographed by the author in the seacoast area of South Carolina. The chimney is built of crossed sticks of wood plastered with mud. The house was occupied to overflowing at least as late as 1940.

succeeding decades. Meanwhile, the growth of traffic, lowered costs of materials, greater efficiency, and, not least, state regulation of rates within their own borders, had brought many costs of transportation down, and the farmers began to benefit.[7]

MARKETING

Almost if not quite as great a source of grievance as the railroads were the marketing agencies, and in the case of elevators they were often one and the same. The primary grain markets of the Middle West, in 1860, were at Cincinnati, Toledo, Chicago, Milwaukee, and St. Louis, but the westward movement of the cereal belts brought such other centers into prominence as Peoria, Minneapolis, Duluth, and Kansas City. In these cities there were large elevator companies that built hundreds of branch elevators throughout their areas. But a wheat-growing section often developed before any such accommodation was provided, in which case the grain was likely to be piled along the tracks, probably to spoil, until the railroad company supplied cars for shipment. It was under such conditions that the railroad companies began to build their own elevators, and sometimes it was difficult to get them to haul the product of competitors. The farmer was usually so pressed for ready cash to pay his taxes, interest, wages, installments on machinery, and store bills that he had to sell as quickly as possible. Hence he had no choice but to sell to the elevator company that was most conveniently at hand. Then it was customary for him to return with his empty wagon, feeling that he had been cheated, but with insufficient information to make a case. Measuring his own wheat and reading the market quotations, he thought he knew what the load would bring him. But the buyer had his own system of grading, and it seems that rarely did he rate the farmer's product as of number-one quality. Number-one spring wheat in the Northwest was classed as "sound, plump and well cleaned"; number two as "sound, reasonably clean and of good milling quality." Number three included "all inferior, shrunken, dirty" grain "weighing not less than

[7] William Z[ebina] Ripley, *Railroads: Rates and Regulation* (New York: Longmans, Green and Co., 1912), pp. 441–486, quotation p. 474; for the main Granger and the Wabash decisions see 94 U.S., 113, 164; 118 U.S., 557.

fifty-three pounds to the bushel." The farmer could take the buyer's rating or haul his wheat back home again.[8]

What this system could mean to the grower is easily demonstrated. In North Dakota a farmer hauled several loads of wheat of good color, but somewhat small size, to the elevator. The buyer rated it as below even number three, or a rejected grade that would bring a very small price. The farmer, not being particularly pressed for cash, decided to ship it himself, along with enough more that had been called number three to make a total of five thousand bushels. The buyers in the central markets paid him number-two prices for seven of his eight carloads and a cent lower on the bushel for the other one. In this way he saved $282.75 that would have gone to the local buyer had he not been financially able to wait a while for the return. But the elevator men had still other tricks for making profits by judicious sorting. They could mix the two upper grades in such a fashion as to make it all resell as number one, the secret of the business being the knowledge of just how much number-two wheat the bin could take without converting it all to that level. The central elevators got their stores from so many places that they had plenty of varieties for expert mingling. What the producers needed was impartial grading by public officials.[9]

To a farmer selling in the local market it made hardly any difference whether the elevator was owned by the railroad company or by an "independent." In any case the railroad had the upper hand and demanded a division of the receipts. Whether the producer stored his grain or not, even if it did not pass through an elevator, he paid the elevator toll to the carrier or else he did not ship at all. In the central markets a like system of fraud was practiced. All the agencies pooled their interests for further extortions. Unless the farmer had already sold his grain at the offered price, it was dumped in whatever warehouse the railroad agent designated and held for storage at ruinous charges. If the owner did not sell quickly he might as well donate the proceeds of his year's efforts to the railroads and middlemen.[10]

[8] Lewis Walker, "Abuses in the Grain Trade of the Northwest," American Academy of Political and Social Science, *Annals*, XVIII, No. 3 (November, 1901), 488–490.

[9] *Ibid.*, p. 490.

[10] D. C. Cloud, *Monopolies and the People* (Davenport, Iowa: Day, Egbert & Fidlar; Muscatine, Iowa: Allen Broomhall, 4th ed., 1873), pp. 136–139.

In 1874, Chicago had fourteen elevators to handle the business of inspection, grading, and mixing the grain. These were owned by about thirty persons but controlled by nine firms that agreed closely on storage charges. Nearly all the marketed wheat of seven or eight states, sooner or later, passed through the hands of this monopoly.[11] It was against this strangle hold that the Grangers fought in the 1870's, and it should be remembered that the Munn vs. Illinois decision of the Supreme Court in 1876—the fundamental Granger case in fixing the principle of the right of a state to regulate railroads—grew out of the Illinois Warehouse Act of 1871. This law had established rates that might be charged for storage in railroad-owned elevators, and the court upheld the practice as long as the rates were not confiscatory or in violation of charter stipulations.[12] The copying of this law in other Prairie states furnished relief from one of the worst forms of earlier robbery.

The operations of the Chicago wheat pit were another factor in regulating the prices paid to farmers. Without descending into pure economics for an explanation, it can be stated, as well as demonstrated, that the ordinary activities of traders in such an organization as this can have a benign effect on the farmer himself. The detailed information gathered by the speculators regarding world-crop and weather conditions, political turmoils, holdovers from previous years, and myriad other factors controlling supply and demand, permits them to buy for future delivery in such a way as to stabilize prices so that the harvest season does not result in a seeming glut that would justify sacrifice prices. This is not the same as saying that the practices were always fair. In fact, before the system of trading in futures was thoroughly established there were several wildly speculative attempts in the Chicago Board of Trade to corner the wheat market, and some of these were successful.

Such corners were rarely beneficial to the farmers. If the price was advancing when the crop went on the market, the producer might have his crop stored, if the rates permitted, only to release it too late, just after the corner was broken and prices were hitting bottom. If the corner held long enough, there was an inducement to plant too much the next year and be confronted with a glutted

[11] *House Executive Document* No. 46, 44 Cong., 2 Sess., II, App., 230.
[12] Buck, *Agrarian Crusade*, p. 57.

market. The last successful corner on the Chicago market was in 1888. Ten years later a trader named Joseph Leiter monopolized the American wheat supply for a few weeks, but Russia, India, Argentina, and small holders everywhere began dumping their stores. A new crop, bigger than Leiter had expected, was on its way, and, before he could sell, prices were low and he lost all his profits. Leiter's father is reported to have given $9,750,000 in helping the son out of his predicament.[13]

In general, throughout the period, the producers had almost no voice in the control of their marketing. State laws trimmed a few of the abuses, but the farmers had not enough political or economic organization to make any reforms thoroughgoing or permanent. First the Grange and, later, the Farmers' Alliances tried cooperative marketing, with a full conception of the desirability of lessening the spread in prices between themselves and the consumers, but both ventures were short-lived and failed of long-time benefits. The farmer was still an individualist, and the lessons of cooperation were postponed to some distant future. Even the efforts to withhold grain from the market, for higher prices, were not extensive enough to achieve the desired ends.[14]

Since so much of the corn was converted into meat on the farm, the tactics of the meat packers probably affected more producers than did the grain markets. In 1863 Chicago took the lead over the old "Porkopolis" of Cincinnati in the meat-packing business, and before long Milwaukee, St. Louis, Kansas City, Omaha, and even St. Joseph were to surpass the old records of the Ohio city. The stockyards district of Chicago soon became, as it was called, a veritable Packingtown, "with its own banks, hotels, Board of Trade, postoffice," and other appurtenances of a business center. Before 1870, the conditions of transportation to such markets were such as to lower prices that were paid to the farmers. To that time, Chicago was mainly a distributing point for live animals. The stock was bought from the Prairies and westward, shipped to Chicago, pur-

[13] George F. Redmond, *Financial Giants of America* (Boston: The Stratford Company, 1922), II, pp. 212–213: James E[rnest] Boyle, *Chicago Wheat Prices for Eighty-One Years* (Ithaca?: 1922), p. 3; "Mr. Leiter's 'Corner' in Wheat," *The Spectator* [London], LXXX, No. 3,651 (June 18, 1898), 854–855; see also "Levi Zeigler Leiter," in *Dictionary of American Biography* (Allen Johnson and Dumas Malone, eds., New York: Charles Scribner's Sons, 21 vols., 1928–1937), XI, 157.

[14] Herman Steen, *Coöperative Marketing* (Garden City: Doubleday, Page & Company, 1923), pp. 211–212; see also Chapter XIV, herein.

chased there by brokers, and reshipped to the places of consumption. The inadequate cars, crowding of animals, and other bad shipping practices (to be described at greater length in connection with the Great Plains livestock business), resulted in shrunken and unfit beasts which sold so low that, in anticipation of this result, the buyers paid correspondingly lower rates to the farmers. The correction of these practices was slow but, as will be seen, there was a considerable improvement after 1880. As better cars, proper loading, ample attention to feeding and watering, and other reforms brought better cattle and hogs to the marts, the improvement in prices was reflected back to the barynard and corral.[15]

There was another innovation of the 1870's that should have been beneficial to livestock growers, but was not. This was the concentration of packing in the great stockyards cities. The reshipment of animals to little slaughterhouses all through the East had been made necessary because of the lack of effective refrigeration of meats for long journeys. Before 1880, Swift, Armour, and others had proved beyond a doubt the utility of the refrigerator car. Some of the early experiments in icing cars were not very successful, but as soon as the problem was mastered, the "beef trust" began to exert its power, and meat products, rather than live animals were shipped from the great marketing centers. It was the fact of the combination of the great packers such as Armour, Swift, Morris, Cudahy, Schwartzschild and Sulzberger, and the National Packing Company into the beef trust, in the 1880's that prevented the benefits of the concentration of meat packing from being passed on to the stock growers. But it was apparently not till about 1900 that the monopoly became strong enough to eliminate competition in buying, so as to fix a price on live animals that would be identical whether in Kansas City, Omaha, or Chicago.[16]

CREDIT RELATIONS

Credit relations were often quite as onerous as the perplexities of transportation and marketing, and the outcries of farmers against

[15] Redmond, *Financial Giants of America*, quotation p. 212; U.S. Commissioner of Agriculture, *Report*, 1870, pp. 250–251; George G. Vest, chm., "The Transportation and Sale of Meat Products," *Senate Report* No. 829, 51 Cong., 1 Sess., p. 18.

[16] J[onathan] Ogden Armour, *The Packers, the Private Car Lines, and the People* (Philadelphia: Henry Altemus Company, 1906), pp. 19–24; Charles Edward Russell, *The Greatest Trust in the World* (New York: The Ridgway-Thayer Company, Publishers, 1905), for activities of beef trust.

the bankers, insurance companies, land mortgage associations, and
other creditors were loud and fairly continuous. Hardly was the
Civil War over when the agriculturists began their thirty-year period of repayment for their brief reign of greenback prosperity.
During the year 1864, greenbacks (United States notes) had sometimes been below forty cents on the dollar in exchange for gold.
At such a time, the farmer naturally went into debt to expand his
operations, in expectation of a long succession of years of high
prices. But the war was not over before the deflation movement was
under way. From 1865 to 1870, the stock of money in the United
States declined from $1,180,000,000 to about three fourths of that
amount, and the per capita of circulating medium fell from $31.18
to $20.10. Inasmuch as the federal Civil War currency had all been
in the North, the strain on the financial structure was all the worse
when the Confederate states re-entered the Union and the diminished money supply had to do service over the whole reunited
country. The deflation was accompanied by a drop in the base-price
index of general commodities from 132 to 87 by 1870 and to 46.5
in 1896. Farm products at the latter date stood at 39.5, according to
the same calculations.[17] This was not solely due to a money shortage. In fact, greater economies in production seem to have been a
major factor. But the effect of monetary deflationary tendencies
has not been utterly swept away by all the recent studies of economists who have involved themselves in theories regarding currency
and credit as a basis for prices. One's confidence is shaken when
Rufus Tucker tries to show that the gold of California and Australia had almost no effect on prices after 1849, and buttresses his
argument by such utter negation of historical fact as to say that,
in the years just after 1849, "the increases in the gold stock of the
world were on a scale never reached before or since. . . ." [18]

To be sure, prices were also affected by the credit situation:
mortgages, short and intermediate loans, checking accounts, and
the like. But farm mortgages merely meant the drainage of needed
cash for interest payments; short and intermediate loans were so

[17] Davis Rich Dewey, *Financial History of the United States* (New York: Longmans, Green and Co., 8th ed., 1922), pp. 292–293; *Statistical Abstract of the United
States*, 1931, pp. 249, 334–335, base price of 100 is for 1926. For more complete
data on this point, see graph page 294, below.

[18] In Charles O[scar] Hardy (Appendix by Rufus S. Tucker), *Is There Enough
Gold?* (Washington: The Brookings Institution, 1936), p. 193.

seldom available to the Western farmers that they were of minor importance as far as any stimulation to farm prices is concerned. The mortgage situation must be considered from time to time hereafter, but no attempts at estimating the totals of such debts for any year or area can be made. Even the census takers ignored the problem before 1890, and then for another thirty-five years they merely included mortgages on farms wholly owned by their operators, thus excluding about half of the farms of the nation, and the great bulk of the farms in the areas hardest hit by agricultural depression. On the basis of this meager evidence, the average farm mortgage (on those counted) was $1,224 in 1890. The census takers ignored the problem again in 1900. In 1910, when farmers were more prosperous, the average was $1,715; and in 1920, just before an inflationary bubble broke, it was $3,356.[19]

Shorter loans, for the carrying on of needed farm operations, were hindered by the inadequacy of banking facilities. In this respect, the old wildcat banks of the prewar era were of more use to the farmers of the West than were the national banks of the later period. In 1863, some $267,000,000 of the $649,000,000 in loans and discounts of the state banks, or 41 per cent, had been in the Middle Western states, a greater sum even than in the East. But, at the same time, the farmers of the same area were being plagued and robbed by the larger amount of wildcat notes. After 1865, the 10 per cent tax on state bank notes drove nearly all of these banks out of existence, but the new national banks could not be organized with less than $50,000 capital. Most of the Prairie farmers lived long distances from centers where sufficient money could be raised to organize a national bank; and the roads were usually bad. Bankers and farmers were not acquainted with each other, and it was difficult for the banker to estimate the need, reliability, or stability of location of the farmer. The banking regulations prevented very much of the speculative type of loans such as those to farmers would be under such conditions. Hence, even the farmer who could get to the county seat for a loan was discouraged by the meager-

[19] See V[ictor] N[elson] Valgren and Elmer E. Englebert, "Farm Mortgage Loans by Banks, Insurance Companies, and Other Agencies," U.S. Department of Agriculture, *Department Bulletin* No. 1,047 (Washington: Government Printing Office, December 28, 1921), pp. 1–2: David L[awrence] Wickens, "Farm-Mortgage Credit," U.S. Department of Agriculture, Division of Publications, *Technical Bulletin* No. 288 (Washington: Government Printing Office, February, 1932), p. 7; Ivan Wright, *Farm Mortgage Financing* (New York: McGraw-Hill Book Company, Inc., 1923), p. 44.

ness of such an advance as he might get, and by the higher rate of interest than was charged to the local business man, who attended the same lodge as the banker. Again, all efforts of the federal government to redistribute bank notes, so as to keep a sufficient amount in the agricultural regions of the West, failed of any permanent effect. Even the removal of harsh restrictions on note issues, in the Resumption Act of 1875, failed to give the currency the desirable kind and amount of elasticity (see page 315, below).[20] Though data are lacking on the amount of farmers' notes held at any one time by the national banks, the evidence is clear that it was always very small in comparison to needs. The scarcity of short and intermediate credits, as well as of currency, in the West and South is sufficient to explain the sectional demand for inflation.

Dependent to such an extreme on the money supply, the farmer found, as the value of greenbacks began to rise toward their ultimate parity with gold in 1879, that the receipts from his crops were insufficient to pay the installments on his mortgage. This was all to the benefit of the creditor, who could foreclose whenever it seemed that even the interest could not be paid, or who otherwise demanded an increase in interest for the renewal of the mortgage. Sometimes he demanded a bonus as well. The expanding national wealth of the period was being concentrated in the Eastern cities, while many creators of the wealth were sinking to the status of tenancy. It did not soothe Western feelings a particle to learn by 1868 that the government, which paid in greenbacks for anything bought from a farmer, was redeeming government bonds in the more precious gold. These bonds represented the bloated prices paid for munitions, equipment, and the like, to profiteers during the war. They had been bought with greenbacks at their face value, though depreciated to as low as 40 per cent in gold. Thus, the 6 per cent interest, paid in gold, really meant 15 per cent on the actual investment. And now the Eastern bondholder, who also no doubt owned Western mortgages, was to be given a bonus of 150 per cent on his bonds. Hence came the Democratic cry in the presidential campaign of 1868 for "the same currency for the bondholder as for the plowholder." Though Horatio Seymour, who did not relish the

[20] Ivan Wright, *Bank Credit and Agriculture* (New York: McGraw-Hill Book Company, Inc., 1922), pp. 45–55.

slogan, made a good race partly on that issue, his defeat was followed on March 18, 1869, by the public-credit resolution of Congress, ordaining that the discrimination should continue.[21]

In the first decade after the war, there was a great deal of wabbling about on the question of resuming specie payments for greenbacks. Since 1861, the United States had been operating on a purely paper-money basis. Finally, after the Democratic Congressional victory in the election of 1874, the Republicans experienced what was called a "death-bed repentance," and in their lame-duck session passed the Resumption Act of January 14, 1875. Aside from the provision that, after 1878, gold would be paid for greenbacks on demand, the law also arranged for a gradual reduction of the permanent supply of greenbacks to $300,000,000. Several readjustments of the greenback circulation had already been made since the original authorization of $450,000,000 in 1862 and 1863, and in 1875 the volume was $382,000,000. Now the proposal was to substitute five dollars in national bank notes for each four dollars of the $82,000,000 in greenbacks retired, or in other words, to issue $102,500,000 in new national currency. If this subterfuge was intended to mollify the debtors of the West and South, it failed of its purpose. Greenbackism was already rising, and its adherents, forerunners of the managed-currency advocates, were demanding a monetary system that would be adjusted to general prices, so as to prevent eras of inflation and deflation, with their accompanying general disturbance of business and distress of farmers.[22] National bank notes as a substitute for greenbacks would produce the exact opposite of the desired effect, being too plentiful in boom times and too scarce in periods of depression. (See pages 314–315, below.) The bulk of the greenback adherents after 1872 cared little for theory. They had a practical concern with a way of coping with their debtor position and providing adequate credit facilities.

When the retirement provision of the Resumption Act had less than half accomplished its purpose, it was repealed in May, 1878, with $346,681,016 in greenbacks still in circulation. This volume was never changed afterward, and both sides to the controversy

[21] Daniel R[eaves] Goodloe, "Western Farm Mortgages," The Forum, X, No. 3 (November, 1890), 346–348; Dewey, Financial History of the United States, pp. 344–352.

[22] Dewey, Financial History of the United States, pp. 333–344, 352–354, 360–362, 372–374, 378–382.

were dissatisfied. But the greenbackers were justified in their main contention, for during the remainder of the century the circulation of national bank notes was seldom if ever in keeping with the need. The West also criticized the geographic distribution of the bank notes. In 1869, over half the total was in New York and southern New England, and later efforts at redistribution were of scant effect. The fact was that interest rates were so high in the West and South that the local bankers profited amply without resorting to note issues. The whole contest between "soft" and "hard" money men was a good deal more than a difference of opinion between debtors and creditors. The officials of the Department of the Treasury itself differed on the matter.[23]

The lack of any federal farm-loan agency resulted in excessive interest charges on the farmers throughout the period. Bank loans of from thirty to ninety days were too short to help produce and market a crop, or to finance farm expansion in land or equipment. Consequently, the farmers, especially in frontier regions, had to depend for credit on merchants, commission men, or implement dealers, who themselves could procure loans and pass them on at advanced rates. In order to relieve this condition, Western states, such as Wisconsin, Nebraska, Kansas, Oklahoma, and the Dakotas, authorized the establishment of state banks with as little as five thousand dollars' capital, and rarely elsewhere was the minimum above fifteen thousand. But such banks seldom had any place to rediscount their notes, and thus they reached the limit of their ability to loan just at the time when the moving of crops created a special demand for liquid capital. Hence, even after 1900, Western interest rates were often 12 and 15 per cent, while Eastern banks had idle funds awaiting offers of 3 or 4 per cent. In periods of financial stringency, the farmer was often unable to renew his loan at any rate of interest.[24]

Farm mortgages were usually negotiated through private loan companies, and the stipulated interest rate was often the lesser part of all the charges paid. These included fees of several kinds and a commission to the agent making the loan. Thus, even a 6 per cent rate was easily translated into at least 10. After the Panic of

[23] *Ibid.*, pp. 383–391; *Statistical Abstract of the United States*, 1931, p. 248.
[24] Claude L[eon] Benner, *The Federal Intermediate Credit System* (New York: The Macmillan Company, 1926), pp. 18, 20–23.

1873, the condition of the debtor became steadily worse, and the farther west the location the harder was the farmer's lot. In the cattle-grazing areas of the Flint Hills in Kansas the records of loss of property to loan companies in the 1880's are quite startling. The New England Loan and Trust Company is cited in the books of Wabaunsee County, a dozen or more times to the page, as taking over farms for debts. Homesteaders who had outlived the grasshopper plagues, hailstorms, and drouths were becoming tenants on their former holdings, or were giving up the effort entirely to become competitors for jobs in cities farther to the east. By 1889, there were 134 mortgage companies incorporated in Kansas and Nebraska and, with companies organized elsewhere but doing business in the two states, the total number was 200 or more.[25]

Down to about 1885, mortgages on farms in the western Prairies were about as safe an investment as could be found, and thousands of little offices were set up in the East to collect money for such loans. Land in the West was increasing in value yearly, and crops were good. Before long, it was difficult to find enough mortgages to absorb all the money available. Consequently, rather than reduce the interest rates, solicitors were given large commissions to drum up trade, and many a Western farmer was induced to procure a loan for expansion purposes when he had all he could do to manage his existing property. Then the business collapsed. There were crop failures in 1886 and 1887, and the borrowers no longer could meet their installments or the interest. Then it was found that the loans were greater than the sale value of the land, and Eastern creditors were loaded with frozen assets. A sampling of 215 farmers living in all parts of the state of Nebraska was made at about that time, showing that the small operators were less bothered with mortgage obligations than the greater landowners. Over half the farms were mortgaged, but a larger percentage of persons saving money was among farmers owning quarter sections or less, while the losers were more among those with holdings of 320 acres and upward. Nemesis at last had caught up with the speculative farmer and the usurer at the same time.[26] During the remainder of the century, credit was so tight that the freeholder who retained his status was

[25] Goodloe, "Western Farm Mortgages," p. 351; W. F. Mappin, "Farm Mortgages and the Small Farmer," *Political Science Quarterly*, IV, No. 3 (September, 1889), 435; Registries of Deeds in the Wabaunsee County Court House, Alma, Kansas.
[26] Mappin, "Farm Mortgages and the Small Farmer," pp. 438–441.

forced to live largely from hand to mouth, with no offers of loans to tempt him.

In foreign markets, as well as domestic, the main products sold from the Prairies were wheat and meat. The Prairie purchases of imports were so intermingled with like goods of American make that it would be difficult, if at all possible, to determine the amount. But since the bulk of the wheat and pork and a large part of the beef were produced in the Middle West, it is a safe guess that most of the exports of such goods (possibly excepting beef) were from the same region. Though the home market began to absorb an increasing percentage of the products in the last quarter of the century, the United States was still the major outside granary and larder of Western Europe. The exports of wheat, rye, and flour grew from a value of $20,000,000 in 1860 to an average of $152,000,000 for the last five years of the century. For the same dates, the exports of meats and other animal products increased from nearly $15,000,000 to $173,000,000. Wheat and its flour alone, in 1898, were exported to the amount of $215,000,000, and in 1900 meat products exceeded $200,000,000. Even on a percentage basis of foodstuffs (crude and prepared) to all exports, the figures show gains from 22.82 in 1866–1870 to 42.91 in 1896–1900, but they reached the climax of 48.32 in 1876–1880. Manufactures exclusive of foods (finished and partly finished) rose only from 19.57 per cent in the late sixties, to 30.97 in the last five years of the century. The corresponding decline came in crude materials, including cotton.[27] It was the balance of trade created primarily by the products of the farms, and especially foods, that brought to America a portion of the capital for the rapid growth of her industries in the cities.

It was not till 1861 that exports of wheat and flour reached imposing proportions. The record before that date was in 1857, when about 14,600,000 bushels of wheat and 3,700,000 barrels of flour sold for $22,000,000 and $26,000,000, respectively. But by 1860, wheat exports had fallen back about to the average of the preceding fifteen years, or some 4,000,000 bushels at a price a little

[27] *Statistical Abstract of the United States*, 1931, pp. 493, 522.

under a dollar. In that year and following, as late as 1878, flour exports ranged between 2,000,000 and 5,000,000 barrels a year. Thereafter, with improved milling practices, the ratio of the value of flour to wheat declined somewhat, and the exports of flour increased with a fair degree of regularity to more than 18,000,000 barrels a year by the end of the century. The violent fluctuations were in the whole grain. In 1861, a new record was set at above 31,000,000 bushels, with 37,000,000 in 1862 and 36,000,000 in 1863. Then, as European crops recovered, there was a fall of a third in the exports of 1864 and of 70 per cent in 1865, the total that year being less than 10,000,000 bushels. If a greater need of Northern wheat than of Southern cotton was a factor in withholding British recognition of the Confederacy during the first two years of the war, the same was not the case in the last two years, but this is not the place for a full explanation of that enigma. England was really suffering for lack of cotton during the last half of the war, while she had ample sources outside the United States for wheat.[28]

European abundance continued through 1866 and 1867, and then, wars and rumors of wars on the continent were combined with occasional crop failures, where there was no other disturbance, to bring American wheat exports, with a fair degree of regularity, up to a new record of 153,000,000 bushels (not including flour) in 1880. Though this figure was exceeded slightly in 1892, the receipts of $191,000,000 in 1880 were not exceeded, or even closely approximated, till during the World War, in 1915. With this much of exposition of general trends, it would seem better to leave further analysis of the relations between acreage, yield, farm price, exports, and export prices to individual study of a table (see Appendix, page 417, and graph, page 192).[29] Even by such a short cut, all matters cannot be made clear. For example, farm prices as of December 1 in each year are not necessarily in accord with the average prices or export prices for the same year. In fact, the exports of a given year are, at least in part, from the crop of the preceding year. Nevertheless, the general wide spread between the farm price and the export price is indicative of the charges made by shippers and middlemen.

[28] See Frank Lawrence Owsley, *King Cotton Diplomacy* (Chicago: The University of Chicago Press, c.1931); figures from Guetter and McKinley, *Statistical Tables*, p. 25.

[29] *Agricultural Yearbook*, 1899, p. 760, data for graph.

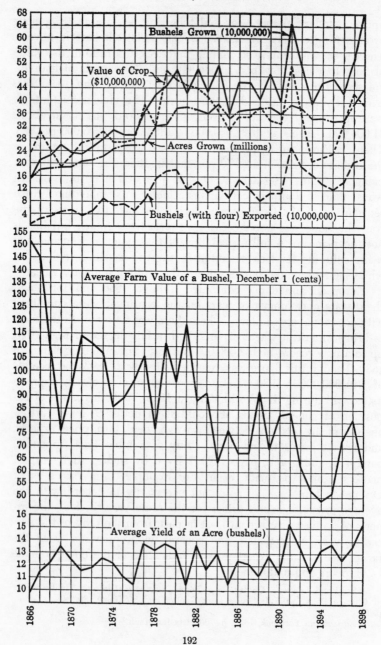

Though corn was by far the greater crop, most of it was marketed in the form of animals and dairy products. Old World peoples did not appreciate the value of corn as a food for human beings, and they grew most of their own feed crops for livestock. Therefore, corn did not enter into the exports from America in such large proportions, according to the size of the crop, as did wheat. As the statistician for the Commissioner of Agriculture said in 1868, the farmer exported only ten bushels of corn out of a thousand he grew, got two dollars for it, and the cost of shipping it from the Prairies to Europe was the price of thirty bushels. Consequently, a crop so exhausting to the soil ought to be kept at home. His ratio for the exported product was fairly accurate for that time. But it was multiplied by three or four in the 1880's, and reached 7.83 per cent in 1897. During the remainder of the century, it was higher yet. When it is noted that four tenths of the wheat crop of 1894 and 1898 was exported, and that the proportion frequently exceeded a third, the figures for corn will be better appreciated.[30]

Dried and salted meats had been shipped from the United States since colonial days. These were products somewhat like the pickled pork and "salt horse" fed to the soldiers during the Civil War, except that the exported product could not have been as revolting as the wretched stuff furnished the American army by contractors.[31] Customers abroad could refuse to buy the product deemed good enough for America's soldiers. The exports of meats, animal fats, and leather, in 1860, amounted to less than $15,000,000 in value, the leather then and in later years representing less than a tenth of the total. This sum had been approximated several times in the 1850's, but it was more than doubled during the war, and was tripled in 1863. The loss of Southern markets explains this temporary activity in foreign trade. The war-year records were not equaled again till 1872, when a new level of $55,000,000 was reached. Then there was a steady growth to $134,000,000 in 1881. The development of effective refrigeration on railroad cars and ships explains the sudden rise, but the record of 1881 was reached

[30] U.S. Commissioner of Agriculture, *Report*, 1868, pp. 50–51; *Statistical Abstract of the United States*, 1911, p. 563.
[31] Shannon, *Organization and Administration of the Union Army*, I, 62, 69, 72, 73, 79, 209.

only once again before 1898. For some of the years, the decline was more than a third below the peak.[32]

The reason for the sudden drop was an early surge of economic nationalism in Europe. American pork was underselling the foreign product, so European hog growers began defaming the American meat. Italy started the exclusion of pork coming from the United States, in 1879, on the charge of unwholesomeness. Portugal, Spain, France, Germany, and Austria-Hungary soon copied the policy. The loss of the markets in Germany and France was felt most seriously, for those countries had been the heaviest buyers. There was no sound reason for this discrimination, on the basis of sanitation. The packers had been shipping better meats than they sold at home, and the "embalmed beef" scandal had to await another war. But, since the European butchers could not compete with American packers, the ban was not readily lifted.[33] The relative values of pork, lard, beef, and cattle exported in the years following the Civil War will be presented in graphic form (see next page).

It will be noted that, while beef exports remained far behind pork, there was no period of actual decline in demand. This was because beef was a lesser competitor with products in the countries to which it was shipped, and especially because the British were the greatest beef eaters in Europe and their country merely asked for good quality. The first continuous shipments of refrigerated beef to England were made by Timothy C. Eastman of New York in 1875. John J. Bate had patented the process of which Eastman became the owner. By inclosing the beef in an air-tight room and forcing cold, dry air over it, Bate could preserve sixty tons of beef for the journey, with fifty tons of ice. The British preferred American beef to all other, as being the juiciest, most flavorful, and properly streaked with solid fat. The grass feeding of the West, previous to forced fattening on corn and fodder, made the difference.[34] The blue-stem grass of the western Prairies and

[32] *Statistical Abstract of the United States*, 1931, p. 522; Guetter and McKinley, *Statistical Tables*, pp. 25–26.

[33] Charles H. Cochrane, "Past, Present and Future of American Meats," *Moody's Magazine*, V, No. 1 (December, 1907), 38–39.

[34] "Meat Animals and Packing-House Products," U.S. Department of Agriculture, Bureau of Statistics, *Bulletin* No. 40 (Washington: Government Printing Office, 1906), pp. 7–8; U.S. Commissioner of Agriculture. *Report*, 1876, pp. 314–315; *ibid.*, 1877, p. 345; Rudolf Alexander Clemen, *The American Livestock and Meat Industry* (New York: The Ronald Press Company, 1923), pp. 275–276.

lower Plains, particularly the Flint Hills of Kansas, then and later produced the prize beef of the country. The shipment of live cattle being an industry in which the Plainsmen were chiefly interested, the discussion of that topic will come in a later chapter.

During much of the period from 1860 to 1900, the farmer was quite doubtful of the effect of the tariff on his markets and pros-

Exports of Meat Products and Cattle, 1866–1900 [35]

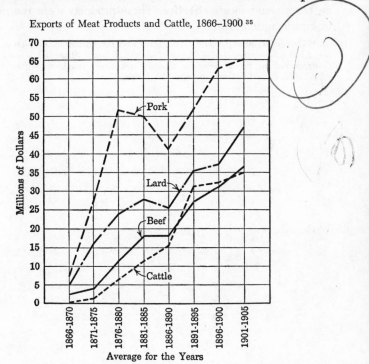

perity. The main objective of many protective schedules is to make consumers pay more for what they buy. It is doubtful whether any large percentage of laborers got any benefit from the tariff, for the most highly protected industries were usually the least organized, and in them the laborers got the smallest pay. But it is certain that the farmer was a consistent loser. It is equally certain that producers of surplus products beyond the domestic demand (see page 176, above) cannot, even with a tariff, raise the domestic price

[35] Cochrane, "American Meats," p. 38.

unless they employ monopoly tactics of output. The farmers did not have this degree of organization. Yet, when tariffs on all they bought kept rising, they fell an easy dupe to protectionist arguments. In 1890 they were taken into the tariff partnership, and thereafter they sacrificed a wonderful political argument.[36] It was more than forty years before anything was done to make the tariff on cereals and meats effective. These products were the mainstay of Prairie agriculture.

[36] George W[illiam] Norris, "The Tariff and the Farmer," *The Nation*, CXXIII, No. 3,191 (September 1, 1926), pp. 192–193; Edward Stanwood, *American Tariff Controversies in the Nineteenth Century* (Boston: Houghton Mifflin Company, c.1903), II, 263–266. See also page 319, herein.

CHAPTER IX

The Livestock Frontier and the Great-Plains Farmer

ORIGINS OF THE RANGE CATTLE BUSINESS

THE range cattle industry, as it flourished in the Great Plains and farther westward in the last half, and particularly in the last third, of the nineteenth century, was essentially an outgrowth of a much older Mexican frontier economy. The Mexican longhorn cattle, later to dominate the Texan pastures and for a few years to replace the buffalo on the northern Plains, were descendants of Spanish breeds, and had physiques admirably fitting them for shifting for themselves in a wild country. From the point of view of ability to cope with nature in a dry area, they were perfect physical specimens, but, to butchers and beef eaters, they lacked the rotundity, tenderness, and succulence of the shorthorn, Hereford, or Angus. To create prosperity for the growers and joy at the dinner table, all that was needed was a little crossbreeding of the longhorns with the heavier types, in order to eliminate their ranginess while preserving their stamina. Not only the cattle but the methods of herding and the life of the cowboy were developed in Mexico hundreds of years before the great drives to the cow towns of the northern Plains. For some years before his final return to Spain in 1540, Hernando Cortés was in the cattle business and made use of the branding iron.[1]

[1] William Curry Holden, *Alkali Trails* (Dallas: The Southwest Press, c.1930), p. 21.

But the English colonies and the Atlantic seaboard, hardly more than a hundred years later than the Spanish, also got a start in the range cattle industry, even if in a somewhat more modest way. Seventeenth- and eighteenth-century laws in Maryland, the Carolinas, and elsewhere dealt with such matters as roundups, branding, overstocking the range, and stealing. Cattle thieves were sometimes lynched, and there was perennial conflict—often over fences—between the cowboys and westward-moving farmers. Cowpens, or branding corrals, were a commonplace on the frontier. But this was all on land excellently suited to general farming and, in consequence, the cattlemen's fringe, just beyond the squatters' frontier, was constantly shifting. In 1776, there were herds of as many as six thousand cattle between the Ogeechee and Savannah rivers in Georgia, and it was estimated that the pastures of Louisiana at about the same time contained no less than three hundred thousand head. As American settlement continued and the cattle range moved onward toward the Mississippi River, Louisiana was annexed. But this was already a cattlemen's paradise, some of the greater owners branding from three thousand to five thousand beasts annually. By 1850, Florida also had great numbers of range cattle, and one savannah alone was said to pasture as many as ten thousand. At the same time the pine regions and coastal prairies of southern Alabama and Mississippi produced about a million cattle a year. As they were sold at the age of three or four years, it would seem that the total herds amounted to three or four million. Such cattle were driven hundreds of miles to Atlantic coast markets.[2]

As late as 1835, some Ohio ranches had as many as a thousand cattle each, but the open range had already moved far out on the Prairies. In earlier years, Middle Western cattle had been driven as far as a thousand miles to the New York market. This range country in the years before 1860, was generally a rather narrow strip, as compared with the later industry of the Great Plains, but it kept on moving as the plow advanced behind it, till the Plains themselves were reached. It existed in east Texas before the coming of the longhorns. Many cattle of the Eastern breeds were kept by the Indians in the later Oklahoma, and also by herders in Kansas

[2] Lewis Cecil Gray, *History of Agriculture in the Southern United States to 1860* (Washington: The Carnegie Institution of Washington, 1933), I, 140–145, 147–151; II, 833–834, 841.

and Nebraska. The range industry was getting a small start in Wyoming and Montana before the day of the cattle drives out of Texas, and one rancher is known to have amassed a fortune of $75,000 in those days. By 1861, John W. Iliff of Colorado was utilizing a seventy-five mile strip of pasture along the South Platte River, his beef being sold largely in the mining towns. Contractors for the Indian reservations comprised an extensive market for other prelonghorn ranchmen.[3]

It is uncertain at how early a period transcontinental travelers, freight companies, or cattle-herding Indian tribes learned that buffalo grass, curing instead of dying as it stood on the ground, made excellent forage that would keep cattle in good condition all winter through. But it is known that a freighting firm wintered fifteen thousand head of work cattle on the open range in 1857–1858. As long as the cattle could dig the grass out of the snow, the feed was good.[4] It was this fact that made the northern Plains range cattle industry a possibility at an early date. That it would have expanded gradually from the older American breeds, already on the Plains before 1865, seems inevitable. And perhaps it would have been better for the business to have grown in that way. A gradual expansion would have avoided the rapid overstocking of the range, with its consequent glut of the market, ruinously low prices, and the destruction of the pasture land itself. It was conditions in Texas that led to the too rapid stocking of the northern range. The cattle business of Texas was growing at the time the state was annexed by the United States. In 1846, Edward Piper of Illinois drove a thousand Texas cattle to an Ohio market. In 1850, other herds were driven to California. In 1854, they were being driven to the corn-feeding grounds of Illinois, and, by 1856, they were driven to Chicago or were herded to the railroad terminals of Iowa towns, for shipment to Chicago.[5]

Then, during the Civil War, the markets were cut off, and the Texas herds became too large for comfortable management. As soon as the war was ended and conditions would permit, the northward

[3] Bidwell and Falconer, History of Agriculture in the North, pp. 177–179; Edward Everett Dale, The Range Cattle Industry (Norman: University of Oklahoma Press, 1930), pp. xiii–xiv, 27, 74, 77–78, 80, 88; McCoy, Sketches of the Cattle Trade, pp. 419–420; Ernest Staples Osgood, The Day of the Cattleman (Minneapolis: The University of Minnesota Press, 1929), pp. 10–12, 16–18.

[4] Osgood, Day of the Cattleman, pp. 16–17; Dale, Range Cattle Industry, p. 61.

[5] Bidwell and Falconer, History of Agriculture in the North, pp. 398, 400–401.

drives began anew, and soon reached proportions altogether incomparable with the prewar efforts. In 1866, a herd was headed toward Sedalia, Missouri, to be shipped over the Missouri Pacific railroad. But the Missourians objected to this invasion of what they considered scrub stock, so the expedition was broken up and scattered by a group described by the drivers as border ruffians, and who fitted De Voto's description of the Western "butcher-knife boys, flat-footed boys, huge-pawed boys." Regardless of the marauders' knifing tactics or physical attributes, the bold Texans in following years struck farther west with their herds. In 1867, Joseph G. McCoy made arrangements with the Kansas Pacific and with the Hannibal and St. Joseph railroads for shipment, and in that year the long drive on a grand scale was begun. Abilene, Kansas, which the railroad had just reached, was the first of the cow towns, and was to be succeeded by points such as Ellsworth, Newton, Baxter Springs, and Dodge City, all in Kansas. Later shipping towns, but mainly for Northern-grown herds, included Ogallala in Nebraska, Miles City in Montana, and Regina and Moose Jaw in Canada. Down to 1880, about 4,223,000 longhorns had been driven northward, and the end of this sort of activity was in sight. The bulk of these cattle were headed directly to Eastern butchers, but a sixth of the drives of 1880 were for stocking Northern ranches. It is likely that in the preceding decade the percentage kept for breeding purposes was considerably larger.[6]

The stories of the Chisholm and other cattle trails, used in the long drives before 1885, are interesting in themselves, as are the tales of hell-roaring adventures in the mushroom cattle towns. But the trails experienced only a few years of activity, and then they were memories, to grow mellow in recollections. Texas fever, transmitted to the northern Plains by tick-infested longhorns, roused Kansas farmers to armed opposition. With their rifles, they blocked the trails and compelled the drovers to move out farther westward for new shipping centers. Then the old cow towns, after a few seasons of exciting activity, slipped back to the status of sleepy country villages with, occasionally, a "boot-hill" graveyard to commemorate the heroic days and furnish inspiration for later missives

    [6] McCoy, *Sketches of the Cattle Trade*, pp. 20–30, 39–44; *Tenth Census: Agriculture*, bottom folio, pp. 973–975; Bernard [Augustine] DeVoto, *Mark Twain's America* (Boston: Little, Brown, and Company, 1932), p. 58.

to the newspapers and secretaries of state historical societies. By 1873, the Missouri, Kansas & Texas railroad had reached the Texas cow country, and a year later McCoy was telling the Southern herdsmen to mend their shiftless ways, improve their herds, fatten them at home, and save money by using the railroads all the way to market, if they hoped ever to become prosperous. Kansas was already stocked with cattle, the ranchers were hybridizing their herds with imported shorthorn bulls, and were sick of the sight of the invading longhorns. "In Colorado it is made by statute, a punishable offense to permit a Texan, or scrub bull, to run at large," said McCoy, "and ranchmen are authorized to shoot down such whenever and wherever they may meet them. . . ." on the open range. The first generation of cattle sired by shorthorn bulls showed hardly a superficial trace of the Texan ancestry, and the Northern cattlemen were going to prevent any reversion to the more primitive type. By 1885 both Colorado and Kansas had effective quarantine laws against Texas cattle (see pages 240–242, below), and the long drive, as a flourishing practice, was at an end.[7]

CATTLE ON THE NORTHERN PLAINS

In the meantime, the range cattle industry had spread all over the Great Plains, into nearly every semilevel spot of the Rocky Mountains, and to a certain extent into the valleys of the Great Basin. By 1875, the buffalo herds had been almost exterminated by professional hide hunters and Eastern sportsmen. With this source of living gone, the Indian tribes were soon impoverished, cowed, and driven on to reservations as soon as the United States army really got serious about the matter. Then the only hindrances to the spread of the cattle industry were the weather, the railroads, the packers, the exhaustion of the range, and such annoyances as might be encountered with desperados, sheepherders, cattle thieves, and occasional homesteaders. But cattle thieves turned respectable as soon as their herds got large enough to be menaced by other cattlemen "on the make." Stories, to hoodwink "tenderfeet," are told of one man or another who started out with one steer and, by expert

[7] Pelzer, "Trails of the Trans-Mississippi Cattle Frontier," pp. 148–161; Parrish, *The Great Plains*, pp. 316–319; McCoy, *Sketches of the Cattle Trade*, pp. 237–238, 252, 418–427; Dale, *Range Cattle Industry*, pp. 69–70, 106.

methods of animal husbandry, including a deft hand at the running iron, in a few years bred this into a herd of thousands. Every cow brute was a maverick that was roped out of the sight of someone else. Then the new rancher would join the cattlemen's association to lynch other "rustlers." Professional bad men were generally no serious menace. For every McCannles gang or Billy the Kid there was a Wild Bill Hickok or some other avenger as a checkmate. Blizzards were indeed a menace, but the cattlemen's own fences caused the greatest losses in bad weather. Cattle could survive most storms as long as they drifted with their rumps toward the tempest, but when they came to a fence they sometimes perished by the thousands.[8]

Even then, there was some consolation. Gullible Easterners could often be induced to buy a ranch, including the cattle as their numbers were entered in the books. A herd of cattle, like the visible stars, always looks more numerous than it really is. The "tenderfoot," looking the cattle over, decided the rancher was blind or half-witted to estimate the herd so low, and thought to make a wondrous bargain by hastily accepting the book count. After a disastrous blizzard, the bartender in the nearest town could generally cheer the despondent ranchers, and sell another round of drinks, by remarking that, whatever else might happen, the books would not freeze. Ice storms were another menace, sometimes covering thousands of square miles with a solid coating two, three, or even more than four inches in thickness. The cattle could get no feed and many of them fell only to die, suffering where they lay unless they were found and shot.[9]

The story of the daily life of the cowboy, as well as his night life and occasional sprees in town, is perhaps too well known to bear another repetition, but a glance at the sober literature of the subject has a salubrious effect on the overwrought imagination.[10] Most of his work was of the prosaic, monotonous, and deadeningly tiresome kind. "It requires no small amount of determined will, and stamina, as well as practical knowledge of handling cattle on

[8] E[dward] Douglas Branch, *The Hunting of the Buffalo* (New York: D. Appleton and Company, 1929); Shannon, *Critiques*, pp. 64–66; Osgood, *Day of the Cattleman*, pp. 193, 220–222; Dale, *Range Cattle Industry*, pp. 108–110.

[9] Shannon, *Critiques*, pp. 22–23.

[10] See [Edward] Douglas Branch, *The Cowboy and His Interpreters* (New York: D. Appleton and Company, 1926); Philip Ashton Rollins, *The Cowboy* (New York: Charles Scribner's Sons, 1922).

the plains," said McCoy, "to be a successful Northern drover. Their hardships and privations are four-fold greater than are endured by the average driver from Texas to Kansas. The trail is through an unsettled country. The weather stormy and soon bitter cold winter sets in. . . ." [11] But of more importance to this account are the business aspects of the occupation. Almost from the start, the better ranchers began bringing in shorthorn bulls, to provide a less leathery meat that would sell well in the East. Andrew Wilson, Joseph P. Farmer, and Albert Crane have received particular mention for their herds, well improved before 1874. In 1873, Wilson held a sale of superior stock in Kansas and took in $24,000 in two days. Some of his bulls sold as high as $1,000 each.[12] Later on, Angus and Galloway stock were tried out, but, before 1900, the Hereford proved its pre-eminent fitness for the Plains, and soon very few except the "white-faced" cattle were to be seen.

Before many years, so rapidly did the industry grow, choice grazing lands, not already claimed and guarded by gun law, became scarce. Then the encroachment of new enterprisers was bitterly resented. Although nearly all the land belonged to the federal government, the states, or the railroad companies, not a cent of rent was paid to the government. Small ranchers were a nuisance, largely because it was feared that they would become great, and that they would do so by finding too many mavericks. Also, the sheepmen had to be guarded against, because the "woollies" cropped the grass too short, polluted the drinking water, and were said to leave an odor in the ground that repelled cattle. A fence might prevail against the small rancher, but sheep ignored such flimsy barriers. So the rifle, the Plainsman's weapon when any serious business was at hand, was freely used in wars between the disparate advocates of animal husbandry. Toward the end of the century, the homesteader also received his share of fervent cursing from the cattlemen, but the farmer was more a symbol of changing conditions than a real menace in most of the range country. The mere fact that the range was getting overcrowded led ranchers to think about fencing in the public domain, and to act on the impulse. But fences were also a nuisance; homesteaders used fences to keep the cattle out of their crops; therefore, "nesters" were

[11] McCoy, *Sketches of the Cattle Trade*, p. 70.
[12] *Ibid.*, pp. 238–243, 342–345, 397–399.

anathema. As a matter of fact, very few farmers had got out to the Plains before the fences were built; most of those who came soon failed and left again; and their encroachment was on only a very small part of the open range. Homesteaders in the short-grass country were, in fact, more often than not the paid employees of the cattle kings themselves. Iliff pastured 35,000 head of cattle on a range with thirty miles of frontage on the South Platte River. He acquired title to this tract by buying out homesteaders, many of whom were on his regular payroll.[13]

In the early 1870's, and this was long before the coming of homesteaders who intended to do any farming, cattlemen were securing title to all the river banks they could acquire under the lax federal laws, and were being advised to acquire still more. Over a decade later, Walter Richthofen, one of the early cattle barons of Colorado, considered the hundreds of thousands of square miles of the Far West and decided that very little of it could "be used for agricultural purposes," and that "cattlemen need never fear of being crowded out by farmers." Not till after 1885 were actual plowmen entering the Great Plains in numbers sufficient to be considered, and by that time the fencing of the range was already well under way. But the winter killing of cattle in 1886–1887, and low prices following, convinced the herdsmen that unless they fenced their range it would, with the next boom period, become so overstocked that their ruin would be complete. This was not a problem of farmers fencing in the water holes. Rivers furnished the main supply of drinking places on the Great Plains, and water holes were not the herders' big reliance until the Rocky Mountains had been crossed. In the Great Basin, a homesteader might stake out a water hole, but it did not take him long to starve alongside it. Fencing on the Great Plains, then, was mainly a big land steal, to stabilize the cattle industry by limiting the number of owners; and more harm than good was to come from the fence as a device to gain this end.[14]

The first cattle fences on the Plains were of Osage hedge, wire

[13] Louis Pelzer, *The Cattlemen's Frontier* (Glendale, Cal.: The Arthur H. Clark Company, 1936), pp. 157–180.

[14] McCoy, *Sketches of the Cattle Trade*, p. 340; Walter Baron Von Richthofen, *Cattle Raising on the Plains of North America* (New York: D. Appleton and Company, 1885), p. 11; Osgood, *Day of the Cattleman*, pp. 241–243; Dale, *Range Cattle Industry*, p. 111; Pelzer, *Cattlemen's Frontier*, pp. 173–191.

and post, post and board, and sometimes, where timber was available, of rails. Even when, in 1874, Joseph F. Glidden won his initial fight over barbed-wire patents, and began putting the product on the market, the cattlemen were slow to find any virtues in the newfangled material. Down to the end of the decade, only a few of them would try it. As late as 1880, only forty thousand tons were manufactured in a year, but in the next decade barbed wire became more popular, and 125,000 tons were produced in 1890. This figure was nearly doubled by 1900. A good part of the product, before the latter date, was going to the cow country, for this was something that would stop the strongest bull without serious injury, that cost but little as compared with other materials, and overcame the difficulty of a scarcity of Western timber. Then the cowboy had to get down from his horse, dig post holes, haul posts from the railroad station or cut them along the creek bottom, jack up a hind wheel of the wagon to use as a wire tightener, and, in general, indulge in work as unbecoming to his dignity as substituting for the camp cook.[15]

From that time onward the range cattle business underwent a transformation to the fenced-ranch phase, and the cowboy even had to suffer the humiliation of working in the corn field, where any corn could be grown. The days of magnificence were passing, but the West began growing a larger percentage of the nation's beef than ever before. Yet, always more beef was produced on farms to the eastward than on the Western range or ranches. In 1900, the states from Texas to North Dakota and out to the Pacific reported nearly 15,000,000 out of less than 28,000,000 beef cattle in the United States, but many of the West's contribution were from east of the Great Plains range and ranch country. A large share of the 4,417,000 in Kansas, Nebraska, and the Dakotas, many of the 4,353,000 in Texas, and a good share of the 1,395,000 in the Pacific states were on general farms. These figures from the Department of Agriculture vary considerably from the census enumeration, but on any basis of calculation the sectional ratio is not greatly

15 McCoy, *Sketches of the Cattle Trade*, pp. 336, 397; Osgood, *Day of the Cattleman*, pp. 56, 191; William Curry Holden, *The Spur Ranch* (Boston: The Christopher Publishing House, c.1934), pp. 64–79; Dale, *Range Cattle Industry*, p. 121; "Barbed Wire," *Encyclopaedia Britannica*, 11th ed., III, 385; *ibid.*, 14th ed., III, 97.

different.[16] Of late years, many more cattle have been shipped out of Texas each year for fattening on the blue-stem grass of the Flint Hills of Kansas than ever were driven to that state in a like time before 1885.[17]

Nearly all of the early fences of the Plains country were illegal, though this matter had to be clarified by additional legislation, to be considered later. Oftentimes many square miles of the public domain were thoroughly barricaded, in serene defiance of the law, and the person who cut the wires was inviting homicidal consequences. Again, the land would not be actually enclosed, but drift fences were built so nearly all around the range that the cattle could easily be outflanked and turned back when they came near a point of egress. In 1883, the Secretary of the Interior advised settlers to destroy any such barriers to the public lands, and in 1885 the law against enclosures was passed (see page 218, below), but this did not stop the practice. As late as the 1940's, ruins of rail drift fences could still be traced in the mountain parks of Colorado. The urge for the building of barbed wire fences must have been great, for the cost of labor alone was $15 to the mile, and the total expense declined from $175 a mile in 1885 to $136 at the end of the century. By the latter time, the Spur Ranch in Texas had 247 miles of fence, costing $37,250 besides upkeep, while all buildings and corrals were valued at another $9,000. Maintenance of the fence for twenty years equaled the original cost, for men were employed on full-time duty riding the circuit and making repairs.[18]

Another consequence of fence building was the necessity of drilling wells and the erection of expensive windmills and tanks in pastures that were cut off from the watering places. At any long distance from the rivers, water was not reached except at great depths. In the Panhandle country, wells had to be drilled for from three hundred to eight hundred feet. Down to five hundred feet, the sinking and casing of a well cost from a dollar and a quarter to two dollars a foot, and deeper holes ran to a higher ratio. In early days the cost was greater yet. An estimate for the average well,

[16] *Agricultural Yearbook*, 1899, p. 820.

[17] For the Flint Hills cattle industry see James C[laude] Malin, "An Introduction to the History of the Bluestem-Pasture Region of Kansas," *The Kansas Historical Quarterly*, XI, No. 1 (February, 1942), 3–28.

[18] Dale, *Range Cattle Industry*, p. 125; Holden, *The Spur Ranch*, pp. 73–74, 76.

with windmill and tower, tank, and reservoir runs to about $1,000 for some parts of the Plains, and twice as much in others. This was more than the homesteader or little stock farmer could pay, but big ranchers often had to have several wells, each watering from 350 to 500 cattle. Barnes gives a picture of a windmill in New Mexico costing from $1,500 to $5,000 for mill, tower, and well, the variation depending on the depth of the vein of water. He also shows a tank in Arizona running in cost from $1,000 to $3,000. The expense of maintenance, repairs, and replacement was also high, but these devices alone made grazing possible in large areas. Toward the end of the century some farmers also were using windmills, but they generally settled close enough to the streams that such costly equipment could be avoided, and such mills as they used were usually of the cheaper variety, set up on towers of the farmers' own construction.[19]

The daily life on the range—riding around the herd to prevent improper straying; tending sick cattle; sniping at coyotes trying to steal calves; shooting at lobo wolves, which were much more dangerous; rounding up the cattle; cutting out and castrating young bulls; branding calves; sometimes even cutting prairie hay or growing corn for winter feed—cannot be told in brief space with sufficient vividness to offset the glamour of cowboy literature and Western "movies," most of which are as fictitious as "Howdy, podner!" and "which same I would rise to explain." As to the trusty six-shooter, the characterization by Rollins, himself a cowboy, might well be considered. The Colt forty-four or forty-five weighed two and a quarter pounds, plus ammunition, and the cow hand ordinarily did not care to be bothered with it, though there were occasions when it was desirable to carry one along. It was always present when a call was made in formal fashion on a sweetheart, merely because the revolver was "an integral part of full dress."[20] There were other excitements and annoyances about life on the range, but they will best be understood after the problems of the sheepmen and homesteaders have also been considered. What the dude-ranch student of cowboy glamour should do is follow all day in the footsteps of the arid-country "puncher," when the grass has

[19] Dale, *Range Cattle Industry*, pp. 99, 121–122; Barnes, *The Story of the Range*, pp. 29–30, plate facing p. 29; Holden, *The Spur Ranch*, pp. 80–89.
[20] Holden, *The Spur Ranch*, pp. 173–174; Rollins, *The Cowboy*, p. 41.

all shriveled up, and watch him burn thorns from the prickly pear with a blowtorch, while the cattle follow him hungrily from clump to clump.

THE WESTERN SHEEP INDUSTRY

If cattle in the Far West did not equal in number those east of the Great Plains, it can also be said that, before the end of the century, when the cattle industry was at its peak, they were in the minority among the livestock even of their own section. The seventeen states from Texas to North Dakota and westward had over 14,000,000 of the nation's 63,000,000 hogs in 1900, and this was more than 45 per cent of the number of cattle in that region. Nebraska had far more swine than cattle, and Kansas had nearly as many. The hogs of either of these states, or of Texas, outnumbered the cattle of any of the Mountain or Pacific states. Though many of these numbers were east of the Great Plains proper, hogs ran to more than 100,000 in Colorado and in Idaho. Throughout his book, McCoy mentions swine on the cattle ranches in the 1870's, particularly wherever grain feeding was done. But, as far as numbers go, sheep had come to be supreme in the same section, numbering nearly 38,000,000 in 1900, or over six tenths of the 61,500,000 in the United States. Sheep also far outnumbered cattle, in the section as a whole. This does not mean that sheep and cattle were generally in the same areas. While cattle dominated the Great Plains, seven tenths of the sheep were in the Mountain states, and outnumbered cattle in each of the eight. Montana had between six and seven sheep for each cow.[21]

During the Civil War, the sheep growers of the East were unusually prosperous, mainly because of the dearth of cotton, but, as soon as the South resumed its accustomed place in the supplying of Northern mills, the sheepmen began to feel depression. The average price of sheep dropped from $3.37 a head in 1866 to $2.17 in 1868. Wool production had increased 70 per cent since 1860, and now Australia, South Africa, South America, and Europe were redoubling their competition, so that wool prices tended to move downward throughout the next twenty years. Consequently, Ohio

[21] *Statistical Abstract of the United States*, 1926, pp. 608–609.

sheep growers diminished their flocks by two and a half million between 1867 and 1869, and other Eastern states showed a like trend. Culls and other low-grade sheep were gladly sold to the butchers for the seventy-five cents to a dollar and a half that would be paid for their hides and tallow. Some growers went out of the business entirely, many reduced their flocks, but others decided to stay with their specialty, by profiting from the experiences of Africa, South America, and Australia. Sheepherders there could ship their wool all the way to the United States and then undersell the domestic grower. The reason was that these outlanders had cheap ranges that could be grazed the year round, and they had to buy no hay or grain for winter feeding. This, as the Commissioner of Agriculture pointed out in 1870, was a situation that could be imitated to perfection in the great American West. Advice came from the West, as well, urging the Eastern wool growers to sell their fifty-dollar land and drive their flocks to a place that was profitable. And so the movement began, not by the actual driving of great numbers of sheep from Ohio to Montana, but by the migration of growers deciding to make a new start. The shift was first noticeable in Texas, New Mexico, and on the Pacific coast, but by 1880, sheep were becoming numerous in all the Mountain states.[22] Perhaps no great proportion of the new growers were direct from the sheep farms of the East, but some of them were.

Since wool was a product of which the United States did not produce a surplus, the tariff could be of real benefit to it, and so the Act of 1867 was intended to be. But American wool markets were so glutted at the time that the new law was not enough to save the industry in the East. Later on, the Western competition behind the tariff wall was too keen for Easterners to make the effort, except

[22] L[ouis] G[eorge] Connor, "A Brief History of the Sheep Industry in the United States," American Historical Association, Annual Report, 1918 (Washington: Government Printing Office, 1921), I, 129, 138; U.S. Commissioner of Agriculture, Report, 1866, p. 67; ibid., 1868, p. 46; ibid., 1870, p. 307; Twelfth Census: Agriculture, I, ccxiii, 708; Flint, "Agriculture in the United States," p. 60; J[acob] R[ichards] Dodge, "Sheep and Wool," U.S. Department of Agriculture, Report No. 66 (Washington: Government Printing Office, 1900), pp. 44–45; Chester Whitney Wright, Wool-Growing and the Tariff (Boston: Houghton Mifflin Company, 1910), pp. 269–271; Letter from Amos Duffield of Beatrice, Nebraska, "Nebraska for Sheep Husbandry," The Prairie Farmer, XL, No. 23 (June 5, 1869), 178; Letter from Albert Griffin of Manhattan, Kansas, "Send on the Flocks," The Prairie Farmer, XLI, No. 7 (February 19, 1870), 50.

with sheep as a side line to general farming. The Western herders also found the Pacific railroads indispensable to their success.[23] The driving of sheep from Montana to Omaha would be a far different matter from the driving of cattle from Abilene, Texas, to Abilene, Kansas. Other matters the stockmen had to adjust for themselves. Sheepherding on the open range was so distinct from sheep farming in the East that the two were almost entirely different enterprises. The vastness, and in many places the roughness of the range, the climatic conditions, and the marketing methods of the new regions—the very bigness and nomadic character of the new business—were things that Eastern farmers had not experienced. Also, it took years to learn what new lands could be kept open to sheep, as the advancing farmer and the powerful cattleman appropriated the choicer spots. States that ranked low in the sheep industry in 1880 were the leaders by 1900, while California and Texas, first and fourth on the list in the earlier year, ranked eighth and tenth respectively at the end of the period.[24]

Though General Brisbin may have been even more than usually enthusiastic when he prophesied, in 1885, that Wyoming could care for all the sheep in the United States, Australia, and Argentina, producing 300,000,000 pounds of wool worth $100,000,000 a year, he did know a good thing when he saw it. By 1910 Wyoming, with second rank in sheep, was outdistancing Montana in wool, with 13 per cent of the amount Brisbin had calculated a quarter of a century earlier. In order to achieve such rapid results, the sheepherders, like the cattlemen, helped themselves to free rent on the government domain. By 1890, most of them owned a little land around the watering places, and then spread out, for grazing, on everything they could keep others off. When on railroad land, they had to pay a rental of five cents an acre each year. As the industry expanded. conflict with the cattle kings became almost inevitable, and warfare did break out in the 1890's. The prices of beef, wool, and mutton were rising; free rent meant quick fortunes; so the rule of first come first served was invoked. When the deadline was crossed, the injured herder saw his wealth in danger of vanishing, so he polished up his "shooting irons" and fared forth to do battle

[23] Wright, *Wool-Growing and the Tariff*, pp. 247–251.
[24] *Twelfth Census: Agriculture*, I, 708.

for his "rights," the worst friction occurring in Wyoming and Colorado.[25]

The old charges of sheep ruining the range were reiterated and answered, in turn, by the ovine defenders. The stories, it was said, were mere concoctions, to amaze the "tenderfoot." But most effective of the replies were citations of instances where sheep owners were also among the greatest of cattle herders, who used the same range and watering places for both. However hot the arguments and lead became, neither side wanted to drag the contest into the courts, and expose legally the fact that they, as trespassers on public lands, had no legal rights. Whatever happened was not noised about and, though rumors got abroad of shocking experiences, the distant public rarely knew the issues or the outcome. In general the cattlemen took the initiative, with shooting, slaughtering, arson, and raids as common events. In the 1890's, along the Colorado-Wyoming border, it was estimated that at least twenty men were killed and a hundred injured. Possibly 600,000 sheep, worth $2,000,000 were destroyed, but the figures are controversial. When a gang of cow "punchers" overtook a lone sheepherder with as many as 3,000 sheep under his care, he had no chance. A sport highly favored was the driving of the sheep over the rim of a steep precipice. Stampedes and scattering were also resorted to, the lost sheep being an easy prey to wild animals. Sometimes the flocks were poisoned. It was generally the nomadic sheepherders who got into trouble, while those who stuck to one range, without overcrowding, were rarely molested.[26]

[25] James S[anks] Brisbin, *The Beef Bonanza; or How to Get Rich on the Plains* (Philadelphia: J. B. Lippincott and Co., 1885), p. 103; *Agricultural Yearbook*, 1910, p. 637; Ezra A[yers] Carman, H[ubert] A. Heath, and John Minto, *The History and Present Condition of the Sheep Industry of the United States* (U.S. Department of Agriculture, Bureau of Animal Industry, *Special Report*, Washington: Government Printing Office, 1892), p. 790; A. W. North, "The Warfare on the Ranges," *Harper's Weekly*, LIII, No. 2,742 (July 10, 1909), 11.

[26] Charles Stedman Newhall, "Sheep and the Forest Reserves," *The Forum*, XXX, No. 6 (February, 1901), 710-716; E. V. Wilcox, "Sheep Ranching in the Western States," U.S. Department of Agriculture, Bureau of Animal Industry, *Nineteenth Annual Report* (Washington: Government Printing Office, 1903), pp. 85-86; Charles Michelson, "The War for the Range," *Munsey's Magazine,* XXVIII, No. 3 (December, 1902), 380-382; E. P. Snow, "Sheepmen and Cattlemen," *The Outlook,* LXXIII, No. 14 (April 4, 1903), 839-840; Henry F. Cope, "Sheep-Herder vs. Cow-Puncher," *The World Today*, VII, No. 2 (August, 1904), 1037-1045; Charles Moreau Harger, "Sheep and Shepherds of the West," *The Outlook,* LXXII, No. 12 (November 22, 1902), 689-693; Joseph E[lwyn] Wing, *Sheep Farming in America* (Chicago: Sanders Publishing Co., new ed., 1909), pp. 226-227.

By the closing years of the century, many a cattleman, who had bitterly fought the woolly advance for years, turned to sheep raising himself. This was particularly noticeable in the old beef strongholds of Montana, Wyoming, and Colorado. Sheep were better protected by nature against the Northern winters; they could thrive where cattle would starve, and reach grass where a cow could not climb. A still more convincing fact was that the profits from sheep were twice those from cattle, and it cost only a third as much to stock the ranch. It was the sheepherders who set the example for cattlemen of storing feed for winter use. The sheep range, as well as the cattle range attracted pseudo homesteaders. Herders were known to hire as many as twenty-five persons, and probably more, to stake out claims for the employers' ultimate control of the water front. Sometimes the roving settlers themselves took the initiative, pooling their interests and charging a watering fee, though this did not proceed so far as to be an actual menace to the herdsmen. After a few seasons of adversity and conflict, the newcomer was generally anxious to sell out and move on. As the range became crowded, the sheepman, like the cattleman, wanted to acquire the necessary minimum of land for security, and the homesteaders and lax land acts were more of a necessity than a nuisance. Even irrigation, at first feared as a lethal blow to the industry, became an asset. By 1889, it was widely practiced in Wyoming for the growing of hay and grain for winter feeding, to replace the supplies that before then were shipped in. The Western hay also was of superior feeding qualities. Thus the 2,700,000 acres of irrigated land in the Rocky Mountain area, as of 1870, were doubled by 1890, and continued to grow at the same rate.[27]

The sheepherder's life was not a luxurious one. If of the nomadic type, his home was a bedroll, carried with him from day to day. In settled localities, the house was generally just "a roof over his head," and even this was often merely a thatch of bear grass. As

[27] Edwin L. Sabin, "On the Western Sheep Range," *Appleton's Booklovers Magazine*, VI, No. 5 (November, 1905), 541; Fred[eric] S[amuel] Hultz and John A[rthur] Hill, *Range Sheep and Wool in the Seventeen Western States* (New York: John Wiley & Sons, Inc., 1931), p. 8; H[ubert] A. Heath, "Condition of the Sheep Industry West of the Mississippi River," U.S. Department of Agriculture, Bureau of Animal Industry, *Sixth and Seventh Annual Reports*, pp. 247, 255; Wilcox, "Sheep Ranching in the Western States," p. 97; Randall R. Howard, "The Passing of the Cattle King," *The Outlook*, XCVIII, No. 4 (May 27, 1911), 204; Oliver E[dwin] Baker, "Agricultural Regions of North America, Part 10—The Grazing and Irrigated Crops Region," *Economic Geography*, VII, No. 4 (October, 1931), 325–364.

the lower range began to parch, near the end of spring, the herder would drive his flock of from fifteen hundred to three thousand sheep to the mountain pastures, there to remain out of contact with any other human being, except for a visit or two of the supply-wagon driver, from June to September. The more opulent owners furnished the herder with a covered sheep wagon, fitted out with a stove, bed, and other things simulating a home. Others provided a tent.˙ On the southern range, the herdsmen had to remain a good part of the year in the mountain pastures. These were usually Mexicans, getting from twenty to thirty dollars a month and food, and were at the bottom of the Western social scale. On the northern range, the wage was from thirty-five to fifty dollars a month and board, the workers generally being native Americans. A survey of Western asylums for the insane showed an undue proportion of former sheepherders among the inmates. The reasons given were the solitude of the life and the "queer" type of mentality that could be tempted into the pursuit in the first place.[28]

Extra help and special care had to be employed during the May lambing season, for a lamb lost from its mother for a few hours was disowned by the ewe and became a "bum," requiring hand feeding if it was to live. Small corrals were often provided for the first ten days, to keep the ewes acquainted with their young. At the end of that time, docking and castration took place in a very few days, and the count of tails showed the increase of the flock, which was often as much as 80 per cent. Sheepshearers, like the harvest hands in the western Prairies, followed the season north. Beginning at the Mexican border early in March, they finished at the Canadian line in June. Until machines were introduced in the early nineties, all clipping was done by hand. One man could take care of from eighty to a hundred sheep in a day, receiving from eight to ten cents each. The wool was then packed in bags of three or four hundred pounds and hauled, sometimes for long distances, to the railroad storehouses. The sheep received a dipping, preferably in a tobacco (or lime and sulphur) solution, about two weeks before shearing,

[28] E. C. Reynolds, "On a Texas Sheep Ranch," *Lippincott's Magazine*, XXXVI, o.s., No. 4 (October, 1885), 324, 326–327; Cope, "Sheep-Herder vs. Cow-Puncher," p. 1044; Carman, Heath, and Minto, *Sheep Industry*, p. 714; Randall R. Howard, "The Sheep-Herder," *The Outlook*, XCVI, No. 17 (December 24, 1910), 943–950: "In the Wake of the Western Sheep," *Blackwood's Magazine*, CXCIV, No. 1,173 (July, 1913), 105–106.

to cleanse the wool, and again, immediately after the clip, to heal cuts and kill parasites. The weight of the fleece and its quality depended largely on the plentifulness of proper feed, so herders who gave the greatest care to their flocks prospered most.[29]

The sheep industry had moved into the Mountain states from all directions but the North. Like the Western cattle business, it was very largely Mexican in origin. New Mexico, though not the greatest, was the most consistent producer through the decades. California also had an early start with Mexican stock, herding methods, and herdsmen, but an increasing scarcity of cheap land and severe drouths in the late seventies brought a change, and her supremacy was surrendered soon after 1880. Arizona was the first to profit from the Californian exodus, but Indian raids checked growth, and the herds were driven northward. Oregon and Washington also got a start from the California industry, and the geometric ratio of reproduction permitted rapid growth from small beginnings. In fact, the Mormons had brought sheep to Utah and started large flocks twenty years before the impulse in any of the other northern Mountain states. The sheep in Colorado, before 1865, were along the southern border, and were merely an overflow from New Mexico.

The migration into Idaho, Montana, and Wyoming came out of the Pacific states and Utah. Some sheep were brought from the East, in the late sixties, and the importation of rams from that direction continued. Stock sheep cost the rancher about $3.00 a head in 1879, and $2.25 in 1888, the difference being attributed to many things, including the tariff of 1883, which had lowered the duty on wool slightly. But, inasmuch as the average price in 1877–1879 had been from $1.00 to $1.25, while from 1888 to 1890 mutton was becoming a profitable source of revenue (and before the McKinley Act), it may be suspected that the growers were led to pay too much attention to the tariff laws. High-priced beef for a few years after the hard winter of 1880–1881 led to a popular demand for more mutton, and this was soon reflected in the breed-

[29] Wilcox, "Sheep Ranching in the Western States," pp. 81–82; Traveler (pseud.), "Sheep in Utah," *Wool and Sheep Facts: The American Shepherd's Yearbook, 1895* (Boston: Frank P. Bennett, ed. and proprietor, c. 1895), p. 114; William Draper Lewis, *Our Sheep and the Tariff* (Vol. II of University of Pennsylvania, *Political Economy and Public Law Series,* Philadelphia: University of Pa. Press Co., 1890), pp. 71–72, 82; William A[rthur] Rushworth, *Sheep and Their Diseases* (Chicago: Alexander Eger, 2d ed., 1903), pp. 73–74.

ing practices of the West. Shropshires, Southdowns, and Cotswolds began to replace some of the Merinos. The perfection of cold storage and refrigerator cars further aided the demand for mutton, but it was not till after 1900 that the carcasses became more valuable than the fleeces.[30]

THE FAR WESTERN FARMER

Except in an experimental way, and for relatively small localities, the plow farmer made little inroad on the semiarid and arid regions before 1900. Most of that vast area has continued to remain closed to him and seems likely to remain so, and the reason is the insufficient rainfall. Dry farming cannot flourish where the year-by-year annual average of precipitation is less than fifteen inches. The occasional good years are not enough to make up for the total failures. To speak of irrigating more than a minor fraction of the region is to utter nonsense. Water, whether derived from reservoirs, from beneath the ground, or from direct rainfall, must, before all, come from the clouds. Irrigation from impounded mountain water can never extend far, for there would not be enough to go around even if it could be transported. Irrigation from rivers pumps the streams dry near their sources, and then does not supply more than the bottom lands. Artesian basins, such as the Dakota, Roswell, and lesser ones, can serve no more than their restricted localities. Ground water is merely accumulated rainfall, and its use for irrigation soon exhausts the supply. Therefore, since average crops require thirty or more inches of rainfall a year, any large region getting in the neighborhood of ten inches or less can never be farmed profitably, except in the favored localities where the precipitation over a wide area can be concentrated on a small one.[31]

The Mormons in Utah, and the farmers in various mountain mining regions, as earlier noted, found some of the irrigable spots,

[30] *Tenth Census: Agriculture,* bottom folio, pp. 1006, 1036, 1072; Wright, *Wool-Growing and the Tariff,* pp. 221, 256; U.S. Commissioner of Agriculture, *Report,* 1870, p. 308; Connor, "History of the Sheep Industry," pp. 140–142; Brisbin, *Beef Bonanza,* p. 112; Lewis, "Sheep and the Tariff," p. 143; Heath, "Condition of the Sheep Industry," pp. 262–263; J[oseph] Russell Smith, *Industrial and Commercial Geography* (New York: Henry Holt and Company, c.1913), p. 174; Carman, Heath, and Minto, *Sheep Industry,* pp. 714, 718.

[31] Nevin M[elancthon] Fenneman, *Physiography of Western United States* (New York: McGraw-Hill Book Company, Inc., 1931), pp. 87–88.

and occasionally they did remarkably well with their opportunities.
By 1900, the Mormons had over six million acres irrigated, at least
in part, in numerous little settlements. Sometimes they did this
by diverting mountain streams, and again, as south of the Great
Salt Lake, by finding artesian sources. The Desert Land Act, as
before stated, did very little for actual irrigation, and it was not
till the Carey Act of 1894 that the federal government bothered
itself again with the problem. Then it did so in a bungling way.
The arid states were allowed a million acres of land each, to be
sold at fifty cents an acre. Private companies were allowed to install
the irrigation works. The water, thus supplied, cost from thirty
to forty dollars an acre, which sum was to be paid the companies
in ten yearly installments, after which the works were transferred
to associations of users. The act was not interstate in character,
and it provided no general plan of conservation of water. Also, no
arrangement was made whereby the farmers could reconstruct the
dams after great washouts. Not till after 1900, and then only slowly,
did the federal government proceed to a thoroughgoing solution
of this problem. As late as 1902, less than nine million acres of land
in the United States were systematically irrigated, or an area about
a sixth the size of the state of Kansas. Only about a quarter of a
million acres had been redeemed under the Carey Act, in place of
the seventeen million allowed for. The great bulk of all the major
irrigation enterprises was along the Missouri River and a number
of Pacific coast streams, including the Columbia and Colorado
rivers. The Mormon works must have been mainly the efforts of
individual farmers, for only 1,639,000 acres were credited to the
entire Great Basin.[32] Except for the Pacific coast, irrigation was
primarily for forage crops and general farming. Imperial Valley
lettuce was not marketed in New York in those days.

By the time that the plowman's frontier reached the Great
Plains, the long drive was becoming an anachronism, the public
domain was already well enclosed in the eastern ranges, and the
stockmen were dominant. Not till 1886 did the railroad companies
lure settlers into western Nebraska, but thereafter more speed was
shown, and in 1888 the land seekers were invading Wyoming. That

[32] Katharine Coman, *The Industrial History of the United States* (New York:
The Macmillan Company, ed. of 1914), pp. 401–402; *Statistical Abstract of the
United States*, 1926, p. 570.

these interlopers could enrage the neighboring cattlemen should not excite any astonishment. But it was not because of their fences. The state law of Nebraska required farmers to fence their crops, or else they had no protection against range stock. The same sort of law had prevailed when the cattleman's frontier was in colonial Virginia and the Carolinas. But in Nebraska the early farmers had their own ideas as to what constituted a fence, and the law was not strict. They merely plowed a furrow around their fields, called this an adequate barricade, and shot any encroaching cattle. If a fence was to be cut, it was usually because the illegal enclosures of the cattlemen severed all access to highways, railroads, and streams. Even by 1882, serious complaints had been made by the scattering vanguard of the homesteaders against this impediment to settlement and transit.[33]

In some cases, state legislation tended to make the federal Pre-emption law ineffective, and honest-intentioned settlers were evicted by judicial decree from portions of the public domain. The Supreme Court of the United States, in the cases of Atherton *vs.* Fowler, Hosmer *vs.* Wallace, and Trenouth *vs.* San Francisco (1877, 1878, 1879), had held that no right of pre-emption could be established on land in the actual use of another, regardless of whether the previous occupation was legal or not. This was interpreted in the state courts as excluding settlers from the enclosed range, as in the case of Davis *vs.* Scott in California (1880). Thus, a homestead or pre-emption claim was likely to be contested as trespass, and few settlers could afford protracted litigation. Sometimes stockmen cut each other's fences, when the only purpose of the enclosure was to establish legal claim to small tracts under the federal land laws. Certainly, it was time for the whole matter to be cleared up, and, as early as 1882, efforts were being made to get legislation to stop the fencing of public lands except by regular legal entry. The failure to secure the passage of such an act through Congress was what led the Commissioner of the General Land Office to recommend the cutting of the wires in 1883 (page 206, above). This notice was circulated by special agents, but it had little effect

---

[33] Osgood, *Day of the Cattleman*, pp. 241–242; Gray, *Agriculture in the South*, I, 199; General Land Office, *Report*, 1883 (Washington: Government Printing Office, 1883), p. 30.

one way or the other, for lack of a law to provide means of enforcement.[34]

So the nuisance continued, and the little fellows, whether stockmen or occasional homesteaders, met with violence, or the threat of it, when compelled to pass a fence. At intervals along the barriers would be posted signs such as "The Son of a Bitch who opens this fence had better look out for his scalp." Many of the enclosed areas were controlled purely by foreign capitalists, like the Prairie Cattle Company (Scotch) with over a million acres. Wyoming alone had upward of 125 such corporations, both foreign and domestically controlled, each of huge dimensions. Even the post roads were crossed by their barbed wire. Though for a long time the cattlemen had the upper hand, the homesteaders, as they became more numerous, grew strong enough to retaliate, and along the edge of the Plains their fences became so continuous that there was no place to hold a large herd of cattle for shipment; but the vaster area of the cattle country was in no wise thus molested. Meanwhile, the Illegal Fencing Act of February 25, 1885, had been adopted, followed by President Cleveland's order for enforcement. While the legislation put the burden of proof on the range hog, the actual removal of the fences was slow and the use of bogus homestead entries for engrossment was multiplied. As late as 1908, a number of illegal enclosures were still to be found, and an act of March 10 of that year was adopted to end the practice.[35]

The clarification of this legal right of the farmers may have been a gratification to the pugnacious spirit handed down by generations of frontiersmen, but it did not signify that farming on the High Plains could now proceed unimpeded. Just as the natural limits of slavery expansion had been reached before 1850, so the natural limits of general farming were pretty generally established by 1890. Farmers might push farther out on the Plains in wet years and be starved back in dry ones. The often-told story of the rush of

[34] 96 U.S., 513; 97 U.S., 575; 100 U.S., 251; 56 Cal., 165; *House Report* No. 1,809, 47 Cong., 1 Sess., pp. 1–2; Donaldson, *Public Domain*, pp. 1171–1179; Public Lands Commission, *Report Relating to Public Lands in the Western Portion of the United States and to the Operation of Existing Land Laws*, this being *House Executive Document* No. 46, 46 Cong., 2 Sess., samples of local Western opinion on pp. 492–511; *House Report* No. 1,325, 48 Cong., 1 Sess., pp. 1–5.

[35] General Land Office, *Report*, 1883, p. 30; *Senate Executive Document* No. 127, 48 Cong., 1 Sess., pp. 1–45; 23 *Statutes at Large*, pp. 321–322; *Public Land Statutes of the United States*, 1931, pp. 745–746; *House Report* No. 1,325, 48 Cong., 1 Sess., pp. 6–7.

homesteaders into Oklahoma, as strip after strip of that territory was opened to settlement between 1889 and 1893, is eloquent testimony to the preference of farmers for land where there was sufficient rainfall to insure crops. There was far more homestead land still available west of the hundredth meridian than was to be had in Oklahoma east of that line. But the Western land was a natural pasture and, except for a few spots, ought never to have been used for anything else. The federal government would have been doing the small farmer a favor if, instead of forbidding the enclosures and encouraging homesteading, it had adopted a rational leasing act, dedicating the range country to cattle and sheep, under strict limitation as to the number that could be pastured in any area. Thus, the grass and the land might have been preserved, the industry legalized, and the rancher compelled to pay his rent. Also, the farmer would have been prevented the harrowing experience of trying to make a living where nothing but erosion and starvation could ensue. It was not till after 1900 that anything was done even to allow enlarged homesteads in the subhumid belt suited to dry farming, and then the allotment was only enough to encourage further starvation efforts.

The story of farming on the Plains is largely a repetition of the experience in the western Prairies, except that the percentage of successful crops over a period of years became less with each frontier advance. In Edwards County, Kansas, slightly east of the hundredth meridian, sundry experiments in dry-land farming were being tried in the 1880's. Sorghum, kaffir corn, and Turkey wheat were found adaptable, as were some other varieties of forage crops and cereals, but all were hazardous, because of the climate and chinch bugs. Before 1900, the disc plow was coming into favor, because it left the stubble on top of the ground and thus checked wind erosion. Listing for wheat was also practiced, the ridges being "busted" before planting, thus providing extra soil working and allowing a deeper penetration of moisture.[36]

Other methods of dry farming were also being tried out, the experiences of the Pacific states being copied. Deep plowing, from twelve to fourteen inches, in the fall (practicable because of the great depth of the true soil), followed by replowing and harrowing

[36] James C[laude] Malin, "The Adaptation of the Agricultural System to Sub-Humid Environment," *Agricultural History*, X, No. 3 (July, 1936), 118–141 *passim*.

to a dust mulch in the spring, tended to conserve moisture. Deep and scanty planting of the seed, and fallowing with continued plowing and dust mulching every other year, made crops possible in years when rainfall did not get too near the ten-inch deadline. This method made little progress on the Plains before 1900, though Colorado and Wyoming, as well as Utah, had model state farms for demonstration purposes by that time. Dry farming was known on California wheat ranches about fifty years earlier, and this was a modification of a practice of respectable antiquity in certain Old World areas.[37] It was futile to attempt this system on less than a full section of land, and the repeal of the Pre-emption and Timber Culture acts (in 1891), as well as the 320-acre limitation of 1890, prevented the legal acquisition of so much from the government. Even the Mondell Act of 1909, raising the homestead limit to half a section in the semiarid and arid regions, was a delusion that merely tempted farmers on to lands where they could not exist without the purchase of much more. So the end of the century came with the farmer on his last frontier, always hopeful that the next year would reverse his luck but never sure that he could "keep his belt buckle from chafing his backbone" till the next crop was raised.

[37] Coman, *Industrial History of the United States*, pp. 406–407.

CHAPTER X

Finance and Marketing Problems of the Range Country

CREDIT RELATIONS, CYCLES, AND PROFITABILITY

THOUGH individualism was almost the universal creed of American farmers, nowhere else was it more strikingly exemplified after 1860 than in the range country. There is nothing surprising in this fact, for dependence on himself and nature had been an outstanding characteristic of the pioneer on every preceding frontier, and this was the last of the series. Yet, on no earlier frontier had the actual need of cooperative enterprise been more evident, as the preceding chapter should have disclosed. Though the stockman may have felt that he led a wholly self-sufficient and satisfying life, he was actually as dependent on conditions outside his control as was the Southern cotton grower. The cattleman got his hat from Connecticut, his gloves from New York, his overalls and shirts from Eastern sweatshops, his boots from Massachusetts, his socks and underwear from Pennylvania, his saddle, bridle, spurs, rifle, revolver, and even his rope from various distant Eastern localities. Surrounded by cattle, he imported canned milk for his coffee. Rarely did he grow any food except meat. He even waited till he arrived at some Eastern shipping point, such as Kansas City, to go on a protracted drunk. Perhaps it was not the "rootin, tootin, shootin" variety. Perhaps the whiskey was of a higher grade than that of the range-town saloon. But the testimony is that it was satisfying. The stockman was also wholly dependent on the railroads, cattle markets, customer demand, and banks, all controlled by Eastern people or financial interests. All that he could do for himself was to regulate the factors of production, and this, to be done effectively, required far more regional cooperation than the stockmen's associations and horse-thief vigilantes nurtured.

Credit for the establishment of a cattle ranch was not a serious problem in the 1860's and early 1870's, before the range was over-stocked, for not much capital was needed. A young cattle hand might save his wages for a few years and get a start for himself, or he could take his pay in calves, to be marked with his own brand and herded with those of his employer. With a good horse and a long rope, he might add to his growing herd more rapidly than if everything was left to nature. When his herd grew large enough to require his whole attention, he could move out on the range for himself, knock a cabin together, cut a few poles to build a corral, and be independent in a small way. When he began to need extra help, he already had some money hid about the house for the buying of provisions, and the hired hands would wait for their wages till the cattle were marketed.[1]

The drovers, who bought cattle on the ranches and marketed them in the East, were the first to need extensive credit. In the earlier days, they simply gave receipts to the different ranchers with whom they dealt, and paid for the cattle when they returned from their sales. But this was a business that could be entrusted only to a man whose honesty was well known. As the range became wider, and the number of drovers increased, it was not always possible to sell through a dealer of proved integrity, and, therefore, the buyer had to have cash on hand. Here, the bankers entered the scene, advancing money to the drover as far as they trusted him to come that way again. Such bankers had to be as much judges of people as of securities, and some of their practices would not have been tolerated if detected by the examiners, but it was affirmed that they rarely judged wrongly. The drover was in the business for more than the profits on one herd, and he could not remain if he dodged his debts. The banks and trust companies began to grow active in the livestock industry, by the early seventies, pioneer

---

[1] Louis Pelzer, "Financial Management of the Cattle Ranges," *Journal of Economic and Business History*, II, No. 4 (August, 1930), 723; Charles I[seard] Bray, "Financing the Western Cattleman," Colorado Experiment Station, *Bulletin* No. 338 (Fort Collins: Colorado Agricultural College, December, 1928), pp. 7–9.

houses being in San Antonio, Austin, and, a little later, in Dallas and Fort Worth. But the Kansas City banks provided the central clearinghouse for the range country, until the crash following the cattle boom of the early eighties. The First National Bank of Kansas City, founded in 1865 with a capital of $100,000, established an office at Abilene, Kansas, soon after the cattle trade of that town began. Before long, it was patronized by stockmen of the whole Plains area. Still later St. Louis and Chicago banks began offering credit through the small-town financial institutions of the range country.[2]

The rancher himself, though he may have built up a herd without much financial assistance, often needed credit for many other things. Especially when he handled the marketing of his animals himself, he needed loans of from thirty to ninety days. Then, as the great cattle markets arose, special stockyards banks made loans to ranchers their chief business. Commission men, dealing with cattle raisers, also often indorsed notes at the banks, and ultimately began making loans of their own. A few cattle-loan companies also developed in the marketing centers, and became somewhat numerous after the middle eighties. Both they and the commission firms usually discounted the cattle notes at the regular banks. Sometimes the cattle-loan companies dealt directly with the stockmen, and again they took over the commission-house paper as intermediary between them and the banks. Every section of the range country soon had at least one financial agency capable of taking care of its needs.[3]

By 1871, the market was becoming oversupplied, and in 1873 there was a serious glut. Prices went so low that many southern herds were held on the northern range for later selling. But this meant that the Texas drovers had to make unusual demands on the bankers. By September, 1873, they owed more than $1,500,000. Then came the panic; the notes could not be renewed; and unfinished cattle had to be sold at ruinous prices. Many were slaughtered for their hides and tankage, and others were scattered among rising

[2] T[roy] J[esse] Cauley "Early Business Methods in the Texas Cattle Industry," *Journal of Economic and Business History,* IV, No. 3 (May, 1932), 476–477; McCoy, *Sketches of the Cattle Trade,* pp. 323, 325–326; Bray, "Financing the Western Cattleman," p. 10.

[3] McCoy, *Sketches of the Cattle Trade,* pp. 322–323; Dale, *Range Cattle Industry,* pp. 169–170.

northern ranches for further feeding. This helped the rapid expansion of the cattle business, especially in Colorado, Wyoming,
and Montana. Then, as new pastures became scarce and the mania
for fences spread throughout the industry, other funds had to be
raised for barbed wire, posts, and additional labor. The small cattleman was now (in the 1880's) being crowded out, and the cattlemen's associations would not respect his rights unless his section of
the range was fully stocked. So he borrowed money, even at
usurious rates of interest, in order to buy more cattle.[4]

Down to this time, financing was largely on a personal basis.
Loans, except in the panic year, were easy to get, but interest
charges were very high. Cattle paper was considered one of the
safest of investments. Neighbors signed each other's notes, and
chattel mortgages were rare. The early ranchers made money
rapidly, and could afford high rates. Then, as the years passed, the
greater cattlemen found that competition for their trade allowed
them to secure lower interest. But this tended to make their competitors more cautious, and so the lower rates tended to spread.
As one of the early drovers, Ike T. Pryor, said, he sometimes borrowed as much as $200,000 on his own note at Texas banks. Then,
one or two hundred miles west of Austin, he would buy herds of
cattle, paying in hundred-dollar drafts that passed as currency on
the range. In the North he would sell again to cattlemen, who
borrowed at 12 per cent in Pueblo, Cheyenne, Denver, or Kansas
City. Often, when he returned to Austin he would find nearly all
of his original loan untouched, because the drafts had been so slow
in returning. It was customary to lend half the full value of the
collateral, but 12 per cent was far from being the maximum rate.
When real-estate loans cost 8 or 10 per cent, cattle loans brought
12 and upward. In periods of great financial uncertainty, 3 per cent
a month was charged and paid. Even the customary 12 became 15
when additional fees were included. Brisbin speaks of 10 per cent
as though it were common, but mentions that it was possible to succeed in the business in spite of interest charges of 25 per cent.
Dale confirms this extreme usury. [5]

[4] McCoy, *Sketches of the Cattle Trade*, pp. 250–251; Bray, "Financing the
Western Cattleman," p. 11.
[5] Cauley, "Early Business Methods in the Texas Cattle Industry," p. 477; Bray,
"Financing the Western Cattleman," pp. 13–14; Dale, *Range Cattle Industry*, p. 172;
Brisbin, *Beef Bonanza*, 55.

In the period of the "beef bonanza," following 1873, the individual operator was largely eclipsed by new corporations. Reports of enormous profits attracted Eastern capital, and many of the greater companies were financed from Europe. By the early eighties, there was a long list of companies with upward of a million dollars of capital each. Some, like the Prairie Cattle Company, the Texas Land and Cattle Company, and the Arkansas Valley Cattle Company, paid annual dividends of from 10 to 20 per cent. The Nebraska Land and Cattle Company (British) bought properties valued at over $900,000, mostly for cash in ninety days. In 1884, the company of Carey and Brother of Wyoming valued its ranches, equipment, 32,287 cattle, 436 horses, and good will at $1,200,000. In 1883, the Union Cattle Company was incorporated in Wyoming with $3,000,000 in stock. Three years later, it floated a loan of $1,400,000 at 7 per cent for ten years, with the International Trust Company of Boston. By 1888, the company was insolvent, and was in receivers' hands for five years before reorganization. One of the lesser creditors was Henry Cabot Lodge, who in 1887 had lent $15,000 and got a little of it back. Untold quantities of Eastern money went into the bonanzas, and not much of it returned. Most of the records of the corporations vanished during and following the collapse of the late eighties.[6]

In the era of wild speculation, few persons stopped to consider the possibility of exhausted ranges or glutted markets. By 1884, the bonanza period was tottering for a fall. Prices dropped and investors lost, but other speculators continued pouring in money. Then the weather took its toll. The winters of 1885–1887 were unusually severe, the grass being so covered with snow and ice that it was beyond the reach of stamping cattle. The dry summer of 1886 between the two winters added further calamity. At such a time as this, cattlemen who had piled up earlier savings and were out of debt could pull through by the use of strict economy, but heavy borrowers were quickly eliminated. Cattle prices were low during the succeeding decade, and money was hard to borrow. At this time the fortunate rancher was the one who sold his surplus cattle

[6] Pelzer, *Cattlemen's Frontier*, pp. 160–169; Dale, *Range Cattle Industry*, p. 169; Bray, "Financing the Western Cattleman," p. 15.

to buy land. Others borrowed money at outrageous rates, to rent pastures or buy feed, and then lost everything.[7]

Soon after 1890, as the cattle business began to achieve a new stability, many new cattle-loan companies were formed, sometimes financed by the packers and again affiliated with large banks. The Panic of 1893 did not hit the cattle country as hard as it did the East, largely because of the previous liquidation, reorganization, and consequent sounder financial structure. While great Eastern banks were failing, those in the cattle-loan business remained solvent. Hence, cattle-loan paper was again in demand. In succeeding years there was some improvement in prices, and at the same time there was a revival of the old tendency to fatten the cattle, for final sale, on the farms of the corn belt. To finance these feeders, the commission men borrowed in the East at 4 and 5 per cent, and reloaned the money to the feeders at doubled rates to buy cattle. In order to get plenty of this easy money, the commission men took unnecessary risks with other people's capital.

Many ranchers were also bitten by the bug of quick profits. A cattleman with $15,000 worth of stock might borrow $12,000 on them to buy more, then borrow $10,000 on the new stock to buy still more, and continue the process till the loans became too small to bother with. By 1898, this practice was becoming almost universal. Some men were pasturing cattle representing several times their original capital, and the commission men were repeating the process by presenting mortgages to banks as collateral for new loans. Then there was another succession of severe winters, and in the late 1890's the collapse of the preceding decade was repeated. One speculative feeder in Kansas, who had started without a dollar in 1894, built up a paper fortune and in November, 1898, failed for $1,500,000, thus getting back again to his starting point. By 1900, the crisis was over and an industry, again reorganized, was reaching out tentatively for loans. By this time, interest rates were down to about 8 per cent, but investments were cautiously made.[8]

[7] Bray, "Financing the Western Cattleman," pp. 15–17; Edward Everett Dale, "The Cow Country in Transition," *Mississippi Valley Historical Review*, XXIV, No. 1 (June, 1937), pp. 18–19.

[8] Dale, *Range Cattle Industry*, p. 170; Clemen, *Livestock and Meat Industry*, p. 503; Bray, "Financing the Western Cattleman," pp. 18–20.

THE TRANSPORTATION PROBLEM

In transportation, as in credit relations, the experiences of the range country can well be exemplified by the cattle industry. The problems of sheepmen were not essentially different from those of the cattlemen, and the troubles of general farmers were similar to those of the western Prairies, accentuated by a little more distance. The story of Far Western transportation might well go deeply into detail on the wagon freighting companies, the stage coaches, and the pony express, but such agencies were mainly occupied in getting persons, materials, and messages across the Plains, rather than in supplying the needs of plainsmen themselves. Inasmuch as the expansion of the cattle industry coincided with the building of the Western railroads, the problem was one involving mainly the relations of shippers with the railroad companies.

Even before the first carload of cattle was shipped from Abilene, there was discussion as to the intelligence of railroad officials in dealing with this sort of traffic. McCoy said that when he interviewed the representatives of the Missouri Pacific for carload rates from Kansas City to St. Louis, he could not interest them at all and was ordered from the office. He then secured an agreement with the Hannibal and St. Joseph line for rates to Quincy, Illinois, whence the cattle could be shipped to Chicago. After some further hesitancy on the part of the Kansas Pacific to build a siding at Abilene, and furnish cars, the first trainload left that town in September, 1867. About a thousand carloads were shipped within a year, each car holding some twenty head. The cattle sold for from twenty-five to twenty-eight dollars each in Chicago, and the freight alone from Abilene was eight dollars. But, considering the fact that the price in Texas at the beginning of the drives was only from three to six dollars each, there was still much money in the business after the long drive and haul. There was some difference of opinion as to the eating qualities of the beef thus supplied to the East, but, even though as stringy and tough as generally described, it was cheap and the demand was great. The unfortunate outcome of attempts to ship cattle by river boats, in 1868, added to the popularity of the rail route from Abilene. Loaded at the mouth of the Red River on the lower Mississippi, packed so closely on the boat decks that they could not lie down, and going for a week or more without feed or water before unloading at Cairo, the cattle were in such bad condition as to discourage further efforts of that kind.[9]

An additional stimulus to railroad shipments came from a fierce rate war between the railroads from Chicago to the Atlantic coast in 1870. For a time the charge on a carload to Buffalo, Albany, or New York was as low as a dollar. Then some lines tried hauling free of charge, and there were cases of a bonus being paid the shipper for the privilege of carrying his cattle. Though this practice prevailed only east of Chicago, it allowed dealers there to pay higher

CATTLE RATES FROM THE NORTHERN PLAINS TO CHICAGO, IN 1884

On the Union Pacific Railroad			On the Northern Pacific Railroad		
From	Carload	Head	From	Carload	Head
Green River, Wyo.	$176.00	$8.80	Mandan, Dak. Ty.	$ 95.00	$4.75
Bitter Creek, Wyo.	166.00	8.30	Dickinson, Dak. Ty.	100.00	5.00
Rock Creek, Wyo.	133.00	6.65	Glendive, Mont.	124.00	6.20
Laramie, Wyo.	128.00	6.40	Miles City, Mont.	133.00	6.65
Cheyenne, Wyo.	119.00	5.95	Billings, Mont.	157.00	7.85
Pine Bluffs, Neb.	112.00	5.60	Livingston, Mont.	179.00	8.95
Ogallala, Neb.	95.00	4.75	Boseman, Mont.	190.00	9.50
Plum Creek, Neb.	95.00	4.75	Helena, Mont.	195.00	9.75

prices, and thus resulted in a rush of shipment from the West.[10] Such a state of affairs could not last long, and the later rate agreements and pools of the Eastern lines resulted in charges high enough to offset any earlier losses. The "Evener Combination" of 1873 was a pooling arrangement of the Pennsylvania, New York Central, and Erie lines to maintain rates of $115 a carload on cattle from Chicago to New York, with a $15 rebate to favored Chicago shippers known as the "Eveners." Aside from the great increase in rates, this agreement (terminated in 1878) tended to destroy the St. Louis market in favor of Chicago. While the earlier rate wars lasted, they were a great stimulus to the spread of the cattle industry on the northern Plains. In 1869, George Thompson shipped the first cattle out of Colorado, and three years later some fourteen

[9] McCoy, *Sketches of the Cattle Trade*, pp. 20, 42–43, 51–53, 104–105, 108–109, 148–149, 190–192, 236; J[acob] R[ichards] Dodge, ed., "The Texas Cattle Trade," U.S. Commissioner of Agriculture, *Report*, 1870, p. 350; Clemen, *Livestock and Meat Industry*, p. 193; Osgood, *Day of the Cattleman*, p. 27.

[10] Clemen, *Livestock and Meat Industry*, pp. 179–180.

thousand were sent by rail from that state. Then came the panic, when cattle were killed for their hides, horns, and tallow.[11]

At the height of the cattle boom, in 1884 and 1885, cattle rates over the Union Pacific and Northern Pacific railroads were considered rather low. The managers of those lines, at the time, were following a policy of encouraging the Plains cattle business. Some sample rates on these two railroads are presented (page 228) by way of illustration.

These rates averaged around 56 and 60 cents a hundred miles for each animal, which, contrary to many Western rates (see page 296, below), was not much above the 53 cents a hundred miles from Chicago to New York.[12]

As the breeds of cattle improved and higher prices arrived, in the late seventies, the new high rates on Atlantic coast shipments were easier to meet, but there was still some discontent over the fact that charges for beef were so much lower in proportion than on live cattle. This hampered the shipment of animals direct to the Eastern butchers. The rebates to Chicago shippers, coupled with increased rates on beef, quieted this complaint, but the benefits seem to have gone to speculative shippers rather than to the stock growers. Though, in later years, the cattlemen apparently were no more discriminated against in rates than unfavored Western interests in general, they did have a real grievance against the type of service furnished. In the earlier years, the cars were small and ill adapted for cattle, and, because the rates were by the carload, the tendency was to overcrowd. The roadbeds were rough; the couplers were of the link-and-pin variety, making stops and starts jerky. Consequently, when the weaker animals were thrown, they were trampled and sometimes killed by the others. When a prostrate brute was discovered in time, it was prodded with a sharp iron spike fastened to a long pole, and pulled by the tail with a screw-tipped pole hooked into the matted hair, till on its feet again. The number killed in transit averaged only about three in two thousand, and insurance was available at the rate of thirty cents a head. But the seven-or-eight-day trip had other bad effects. Many cattle were

[11] *Ibid.*, p. 180; Ora Brooks Peake, *The Colorado Range Cattle Industry* (Glendale, Cal.: The Arthur H. Clark Company, 1937), p. 260; Vest, "Transportation and Sale of Meat Products," pp. 2–3.

[12] Joseph Nimmo, "Range and Ranch Cattle Traffic," *House Executive Document* No. 267, 48 Cong., 2 Sess., pp. 59–60. Table, p. 228, is from this source.

so bruised as to make inferior meat, and the shrinkage from lack of feed and water took from one hundred to five hundred pounds from each animal. There was further complaint that the railroads, in league with the packers, would not furnish cars enough, presumably to beat down prices. On the other hand, since all cattlemen wanted to ship when the market was at its peak, the supplying of sufficient cars was a hard problem.[13]

Some of the shippers' grievances seem to have been well founded. An official investigation of 1871 showed that cattle trains were shunted to sidings, to wait for hours, giving precedence on the rails to most other kinds of service. The slowing up of transportation added to the disadvantages of the lack of feed and water, the inadequate ventilation, and the crowding. As to the car supply, early shippers sometimes put in their orders two or three months ahead of time, and then had to hold their herds at the shipping point for another month, or longer. Numerous lawsuits against the railroads resulted from losses caused through carelessness, and sometimes the shippers recovered damages. Shortly after 1880, the profits from cattle hauling, in addition to the pressure of public opinion, led to some needed improvements. Chutes were provided for loading and unloading, air brakes were installed on the cattle-express trains, which also carried parlor and dining cars for the use of shippers accompanying their cattle. Such trains were given the right of way, in preference even to mail trains. Some railroads also began to install "cattle restaurants," where the stock might be fed and watered every two hundred miles or twelve hours. Some cars had feed and water troughs that could be filled from the outside. Ordinary cars were unloaded three times between Denver and Chicago, to feed and water the cattle and rest them in the yards. Before 1890, numerous patents were granted for safe cars and for feeding and watering devices. The Newell car had collapsible troughs and feed racks; others had compartments to prevent injuries. The Mather car was said to decrease shrinkage by 65 per cent.[14]

---

[13] Frederic Logan Paxson, "The Cow Country," *American Historical Review*, XXII, No. 1 (October, 1916), 81; James E. Downing, "Pioneer Transportation for Livestock," *Breeder's Gazette*, LXXX, No. 8 (August 25, 1921), 249; U.S. Commissioner of Agriculture, *Report*, 1870, p. 251; Vest, "Transportation and Sale of Meat Products," p. 18; Peake, *Colorado Range Cattle Industry*, pp. 262, 264–266; Clemen, *Livestock and Meat Industry*, pp. 195–197.

[14] Peake, *Colorado Range Cattle Industry*, pp. 261, 263, 265–266; Charles

Shipment by carload rates, instead of by weight, prevailed east of Chicago till 1879, east of St. Louis till 1888, and east of Cheyenne and Denver until 1908. William H. Vanderbilt's slogan of "the public be damned" was applied by the cattle haulers wherever they could make it effective. In addition to the "Evener" charges of 1873–1878, the freight from the range to Chicago or other centers was correspondingly high. A hundred dollars a car from Laramie and two hundred from Nevada, to Chicago, were considered special rates. Favored shippers could get rebates, which further spread discontent among their rivals. There were also yardage charges of twenty-five cents and commission fees of fifty cents a head. In 1885, the freight on beef from Chicago to New York was seventy cents a hundredweight, which was a fair equivalent to the forty cents for live animals. As an example of what these charges amounted to, in 1879 the Wyoming shipper had to deduct from $6.90 to $12.50 from what he got for each cow, to cover the freight to Chicago; and the Chicago price was lower than that of the Atlantic coast because of additional rates to the ultimate destination.[15]

RELATIONS WITH PACKERS: MARKETS

Before the Texas cattle moved to the northern Plains the Chicago livestock market had experienced years of growth. The Union Stock Yards on Halstead Street, opened on December 25, 1865, became the market for the animals of the Middle West. Packing at that time was largely a seasonal affair, for, without adequate refrigeration, the drying, smoking, and pickling of meats could not well be carried on in the warm and hot months. Pork was still the main product handled. In the season of 1867–1868, over 796,000 hogs and 35,000 cattle were packed at Chicago. But some 1,618,000 live and 265,000 dressed hogs had been received, of which over 1,000,000 had been reshipped. Also, nearly 314,000 live cattle had arrived,

---

S[umner] Plumb, *Marketing Farm Animals* (Boston: Ginn and Company, c.1927), pp. 29, 116–119; Clemen, *Livestock and Meat Industry*, pp. 195, 198–200.

[15] Plumb, *Marketing Farm Animals*, p. 77; Clemen, *Livestock and Meat Industry*, p. 200; Josiah Bushnell Grinnell, "The Cattle Industries of the United States," *Agricultural Review and Journal of the American Agricultural Association*, II, No. 2 (May, 1882), p. 16; Peake, *Colorado Range Cattle Industry*, p. 267; Clara M. Love, "History of the Cattle Industry in the Southwest," *The Southwestern Historical Quarterly*, XIX, No. 4 (April, 1916), 399; Osgood, *Day of the Cattleman*, p. 51.

two thirds of them for live resale. Nelson Morris and Philip D. Armour got started on a big scale, at Chicago and Milwaukee respectively, as a result of Civil War contracts, and the firm of Plankinton and Armour helped make Milwaukee a worthy rival of Chicago in the industry. In fact, as late as 1882 that company handled nearly 422,000 of the 486,000 hogs packed in the Wisconsin metropolis.

It was not till nearly 1870 that the packing industry entered the new era of development based on range beef cattle. As early as 1863, the Commissioner of Agriculture had pointed out the reduced ratio of cattle to population, a situation that was growing worse east of Ohio, but he felt that Texas cattle could not be depended on to remedy the deficiency, because they were too wild "to be driven east in great numbers." Then, in the later sixties, the growing centralization of industry, and temporary national prosperity, led to a still greater demand by the city workers, who were becoming beef eaters. The packers played a definite part in the stimulation of this demand. Philip D. Armour told the Vest committee that the cattlemen were "indebted to the dressed-beef industry . . . for the successful efforts of its promoters in opening up new markets in communities which were not formerly beef consuming." [16]

Although Armour may have been entirely correct in his statement, it is at least as certain that the packers, like the railroads, wanted to get all the profits from the business that could be obtained, and the demand for beef was not such as to give great profits to all. While the cattlemen would not cooperate sufficiently to regulate production and preserve the range, yet they were driven into defensive organizations to combat the packers. But the resulting contest was like that between the producers of crude petroleum and the Standard Oil Company in the same years. The packers' combination was smaller than any devised by the cattlemen, more closely knit, better financed, and powerful enough to dictate. Especially after the Panic of 1873, the cattlemen began to organize,

[16] Clemen, *Livestock and Meat Industry*, p. 173; Chicago Board of Trade, *Tenth Annual Statement of the Trade and Commerce of Chicago, 1867–1868* (John F. Beaty, comp., Chicago: Horton & Leonard, Book and Job Printers, 1868), pp. 56, 58, 64; Milwaukee Chamber of Commerce, *Twenty-fourth Annual Report of the Trade and Commerce of Milwaukee, 1881–1882* (Wm. J. Langson, comp., Milwaukee: Sentinel Company, 1882), p. 111; U.S. Commissioner of Agriculture, *Report*, 1863, p. 257; Vest, "Transportation and Sale of Meat Products," p. 423.

corporations entered the business, and marketing pools were formed. Stock growers' associations, local, state, and interstate in scope, tried to influence the activities of the packers as well as those of the railroads, and used the boycott as their principal weapon.[17]

The Wyoming Stock Graziers' Association, established in 1871 by herdsmen in the vicinity of Cheyenne, was apparently the first state organization. But, within a short time, the Colorado Stock Growers' Association and the Southern Colorado Association were also formed, to stem the flood of Texas cattle. The first-mentioned Colorado organization was the stronger, and it invited delegates from neighboring territories to attend its meetings. Then, in 1873, the Laramie County Stock Growers' Association, destined to become the most powerful on the High Plains, was formed. In 1879, the name was changed to the Wyoming Stock Growers' Association. By 1885, with a membership of 363, it reigned supreme in Wyoming and also held jurisdiction in Dakota, Nebraska, and Montana. Other associations were founded in Montana and elsewhere. In November, 1884, and again a year later, a national convention of cattle growers and shippers was held in St. Louis, where the grievances against railroads and packers were aired. The members also discussed the idea of a national cattle trail from South to North, to be unobstructed and so guarded as not to interfere with quarantines. But this was merely the death rattle of the long drive, and the trail was never opened. The setting up of a Bureau of Animal Industry in the United States Department of Agriculture has been attributed to the agitation of the first St. Louis meeting; but agitation over this matter was already strong before the convention met, and the bureau might well have been established anyway. Western cattlemen at the time were wanting a quarantine against Eastern bulls infected with pleuropneumonia, and the packers were opposing any federal legislation on the subject lest it might also result in a check to the flow of Texas cattle to their markets. The bureau was a sort of compromise.[18]

The original bill would have given the President authority to

[17] Paxson, "The Cow Country," pp. 78–79; Osgood, *Day of the Cattleman,* p. 106; Pelzer, *Cattlemen's Frontier,* pp. 76–77; Peake, *Colorado Range Cattle Industry,* pp. 103–168 *passim.*

[18] Osgood, *Day of the Cattleman,* pp. 118–132, 169–172, 179–181; Pelzer, *Cattlemen's Frontier,* pp. 73–84; *Breeder's Gazette,* V, No. 15 (April 10, 1884), 542–543; D. E. Salmon, "Pleuro-Pneumonia in Illinois," *Breeder's Gazette,* VI, No. 12 (September 18, 1884), 421–422.

declare any state or territory under quarantine, if it failed to co-
operate, but the measure, as adopted, merely gave the bureau the
authority to make rules to suppress diseases, to invite state and territorial cooperation, and to bar cattle actually diseased, from transportation. The failure of the measure to provide vigorous quarantines led the Western interests to feel that they had been sold out
to the packers, but it also seems likely that the passage of any bill
at all was partially due to the fear of the Chicago packers and buyers that, otherwise, they would too far antagonize the Wyoming
Stock Growers' Association.[19]

In their resentment against the packers' show of power, the cattlemen began looking for other markets, and gave attention to
Moreton Frewen, the English manager of the Powder Cattle Company. His scheme was for the exportation of cattle, by way of
Canada, to England. The Wyoming Stock Growers' Association authorized Frewen to place the plan before the Privy Council, representing the advantages to English farmers of getting cattle they
could fatten in a few months, instead of relying on the Irish yearlings that required two years. Before this time, the Privy Council
had placed restrictions on the importation of inferior American
cattle, and needed to be convinced that the Western animals had no
pleuropneumonia. The Council was friendly to Frewen, but decided
that Canadian consent would also have to be secured. Here was an
obstacle that could not be overcome. The Canadians wanted the
English market for themselves, said they could supply it, and trem-
bled at the outcropping of Texas fever on the ranges of Wyoming
in recent months. Yet, as was pointed out, the Canadians allowed
shipment over their railroads to Duluth, and many American cattle were matured on the Canadian range without spreading the
disease.[20]

Another device to circumvent the packers, during the boom
period before 1885, was the erection of packing houses on the
Plains. A Frenchman, the Marquis de Mores, as he was called, led
in this effort. He held about seven thousand acres around Medora,
(North) Dakota, the headquarters for 27,000 cattle and 10,000
sheep. Married to the daughter of an American banker, he could

[19] Osgood, *Day of the Cattleman*, pp. 172–173.
[20] *Ibid.*, pp. 108–112; [Great Britain] Parliamentary *Accounts and Papers*, 1884–
1885, LXXIII, No. 19, pp. 3–12.

get capital from New York, and with it he built slaughterhouses at a number of places in Dakota and Montana. He also erected several cold-storage houses, and procured refrigerator cars to deliver fresh beef in Duluth, St. Paul, Chicago, and New York. The Nimmo report of 1885 declared:

This enterprise and a few kindred ones of lesser magnitude operating in other portions of the cattle belt have got beyond the experimental stage, and are evidently destined to further development. They encounter the opposition of a large interest engaged in the handling of live-stock in transit, and especially of those vested in extensive stock yards in Chicago. . . . The railroad companies being fully equipped with cattle cars naturally take a conservative view of and are disposed to look with small favor on a change that will make this equipment useless and would require the construction of expensive refrigerator cars.

In 1884, about 8,000 cattle were slaughtered in Montana and the dressed beef was shipped to the East.[21]

But the hopes of the Western packers were not realized. Because the supply of matured beef was not year round, slaughtering on the Plains proved impractical except for taking care of the local market. At Medora the cattle came in during a ninety-day period, and in the remaining nine months of the year the plant was idle. Furthermore, only medium-grade cattle were offered, and the small slaughter houses were not equipped to make use of the by-products that furnished so much of the profits for the greater packers. Then, because of the large amount of capital needed to operate the large ranches, there was not enough surplus to finance big packing enterprises. The cattlemen themselves supported the endeavor very slightly, for they loved the annual trips to the Eastern markets. So they complained of the treatment they received at Chicago, Kansas City, and elsewhere, and continued to support the system.[22]

After 1885, the cattlemen found themselves more than ever at the mercy of the packers. A crowded range and bad weather were combined with falling prices. In five years following January, 1884, the price of Western cattle declined from $5.60 to $3.75 a hundred pounds, and for a time in 1887 they reached $1.00, while the price of beef to the consumer was little changed. The Matador Land

---

[21] Nimmo, "Range and Ranch Cattle Traffic," pp. 64, 81 (quotation); Osgood, Day of the Cattleman, pp. 107–108.

[22] John Clay, My Life on the Range (Chicago: privately printed, c.1924), pp. 195–196.

and Cattle Company complained, in 1886, that the Chicago industry was in the hands of a small clique that fixed the price of cattle and prevented extensive competition. The findings of the Vest committee of the United States Senate came to the same conclusions. Its report pointed out that, in a brief time, the methods of distribution in the cattle industry had been revolutionized. Whereas the buyers and butchers had once gone from one stockman to another, competing in their bids, now the growers could market their animals in large numbers in a few cities only, such as Chicago, Kansas City, Omaha, St. Louis, Pittsburgh, and Cincinnati. The last two catered mainly to the local territory. The Chicago packers—Armour, Swift, Morris, and Hammond—dominated their own market and controlled prices elsewhere.[23] Emphasis was placed on interrelations between railroad combinations, stockyard companies, and the leading packers.

This revolution in the manner and markets for selling cattle has been caused by the construction of railroads, subsequent combination between these corporations, and the establishment of stock-yards owned by parties controlling the railroads upon whose lines these yards are located, but especially by the fact that a few enterprising men at Chicago, engaged in the packing and dressed beef business, are able through their enormous capital to centralize and control the beef business at that point.[24]

Conditions in the cattle business remained bad for several more years. In 1890, prices took a new drop, largely because of over-production in relation to market conditions. But this was a matter the herdsmen now tried to correct. For three more years they shipped even more cattle to market, and spayed heifers till there was danger of a cattle famine. Cattle were considered poor property, and owners tried to get rid of them. A Kansas City market paper said: "If you don't believe the cattle market is busted, come in and see for yourself, but don't bring any cattle with you." There was noticeable improvement in 1897, and this continued through the next year. More cattle were fed in Kansas and Nebraska by 1898 than ever before, and in Colorado, Wyoming, and Nevada the herdsmen were feeding every animal they could get. It would

---

[23] Vest, "Transportation and Sale of Meat Products," p. 1; Osgood, *Day of the Cattleman*, pp. 105–106; Clay, *Life on the Range*, p. 319.
[24] Vest, "Transportation and Sale of Meat Products," p. 2.

seem that the efforts at restriction of output in the earlier years had not gone as far as was expected. Yet, the peak of 37,651,000 beef cattle in the United States in 1892 (as counted by the Department of Agriculture, the enumeration being rather confusing in those years) had been lowered to 29,264,000 in 1898, and was to decline to 27,610,000 by 1900.[25] The problems of relations with the packers remained unsolved.

The marketing of sheep and wool was somewhat different. The wool dealers were mainly in the big cities of the East (particularly Boston), but they sent their representatives out on the range before or during the shearing season, and bought directly from the growers or from local merchants. The buyers spent much time going over the wool, fleece by fleece. As the methods of cleaning improved, it became possible, about 1900, to inspect only a sample from a group of bales. The original Mexican sheep had a very light fleece, but the improvement of the breed could be rapid. Better grades of animals in Nebraska averaged eight-pound fleeces, and Grinnell gave some credence to a ram that produced forty pounds. The price of sheep in 1880 was from $5.00 to $6.40 a hundred pounds, but by 1893 they were down to $1.00 and $2.00 in Chicago. At that time the wool market was stagnant, and Australian sheep were killed for their pelts alone, for which there were many uses.[26]

The importance of the Chicago livestock market, and the center there of the beef trust, brings it special attention in the literature of the subject. But other, older centers were still prominent. In the twenty years before 1884, the cities of New York and Buffalo had exceeded all Western rivals except Chicago, while Cincinnati and Philadelphia had approximated Kansas City. In the same period Chicago had received 18,000,000 cattle and shipped 12,000,000; the figures for St. Louis being 5,900,000 and 3,500,000. From the

[25] John T. McNeeley, "The Cattle Industry of Colorado, Wyoming, and Nevada, and the Sheep Industry of Colorado in 1897," U.S. Department of Agriculture, Bureau of Animal Industry, Fifteenth Annual Report, 1898 (Washington: Government Printing Office, 1899), pp. 377–379; Peake, Colorado Range Cattle Industry, quotation, pp. 276–277; Agricultural Yearbook, 1899, p. 818. See Twelfth Census: Agriculture, I, clxii–clxiv, for explanation of discrepancy in the enumeration of cattle, 1890–1900.

[26] Arthur Harrison Cole, The American Wool Manufacture (Cambridge: Harvard University Press, 1926), II, 74–76; Grinnell, Cattle Industries of the United States, p. 16; Alvin T. Steinel, History of Agriculture in Colorado, 1858–1926 (Fort Collins: State Agricultural College, 1926), pp. 148–149.

opening of the Kansas City Stockyards in 1871, until November, 1884, that market had received over 3,600,000 cattle, of which 2,800,000 were reshipped to the East, the remainder being for local consumption and packing. Then, toward the close of the 1880's the Chicago companies began establishing branch plants at such places as Kansas City, Omaha, and St. Joseph. Such houses handled pork and mutton, as well as beef, and specialized in by-products. The Armour company even became involved in wheat deals. Before 1900, there were also important markets at Denver, Fort Worth, Wichita, Sioux City, Cedar Rapids, Ottumwa, and Mason City. In the four Iowa towns there were several small but important firms.[27]

PUBLIC POLICY ON THE RANGE: FENCES

From the time of the occupation of the range country till the end of the century, territorial and state laws reflected the supremacy of the stock raiser; and the activities of the Wyoming Stock Growers' Association are typical of the organized efforts on the range. This group combated cattle thieves, fought the railroads and packers, made regulations for roundups, and got legislation for stock inspection, sanitation, and means of determining the ownership of mavericks. Congress itself was influenced by its lobbyists. Though the associations or groups of neighborhood vigilantes might pay personal attention to newcomers on the range, to cattle-and-horse thieves, and homesteaders, they relied mainly on the legislatures for the solution of many other problems. Or it might better express the case to say that they sought legislation to give legal covering to policies they were determined to evolve anyway, on such things as fencing, quarantines, leasing of lands, and water rights.[28]

The earlier laws regarding fences reflect accurately the extent of power of general farmers as opposed to range riders in the various states and territories. Wherever the livestock were to be

---

[27] Edward W. Perry, "Live Stock and Meat Traffic of Chicago," U.S. Department of Agriculture, Bureau of Animal Industry, *First Annual Report*, 1884 (Washington: Government Printing Office, 1885), p. 247; Louis F[ranklin] Swift, in collaboration with Arthur Van Vlissingen, *The Yankee of the Yards: The Biography of Gustavus Franklin Swift* (Chicago: A. W. Shaw Company, 1927), pp. 131–137; Clemen, *Livestock and Meat Industry*, pp. 451–461; Frank S. Hastings, *A Ranchman's Recollections* (Chicago: The Breeder's Gazette, 1921), pp. 141–142.

[28] Dan W. Greenburg, *Sixty Years: . . . The Cattle Industry in Wyoming. . . .* (Cheyenne: Wyoming Stock Growers Association, 1932), pp. 15–31 *passim*.

fenced away from the farms, the farmers were in control; where the farmer had to see to the protection of his crops, the stockman had the upper hand. Likewise, the degree of strictness or laxity of such legislation reveals the source of control. The supremacy of farming interests in Kansas and Nebraska is only to be expected. Yet, down to the end of the century western Oklahoma was still "declared a free range country." [29] But, as fencing became the established practice of stockmen themselves, the problem grew more complex. In general, laws were adopted, repealed, and repassed, with the trend toward enclosure ascendant. The whole matter is also closely connected with federal land policy and the leasing regulations adopted by the states. As late as 1879, the Wyoming Stock Growers' Association inveighed against cattle fences as unwise and dangerous to the animals, and, as has already been shown, there was much truth to this contention.[30]

If the herdsman was to be held liable for damages done by his animals in breaking through fences, he was determined that the law should be quite specific on what constituted a fence. So, in a short time, the statutes of every territory and state in the range country contained definitions in minute detail. The construction and materials had to come up to standard requirements, or else the builder of the fence must assume his own responsibility. Nebraska, with a large farming population, was laxest: "Any structure or hedge or ditch in the nature of a fence, used for purposes of enclosure, which is such as good husbandmen generally keep, shall be deemed a lawful fence." Official fence viewers were empowered to settle disputes. Colorado defined barbed-wire fences in 1879, and Kansas in 1883. In 1885, Montana specified four strands (or three and a top pole), but, in 1888, Wyoming stipulated only three. In the early sixties, before the swarm of cattle on the Plains, fencing laws favored the farmers in Colorado as much as in Kansas. Farmers might plant without enclosures, and it was the responsibility of owners of livestock to pen them up or keep them herded off land in crops. But, in the 1870's, with the coming of an open-range economy, the liability was shifted to the farmers, though in

[29] Oklahoma, *Session Laws,* 1899 (Guthrie: 1899), pp. 58–59. The state and territorial laws appear under such a variety of names and publishers that, hereafter, they will be referred to merely by the name of the commonwealth and the year of enactment.

[30] Greenburg, *Cattle Industry in Wyoming,* pp. 23–24.

general the matter was put on a county local-option basis. On the petition of a given number of landowners in the county, a special election could be held to determine whether a district might be fenced off entirely from animals. Elsewhere the open range would prevail.[31] On the whole, this seems to have been a very sensible solution of the problem. In 1872, Colorado permitted the Union Colony, three fourths of its members consenting, to enclose as much of their land as they desired, for three years. In 1888, Wyoming, by requiring removable sections of specific design across public roads, took care of the interests of farmers who were cut off from the world by the fences of grazing syndicates.[32] By 1890, the influence of the federal government regarding illegal fences was beginning to be felt, but contests between ranchers and farmers continued.

PUBLIC POLICY: QUARANTINES

In view of the fact that Texas fever disappeared among cattle after a single winter on the northern Plains (even in Kansas), it would seem that, after the first scare, there were other reasons for the efforts to shut out Texas longhorns. The desire to prevent improved cattle from reversion to the earlier type and the determination to preserve the range for their own herds seem to have been uppermost in the minds of the quarantine advocates. If the Texans might drive their yearlings northward, they could preserve the Southern pastures at the expense of the other section. Thus, when the Cattle Growers' Convention of 1884, in St. Louis, opposed the idea of a national cattle trail, the fear of Texas fever was only an excuse to prevent any admission of the true motives, which would appear to have been defensible enough in themselves. This effort to protect the grass had an even earlier origin than the longhorn invasion. In 1861, Colorado barred nonresident grazing in some counties, and added to the list in 1862. In 1879 the state imposed an annual grazing tax of fifty cents each for cattle and twenty

[31] Kansas (1860), p. 123; Kansas (1864), p. 64; Kansas (1883), pp. 167–168; Colorado (1862), p. 68; Colorado (1864), pp. 87–88; Colorado (1865), p. 61; Colorado (1866), pp. 55, 86; Colorado (1872), p. 183; Colorado (1874), pp. 132–134; Colorado (1879), pp. 68–69, 235–236; Nebraska (1866, Revised), quotation, p. 10; Montana (1871–1872), p. 373; Montana (1885), pp. 76–78; Wyoming (1869), p. 421; Wyoming (1888), pp. 69–70.
[32] Colorado (1872), pp. 129–130; Wyoming (1888), p. 71.

cents for sheep, to be collected from nonresidents. In 1901, Montana enacted a similar law for animals brought into the state. Over-stocking became an acute problem after 1885, when cattle in Wyoming, bought by book count at thirty dollars a head, had to be sold by tally count at fifteen or twenty dollars.[33]

The application of quarantine and inspection laws was of positive benefit in excluding diseased Eastern bulls. The Wyoming association maintained eighteen inspection stations for Texas cattle and nine for Eastern. At these points estrays also were cut out from the herds, and in 1888–1889 these were three out of each hundred inspected. The estrays were sold and the proceeds given to the proper owners, who, in those two years, received nearly $16,000 they otherwise would never have seen. Small as the sum might seem, it was appreciated in those hard years. On grounds of Texas fever, the quarantine laws of Kansas and Colorado were more defensible than for regions to their north. There were no wintering grounds between them and the Southern pastures, and so those states had to take the brunt of whatever infection was carried over their borders. In 1861, Kansas barred the driving of cattle from Texas, Arkansas, or Indian Territory over the state line between April 1 and November 1 of each year. In the remaining months the danger was at a minimum. In 1865, such entries were forbidden at any time. This law was repealed in 1866 but was re-enacted in 1867, with entry narrowed to December, January, and February. The restrictions were modified in 1876, by the setting aside of a quarantine herding ground in the western portion of the state. There, the cattle might be held even in the warmer months. In 1877, the area was extended, but herders of Southern cattle had to secure the written permission of resident owners. In 1881, the older prohibitions were re-enacted, and in 1884 the state Live Stock Sanitary Commission was given quarantine powers. In 1885, the commission required health certificates for cattle admitted between March 1 and December 1, but, in 1891, entry was limited to December and January.[34] Other range states and territories

[33] Frank Wilkeson, "Cattle-Raising on the Plains," *Harper's New Monthly Magazine*, LXXII, No. 431 (April, 1886), 792; Colorado (1861), p. 133; Colorado (1862), p. 96; Colorado (1879), pp. 180–182; Montana (1901), pp. 57–61; W. E. Guthrie, "The Open Range Cattle Business in Wyoming," *Annals of Wyoming*, V, No. 1 (July, 1927), 28–30.

[34] Greenburg, *Cattle Industry in Wyoming*, pp. 32–38; Kansas (1861), p. 280; Kansas (1865), pp. 159–160; Kansas (1866), p. 248; Kansas (1867), pp. 263–264;

passed more or less similar quarantine laws; Colorado in 1867, 1879, and 1885; Wyoming in 1882; Nebraska in 1883, 1885, 1887, and 1901; Montana in 1885; South Dakota in 1893; and Oklahoma in 1895, 1897, and 1901.[35]

PUBLIC POLICY: WATER RIGHTS

Only gradually did the Western commonwealths learn that the English common law as to riparian rights could not be made to work in an arid or subhumid region. The English rule was that the owner of land along a stream could demand that nobody should divert water before it reached him. He was entitled to an undiminished supply. The trouble in the West was that, with not enough water for all, the man who owned the banks of the stream could control the land behind it to the next watershed. Another abuse was that of overappropriation, meaning that certain persons were allowed so much of the water that others had to do without. This ultimately resulted in the rivers being pumped dry for irrigation, near their sources, while farther downstream, probably in another state, farms were left without their earlier supply. A third misapplication of the old common law had to do with private ownership of the water, aside from its use in connection with the adjoining land. The rule of first come, first served was applied in various of the early territorial legislatures. Colorado, in 1862, provided that irrigation canals from streams could be constructed only when they would not interfere with the prior rights of earlier users. A like guarantee was included in the later state constitution, and reaffirmed by an act of 1879. Similar provisions can be traced through the laws of Montana, Wyoming, Nebraska, Kansas, Oklahoma, and doubtless in all the rest of the Far West.[36]

Kansas (1876), p. 316; Kansas (1877), pp. 241–242; Kansas (1881), p. 292; Kansas (1883), pp. 218–219; Kansas (1884), p. 17; Kansas (1885), pp. 308–310; Kansas (1891), pp. 346–348.

[35] Colorado (1867), p. 86; Colorado (1879), p. 191; Colorado (1885), pp. 335–336; Wyoming (1882), pp. 81–85; Nebraska (1883), p. 59; Nebraska (1885), pp. 73–89; Nebraska (1887), p. 82; Nebraska (1901), pp. 49–54; Montana (1885), pp. 31–36; South Dakota (1893), p. 260; Oklahoma (1895), pp. 257–265; Oklahoma (1897), pp. 237–240; Oklahoma (1901), pp. 171–176.

[36] William E. Smythe, "The Struggle for Water in the West," *Atlantic Monthly,* LXXXVI, No. 517 (November, 1900), 646–654, is a good summary of the problem. See also the *Session Laws,* as in the preceding note.

The states were also about equally troubled by overappropriation. Time after time, laws were passed giving lands not on a river's bank rights to the water, and then stating that, if there was insufficient water, it should be meted out among the users at the discretion of a district commissioner. In 1886, Kansas made some effort to avoid this dividing up of the water in ways that gave nobody enough. But Wyoming was first to abandon precedent entirely and deal with the situation in a realistic fashion. In 1888, before statehood, Wyoming adopted an irrigation code requiring that the flow of streams should be measured and existing claims readjusted, and providing adequate supervision. Also, it was the first state to decree that water goes with the land.[37] In view of the fact that there was water enough for the irrigation of only a small proportion of the whole area, it was not only sensible but also humane to apportion the water to places where it could be best used, and to discourage in a positive fashion futile hopes for its diversion elsewhere. The rest of the land was better devoted to stock raising anyway.

The earlier public policy of separation of water and land rights had encouraged settlers to take up homesteads where they thought there was free water, only to find that they had to buy their water rights from monopolists charging all the traffic would bear. For example, in 1893, Colorado provided for deeding water rights the same way as real estate. But two years earlier, Wyoming was setting a precedent that would keep the two rights together. By 1898, Governor William A. Richards of Wyoming was demanding that federal lands be ceded to the state so that the policy could be further worked out. Not till 1901 was Colorado beginning to catch up with Wyoming.[38] But, even then, the problem could be solved only in part. Most of the best rivers for irrigation were interstate in their flow. Often, as at Garden City, Kansas, the first use of the river had occurred remote from the source. At Garden City, a profitable irrigation system of farming was developed. Then the practice was copied in Colorado, which was upstream. With no

[37] Colorado (1861), pp. 67–68; Montana (1867), p. 33; Colorado (1879), pp. 96–97; Kansas (1886), p. 154; Wyoming (1888), pp. 115–122.
[38] Smythe, "Struggle for Water in the West," pp. 648–649; Colorado (1893), p. 298; Wyoming (1890–1891), pp. 335–336; National Stock Growers' Convention, *Proceedings*, I (Denver: News Job Printing Company, 1898), 86; Colorado (1901), pp. 83–94.

coordination between the laws of the two states, Garden City was desolated. What was needed here was federal regulation of water rights, if interstate agreements could not be negotiated.

At the end of the century, many of the problems of the range country were still unsolved. The upward curve of gold supply, along with other forces operating the world over, was bringing back higher prices for cattle, wool, sheep, and wheat. A few years of relative prosperity were ahead, after which the enigmas were to return in bewildering perplexity. But before 1900 the lines of future activity were well drawn and visible. Individualism was still at its height. A new cycle of wet years was enough to tempt farmers and farming corporations farther west than they could permanently endure. The hard experiences of another generation, and more, were still to be withstood, before it could be seen whether the farmers and ranchers would work out their problems together, or have to submit to rigid federal control, alien to their traditions.

CHAPTER XI

Specialized Agriculture and
Eastern Adjustments

CONNECTICUT AS A CASE STUDY

WHILE the agricultural frontier was moving westward with more speed than ever before in the history of the country, farmers in the North Atlantic states often had to make adjustments quite as violent as those of the homesteaders on the Plains. The Easterners, for the most part, lived on farms that had been in the family for generations, and they knew the possibilities of the soil. But the higher price of an acre, the slight fertility of most acres, and a topography that compelled the breaking up of farms into fields hardly larger than a Western corral, unfitted the Eastern farmer for competition with the meat and cereal products coming from vastly larger, more fertile, and cheaper Western farms. Freight charges from the West were generally so high that the Atlantic coast farmer could still grow some animals and grain for strictly local consumption. But the growth of urbanization was so great that, even had the American West not existed, the Eastern farmers would have been totally incapable of meeting the demands. Like England, those states would have had to depend on newer farming areas in other parts of the world—assuming, of course, that urbanization would have been as great without the wealth of the West to draw on. Many adjustments to new conditions had been made before 1860. Already the centers of cereal production had shifted west of the Appalachians. But more new situations had to be faced in the next forty years. Sometimes the farmer sold out and started westward himself. Again, in many cases, he merely abandoned his farm and moved to town. It may be that the study of one state will serve as an illustration of the broader problem. Connecticut may not be typical of the East, but it is in the very heart of the great industrial area of America, and it is chosen as a case study to which conditions in other states may be compared.

THE INFLUENCE OF WESTERN COMPETITION

The influence of Western competition was well understood by Professor William H. Brewer when, at the beginning of the 1890's, he told the Connecticut Department of Agriculture that the enormous crops of the West, under the new methods of agriculture, created a situation such that "the New England farmer has found his products selling at lower prices because of the new, fierce and rapidly increasing competition. One by one he has had to abandon the growing of this or that crop because the West crowded him beyond the paying point. . . ."[1] In 1897, another phase of the subject was considered in these words: "Ours is a grazing country. The pastures are extensive, well watered, well sheltered; and hay is considered dear when it sells at ten dollars per ton. But in raising sheep the profit is doubtful; and as to fattening cattle, that industry, once a leading one in this part of New England, was long since abandoned owing to Western competition."[2]

That such estimates as these were no mere dolorous clamorings is attested by the census and by figures from the Department of Agriculture. In 1860, New England had grown over 1,000,000 bushels of wheat; in 1899, less than 137,000. Corn declined in the same period from 9,165,000 bushels to 6,615,000. Oats remained about stationary, around 11,000,000 bushels. Rye fell from nearly 1,500,000 bushels to less than a third that amount; beef cattle from 625,000 head to 474,000; sheep from 1,780,000 head to 585,000. The yield of barley was slightly increased, but it was little more than 1,000,000 bushels. The hay crop was less than 4,000,000 tons at each reckoning. Dairy cattle had increased from 680,000 head

[1] William H. Brewer, "The Past and Future of Connecticut Agriculture," Connecticut Board of Agriculture, *Twenty-Fourth Annual Report*, 1890 (Hartford: The Case, Lockwood & Brainard Company, 1891), p. 165.
[2] Philip Morgan and Alvan F. Sanborn, "The Problems of Rural New England," *The Atlantic Monthly*, LXXIX, No. 475 (May, 1897), 584.

to 960,000.[3] In none of the last three items was the increase anywhere near that of the population, nor was the total growth anywhere closely correlated with the decline of crops in general. By the end of the century, it was also noted that it required from about seven to nine dollars in labor cost to grow an acre of corn in the Middle West, but nearly seventeen dollars in New England.[4]

During the same forty years, the improved land in New England decreased from 12,216,000 acres to 8,134,000, or approximately a third, while the increase in the Middle Atlantic states (from 27,000,000 to 31,000,000) was hardly enough to make up the deficit for the Northeast as a whole. The bulk of New England's improved land, in 1900, was in Maine and Vermont, in which more nearly frontier conditions prevailed. Connecticut had 2,312,000 acres in farms, but only 1,065,000 acres were improved.[5] In the same year it was said that "the most unobservant of travelers through the agricultural districts of the Nutmeg State cannot fail to note the brush-grown highways, the down-fallen walls, the decayed fences, dilapidated buildings and neglected fields which mark the decadence of the true agricultural spirit." Complaints would be heard that "farming does not pay," and also that "most of the hired labor . . . is of foreign birth, transient, ignorant and unreliable. . . ." The conclusion would be that, "notwithstanding the many splendid, well kept farms in the state, Connecticut farming has fallen far below its high standard of a half century ago." [6] The Secretary of Agriculture, commenting on the abandoned farms of New England, at the same time, said: "A personal inspection of some of these farms shows that they are not abandoned on account of sterility of soil, but are in many cases capable of affording a good living to industrious farmers, and under more favorable auspices than are farms in some of our newer States, on account of nearness to market, educational institutions, and other desirable environments." [7]

[3] *Eighth Census: Agriculture,* pp. 184–187; *Agricultural Yearbook,* 1899, pp. 765–770, 820–821.

[4] Frederick Irving Anderson, *The Farmer of To-morrow* (New York: The Macmillan Company, 1913), p. 18.

[5] *Eighth Census: Agriculture,* p. vii; *Twelfth Census: Agriculture,* I, 142; *Statistical Abstract of the United States,* 1926, pp. 580–581.

[6] C. N. Hall, "Some Features of Old Connecticut Farming," *New England Magazine,* XXII, n.s., No. 5 (July, 1900), 549.

[7] *Agricultural Yearbook,* 1899, p. 60.

ABANDONMENT OF FARMS

The most noticeable adjustment to Western competition, and the one getting the most attention, was the abandonment of farms. As the term was used, an abandoned farm was one formerly kept up and cultivated, but now no longer occupied, and falling to decay. Sometimes the meadow land might be mowed, but nothing was being done to build up the soil, and vegetation was allowed to run wild. One such farm, characteristic of many, was advertised for sale in the following terms.

Farm of sixty acres; mowing, eight; pasture, eighteen; woodland, thirty-four; suitable for cultivation, twelve. Almost all the grass can be cut with a machine. One-story house, five rooms, in need of some repair. Small barn, in good repair. Good well at house, and running water back of barn. Twenty apple and twelve other fruit trees. Railroad station, Leverett, six miles; post office, Shutesbury, one mile. Price, $400; cash at sale, $100; interest on balance, four per cent.[8]

The truth about a good number of such farms is that abandonment was the proper remedy. Because of their location, lack of original fertility, soil exhaustion, rocky nature, and the like, they were best adapted for growing wood and timber, or at most for pasturage, rather than for general farming. Occasionally the farm had been used to cater to small business centers that had moved out, leaving no demand such as had once existed for local produce, and the hauling charge to the larger but more distant towns was more than the price of the goods could justify.[9] The owners of the farms thus deserted might try their luck in another neighborhood, or might take up day labor in the mill towns. Some of the more adventurous type went west. In one recorded case near New Haven, one son in the family moved to California to try for riches in the mines, another acquired a Western farm far larger than that on which he was reared, and two other sons made fortunes in coal.[10] The lure of new scenes to the younger people on New England farms was described in 1893 as follows.

[8] Clifton Johnson, "The Deserted Homes of New England," *The Cosmopolitan*, XV, No. 2 (June, 1893), 220.
[9] Frederick H. Fowler, "Abandoned Farms," *Cyclopedia of American Agriculture*, IV, 104–105.
[10] William Henry Bishop, "Hunting an Abandoned Farm in Connecticut," *The Century Magazine*, XLVII, o.s.,No. 6 (April, 1894). 922.

The newspaper and literature give wide outlooks from one end of the world to the other to the humblest home. In the reader's ears, however remote his habitation, is a continual hum of strange sounds,—the waves of the sea, the din of crowded city streets, the thud of the pick as the miner searches for treasure in the far west, the clicking of the reapers in the wide grain fields of the prairies, and the ring of gold and silver money as it changes hands in the world's trade and commerce. The dweller in the weatherworn little house among the secluded New England hills hears all this, and as he follows the slow plow across the rocky fields or swings the scythe beneath the hot skies of summer, is it any wonder if he sees visions of fortune or fame beckoning him? At the very best there will be whispers in the breezes of quicker gains for lighter labor, and of enlivening sights and sounds to be gained by a change of abode. All this makes the bonds of seclusion chafe, and many go and few return.[11]

Under such temptations it was futile to sing the plaintive melody of the day:

> Come, boys, I have something to tell you,
>   Come near, I would whisper it low;
> You are thinking of leaving the homestead.
>   *Don't be in a hurry to go.*
> The city has many attractions,
>   But think of the vices and sins,
> When once in the vortex of fashion,
>   How soon the course downward begins.
>
> Chorus:
> Stay on the farm, stay on the farm,
>   Though profits come in rather slow.
> Stay on the farm, stay on the farm;
>   Don't be in a hurry to go.

The boys had to find out for themselves, and they went.

Not always was the farm entirely abandoned. As rapid transit developed from the larger cities, many business and professional people desired country homes where they could spend a part of the year away from their regular life of noise and hurry. They might, if the location was not too far distant, even want to live permanently in the country, riding to and from their work. Where farms were sold to persons such as these, the buildings no longer ran down, but were improved instead, and, though the land was no

[11] Johnson, "Deserted Homes of New England," p. 216.

longer devoted to agriculture, at least it was developed as a sort of show place. In time, whole communities of city workers accumulated near such cities as New York, New Haven, Bridgeport, and Hartford. Sometimes these settlements took the form of artists' colonies. In later years many people took up summer homes in Vermont, New Hampshire, and Maine.[12]

In other cases, farms no longer desired by native Yankees were sold to immigrants, who, because of their accustomed life of little comfort, were able to live on less than what the older inhabitants deemed a respectable standard. If too many people of alien language and ways thus moved into a neighborhood, this led other established owners to want to sell. Particularly was this true among former city dwellers who were getting tired of the new life, and homesick for the noise and confusion from which they had once been so glad to escape. As one woman of education stated her case (though some years after 1900), the distance from schools, the presence of Italians in the neighborhood, with whom her daughter would have to associate (perhaps compete) in school, and remoteness from the cultural refinements to which she had become accustomed, were sufficient reasons for putting her property up for sale.[13]

Other families managed to hold on to their lands by taking in summer boarders from the cities, but such farmers were not as numerous as those who moved to town. New Britain, Bridgeport, Bristol, Waterbury, and Willimantic, in Connecticut, were typical of the cities to which the people came in search for day labor. But the growth of the cities also created markets to keep farmers where they were. Some of the migrants to the cities sought something more than day's wages, becoming shopkeepers or going into the selling of insurance. In this exodus from the hillside fields, the farmers were only following a general trend. In earlier years there had been many country mechanics, blacksmiths, wagon makers, and the like. There had been lawyers and storekeepers. These were the first to be attracted to the industrial towns, and the stories of their

---

[12] See Bishop, "Hunting an Abandoned Farm," pp. 915–924. The song is the first of four stanzas, as printed (with the correction of one obviously typographical error) in *Bonham's Rural Messenger*, II, No. 2 (February 1, 1869), 214. The chorus, not given in the *Rural Messenger*, is traditional.

[13] J[ames] Madison Gathany, "What's the Matter with the Eastern Farmer?" *The Outlook*, CXXVI, No. 3 (September 15, 1920), 106–107.

successes (failures were usually kept quiet) were a temptation to the plowmen.[14]

NEW FARMING METHODS

The exodus from the farms was not altogether bad for agriculture in the section as a whole. New England farmers were about as fecund as people elsewhere, and there was little room for more than one son in a family to engage in the same occupation as his father, if in the same area. The surplus had to go elsewhere. Then, too, it was not always the more energetic man who abandoned his farm. If the land was of the better sort, it was the lazy or shiftless man who generally failed first. When he was more capable, then he was the possessor of acres that had always been too poor for anything but the meagerest of subsistence agriculture, and the day when the Jack-of-all-trades, including farming, could compete with the commercial farmer was in the past. If not always the more intelligent, the owners of the better lands, at least, were left behind, and it was possible for such as they to find at home a solution for their difficulties. In consequence, there were marked changes made in agricultural methods before 1900.

An early aid to readjustment was the establishment of the Connecticut Board of Agriculture in 1865, which was to become the fountainhead of rural progress. Through its experiment stations, new ways of making the best of the state's resources were discovered, remedies were evolved for plant diseases, and other services were given, as was becoming the common practice in most of the states. The new discoveries were broadcast among the farmers in the board's bulletins and reports, which also contained suggestions and hints from practical farmers who were trying out their own experiments. For example, a George M. Clark told how he produced "Large Hay Crops," and others wrote about the sheep industry, tobacco crops, seed growing, and other matters. Agriculturists were informed as to what the markets could absorb of products that they might grow in place of unprofitable ones. Then, in 1881, Charles and Augustus Storrs gave the state 170 acres, with buildings, in addition to $6,000 for equipment, for the fostering of

[14] Charles C. Nott, "A Good Farm for Nothing," *The Nation*, XLIX, No. 1,273 (November 21, 1889), 406–408, for general factors, with ample blame on federal governmental policies; Brewer, "Past and Future of Connecticut Agriculture" pp. 161–162.

agricultural education. The state was indeed slow in this respect, but the Storrs Agricultural School, thus established at Mansfield, was rechartered by the state as the Storrs Agricultural College (coeducational) in 1883, and sixteen years later it became the Connecticut Agricultural College.[15] Since 1939 it has been the University of Connecticut.

Many farmers sent their sons to "Storrs," as the institution continued to be known, for the scientific and practical knowledge they were needing. Also, the college became the center of research, with notable results in cattle breeding, poultry raising, and general animal husbandry. But progress in the state was also made through the examples of successful individual farmers. Their less prosperous neighbors found efficient management worthy of imitation and began diversifying instead of adhering to their old practice of a single crop of corn. More slowly than the West, but steadily, they also started to abandon the scythe and primitive plows, for the newer machines, and to adopt the use of manure spreaders, disc harrows, tedders, and modern hay rakes, along with other machinery.[16] Increasing attention was paid to the growing of truck crops of a perishable nature, for the neighboring city markets. The time was to come, but not before 1900, when even California and Texas would be competing for this market, though mainly in the off seasons for chilly New England. The produce raised in 1900 by A. N. Farnum, near New Haven, can be taken as a sample of what the new agriculture was achieving in the way of diversification and specialization. The data follow.

1,296 bushels Lima beans, 276 bushels dandelions, 3,575 dozen bunches beets + bushels [not explained], 414 bushels string beans, 160,528 ears sweet corn, 4,206 dozens cucumbers, 8,367 citron melons, 6,536 watermelons, 4,000 lettuce, 2,187 bunches onions, 3,000 bushels onions, 400 bushels peppers, 4,879 bushels potatoes, 1,500 dozen radish, 2,100 dozen squash, 680 bushels spinach, 49,292 quarts strawberries; 7,792 baskets tomatoes, 3,890 quarts raspberries, 8,791 quarts blackberries, 1,091 bbls. kale, 10,388 lbs. grapes, 10,079 quarts currants.[17]

[15] T[heodore] S[edgwick] Gold, *Handbook of Connecticut Agriculture* (Hartford: The Case, Lockwood & Brainard Co., 1901), pp. 32, 41–88 *passim*.

[16] Joseph B. Walker, "The Progress of New England Agriculture during the Last Thirty Years," *New Englander and Yale Review*, XLVII, No. 211 (October, 1887), 233–245.

[17] Gold, *Handbook of Connecticut Agriculture*, pp. 80–81 (quotation); Connecticut Board of Agriculture, *Thirty-fifth Annual Report*, 1901 (Hartford: The Case, Lockwood & Brainard Company, 1902), pp. 111–132.

Not all could be successful imitators of Farnum, for his farm was large and adapted to high specialization, but the census figures show that agriculturists in general were shifting to a new basis. Between 1860 and 1900, Connecticut's potato crop nearly doubled, from 1,800,000 to 3,500,000 bushels. It was not till 1890 that the apple harvest was evaluated, but in the next ten years the reported amount grew from less than 2,000,000 bushels to 3,700,000. Peaches also were becoming noticeably abundant during the same decade. The growing of tobacco, practiced even in colonial days in the Connecticut Valley, also increased. The broad-leafed cigar-wrapper varieties matured especially well in that region, and, before 1900, virtually the whole lower valley was planted to that staple. In the preceding forty years the output increased from less than 7,000,000 to the nearly 28,000,000 pounds average maintained from 1909 to 1913. Connecticut became the eighth state in volume of output, excelling Maryland and South Carolina, but far exceeded even in the North by Ohio, Pennsylvania, and Wisconsin.

Notable progress was also made in the dairy industry, both in volume and in adjustment to Western competition. From colonial days, Connecticut had been noted for her butter, and especially cheese. In 1860, the state produced 3,898,000 pounds of cheese, but this was cut to 826,000 pounds in 1880 and to 40,600 by 1900. First New York and, later, Wisconsin cheese took over the market. In a like manner, the butter output diminished, as the production of Wisconsin, Illinois, Minnesota, and other Western states became standardized and plentiful. But the West could not supply the Eastern cities with milk, and in this initial stage of the dairying industry Connecticut really began to flourish. Between 1870 (the first recorded figures) and 1900, the milk production expanded from approximately 6,250,000 gallons to 33,879,000, or over fivefold. Whereas the average family, in earlier years, had kept a cow or two, now large producers were in the business, sometimes with hundreds of dairy cows each. Marginal land for cereal crops was turned into pasture and meadow. If Western corn was cheaper than Eastern, so much the better for the dairyman. He would buy corn from Illinois and Iowa, and be glad to get it.

In spite of the high cost of feed, chicken farming would have been one solution for the thousands of acres of unproductive hillsides. Although seven million dozen eggs were produced in Connecticut in 1900, they were only a small fraction of the consuming capacity of the state, and just across the border was the New York metropolitan area that could eat up the whole year's supply in a week or two. Speedy rail and refrigeration service, before 1900, could put Western eggs on the market in New England fresh enough even for poaching; nevertheless, local prejudice prevented their use for anything except cooking purposes. Consequently, local eggs sold at premium prices. But the Yankee farmer looked on chicken raising as "women's work" and he was too slow in grasping the opportunities that chicken farming offered.

Incidental items of specialization were becoming interesting as experiments, even if not prominent, before 1900. Bee culture advanced so that Connecticut honey increased from 100,000 pounds in 1880 to 130,000 in 1890. The raising of silver foxes became profitable on a few farms. There were also specialists in the raising of pedigreed dogs, cattle, horses, and rabbits. Numerous evidences were visible, before 1900, pointing to the fact that farmers who knew how to make drastic adjustments could still prosper. Rural electrification was in advance of any part of the West. Roads were being improved. Libraries, even when small, were available in the town centers. Consolidation of schools was going forward. All these and other things were breaking down the isolation of rural life as typified in 1860. Though farming had diminished in acreage, the farmers themselves were better off than at any earlier date. During all these years the Eastern farmer had remained aloof from such Western phenomena as the Granger movement and the Farmers' Alliances. Why should he join in an agitation that could only result in the greater effectiveness of Western competition? [18]

DAIRYING IN THE PRAIRIES AND EASTWARD

While liquid milk production was on the increase near the Eastern industrial centers, general dairying was spreading out through much of the United States, and particularly in the North Central section. "No branch of agriculture," said the Chief of the Dairy Division of the federal Bureau of Animal Industry in 1899,

---

[18] The evidence for the last few paragraphs is collected from numerous pages in the census reports, and from stray bits of information gathered, often at first hand, from the farmers themselves.

". . . has made greater progress than dairying during the nineteenth century. . . . It is now regarded as among the most progressive and highly developed forms of farming in the United States." It was once thought that the occupation could be followed with success only in isolated spots, constituting about a third of the area between the fortieth parallel and the forty-fifth, from the Atlantic coast to the western Prairies, but it was learned gradually that, wherever beef could be grown, milk products need not be lacking, and cattle could be raised in nearly all parts of the country. Some regions had greater natural advantages, but where these were absent they could be compensated for by more personal attention.[19]

Before 1860, central and western New York, together with the adjacent parts of Pennsylvania and Ohio, became famous for their cheese. In later years, when the supremacy shifted to Wisconsin, the name "New York" remained the distinguishing brand of a particular kind of cream cheese, rather than a designation of its origin. But all forms of dairying were also going forward in New York, in the early years, and it was there that some of the most outstanding improvements originated. Shorthorns were the first improved dairy breed in the United States, probably because they produced excellent beef as well as being good milkers. But, before 1860, some of the more specialized varieties were also imported, the movement continuing for many years afterward. In 1873, a number of Ayrshires were brought to Massachusetts by the Society for the Promotion of Agriculture, and there were additional importations for another generation. Holstein Friesians, Jerseys, and Guernseys also became common, and the first Brown Swiss seems to have been brought to Belmont, Massachusetts, by H. M. Clark in 1869. A few more came several years later. This never became a numerous breed,[20] but Illini Nellie, who died in 1940, was for years known the world over as a champion milker.

Along with improved dairy herds came efforts to develop strains and feeding processes that would result in high milking averages for at least three hundred days in the year. The ordinary cow would give a high yield when fresh and while the pasture was green, then diminish to strippings in a few months, and remain dry the

[19] Henry E. Alvord, "Dairy Development in the United States," *Agricultural Yearbook,* 1899, p. 381.

[20] *Ibid.,* pp. 383, 391; Clarence H[enry] Eckles, *Dairy Cattle and Milk Production* (New York: The Macmillan Company, 3d ed., 1939), pp. 54–77 *passim.*

rest of the year. But, before the 1890's any cow that did not average six or seven quarts for three hundred days (4,000 to 4,500 pounds total) was considered unprofitable. Between 1852 and 1863, Zadok Pratt of New York raised the average butter yield of his herd of fifty from 130 pounds a year to 225, and maintained a seven-year average of 4,710 pounds of milk to the cow. This is considered "the first good record of definite herd improvement." By the 1890's, entire herds were averaging from 300 to 500 pounds of butter a year, and numerous individual cows yielded 2 pounds a day. These records were three or four times the average of forty years earlier.[21]

The manufacture of cheese on a factory basis was begun in the 1850's, by Jesse Williams of the Rome neighborhood in New York. The idea spread in his state, in Pennsylvania and Ohio, and then reached out to other states in the West as well as in the East. In 1869, there were over a thousand such factories in the United States, some of them being of the small, neighborhood cooperative kind. The first butter factory, or creamery, was started in Orange County, New York, by Alanson Slaughter in 1861. Many of the early creameries also made cheese.[22] In 1864, Chester Hazen introduced the New York cheese-factory system in Ladoga, Wisconsin, and by 1870 there were over a hundred such plants in the state, mainly in the southeastern part. Illinois and Iowa were also rapid in dairy development, and the first creamery of the Northwest was opened at Elgin, Illinois, in 1870. While Wisconsin made astonishing progress with cheeses, employing the skill of numerous foreign experts, that state for a long time left butter making to the home and the neighborhood dairy. For some years, a serious obstacle to the wide marketing of Western cheese and butter was the bad reputation they had in the East, the butter being quoted on the exchanges as Western grease. This problem was taken in hand in 1867, by the Illinois and Wisconsin Dairymen's Association, which two years later developed into the Northwestern Dairymen's Association. In the following years, state organizations sprang up as well, all working to eliminate bad practices and raise the quality of the products. The result was that, before 1880, Wisconsin no longer had to give her cheese fictitious Eastern labels, for it was winning prizes in competition with New York, and under the Wisconsin brand. The

[21] *Ibid.*; Alvord, "Dairy Development," p. 392.
[22] Alvord, "Dairy Development," pp. 384–386.

use of refrigerator cars for long shipments, after 1872, also helped in the wider marketing of the product.[23]

Despite the rapid growth of commercial creameries, especially in the newer farming states, 1,000,000,000 pounds of butter were made in the homes in 1899, as compared with four tenths as much in nearly 8,000 creameries. Creamery butter predominated in the larger city markets, but the local trade consumed the bulk of the total output. Iowa led all the states, both in amount of butter and in the percentage made in factories. There were creameries in all but two counties, 780 in all, and 40 per cent of these were co-operative. The cream from 624,000 cows went to these plants, in the course of a year, and came out as 88,000,000 pounds of butter. In addition, some 50,000,000 pounds were made in the homes, the total of the two sources accounting for a tenth of all butter made in the United States.

Immense quantities of the home-made or "country" butter were hardly fit for human consumption. Made with little care as to sanitation, often of half-rotted cream, scalded to make the butter come more rapidly, and the buttermilk only partially worked out afterward—such swill was marketed at the village store. In order to retain the custom of the farmers, the storekeeper took all that came in, paying for it in merchandise, and saved only the best for his local customers. People were in the habit of asking for butter by the name of the maker. If Mrs. Jones's supply was exhausted, Mrs. Johnson's might be the second choice. When the offerings got down to Mrs. Sanders's, oleomargarine would be purchased instead. The grocer took all the cull butter out to the back room and dumped it into an open barrel, unprotected by screen wire, and cared not what was caught and immured in the descent. This "marble butter" was bought up at insignificant prices by a huckster, who hauled it to a renovating plant. There it went through some mysterious process that at least removed the visible signs of impurities, and came out attractively packaged and labeled as "creamery butter." The taste of this stuff was sometimes passable, but occasionally astonishing. The name of the brand had to be changed frequently, to continue the beguiling of purchasers. But it was a great boon

[23] Frederick Merk, *Economic History of Wisconsin during the Civil War Decade* (State Historical Society of Wisconsin, *Studies*, I, Madison: The Society, 1916), pp. 22–30.

to the makers of oleomargarine, whose product could much more easily pass for creamery butter. Before 1900, some states were adopting laws against false labeling. At the end of the century, little butter was exported, but almost none was imported. The average per capita of consumption was about twenty pounds a year, a larger amount than anywhere else in the world.[24]

Throughout the whole period, it required about one milk cow for each four persons in the nation to keep them all supplied with milk, butter, and cheese, and provide a little for exportation. Thus, at the end of the century there were about 17,500,000 such cattle in the country—badly distributed through the various sections. Iowa led, with 1,500,000. New York had nearly as many, while Illinois and Pennsylvania each had about 1,000,000. Wisconsin, Ohio, Kansas, Missouri, Minnesota, Nebraska, and Indiana each had over 500,000. In 1899, the product of 11,000,000 of the 17,500,000 cows, largely in the West, was used to make 1,430,000,000 pounds of butter selling at an average of eighteen cents a pound. A million cows supplied the country with 300,000,000 pounds of cheese at nine cents a pound. The 5,500,000 cows remaining produced a little over 2,000,000,000 gallons of milk selling at about eight cents a gallon. The total product was valued at around $450,000,000 or, with certain by-products added, at more than $500,000,000. In the 1890's, more effort was made to salvage the skimmed milk and buttermilk for feeding animals, whereas formerly most of it had been thrown away. Other by-products were a little milk sugar and casein. The latter "is desiccated and prepared as a baking supply and substitute for eggs, as the basis of an enamel paint, as a substitute for glue in paper sizing, and it is also solidified so as to make excellent buttons, combs, brush backs, handles, electrical insulators, and similar articles." [25]

Not enough was done during the generation to suppress the sale of adulterated milk and milk infected with harmful bacteria. Some steps in the right direction were taken in Massachusetts before 1860, and in 1864 a revised law forbade the sale of adulterated milk or milk from diseased cows or cows fed on stuff spoiling the flavor. Then, in 1868, the Massachusetts law was weakened by fixing penalties only on persons knowingly selling adulterated milk.

[24] Alvord, "Dairy Development," pp. 400–401.
[25] Ibid., pp. 401–402.

In 1870, the Boston inspector reported 520 adulterated samples of milk out of 1,680 examined during the preceding year, and in 1871 the ratio was 610 to 1,700. Sometimes, over half the samples taken were adulterated.[26] Many years later, dairymen were occasionally convicted of preserving filthy milk with formaldehyde. In the 1880's, blackleg sometimes attacked Eastern herds, and so many cattle were found to be tubercular that tests were given wherever the farmers were amenable. At the same time, the plague of pleuro-pneumonia broke out, and in 1887 the Bureau of Animal Industry was given an appropriation to buy afflicted animals, if necessary, to prevent the pest from spreading beyond state lines. New Jersey spent over $12,000 that year in fighting the same infection, and Illinois spent nearly $74,000. Maryland went as high as $106,000, three fourths of which was to pay for slaughtered cattle. In the course of five years $1,500,000 went for this purpose alone, the country over, and the movement was totally effective by 1892.[27]

TRUCK FARMING AND FRUIT GROWING IN THE EAST

Further evidence of Eastern adjustment to Western competition is shown in the expansion of truck gardening and orchard indus-tries. As the population of the country became more urban, the back-yard garden began to disappear, and the little truck patch in the country often expanded into a truck farm. As the transporta-tion facilities improved, it became possible to engage in this form of specialization at greater distances from the large cities, but the cities were rising rapidly in the Middle West as well as growing in the East. Prominent among the truck crops grown were cabbage, kale, spinach, potatoes, sweet potatoes, eggplants, cucumbers, let-tuce, radishes, beets, cauliflower, strawberries, celery, and onions. Where land was very expensive, the system of double cropping was common. Quick-growing vegetables, radishes, lettuce, and the like, were planted between the rows of cabbage and other wide-planted crops. Thus a series of vegetables could be taken off the same ground during the season. Near some of the bigger markets,

---

[26] U.S. Commissioner of Agriculture, *Report*, 1870, pp. 316–320.
[27] U.S. Department of Agriculture, Bureau of Animal Industry, *Fourth and Fifth Annual Reports*, 1887–1888 (Washington: Government Printing Office, 1889), pp. 9–32, 498–499; U.S. Secretary of Agriculture, *Report*, 1890, p. 75; *ibid.*, 1892, pp. 85–88.

such as Boston, many acres would be covered with glass and devoted to tomatoes, lettuce, and cucumbers during the winter months. Other vegetables were also forced in the same manner.[28] The expansion of this sort of farming in the North Atlantic states, Delaware, Maryland, and the East North Central section, in the 1880's and 1890's, can be seen from the following figures. The relatively small growth in some of the New England states in the nineties may well be due to the earlier development there, and to the fact that the possibilities of expansion were more nearly reached by 1889 than in some of the other states.

VALUE OF TRUCK AND SMALL FRUITS SOLD IN THE EAST,
1879, 1889, 1899[29]

(Values in thousands)

State	1879	1889	1899	Per Cent Increase 1889–1899
Maine	$ 145	$ 399	$ 906	127.3
New Hampshire	113	187	394	110.8
Vermont	39	62	202	227.9
Massachusetts	1,697	2,255	4,834	114.3
Rhode Island	262	318	538	69.5
Connecticut	385	371	1,237	233.2
New York	4,212	3,400	11,455	236.9
New Jersey	1,842	2,231	6,142	175.4
Pennsylvania	4,863	1,456	5,481	276.5
Delaware	157	221	1,231	457.2
Maryland	874	1,057	4,767	350.9
Ohio	1,487	1,723	5,661	228.5
Indiana	578	842	3,540	320.2
Illinois	960	1,382	4,314	212.2
Michigan	637	1,243	3,860	210.6
Wisconsin	207	609	2,092	243.7
Sixteen States	$18,466	$17,755	$56,653	218.9

Beginnings in the canning of fruits and vegetables were made long before 1860, but, in the years following, the industry grew with astonishing speed all through the Eastern and North Central states and on the Pacific coast. Nearly any kind of food that could be cooked was canned. By 1885, tinned cans were made in factories by such purely mechanical processes that their price could be

[28] Lee Cleveland Corbett, Garden Farming (Boston: Ginn and Company, c.1913), pp. 1–2, 6.
[29] Tenth Census: Agriculture, bottom folio, p. 285; Twelfth Census: Agriculture, II, 322.

greatly lowered. Pressure cooking in the cans, at temperatures up to 500°, was possible, and, by 1890, most of the processes of canning foods had become mechanical. Even the filling of the cans and the soldering of the lids were done by machines. The rolling on of can tops, without solder, came after 1900. But, despite the rapid growth of this industry, many families still liked the flavor of home-canned foods best, and the kitchen industry has continued.[30] Probably two thirds of the canned vegetables by 1900 were corn and tomatoes, but peas, asparagus, lima beans, green beans, beets, pumpkins, and other products also were canned in large quantities.[31]

VALUE OF ORCHARD FRUITS SOLD OR CONSUMED IN THE NORTH, BY DECADES[32]

(*Values in thousands*)

State	1859	1869	1879	1899
Maine	$ 502	$ 875	$ 1,112	$ 999
New Hampshire	558	744	972	839
Vermont	212	682	641	543
Massachusetts	926	940	1,005	2,700
Rhode Island	84	43	59	212
Connecticut	509	536	456	1,333
New York	3,726	8,347	8,410	15,844
New Jersey	429	1,295	860	4,083
Pennsylvania	1,480	4,208	4,863	9,885
Delaware	114	1,227	847	756
Maryland	252	1,319	1,563	2,490
Ohio	1,929	5,844	3,576	8,901
Indiana	1,259	2,858	2,757	4,630
Illinois	1,126	3,572	3,503	5,455
Michigan	1,122	3,448	2,761	5,859
Wisconsin	79	819	639	1,118
TOTAL	$13,142	$36,757	$34,024	$65,647

The value of orchard fruits, in the same sixteen states considered above, can again be presented most conveniently, decade by decade, in tabular form. The figures for 1899 are not strictly comparable with earlier years, because never before had they been gathered accurately. There are no figures for 1889.

[30] Shannon, *Economic History of the People of the United States*, pp. 556–557, 756.

[31] *Twelfth Census: Agriculture*, II, 302.

[32] *Eighth Census: Agriculture*, p. 186; *Ninth Census: Wealth and Industry*, p. 81; *Tenth Census: Agriculture*, bottom folio. p. 43; *Twelfth Census: Agriculture*, II, 599–600.

HORTICULTURE AND TRUCK FARMING ON THE PACIFIC COAST

Though the data listed above show an extensive development in orchards in many parts of the Northeast, it would seem best to consider horticulture, in its intensive phases, primarily from the point of view of the section where it was most highly developed— that is, the Pacific coast. Nearly all kinds of fruits grown anywhere else in America were produced from California to Washington, and very important other ones as well. The problems of culture were not always the same in the East as in the Far West, and marketing methods were more thoroughly worked out on the West coast. While the Easterner grew fruits mainly for local consumption, the Pacific states were in the business of supplying the nation. Though California, Oregon, and Washington were constantly prominent in the stock-raising business, and while they were also great wheat growers before 1900, in those lines of agriculture their experiences were not widely different from those of the Great Plains. In fact, as has been noted, combines and other heavy machinery for wheat were first developed there. But in fruit growing, the section was distinctive, so it is selected to illustrate that subject, just as Connecticut was taken as an example of Eastern readjustments.

Hardly had the excitement of the first gold rush subsided when, in 1851, an exhibit was held in San Francisco of the wide variety of the new state's agricultural products. The later spirit of the state was also shown in the boast that scarcely a plant existed anywhere in the world that California could not duplicate. In later years, drouth took some of the enthusiasm out of the farmers, but, by 1865, Samuel Bowles reported that more of agricultural products were being raised than ever before. The southern part had figs, oranges, and grapes; the northern section, apples; while peaches, plums, pears, strawberries, and blackberries were produced in nearly every locality. At the same time, the Buena Vista Vinicultural Society had a five-thousand-acre estate, bearing about a million native and foreign vines, and worth half a million dollars. A fifth of this valuation represented wine and brandies on hand and in preparation. Already, the state had markets in Nevada, the territories of Washington and Idaho, and the British provinces of western Canada, and was needing new sales areas.[33] In 1867 C. W.

[33] Samuel Bowles, *Across the Continent* (Springfield, Mass.: Samuel Bowles & Company, new ed., 1869), pp. 162–163, 284–287, 337.

Reed had a nursery of a million trees that was rated the best in the state. Wilson Flint and, later, John Rock were the pioneer "nurserymen." Rock, for a generation after the 1860's, advocated the propagation of the best of anything attempted, and educated many others in his methods.[34] As a result of such teachings, California wines were commended at the Paris exposition of 1867, and, five years later, the state produced ten million gallons, besides two million of grape brandy.[35]

Although, to that time, grapes were the leading fruit crop in value, great progress was made in nearly a score of others. The estimated value of grapes alone in 1870 was $466,000 for 11,654,000 pounds, while apples came second with $415,000 for nearly 21,-000,000 pounds. Peaches, pears, and cherries ranged between $200,000 and $300,000 in value, while strawberries, plums, and apricots each ran above $100,000. Oranges stood eleventh in value, at about $74,000, being exceeded even by blackberries and figs, and lemons were a negligible item near the bottom of the list. The total value of fruits was about $2,280,000. A considerable quantity of the fruit put on the market in that year spoiled in transit, thus adding to the grievance of horticulturists remote from railroad centers, who already were indignant at being compelled to pay higher freight rates than persons at points where there was railroad competition.[36]

Nevertheless, the efforts were redoubled, and in 1879 evidence of an increased interest in citrus fruits was shown at fairs. In the same year a Horticultural Society was established, with members from all parts of the state. This was just a year ahead of the American Horticultural Society, of national scope. Down to this time, the fruit growers had been baffled in their efforts to realize their dreams of national and world-wide markets. The obstacles were the inability of the small Western population (that between California and the East) to consume the products, the high cost of long-distance transportation, the lack of proper facilities and

[34] E[dward] J[ames] Wickson, *California Nurserymen and the Plant Industry, 1850–1910* (Los Angeles: The California Association of Nurserymen, 1921), pp. 27–31.
[35] Albert S[idney] Bolles, *Industrial History of the United States* (Norwich, Conn.: The Henry Bill Publishing Company, 1879), p. 171; R[olander] Guy McClellan, *The Golden State* (Philadelphia: William Flint & Company, ed. of 1876), p. 370.
[36] McClellan, *Golden State*, p. 364.

skill in handling necessary to the delivery of fresh fruits in good
condition, and an ignorance of methods of putting the products
into acceptable and durable forms for distant commercial distribution.[37] After 1880, the completion of the fourth transcontinental
railroad introduced more competition in transportation, and the
development of adequate refrigerator cars maintained the freshness
of the shipments. Even then, there were problems of furnishing a
constant stream of goods, so as to maintain the markets. The inadequate solution of this difficulty contributed to the collapse of a
California real-estate boom in the late eighties.[38]

The effects of this setback were not protracted, and only speculators had been harmed. By 1890, not only were the fruit growers
feeling hopeful, but also the state was beginning to participate, in a
small way, in the growth of the truck-farming business. In the late
fall and early spring, California was supplying the Far West with
truck, and a few products, such as "new potatoes, cabbages, cauli-
flowers, and tomatoes" were sent as "far east as St. Louis, Kansas
City, and Chicago." [39] The Pacific coast shippers, at the same time,
were greatly interested in the different projects for an interoceanic
canal in the Central American area. The success of such a waterway
was expected to put profit into a vastly increased eastward movement of goods.[40] At that time a Fruit Union was in existence, handling shipments of whole trainloads at a time, but the problem of
distribution in the Eastern markets seemed beyond the capacity
even of this agency. In 1894, it was suggested that the producers
might create an express business of their own, dealing directly with
the consumers. As it was, they were reaching only about five million
out of what was reckoned as sixty million potential customers.
Their own express company, they thought, might develop this
possible trade, but that was about as far as the idea got.[41]

Another solution was found in the late nineties. Instead of
employing the usual commission men, they held auctions in the

[37] Wickson, California Nurserymen, pp. 33–40.

[38] Ibid., p. 41; Agricultural Yearbook, 1900, p. 445.

[39] "Truck Farming," The Nation, LII, No. 1,347 (April 23, 1891), 335; Eleventh
Census: Agriculture, p. 593; quotation from The Nation, as derived (almost verbatim,
but without credit) from the Census.

[40] William L. Merry, "Commercial Future of the Pacific States," The Forum, XII,
No. 3 (November, 1891), 411–413.

[41] California State Board of Horticulture, Fourth Biennial Report, 1893–1894
(Sacramento: State Office, 1894), pp. 127–128.

larger cities, with so much success that the great bulk of fresh fruit shipments was disposed of in that way. The extent of growth of the fruit industries is revealed in a production amounting to over $28,000,000 in 1899. Truck gardening was still in the infant stage, but the soils and climate had already shown special fitness for certain vegetables, chief of them being asparagus, cauliflower, cabbage, Brussels sprouts, celery, and onions.[42]

Horticulture in Oregon is said to have begun with the bringing of a few apple seeds from a London dinner party. The story in full is a romantic one, but not particularly significant even if true. The establishment of Henderson Luelling's nursery, in 1847, is something more substantial. But the first settlers in Oregon brought their slips along with them, and soon there was an ample supply of apples, plums, various kinds of berries, wild currants, and barberries, known as the Oregon grape. By 1850, numerous varieties of apples, pears, cherries, peaches, plums (including the Rhine prune), as well as Catawba and Isabella grapes were being grown. For a few years after 1856, the bimonthly steamer shipments to San Francisco, in the fall and winter, ran between three thousand and six thousand boxes, and several individual fortunes were budding. But, in the meantime, California had imported thousands of young trees and root grafts by way of the Isthmus of Panama, and the resulting competition caused several years of decay of the Oregon industry. California could market its fruits a month or more earlier than Oregon, and the northward shipments carried some of the insect pests that California had brought in from Australia and the Eastern states. Consequently, for a time the well-developed orchards of Oregon were neglected, and the fruit rotted on the ground, so creating nice breeding places for aphids and the codling moth. The enormous transportation costs also hampered the Oregon industry.[43]

The organization of the Oregon State Horticultural Society in 1885 was the first step toward the checking of this decadence. Fruit growing at the time was at a low point, while insect pests and tree and fruit diseases were making heavy inroads. But the com-

[42] Twelfth Census: Agriculture, II, pp. 599–600.
[43] Oregon State Board of Horticulture, Second Biennial Report, 1893 (Salem: Frank C. Baker, State Printer, 1893), pp. 98–99; J. R. Caldwell, "The First Fruits of the Land," Oregon Historical Quarterly, VII, No. 1 (March, 1906), 28–38.

pletion of the Northern Pacific railroad, in 1883, also was a stimulus to revival. Soon afterward the whole agricultural system began to take on a new life. Grain lands and pastures were planted to orchards, and Oregon again began to produce numerous kinds of fruits. Immense numbers of apple, pear, quince, and cherry trees were set out. The estimated number of acres in orchards and vineyards in the state in 1895 was sixty-five thousand, as compared with four hundred thousand in California. The state's exhibit at the Chicago World's Fair of 1893 had stimulated interest, and inquiries from fruit dealers all over the United States multiplied tenfold. The extension of the industry was continuous from that time. Not only were individual growers expanding their activities, but localities that never before had exported fruits made good beginnings. In 1898, the state produced "1,606 carloads of green and dried fruits." [44]

Washington, many years later in settlement than California and Oregon, was correspondingly slow in other respects. As late as 1884, the fruit industry of the territory was still inconspicuous. But the coming of the Northern Pacific railroad put shipments from the Puget Sound to Duluth seven hundred miles closer than those from San Francisco to Chicago, and thus gave Washington an advantage in the Eastern markets. So, while the value of orchard products in 1879 had been less than $127,000, twenty years later it was well over $1,000,000, and about equal to that of Oregon. Orchards developed most rapidly in the eastern valleys, but after 1890 there was a noticeable improvement in the western part of the state as well. By 1893, apples, pears, peaches, quinces, cherries, plums, prunes, and various berries were grown successfully. By this time, rapid transit was being tried between the Pacific coast and Europe, and high hopes were expressed in Washington of that not distant day when California would have difficulty in retaining her supremacy. It was generally conceded, as in California, that, with proper refrigeration on ships going by way of an Isthmian canal, the short water route to the East and Europe would be more beneficial to the fruit-growing interests than to any other industry. As

[44] Oregon State Board of Horticulture, *Third Biennial Report*, 1895 (Salem: Frank C. Baker, State Printer, 1894 [*sic*]), pp. 246–247; Oregon State Board of Horticulture, *Fifth Biennial Report*, 1898 (Salem: W. H. Leeds, State Printer, 1898), p. 63.

speedy transportation in refrigerator cars created supply, the Eastern demand rose in response.[45]

As the century came to a close, many problems of the Pacific coast horticulturists still awaited solution. The rise of highly successful cooperatives was imminent but not yet a reality. Though the great inrush of population from other parts of the country came later, before 1900 the Western coast was becoming more alluring. In the 1880's, the population of California increased by nearly a half, to over 1,200,000; Oregon grew by four fifths, to about 318,-000; and the population of Washington was multiplied by four and a half, to 357,000.[46] As yet, the agricultural possibilities of the states were the principal lure. In the nineties, California had only a modest growth, to 1,485,000; but Oregon increased nearly a third, to 414,000; and Washington again surged ahead, with a rise of nearly a half, to 518,000.[47] California was yet to pay for her excessive boasting and "boosting," but the problems of a state of old people, waiting for pensions, came mainly after 1910.

The farmers of the East, as well as of the Western coast, had shown their ability to cope with conditions created by a rapidly shifting agricultural frontier, and it was the newer states of the interior—the granary and larder of the nation—that, along with the South, were suffering most from agricultural depression.

[45] McClellan, *Golden State*, pp. 714, 722; *Twelfth Census: Agriculture*, II, 599–600; Washington State Board of Horticulture, *First Biennial Report*, 1891–1892 (Olympia: O. C. White, State Printer, 1893), pp. 233–236, 242, 263; Merry, "Commercial Future of the Pacific States," pp. 413–414; Caldwell, "First Fruits of the Land," p. 33.

[46] *Statistical Abstract of the United States*, 1931, pp. 8–9.

[47] *Ibid.*

CHAPTER XII

Governmental Activity in Agriculture

STATE AGENCIES

FROM the preceding chapters, it should be apparent that governments had a distinct influence on agricultural advance, even if not always on behalf of the farmer. The federal land laws, for example, were of the most vital importance in the expansion of farming and grazing throughout the West. Always these acts were so worded as to convey the impression that the man of little means was to be benefited, or, as in the railroad grants, that the general welfare was to be advanced. But, at the same time, the legislation was so shaped as to give the main advantage to speculators and other land monopolists. The same interests were served by the public policies of the states. The lien laws and disfranchisement provisions of the South were to perpetuate the control of the section by the landlord-merchants. The agricultural and horticultural boards of the Pacific coast, whose reports to the legislatures show even more than do their names their connection with the state governments, were concerned mainly with combating outside influences that conflicted with the prosperity of the greater landlords. Occasionally, as in the case of the Granger laws of the 1870's, the rank and file of the farmers executed a coup of their own, but never to the extent of relieving the tenant or agricultural wage laborer. Again, it was the landowner fighting to retain his equity. But governments could not ignore the humbler voters entirely, and, in those states where even the tenant and wage farmer had the suffrage, some benefits sifted down to the lower stratum. Furthermore, inasmuch as the activity of the state resulted in the stimulation of better methods and management of farming, control of credit and railroad rates, and the like, the man of little influence has been enabled to get a modicum of the benefits.

In the decades before 1860, when the population in nearly all the states was primarily rural, the governments were mainly concerned with the encouragement of agricultural societies, and occasionally in the establishment of state boards. New York's board of 1819 was composed solely of delegates from the agricultural societies, and the revised board of 1841 was in effect the State Agricultural Society itself. Largely financed by its own members, with a small state subsidy, this organization did good work in a limited way for many years. In 1884, it was necessary for the state to appoint a special agency to enforce the dairy regulations, but no regular department of agriculture was created till 1893. Other states followed the policy of subsidizing private societies until, in 1874, Georgia set up the first state department of agriculture. Five other Southern states created departments by 1889, the year in which North Dakota came into the Union with the first one for the North. Kentucky, New York, and Pennsylvania were the only other states to follow the precedent before the close of the century. Of the ten departments of 1895, seven were in the South. The lack of effective state societies in the South, where any at all existed, and the absence of small governmental units such as the township have been advanced as reasons for the earlier appearance of the state departments of agriculture in that section. After 1900, state departments were created in most of the states everywhere.[1]

It has been the practice in America to relegate agricultural research, experimentation, education, and demonstration to the state colleges and their agencies and affiliates, thus leaving to the agricultural departments mainly the business of regulation; and there was enough of this to occupy the full attention of such bodies. In view of the fact that the regulation of business in general made very little advance before 1900, it is not surprising that less than a quarter of the states by that time had taken any effective steps toward the suppression of abuses that hindered agriculture. The

[1] Edward Wiest, *Agricultural Organization in the United States* (Vol. II of University of Kentucky *Studies in Economics and Sociology*, Lexington: University of Kentucky, 1923), pp. 291–300.

adulteration of dairy products, already mentioned, was one of the early examples of the need of inspection and strict control. The building of an oleomargarine factory in the city of New York, in 1873, called for a new sort of interference. The new product was sold as butter, but it could be made much more cheaply. The imitation was much more likely to be clean than the average country butter, certainly was preferable to the renovated product, and was a healthful food in itself. Nevertheless, it should be sold only under its own name. For this reason, and to protect the dairies, New York and Pennsylvania in the 1870's led in the movement for legislation against such false labeling. But all the efforts of the states were ineffective in the interstate shipments of adulterations and false substitutes, thus compelling federal legislation on the subject after 1900. Quarantines, to prevent the spread of animal and plant diseases, the inspection of feed products for animals and of fertilizers, and sundry other regulatory matters were delegated to the state departments, but the power and scope of the agencies varied widely among the states.[2]

THE FEDERAL DEPARTMENT OF AGRICULTURE

The United States Department of Agriculture was created under a Congressional act of May 15, 1862. It was administered by a commissioner appointed by the President, but who was not to be a member of the cabinet. Yet the commissioner was independent of all the other administrative departments of the government. The advocates of the measure had wanted a secretary of agriculture, with full equality in the presidential family, but there was objection at that time to the representation of special business interests in that way. For several years before the war, there had been a Bureau of Agriculture in the Patent Office, this being the special pet and protégé of Henry Leavitt Ellsworth, Commissioner of Patents. The new department was largely the result of agitation by the United States Agricultural Society. The newly ensconced Republican party had not yet forgotten its debt to the farmers who had played so large a part in its political success, and the new department was one of the first fruits of this alliance. The appropriation for the department in 1863 was eighty thousand dollars,

[2] Ibid.

all of which was spent. The powers of the commissioner expanded rapidly after the war, and, instead of merely distributing seeds and disseminating information, the department began to study plant and animal diseases and methods of combating them; to search out new crops and means of further utilizing the older ones; to find ways for improving pastures, especially in the arid West; to look into the deleterious effects of food adulteration; to gather statistics in directions useful to farmers; and to carry on experiments in numerous lines. The addition of the Bureau of Animal Industry, in 1884, with its powers, through grants-in-aid, to coordinate quarantine work in the states, was the first step toward the direct regulation of individual activities of the farmers.[3]

Appropriations for the study of forestry were received in 1876, and in 1886 a special forestry division was created. Before this time, agitation was renewed for the elevation of the department to cabinet rank, and the specious cry against special privilege and class legislation was revived by the older recipients of governmental favors. But Congress could not hold out forever against the popular clamor, so on February 9, 1889, the new legislation was adopted. Immediately afterward Cleveland elevated Commisisoner Norman J. Coleman to the post of Secretary of Agriculture for the few remaining days of the administration. Thereafter the authority of the department began to broaden. In 1890, it was given the power to inspect all livestock imported from abroad, and to send back any infected animals. Later on, interstate quarantines also were imposed. The ban on foreign stock was largely in retaliation against previous discrimination by European governments against American animals, but its effects were declared by President Benjamin Harrison to be good. By the end of the century, the powers of the department were still rather modest as compared with its later program.[4] If all the statistics and good advice issued by the department and its bureaus, in multitudes of publications, had been generally studied and heeded, agriculture by 1900 might well have been in a much more prosperous condition. The *Yearbook* alone, with its hundreds of thousands of free copies distributed by the

[3] William L[awrence] Wanlass, *The United States Department of Agriculture* (Johns Hopkins University *Studies in Historical and Political Science*, XXXVIII, No. 1, Baltimore: The Johns Hopkins Press, 1920), pp. 16–22.

[4] *Ibid.*, pp. 22–26.

members of Congress, was a storehouse of useful knowledge that
was sometimes applied.

In 1860, there were a few collegiate chairs in the United States
that divided up a didactic consideration of agriculture with other
branches of natural science, but Michigan, Maryland, and Pennsylvania had the only real agricultural colleges, and they were all
new. By that time, however, the demand for state and federal
cooperation in a program for agricultural research and education
was becoming vociferous. In 1838, a petition with six thousand
signatures had been submitted to the New York legislature, asking
for state aid in the education of future farmers. People were beginning to demand more science and less Latin. There were efforts
in other states to supply the need by private enterprise, but the
success of the governments in elementary education, through the
public school systems, convinced growing numbers of the people
that the state or federal governments were the proper agencies
to propagate the new movement.[5] Different educators, such as
Jonathan Baldwin Turner of Illinois College and John P. Norton of
Yale, by their teaching, lectures, and articles, did much to arouse
national interest. Turner pointed to the fact that four out of every
five persons in the United States were, in one way or another,
getting their living from the farms, while less than two hundred
thousand dollars had ever been spent in furthering their interests.
More than that sum had gone for beautifying the grounds around
the national Capitol, five times as much had been expended "on
a single trip to Japan, to the Dead Sea, and to the North Pole,"
while the people who raised the money were far more interested
in the nation's own resources than they were in such distant objectives. Turner's own plan for the establishment of an industrial
university was published in the Patent Office *Report* for 1851, and
his ideas may be considered as forerunners of the provisions of the
later Morrill Act.[6]

[5] Wiest, *Agricultural Organization*, pp. 189–192.
[6] Eugene Davenport, *History of Collegiate Education in Agriculture* (Urbana:
University of Illinois, 1909), pp. 4–9; Edmund J[anes] James, *The Origin of the
Land Grant Act of 1862* (University of Illinois *Studies*, IV, No. 1, Urbana-
Champaign: University Press, 1910), pp. 7–32; Wiest, *Agricultural Organization*,
pp. 192–198.

In 1847, the Commissioner of Patents published the findings of a special agent sent to Europe to investigate agricultural education projects. The commissioner also began urging on Congress the need of federal aid in America. In 1850, he deplored the lack of competent men to fill chairs of agriculture in the colleges, and said that "if a young farmer engaged in stock growing wishes to study the digestive organs, the muscles, nerves, or blood vessels of the horse, cow, sheep, or hog, there is not a museum in all America where this can be done." [7]

In the next two years, the commissioner published letters from prominent agriculturists, asking for a national school for the training of teachers of agriculture, and for other industrial schools. Following numerous petitions to Congress, in December, 1857, Justin Smith Morrill of Vermont presented his first bill to the House of Representatives, asking for two thousand acres of land for each member of Congress in any state, to be given that state as an endowment for a college "for the benefit of agricultural and mechanic arts." The Committee on Public Lands promptly smothered the measure. He presented the bill again two years later, and it passed both houses of Congress, but was vetoed by President James Buchanan.[8] By this time, the bill was being bitterly opposed by Southern members of Congress, on the state-rights issue. Senator Clement Claiborne Clay of Alabama spoke as "an ambassador from a sovereign State" in opposition to this effort to gag the commonwealths by means of subversive grants. In view of the near disfranchisement of professors in land-grant colleges, by the Hatch Act of 1940, it would seem that there was some substance to Clay's fears. A Minnesota senator (Henry Mower Rice) also felt that the land-grant provision would bring a "slow, lingering death" to his state.[9] Considering the land monopolization that actually resulted, there was also some justification for his stand.

Again, in December, 1861, Morrill presented an amended bill which, five months later, was reported adversely by the Committee on Public Lands, though the Southern representatives now were no longer present to obstruct. But a similar measure presented to

[7] A[lfred] C[harles] True, "Education and Research in Agriculture in the United States," *Agricultural Yearbook*, 1894, pp. 89–90.

[8] A. C. True, "Agricultural Education in the United States," *Agricultural Yearbook*, 1899, pp. 166–167.

[9] Wiest, *Agricultural Organization*, p. 200.

the Senate by Ben Wade of Ohio ultimately passed both houses and became law on July 2, 1862. This act was of a comprehensive nature, allowing to each state accepting its terms "the endowment, support, and maintenance of at least one college where the leading object shall be, without excluding other scientific and classical studies, and including military tactics, to teach such branches of learning as are related to agriculture and the mechanic arts, in such manner as the legislatures . . . may . . . prescribe, in order to promote the liberal and practical education of the industrial classes in the several pursuits and professions in life." The endowment was to be thirty thousand acres of public land for each representative and senator in Congress. When any of the land was sold, the proceeds should be invested at a rate of interest not less than 5 per cent. Not more than a tenth of the proceeds could be used to buy building sites or experimental farms, but the rest of the fund, if ever diminished, should be made up again by state appropriations. Since this left the states to supply the buildings and equipment, it was clear that the proposed "endowment, support, and maintenance" from the federal government was to be only partial. In fact, in time the federal grant, together with all later annual donations, constituted only a very minor fraction of the funds needed to run most of the colleges.[10] The act provided an initial stimulus, but left the way open for an amount of federal meddling far out of proportion to the support granted.

Some features of the act were considerably short of ideal. The oldest and richest states—the ones least needing the aid—because of their larger population got the bigger grants. But, since those states had no public lands in their own borders, they could locate their scrip in the most desirable parts of any Western territories or states, whereas the latter had to select within their own limits. On the other hand, the newer commonwealths, because of their small population and slender financial means, could not make an early start; so, after the railroads, Eastern states, and other monopolists had made their selections, the new states were allowed the gleanings. Thus New York, which needed no assistance, got 990,-000 acres of the choicest Western lands, while Kansas and some others got 90,000 much poorer acres. Down to 1898, sixty-four col-

[10] True, "Agricultural Education," pp. 167–168; 12 Statutes at Large, pp. 503–504.

leges and universities (or separate branches), representing each of the forty-five states and three of the territories (all but Indian Territory), had participated in the division, but the total endowment for all was only a little over $10,000,000, most of it in a few Eastern states. As yet, 1,240,000 acres were unsold, and, for the most part, were unsalable.[11] Not only would an outright gift of money to the states have avoided some of the inequity, but it would have prevented the throwing away by the states of millions of acres of lands to monopolists, at prices often as low as fifty cents an acre.

Only seventeen of the states and territories turned their funds over to the regular state university, and, of these, West Virginia split her allotment between two schools, one white and one Negro. All the rest of the states established separate agricultural colleges, and several of them, especially in the South, set up two.[12] In this way many of the states saddled upon themselves the financial overhead—in administration, campuses, buildings, equipment, libraries, and duplication of departments and courses—of maintaining two or three educational institutions where one would have been sufficient. The consequence was often the crippling of them all. But once established, each school had its jealous supporters, so the states that made the initial mistake had either to continue bearing an additional financial burden or else retard their state schools.

For many years after the opening of the new colleges, whether in the state universities or separate, very little was done toward the training of the youth to become expert agriculturists. The idea was held that agriculture was a subject that could be taught by one professor, and it was hard enough to get even this one, if thoroughly trained, for each of the new institutions. The words "liberal education" and "classical studies" in the Act of 1862 meant, as the terms were then used, the same thing—Latin and Greek. The "practical" studies were reading, writing, and arithmetic, and the "professions" were medicine, law, and theology. What happened was that many of the states merely added a few industrial features to their offerings, as an embroidered edging to the usual classical education.[13] It was the next generation that became so practical as almost to eliminate the liberal arts altogether.

[11] True, "Agricultural Education," pp. 168, 185; *Agricultural Yearbook*, 1899, pp. 671–672.

[12] *Agricultural Yearbook*, 1899, pp. 671–672.

[13] True, "Educational and Research in Agriculture," p. 97.

The Populist upheaval of the 1890's did more than any other thing to convert the agricultural colleges of the Middle West into true institutions of higher learning of a distinctive type. The Populist board of regents of Kansas hired Thomas Will to teach economics, then discharged the entire faculty of the Kansas State Agricultural College, put Will in the presidency, and rehired such of the old staff as were amenable to the new dispensation. This was a severe blow to such tradition of academic tenure as may have existed, but the new professors that were hired were the best obtainable for the salary that was offered. Immediately, that college began to emerge from the high school ranks. The University of Illinois did not suffer so severe a shock, but it was not till John Peter Altgeld became governor of the state in 1893 that a real university was created. Altgeld also had some Populistic leanings, which may help to explain why no building on the campus was named for him till 1940—and then only one wing of a building.

In contrast to the slow growth of the general educational services of the colleges, the agricultural curriculum soon grew from a narrow, rigid course, with one or two lecturers, to a well-rounded offering including many electives. By 1898, most of the colleges had departments of general agriculture, animal industry, dairy husbandry, horticulture, agricultural chemistry, general and economic entomology, an experiment station, and an extension department. There was also, usually, a demonstration farm of 125 acres or more, well stocked with cattle, sheep, horses, swine, and poultry, a dairy building fully equipped with modern machinery and appliances, gardens, orchards, and museums. Because of the state control over most of the activities, it was decided that a greater degree of national coordination should exist, and, in 1867, Congress authorized the setting up of a federal Bureau of Education for the purpose of collecting and distributing information. Most of the bureau's reports came from data supplied by the agricultural colleges.[14] An example of the fact that radical reconstruction was not being carried into the field of agricultural education was seen in the extension of time granted Mississippi in 1866 to allow that partially reconstructed state to acquire its land grant, though its application had been too long delayed. During the first year of the

[14] A. C. True, "Some Types of American Agricultural Colleges," *Agricultural Yearbook*, 1898, pp. 63–80.

resulting college, it had a larger enrollment than the state university—a distinction that was held through the 1880's.[15]

Additional federal aid to the agricultural colleges was authorized by the Second Morrill Act of August 30, 1890. An appropriation of $15,000 for each state and territory was stipulated for the fiscal year that had ended two months earlier, and $1,000 over the amount for each preceding year was to be added to that sum annually for ten years, after which the yearly appropriation was to continue at $25,000. This contribution was "to be applied only to instruction in agriculture, the mechanic arts, the English language and the various branches of mathematical, physical, natural and economic science, with special reference to their applications in the industries of life, and to the facilities for such instruction." The law provided that this form of education be offered to all races alike,[16] which helps explain the duplication of schools in the South. This act was a distinct improvement over its predecessor, primarily because it showed recognition that little states needed at least as much help as the larger ones. The annual appropriation itself was far larger than the income from the land endowment in all but a very few of the states. The clause about "applications in the industries of life" led to some peculiar subterfuges. In later years courses in journalism were labeled "industrial journalism," and at least one college offered a course in what was called "agricultural English." The professor who was asked to teach the course felt that farmers' children should learn the same English as the rest, so he decided that his job was to teach pastoral poetry. Perhaps that was the intention. In later years the annual appropriations were increased occasionally, but this came in the next century.

Agricultural education took other forms than instruction in colleges. Prominent among these were farmers' institutes. Something similar to them had been fostered by the earlier agricultural societies, but the states began to take a more active part after the Act of 1862. In that year the Massachusetts State Board of Agriculture called for a four-day public meeting, and in 1866 Connecticut had a farmers' convention. Early in the 1870's, various Eastern states adopted a policy of annual institutes, and the agricultural colleges

[15] Ronald J[ames] Slay, *The Development of the Teaching of Agriculture in Mississippi* (New York: Columbia University, Bureau of Publications, Teachers College, 1928), pp. 41–42, 51.

[16] 26 *Statutes at Large*, pp. 417–419.

of Kansas and Michigan inaugurated their own programs. Before long, other states joined in the movement and the legislatures began making appropriations to further the work. The meetings were generally held in the winter months, one in each township. Part of the offerings were of a light and possibly entertaining sort, but such intervals were interspersed with serious lectures and discussions on matters of immediate importance to farmers. Professors from the agricultural colleges and investigators from the experiment stations took a prominent part. Evening sessions were often of the popular, inspirational lecture variety.[17] Prizes were offered to girls for samples of their cooking, baking, and canning, to boys for their skill in the handicrafts, and to their elders in their own specialties. Music, elocution, and refreshments played their part in getting an audience. But, even aside from the entertainment and serious instruction, the institutes were good things for the people they served. The farmer was too secluded an individual, and his wife was likely to be even more so. She could not go to town, as her husband did, every time a pitman rod broke on the header, and she needed the three or four days' association with other women.

Small beginnings were also made toward the extension of agricultural education down into the secondary and elementary schools. No great proportion of the farmers sent their sons to the agricultural colleges, and even of these students a large number went into the professions instead of returning to the soil. But a much larger number attended the secondary schools, and the state laws were making attendance compulsory in the elementary grades. Here was the real opportunity to start the boys and girls right before they got set in the unprogressiveness of their elders. For years before 1900, Southern Negroes got industrial training at Hampton Institute in Virginia, at Tuskegee Institute in Alabama, and at other similar schools of more modest reputation. Then, in 1895, the University of Minnesota organized a special secondary agricultural school, with a faculty all its own, and Nebraska later adopted the same plan. In the closing years of the century Alabama maintained a secondary agricultural school in each Congressional district. New Jersey in 1894 and Pennsylvania in 1897 each secured a farming

[17] True, "Agricultural Education," pp. 170–171.

school for boys and girls.[18] This very nearly calls the roll of such efforts, but it may also be noted that the agricultural colleges themselves usually had academic departments, and some of the Western ones took regular students direct from the eighth grade. So well did the Kansas State Agricultural College train the local children that Manhattan did not maintain a high school till well after 1900. A movement begun by Liberty Hyde Bailey of Cornell University, in 1894, in a few years was pointing the way toward agricultural instruction in the lower grades. The teaching of nature study in New York, Indiana, Missouri, Rhode Island, and Pennsylvania was also looked upon as training for later more intensive work.[19]

The extension divisions of the colleges were a vital force in adult education. In 1892, the Pennsylvania State College started a "Chautauqua course of home reading in agriculture." The college sent out book lists, offered examinations, and conducted correspondence in regard to the lessons. Where the farmers could not get the books, printed lessons and questions were sent out. By 1899, over 3,400 readers were taking the courses, of whom about one in eight was pursuing the study systematically. By that time, Michigan, New Hampshire, Connecticut, West Virginia, South Dakota, and New York had adopted somewhat similar plans. The New York courses were of a more elaborate nature than elsewhere, and in 1898 some 8,600 farmers were enrolled, all but about 600 of them being residents of that state. Reading clubs were formed and visited by representatives from the university. Itinerant schools also were conducted by Cornell, the experts in charge drilling away for a few days at a time on just those points the farmers were most in need of learning. The expansion of efforts of the experiment stations, and their numerous publications, in time supplied what had formerly been a lack of good books and other reading material within the comprehension of the average farmer.[20] Farmers' short courses were also being offered at the colleges in the 1890's, either during the vacation period or alongside the regular classes. The Wisconsin school offered two twelve-week courses beginning in January, each of a very practical nature.[21] The Granges and the

[18] *Ibid.*, p. 177; A. C. True, "Popular Education for the Farmer in the United States," *Agricultural Yearbook*, 1897, pp. 279–290.

[19] True, "Agricultural Education," pp. 177–178, 188–189.

[20] *Ibid.*, pp. 179–181.

[21] *Ibid.*, pp. 186–187.

Farmers' Alliances were valuable educational agencies whose main work of another nature will be discussed later.

AGRICULTURAL EXPERIMENT STATIONS

As early as 1872, the Commissioner of Agriculture held a conference with representatives of the land-grant colleges to discuss the establishment of experiment stations. Interest was already running high, among the informed leaders, regarding the results of experimentation in Europe. Some progress had already been made, largely through the independent efforts of professors in the agricultural colleges, and, in 1875, Connecticut set up a thoroughly organized experiment station. For some years before this, California also had been making substantial progress toward the creation of a station, a work that was to be continued by the pioneer farm scientist Eugene W. Hilgard. These precedents were followed at the University of North Carolina in 1877, Cornell in 1879, and the scientific school of Rutgers in 1880. In 1886, it was noted by the Committee on Agriculture of the federal House of Representatives that twelve states had thoroughgoing stations, and five more were "carrying on what is strictly experiment-station work as a part of their ordinary duty." Some of these early efforts were mainly the achievement of enterprising and public-spirited individuals like Orange Judd of Connecticut. But most noted of all was Lawson Valentine, who, in 1876, bought several hundred acres in Orange County, New York, which he named the Houghton Farm. This was followed by the employment of Manly Miles (then at Michigan) to start the work of an experiment station. Later, under the management of Henry E. Alvord, Valentine spent about $20,000 a year on experimental work, till his death, in 1888, ended the project.[22]

Another convention of agricultural college delegates met in the federal capital in 1883, to urge Congressional aid in the work, and C. C. Carpenter of Iowa already had a bill for this purpose before the House of Representatives. But Congress was too much wrapped up in the further entanglement of tariff laws to give any attention to such a fanciful notion as scientific aid to common farmers. Nevertheless, the forces of enlightenment persisted. The Cullen bill

[22] A. C. True, "Agricultural Experiment Stations in the United States," *Agricultural Yearbook*, 1899, pp. 514–518.

replaced the earlier one by Carpenter, and another conference, called by Commissioner Coleman in 1885, urged its adoption. All this, and additional agitation, finally convinced Congress, so on March 2, 1887, Cleveland had the opportunity of signing a bill introduced more than a year earlier by Representative William H. Hatch of Missouri. The Hatch Act provided $15,000 a year from the sales of public lands, to be given to each state and territory for experiment-station work. The money was to go to the land-grant colleges except in states where stations were already established and operating under some other arrangement. As much as $3,000 of the first appropriation might go for buildings, and thereafter no more than $750 a year, the rest to be spent purely for the work of investigation. The act went into some detail in specifying the practical nature of agricultural experimentation that was to be pursued. To a large degree the law was a monument to Commissioner and Secretary Coleman.[23]

An oversight on the part of Congress prevented any appropriation during the first year, so it was not till 1888 that progress was begun. In 1894, the Secretary of Agriculture was given authority to examine the financial accounts of the stations. Such a check-up was hardly necessary, but it brought about closer cooperation between the Department of Agriculture and the colleges and stations. Annual visits from the Office of Experiment Stations, and reports to Congress, further emphasized the seriousness of the work. By a series of rulings issued in March of 1896, the stations were assured of their right to use, as they saw fit, the funds created by sales of the products they raised or manufactured. The first outstanding display of the work of the stations was at the Chicago World's Fair of 1893, the exhibits being in nine sections: "botany, soils, fertilizers, crops, horticulture, entomology, feeding stuffs, animal nutrition, and dairying." The total expenditure of federal, state, and station-earned funds in the first year was about $720,000. There were then forty-six stations in thirty-eight states and one territory. In the next year these stations issued 45 reports and 237 bulletins.

[23] *Ibid.*, pp. 518–520; Whitney H[art] Shepardson, *Agricultural Education in the United States* (New York: The Macmillan Company, 1929), pp. 31–32; 24 *Statutes at Large*, pp. 440–442; W[ilbur] O[lin] Atwater, director, "Organization of the Agricultural Experiment Stations in the United States, . . . 1889," U.S. Department of Agriculture, Office of Experiment Stations, *Experiment Station Bulletin* No. 1 (Washington: Government Printing Office, 1889), pp. 6–7, 65–67.

By 1899, there were stations in every state and territory and in Alaska and Hawaii. Exclusive of branches, there were fifty-six stations, with an income above $1,000,000, seven tenths of it coming from the federal Treasury. Together "the stations published 445 annual reports and bulletins" and had a mailing list of over half a million.[24]

The myriad activities of the stations and the cooperation of the federal Department of Agriculture were of incalculable help to the farmers of the nation, but sometimes federal meddling became a nuisance. Experiment-station researchers are serious-minded men, who can best do their work in an atmosphere free of restraint, and if unconscious of bureaucratic control. But the Department of Agriculture has local pressures to divert its energies, and members of Congress prodding it to do something for the mending of political fences. In 1913, Eugene Davenport pointed out some of the malign effects of this sort of officiousness, and he was looking back over a long career, mostly in the nineteenth century, when he announced his conclusions. As he saw it—and none other knew the situation better—too much of the cooperation of the Department of Agriculture had served merely to slow down work, cause embarrassment, and involve the stations in politics. Most of the trouble came because the department was trying to solve some local problem that was best handled independently or let alone, "and with no other excuse than that it had the money and the inclination to do it. . . ." He felt that every conceivable local issue in the whole nation had been dabbled in by the thousands of agents in the department, and with generally poor results. Much avoidable friction arose because of this meddling, beyond the scope of the original law, conducted with the bureaucrat's usual ignorance of the workings of the minds of research experts.[25]

THE LINES OF FEDERAL ACTIVITY

A convenient way to get a view of the range of governmental activity in agriculture is to note the creation of bureaus in the federal Department of Agriculture, and the work they did. The

[24] True, "Agricultural Experiment Stations," pp. 520–523.

[25] Eugene Davenport, *The Relations between the Federal Department of Agriculture and the Agricultural Colleges and Experiment Stations* (Urbana: University of Illinois, 1913), pp. 5–8, quotation p. 6.

first Commissioner of Agriculture was Isaac Newton (1862–1867). During his term, the slender library of agricultural books inherited from the Patent Office developed into the Department Library, but as late as 1875 the collection numbered only 7,000 volumes. Until 1893, growth continued to be slow; the quarters were cramped and the service was limited. Then the librarian was put on the civil service list, the library itself was reorganized, and modern methods were introduced. By 1899, the number of volumes reached 68,000, three fourths of which were strictly agricultural and the rest related. At the same time, sixty-two of seventy-nine American institutions presumably having agricultural libraries reported approximately 187,000 volumes of agricultural books among them. Cornell University had 15,000 volumes, and from that number the series declined to the Alcorn Agricultural and Mechanical College of Mississippi (Negro), with 75.[26] Quite clearly, here was one aspect of agricultural education in which the governments were not wildly extravagant, and the value of many even of this small number of books may well be questioned.

The Division of Chemistry was also established in 1862, and its first report was submitted at the beginning of the following year. It included an analysis of grape juices, sorghums, sugars, sirups, and beets, and contained an article on the chemistry of sugar. Succeeding reports continued to branch out in other lines. By 1868, note was taken of the phosphate rocks of South Carolina, later to prove of great importance, and, in 1869, there was an article on soil analysis. Also of significance was the collection of data on the nitrogen nutrition of plants and the work of bacteria in supplying this chemical to the soil. Increasing attention was paid to soil analysis, physical properties, and fertilization. Much time, after 1883, was given to sorghums, in an effort to utilize them for sugar, and to cereals, the purpose being to ascertain their qualities for new uses. Food adulterations were carefully studied, though the progress of checking their use was disappointingly slow. It was

[26] M[ilton] S[tover] Eisenhower and A[rthur] P[ercy] Chew, "The United States Department of Agriculture: Its Structure and Functions," U.S. Department of Agriculture, *Miscellaneous Publication* No. 88 (Washington: Government Printing Office, 1934), p. 139; Charles H[oward] Greathouse, "Development of Agricultural Libraries," *Agricultural Yearbook*, 1899, pp. 497, 504; *Agricultural Yearbook*, 1899, pp. 757–758. Wiest, *Agricultural Organization*, pp. 21–185, supplies adequate details on the origins, development, and activities of the department and its subordinate agencies; pages not repeated in succeeding footnotes.

recognized that oleomargarine and glucose, as examples, were nutritious foods, but they were an imposition on the public when sold as butter and honey. "The closing of the century," said Harvey W. Wiley, later famous as an advocate of pure food and drugs, "sees in this country an endowment for agricultural research which excites the admiration of the whole civilized world. . . . We find chemistry intimately associated with nearly every line of agricultural progress and pointing the way to still greater advancement." Half or more of the federal money spent "for strictly scientific investigations has been for chemical studies." [27]

The Division of Statistics, created in 1863, collected data on the condition, prospects, and harvests of the main crops, and as to the numbers of farm animals. It operated through many correspondents directed by state agents. Information was also sought from foreign countries. It coordinated and tabulated this information, as well as other data on distribution and consumption, and issued monthly bulletins for the information and guidance of producers, consumers, publicists, and scholars. As a Maine farmer wrote in the early years of the service, "Your monthly reports give me just the information I have wanted for years. Knowing the supply and demand, I am able to sell at my own price." By 1899, a corps of fifty thousand reporters kept the division informed on the condition of staple crops, so that the raisers might be promptly and accurately notified.[28]

The Division of Entomology also came in 1863, and its work was quite as important as that of any other agency of the government. The main objective was to develop methods of insect control and to keep the farmers informed on the newest discoveries. As a result of the Western grasshopper visitations of 1874 and following, in 1876 Congress made a special appropriation of $18,000 to study the Rocky Mountain locust. The Hatch Act of 1887 furthered the work in experiment stations. Four other events gave the division sufficient material to keep it busy during the remainder of the century; the discovery of the gypsy moth and brown-tail moth in

[27] H[arvey] W[ashington] Wiley, "The Relation of Chemistry to the Progress of Agriculture," *Agricultural Yearbook*, 1899, pp. 236–253, quotation p. 258.

[28] Charles H. Greathouse, *Historical Sketch of the United States Department of Agriculture* (U.S. Department of Agriculture, Division of Publications, *Bulletin* No. 3, Washington: Government Printing Office, 2d rev., 1907), pp. 28–29, 51–52, quotation p. 11; W[illet] M[artin] Hays, "The United States Department of Agriculture," *The Outlook*, LXXX, No. 14 (August 5, 1905), 866.

Massachusetts; the invasion of Texas by the boll weevil; the finding of San Jose scale in the East; and a fuller realization of the part taken by insects in the carrying of diseases of man and other animals.[29]

The second Commissioner of Agriculture was Horace Capron. During his term (1867–1871) the Division of Botany was inaugurated (1868), at the suggestion of Joseph Henry of the Smithsonian Institution, who also offered the Department of Agriculture the unmounted botanical specimens of the National Museum. When Frederick Watts (1871–1877) took over the department, there was also a Division of Garden and Grounds. Then, in 1871, Thomas Taylor was put in charge of a new Division of Microscopy. He studied cranberry rot, mildew in grapes, blights in peaches and plums, and, after investigating mushrooms, suggested their cultivation as a profitable business. On slender funds, the department continued to study plant diseases until 1885, when a Section of Mycology was formed, the name being changed in 1888 to Plant Pathology. This was subsequently merged with a Division of Plant Science to make the Bureau of Plant Industry. The researches of this bureau revealed the basic laws of plant disease, evolved methods for destroying fungi by spraying with chemicals, and showed the relation of correct tillage to the control of pests and diseases. In 1890, over five thousand fruit growers were participating in farm tests to demonstrate the use of copper compounds for black rot, mildew, and other diseases.[30] By the end of the century, the heredity of each of the great crop plants was being studied by specialists, and numerous breeders in the experiment stations had taken species to be adapted to the production of better crops under divers local conditions.[31] Before the end of the century, plant breeding had produced distinct improvements in grapes, pears, apples, plums, strawberries, gooseberries, different vegetables, the cereals, cotton, flowers, ornamental plants, and nuts.[32]

A year before William LeDuc became commissioner (1877–

[29] L[eland] O[ssian] Howard, "Progress in Economic Entomology in the United States," *Agricultural Yearbook,* 1899, pp. 135–156 *passim;* Greathouse, *Department of Agriculture,* pp. 10, 18, 51.

[30] B[everly] T[homas] Galloway, "Progress in the Treatment of Plant Diseases in the United States," *Agricultural Yearbook,* 1899, pp. 191–200.

[31] Hays, "Department of Agriculture," p. 865.

[32] Herbert J[ohn] Webber and Ernst A[thearn] Bessey, "Progress of Plant Breeding in the United States," *Agricultural Yearbook,* 1899, pp. 465–490 *passim.*

1881), some forestry work was begun, and in 1881 the Division of Forestry was set up. Ten years later, Congress authorized the system of forest reserves to protect what timber was left on the public domain and to insure a regular flow of water in the streams.[33] In 1893, the forestry service discovered that the hewing of the bark from one side of pine trees for turpentine did not harm the trees. Out of this grew the new industry of the Southeastern turpentine plantations.[34] Appropriations for forestry work increased from $5,000 in 1872 to a maximum of $120,000 in 1893. Then, on June 4, 1897, an act of Congress provided a new system of organization of the forest reserves and placed their administration under the control of the Department of the Interior.[35]

Toward the end of the administration of the next commissioner, George B. Loring (1881–1885), the Bureau of Animal Industry grew out of the work, already begun, of fighting pleuropneumonia among cattle. In 1889, before the disease was conquered, the bureau issued elaborate instructions for the quarantine, inspection, dipping, and sanitary shipment of cattle from areas afflicted with Texas fever. The dipping was a recognition of the fact that ticks were the carriers. An immediate decline in the prevalence of the disease was noted from that time. "The result has been increased prices abroad and a great reduction of insurance on cargoes of cattle. . . ." In 1895, the quarantine regulations were extended to cover hog cholera, tuberculosis, and sheep scab. Scab was a disease easily eradicated, but was allowed to continue as a result of the carelessness with which infected animals were handled. Serum treatments were developed for hog cholera, effecting a saving of three quarters or more of losses in droves that were treated. The possibility of stamping out the disease entirely was anticipated. Work was also done on vaccines for blackleg and tuberculosis among cattle, and other diseases were being investigated. The inspection of exported animals was pursued with great vigor, so as to eliminate all cause for foreign bans. Meat inspection at slaughterhouses became another activity, though not carried far enough, as the embalmed beef scandal of 1898 was to reveal. The inspection

[33] Gifford Pinchot, "Progress of Forestry in the United States," *Agricultural Yearbook*, 1899, pp. 294–295.

[34] Greathouse, *Department of Agriculture*, p. 30.

[35] Pinchot, "Forestry in the United States," pp. 294–295.

of imported livestock was begun in 1890. In 1895, a Dairy Division was added to the bureau.[36]

Norman J. Coleman, Commissioner and Secretary from 1885 to 1889, added important services to the department, aside from calling attention to the possibilities of agriculture in Alaska and agitating for further protection and expansion of the national forests. A recognition of the importance of birds in the control of insects led to the founding of a Section of Economic Ornithology in the Division of Entomology, July 1, 1885. It was set aside as a separate division only a few months later. In 1896, with widened scope, it became the Division of Biological Survey. Its principal work was "(1) To determine as accurately as possible the food of birds of economic importance; (2) to act as a court of appeal to investigate complaints concerning depredations of birds on crops; (3) to diffuse the results of its work and educate the public as to the value of birds." An important early result of the investigations was to show that most owls and hawks were to be numbered among the farmers' best friends, as destroyers of harmful rodents and other pests. In 1885, Pennsylvania had adopted a "scalp law" that was resulting in the extermination of hawks and owls. Colorado, Indiana, New Hampshire, Ohio, Virginia, and West Virginia also offered bounties. The revelations of the ornithologists secured a reversal of this trend till a number of states actually adopted measures to protect what they formerly had sought to destroy.[37] But almost no advance was made toward the protection of those other great foes of rodents, the snakes. The story is told of a farmer who was seen to tear down a wheat shock to kill a bull snake underneath. Asked how he knew the snake was there, he replied: "I kicked the shock and no mice ran out." [38]

The Division of Pomology, of 1886 and following, collected and disseminated data for the benefit of fruit growers, tested the adaptability of orchard trees to the different soils and climates, studied

[36] George F[ayette] Thompson, "Administrative Work of the Federal Government in Relation to the Animal Industry," *Agricultural Yearbook*, 1899, pp. 441–464, quotation p. 452; Eisenhower and Chew, "Department of Agriculture," pp. 60–62; Greathouse, *Department of Agriculture*, pp. 24–25; Wanlass, *Department of Agriculture*, pp. 25–26.

[37] T[heodore] S[herman] Palmer, "A Review of Economic Ornithology in the United States," *Agricultural Yearbook*, 1899, pp. 262–267.

[38] For examples of similar stories see Raymond Lee Ditmars, *Reptiles of the World* (New York: The Macmillan Company, new ed., 1933), pp. 174–175.

the best methods of culture, and introduced new varieties. With this work was also associated the activities of the Division of Vegetable Physiology and Pathology, originated in 1887. Its publications, twelve years later, included bulletins on peach growing for market, spraying for fruit diseases, the pineapple industry, mushroom culture, black rot of the cabbage, fungous diseases of the grape and their treatment, and several others. Then, under the Hatch Act, came the experiment stations, already discussed, through whose aid much of the information for other bureaus, divisions, and sections of the Department of Agriculture was obtained. From time to time, in succeeding years, Congress appropriated extra funds for a number of special investigations, in cooperation with the experiment stations. Some of these were for studies of irrigation, the "nutritive value and economy of human foods," the work conducted by the Office of Public Road Inquiries, and the researches on forage plants of the Division of Agrostology.[39]

The second Secretary of Agriculture, and the first to occupy the post for more than a few days, was Jeremiah M. Rusk (1889–1893). It was he who established the Division of Publications and started the issuance of the *Farmers' Bulletins*.[40] Hundreds of publications were got out each year, many of them for free distribution by members of Congress. For example, 470,000 of the 500,000 copies of the *Yearbook* were for such disposal. A monthly list of publications was a guide to the farmers in selecting their wants, and 426,000 of the lists were issued in 1899.[41] In 1891, the Weather Bureau was transferred from the Signal Service of the War Department to the Department of Agriculture, and among its numerous publications were nearly 500,000 daily weather maps in 1899. Six hundred new weather stations were added soon after the transfer, and the first year's operations cost close to $900,000. With 2,200 observers, the cost could hardly have been less, but its worth was far greater than the expense. By 1900, the extension of observations to the Caribbean region gave advance notice of approaching storms.[42]

The last Secretary of Agriculture for this study was J. Sterling

[39] *Agricultural Yearbook*, 1899, pp. 668–669, 685.

[40] Greathouse, *Department of Agriculture*, p. 23.

[41] *Agricultural Yearbook*, 1899, pp. 676–686.

[42] F[rank] H[agar] Bigelow, "Work of the Meteorologist for the Benefit of Agriculture, Commerce, and Navigation," *Agricultural Yearbook*, 1899, pp. 71–92 *passim*; Eisenhower and Chew, "Department of Agriculture," p. 25.

Morton (1893–1897). He recommended a closer supervision of the experiment stations and also set about enlarging the departmental library. In line with the policies of the Cleveland administration, he greatly expanded the classified civil service in the department. He opposed the old political electioneering device of distributing free seeds, and at least took that duty off the hands of departmental employees, leaving it to the seedmen holding government contracts. In place of the special agents abroad, he established a Section of Foreign Markets under his personal supervision. In 1893, Congress appropriated ten thousand dollars for the study of road building and maintenance, for the publication of information on the subject, and for the assistance of the agricultural colleges and experiment stations in like work. This resulted in the Office of Public Road Inquiries.[43] For nearly a score of years its efforts were purely in the way of investigation and education, but the groundwork was being laid for the later vast program of road building. Further progress was made, in 1894, by the creation of a Division of Soils, separated from the Weather Bureau a year later. From its studies came the beginnings of the soil science that was to become quite revolutionary by the 1930's.[44]

In 1894, Congress made a special appropriation for the study of nutrition in human foods, the work being done by the Office of Experiment Stations. Other appropriations followed, and both technical and popular writings on the subject were published. One investigation revealed what had long been suspected, that there was little relation between the cost of making bread and its retail price. For some time following this exposure, the price of bread dropped in many cities. As to feed for animals, the Division of Agrostology, set up in 1895, soon resulted in A Handbook of Grasses of the United States. Also, there were experiments with domestic and foreign grasses and legumes in all parts of the country, both to improve pastures and to build up depleted soils.[45]

[43] Greathouse, Department of Agriculture, pp. 27–31.
[44] Eisenhower and Chew, "Department of Agriculture," p. 161; Wiest, Agricultural Organization, p. 143.
[45] A. C. True and R[obert] D[enniston] Milner, "Development of Nutrition Investigations of the Department of Agriculture," Agricultural Yearbook, 1899, pp. 410–414; F[rank] Lamson-Scribner, "Progress of Economic and Scientific Agrostology," ibid., pp. 350–355; Eisenhower and Chew, "Department of Agriculture," p. 127; Greathouse, Department of Agriculture, p. 29; Agricultural Yearbook, 1900, p. 12.

From Henry L. Ellsworth's first appropriation of a thousand dollars for the Patent Office in 1839, for work in agriculture, till the
beginning of James Wilson's long career as Secretary in 1897, the
department had cost the people less than twenty million dollars.
What it had contributed to human welfare cannot be calculated,
but the declaration that it was "the greatest research university in
the world" can hardly be questioned.[46] With all this assistance,
then, why were American farmers not prospering?

[46] Hays, "United States Department of Agriculture," p. 863.

CHAPTER XIII

The Agrarian Uprising

THE ENIGMA OF FARM PRICES

THE preceding pages have been replete with references to agricultural distress: cotton that, according to individual testimony, cost six or seven cents a pound to produce, selling at four or five cents, fifty-cent wheat going at hardly half that price, and the like.[1] This was not a constant condition, but it so persisted and recurred that, for much of the three decades before 1897, large portions of the farming population had no financial security, and tenancy was usually on the increase. The individual with an orderly mind would, no doubt, like to see the farmers' balance sheet for these decades drawn up in neat columns and graphs. These should reveal actual costs of production, prices and total receipts for produce sold, and the cost and amount of goods purchased. It would be gratifying, also, to scan accurate data on the total amounts of long, short, and intermediate farm credits, as well as interest rates, by state, geographic section, or area of crop specialization.

Unfortunately, for the meticulous student, no collected data exist for most of these factors. America's rural grandsires were not bookkeepers, and no federal or state agencies wrested the information from them. The best that can be done, even for the prices of farm products before 1908, is to take the federal government reports for December 1 of each year.[2] These reflect what the goods

[1] [U.S.] Industrial Commission, *Final Report* (Washington: Government Printing Office, 1900–1902), XIX, 142.

[2] George F[rederick] Warren, "Prices of Farm Products in the United States," U. S. Department of Agriculture, *Department Bulletin* No. 999 (Washington: Government Printing Office, 1921), p. 66.

brought in the markets, but not what the farmer actually got. Furthermore, since most farmers sold their wheat in June, July, or August and their cotton in January or February, the December 1 prices may often be far from those prevailing at the times when the farmers were getting their share of the proceeds. Even the reports of the various boards of trade are but little more useful in computing the agricultural balance sheet, and for reasons that were made obvious in the preceding chapters, without further argument here. It is doubtful whether sufficient data can ever be collected from such scattered farmers' account books as may exist. The only other, and the only closely reliable, source of information would be the thousands of rural newspapers, both in their general news items and in their local market reports. Some further information might be gleaned from the farm journals. But statistics gathered from such sources will require the lifetime study of many scholars, and it is not likely to be accomplished in this generation.

Yet, some slight indication of the degree of rural prosperity can be shown by tables or graphs of the buying power of an average acre of each crop, in terms of general wholesale prices for December 1 in the same year. But most farmers received much less than the stipulated wholesale price for what they sold, and they paid far more than wholesale prices for what they bought. The following set of graphs for a few crops is offered merely as a suggestion of the trading value of the commodities on the produce exchanges. The index number of 100 is for the years 1910–1914. The December 1 price (of corn, for example) is divided by the average for 1910–1914, and the purchasing power is obtained by dividing the first quotient by the index number of general wholesale prices for the same date. The buying power is represented both in terms of bushel or pound and in terms of an acre of the crop. Consumers were interested in the price of a unit of goods, but the farmer had to depend on the returns by acres. Short crops meant high prices to consumers, but, as the graphs show, the acreage returns to the farmers, in such cases, rarely mounted accordingly. The most striking exception is cotton in 1900. In view of the fact that the average farmer was considered to be in fairly comfortable circumstances from 1910 to 1914, the charts may be of some value for comparison. Before 1900, the index of 100 was never approached

Purchasing Power of Four Different Crops at December 1 Prices, 1867–1900
(Five-Year Average, 1910–1914, is 100) [3]

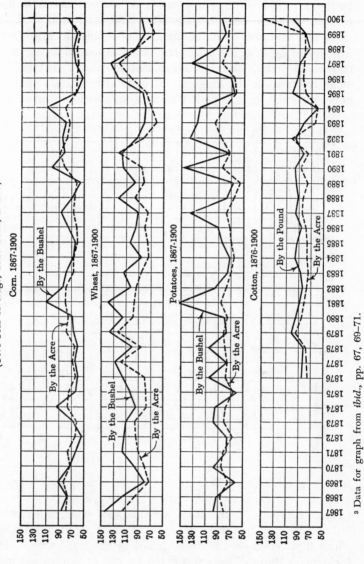

[3] Data for graph from *ibid.*, pp. 67, 69–71.

by the acreage line for corn, potatoes, or cotton. After 1868, it was reached by wheat only in 1877, 1879–1880, 1891, and 1896–1898.

A further study of index numbers of wholesale prices shows that, following 1830, the prices of farm crops tended to rise in relation to all goods, thus indicating that something besides prices alone lay beneath the long periods of farmer distress. Again, the price tendency for the period under consideration is most easily

Index of Wholesale Prices of Farm Products and All Commodities, 1860–1900 [4]

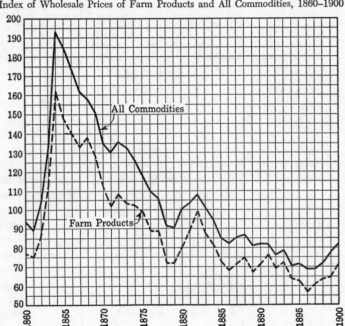

seen in graphic form. The greatest lag of farm prices below the general curve came in 1861–1865, when the divergence increased from 14 points to 37. But these were the war years, when farmers felt prosperous. Then the gap narrowed to 20 points in 1868, after which it widened steadily to 30 points in the panic year of 1873. Incidentally, farm distress was noted for two or three years before the panic. But, in the next four years of general hard times, the lines

[4] Data for graph from tables in George F[rederick] Warren and Frank A[shmore] Pearson, *Gold and Prices* (New York: John Wiley & Sons, Inc., 1935), pp. 30–31.

converged to 17 points in 1877, though the same years were the worst the Midwest farmers had seen in two decades, and were marked by the Granger unrest. Then the space grew to 20 points in 1880, and diminished to 9 in 1882. For the remainder of the 1880's, it remained close to 14. Contrary to the situation before the Panic of 1873, between 1889 and 1893, when the next panic came, the difference between farm and general prices diminished from 14 points to 6. Then the general prices fell most rapidly till 1896, when the gap widened to 12 points, and as prosperity returned to rural areas in 1897 and 1898 only 8 points separated the two lines. But in 1899 and 1900 farmers did not keep pace with general conditions, and the hiatus widened by half, though each year brought additional prosperity and abated unrest to the farms. The results of such a study of price curves, then, seem pretty largely negative in any effort to analyze the causes of rural unrest during those decades.[5]

Nevertheless, the actual prices received by farmers in the newer areas of the West and in the cotton belt—badly reconstructed economically for postwar conditions—were foremost in the list of causes for distress and unrest. Commentators and agitators in the West and South insisted that the farmer got only a small portion of the wholesale prices quoted at the exchanges. The reasons were that the charges made by middlemen and the railroads came out of the producers' pockets, and there is no question that these rates were much higher in those sections than in the Northeast. Another drain on the farmer was the shortage of capital, banking facilities, currency and credit, all of which caused interest rates to be so high as to make profitable agriculture uncertain. The divergence between farm and general prices was in itself enough to cause distress in the 1870's, without the other aggravations. In the late 1880's and the 1890's the problem was more complex.

VALIDITY OF RAILROAD-RATE COMPLAINTS

When the farmers of Iowa, Nebraska, or Kansas complained that it took the value of one bushel of corn to pay the freight on

[5] For further discussion see R[oland] W[illey] Bartlett, "Why Farm Prices Change," *Illinois Agricultural Economics Schools* (Urbana: Prepared for the Department of Economics, University of Illinois College of Agriculture Extension Service in Agricultural and Home Economics, mimeographed, 1935), p. 3.

TON-MILE RAILROAD FREIGHT RATES, BY SECTIONS

(Gold values, in cents)

Year	East of Chicago				Chicago to Missouri River					West of Missouri River				Southern			
	a	b	c	d	e	f	g	h	i	j	k	l	m	n	o	p	q
1860	2.16	1.96	1.67	6.41	2.04												
1861	2.09	1.93	1.71	5.82	1.91												
1862	1.99	1.93	1.80	7.17	1.86												
1863	1.63	1.55	1.43	7.01	1.39	1.91											
1864	1.53	1.35	1.29	....	1.36	1.39											
1865	1.65	1.54	1.39	....	1.76	1.99	2.29	2.38	1.79								
1866	1.75	1.64	1.42	4.66	2.25	2.40	2.45	2.78	2.61					3.55			
1867	1.75	1.50	1.40	3.75	2.09	2.19	2.41	2.83	2.15					3.45	3.01		
1868	1.66	1.32	1.21	3.18	1.75	2.39	2.58	2.53	2.27					3.30	2.95		
1869	1.27	1.23	1.20	3.75	1.84	2.20	2.69	2.30	1.99					3.11	2.45	4.42	
1870	1.27	1.27	1.23	4.10	1.95	2.32	2.61	2.38	2.03		3.60			4.34	2.51	4.53	
1871	1.24	1.21	1.28	4.45	2.08	2.37	2.57	2.29	1.87		2.42			4.85	2.30	4.86	
1872	1.23	1.30	1.26	3.64	1.92	2.23	2.33	2.18	1.74		2.39			3.78	2.05	4.43	
1873	1.16	1.26	1.22	1.91	1.92	2.00	2.05	2.17	1.61		2.15			2.59	1.93	4.21	7.67
1874	1.07	1.16	1.13	1.35	1.88	1.87	1.99	2.14	1.66		1.95	2.75		3.24	1.94	3.62	5.37
1875	.89	.99	.97	1.30	1.69	1.69	1.71	1.83	1.66		2.16	2.12	4.51	2.53	1.69	3.06	4.67
1876	.72	.84	.83	1.06	1.59	1.69	1.58	1.80	1.39		2.21	2.42	3.51	2.62	1.64	3.06	3.95
1877	.81	.95	1.02	1.04	1.72	1.56	1.60	1.95	1.32	4.80	2.14	2.40	3.15	2.16	1.38	2.75	3.69
1878	.72	.91	.87	.99	1.62	1.54	1.58	1.76	1.21	4.38	2.24	2.09	3.21	2.32	1.64	2.83	4.39
1879	.64	.82	.75	.86	1.52	1.43	1.56	1.70	1.11	3.74	1.99	2.51	3.12	2.25	1.53	2.43	4.07
1880	.75	.92	....	.87	1.54	1.21	1.49	1.75	1.08	3.15	....	2.38	3.09	2.47	1.59	2.16	3.11

Year	a	b	c	d	e	f	g	h	i	j	k	l	m	n	o	p	q
1881	.62	.86	.75	.89	1.52	1.22	1.47	1.70	1.16	3.20	2.18	2.28	3.36	2.13	1.50	2.07	2.84
1882	.63	.87	.75	.75	1.42	1.28	1.47	1.48	1.09	3.04	2.10	2.29	2.28	2.07	1.35	1.95	3.75
1883	.73	.88	.79	.72	1.43	1.17	1.43	1.39	1.03	2.72	1.91	1.99	1.76	2.05	1.32	2.06	2.03
1884	.65	.80	.67	.67	1.37	1.10	1.31	1.29	.97	2.46	1.56	1.93	1.65	1.75	1.34	2.09	2.75
1885	.55	.70	.58	.55	1.31	1.04	1.19	1.28	.96	2.25	1.42	1.75	1.56	1.62	1.16	1.95	3.60
1886	.64	.76	.69	.54	1.16	1.07	1.19	1.17	.95	2.04	1.27	1.60	1.67	1.68	1.08	1.93	3.43
1887	.67	.73	.72	.54	1.09	1.01	1.10	1.09	.88	1.82	1.21	1.35	1.46	1.60	1.08	1.92	3.02
1888	.67	.72	.66	.54	1.07	.96	.98	1.02	.79	1.42	1.17	1.31	1.31	1.61	1.05	1.71	2.88
1889	.63	.69	.69	.54	.84	.97	1.10	1.07	.87	1.59	1.17	1.29	1.44	1.43	1.00	1.48	3.16
1890	.64	.66	.69	.56	.94	1.00	.98	1.00	.81	1.53	1.14	1.13	1.25	1.39	.97	1.31	3.13
1891	.63	.66	.70	.53	.93	1.04	1.03	1.00	.86	1.46	1.13	1.18	1.28	1.41	.97	1.42	2.88
1892	.60	.65	.67	.52	.91	1.06	1.01	1.03	.85	1.36	1.08	1.13	1.23	1.29	.95	1.36	2.19
1893	.60	.62	.68	.51	.85	1.04	1.03	1.03	.82	1.33	1.03	1.07	1.14	1.27	.92	1.21	1.81
1894	.59	.61	.65	.48	.84	.99	1.08	1.04	.78	1.32	.97	.98	1.16	1.19	.88	1.13	2.27
1895	.57	.57	.64	.43	.81	1.08	1.14	1.08	.77	1.33	.97	1.05	1.21	1.08	.83	1.05	1.95
1896	.55	.56	.66	.43	.75	1.02	1.02	1.00	.74	1.33	.96	1.03	1.09	1.22	.81	1.03	1.43
1897	.54	.56	.60	.42	.67	.96	.98	1.01	.78	1.28	.96	1.01	1.12	1.11	.79	.98	1.24
1898	.53	.52	.57	.37	.70	.97	.89	.97	.81	1.36	.95	.96	1.04	.99	.74	.93	1.98
1899	.48	.47	.50	.36	.69	1.00	.88	.94	.77	1.16	1.02	.95	1.11	1.04	.73	.90	1.85
1900	.49	.50	.58	.34	.65	.99	.84	.93	.77	1.11	1.05	.93	.97	1.14	.75	.92	1.77

a Lake Shore and Michigan Southern; b Pennsylvania; c Pittsburgh, Fort Wayne, and Chicago; d Chesapeake and Ohio; e Illinois Central; f Chicago, Rock Island, and Pacific; g Chicago and Northwestern; h Chicago, Milwaukee, and St. Paul; i Chicago, Burlington, and Quincy (east of Missouri River); j Chicago, Burlington, and Quincy (west of Missouri River); k Union Pacific; l Atchison, Topeka, and Santa Fé; m Texas and Pacific; n Louisville and Nashville; o Georgia; p Southern; q Galveston, Houston, and Henderson.

another bushel, or when the Minnesota or Dakota farmers said the
same of wheat,[6] often this was no exaggeration and sometimes it
was an understatement. Not only did the Western and Southern
producers have to ship their produce great distances to market,
but the ton-mile rates of the West and the South were frequently
from twice to three times those between Chicago and New York.
A statistical analysis by the Department of Agriculture, in 1901,
shows this to be almost invariably true even for normal rates.[7]
Though reduced to gold values, all rates for the years 1860 to
1874 seem alarmingly high as compared with those of 1900. But,
as the rates diminished in the later years, the ratio between the
Northeast and the rest of the country remained little changed. This
can be well illustrated in parallel columns for the railroads east of
Chicago, those between Chicago and the Missouri River, those of
the farther West, and those of the South. It should be admitted that
some rates in New England were also high, but in that locality the
shipment was never a long one, and the toll from the individual
farmer was, in consequence, never comparable with that from the
wheat grower of Dakota, the corn raiser of Kansas, or the cotton
farmer of Arkansas.

In the table on page 296,[8] probably the most revealing figures
are in columns i and j, for the Burlington line east and west of
the Missouri River. The rates were nearly four times as high west
of the river as east of it in 1877, and were half again as high down
to 1900. No doubt, a similar tendency could be seen in other intersectional railroads, if the statistician had broken down all rates in
a like manner. In fact, this was done for the various lines forming
the Union Pacific system for the years 1881–1896, and with rather
startling results. On the Salina and Southwestern branch, the ton-
mile rate for 1881 was 4.726 cents, and in 1896 it was almost an
even 4 cents. On the other hand, the Kansas Central branch rose
above 3 cents only in one year, while the Carbon Cutoff was as
low as 0.615 cents in 1890. Several other idiosyncrasies are revealed for the eleven lines in the system, which cannot be explained

    [6] John D[onald] Hicks, *The Populist Revolt* (Minneapolis: The University of
Minnesota Press, c.1931), p. 60.
    [7] H[arry] T[urner] Newcomb and Edward G. Ward, "Changes in the Rates of
Charge for Railway and Other Transportation Services," U.S. Department of Agriculture, Division of Statistics, *Miscellaneous Series, Bulletin* No. 15, rev. (Washington: Government Printing Office, 1901).
    [8] *Ibid.*, pp. 21–23, 25–26.

merely on the basis of volume of traffic carried. A record for the
period was, the charge of 44 cents a ton-mile on a little railroad in
the Arkansas-Louisiana area in 1880.[9]

The part that competition, or the lack of it, played in the
determination of rates is well illustrated in the traffic between
Chicago and New York. As stated by Department of Agriculture

Rail and Water Rates on Wheat, Chicago to New York, 1868–1900 [10]
(In cents a bushel)

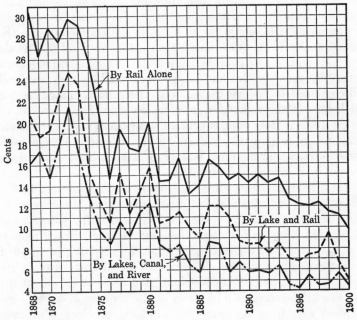

statisticians, the existence of traffic by way of the Great Lakes and
the Erie Canal "constitute[s] a substantial limitation upon the rates
which railway carriers can secure for land transportation." [11] The
bushel rates on wheat by rail alone, by rail and water, and by water
alone are given here, in graphic form, over a number of years by
way of illustration.

The great trouble with all the generalized reports of ton-mile

[9] *Ibid.*, p. 31; *Tenth Census: Transportation*, bottom folio, p. 23.
[10] Newcomb and Ward, "Changes in Rates," pp. 45, 55.
[11] *Ibid.*, p. 54. See Senate estimates on page 177, above.

rates for individual railroads is that they represent averages for the entire year on all shipments. Such rates were not the ones shown by the local railroad agent to the shipping farmer. This volume is not the place to go into detail on railroad abuses that plagued the farmer: rate wars, long-and-short-haul discriminations, rebating, pooling arrangements, traffic associations, and the like. But such things often made the farmer pay far more than the average ton-mile rate reported by the railroad company. When there was a rate war between railroads operating between Omaha and Chicago, for example, shippers at noncompetitive points between the two terminals paid amply for all losses to the corporations on the through traffic. Local rates could be hoisted to any level that would not choke off business entirely. Even after the pooling arrangement of 1870 between the Omaha-Chicago lines, the long-and-short-haul evil continued to bedevil the farmers. The carload charge for the full length of the railroad was often less than for a fraction of the distance, if from noncompetitive points. A few farmers—those within wagon-hauling distance—around the railroad centers enjoyed moderate rates, but the great bulk of all farmers lived where there were no such competitive advantages.

The wheat rate from Fargo to Duluth, on the Northern Pacific railroad, was sometimes almost twice that from Minneapolis to Chicago, though the latter distance was twice the former. But Minneapolis shippers had more than one railroad to choose. Suppose the farmer tried to beat the game by shipping to the first competitive city, and then reshipping to the ultimate market. He found the cards stacked against him. If the wheat grower of the Northwest decided to ship his grain to Minneapolis, in order to get the lower rates from that center to Milwaukee or Chicago, his crop would not be hauled unless he paid the full through rate to the lake port. If he unloaded at Minneapolis, he might sell the "transit" to Chicago or Milwaukee, provided that he could find a buyer. But the market for such services was congested, and a heavy discount was the usual result.[12] Though the rate on grain from St. Paul to Chicago was an unchanging 12½ cents a hundred pounds continually from 1888 to 1900[13] (a suspicious circumstance in itself), the charge from many Minnesota towns to the Twin Cities

[12] Hicks, *Populist Revolt*, pp. 61, 63–64.
[13] Newcomb and Ward, "Changes in Rates," p. 50.

was 25 cents a bushel. The cost all the way from Chicago to Liverpool was less than from some Dakota areas to Minneapolis. Again, local rates were often outrageous. Iowa farmers, shipping in feed corn from the next county, had to pay as much freight as though buying from Chicago. But Nebraska farmers, paying half again as much, thought the Iowa brethren were getting by famously.[14]

Occasionally, high rates were justifiable, as in the heavy shipping seasons when freight cars had to be "deadheaded" to the West, thus doubling the cost of operation. Again, it has been pointed out, Western railroads were so overbuilt that, even with their high charges, many of them did not make money.[15] The weakness of this argument is that where there was the most overbuilding, the rates, from resulting competition, were lowest. "Charge all the traffic will bear," was the rule. The idea of building up traffic by lowered rates was heresy in those days. But official statements of low profits mean little, when the overcapitalization of the roads is considered (see page 175, above). A writer in Poor's *Manual*, in 1884, asserted that all railroad stock was water, the lines being built from bond issues and the stock distributed free among the officials. When so respectable a journal as this could carry such words, perhaps the "wild-eyed" Populists also had some justification for their claims. Jerry Simpson said that the eight thousand miles of Kansas railroads cost a hundred million dollars to build, but were capitalized at three hundred million dollars in stocks and an equal amount in bonds. Apologists for the railroads justified watering, on the basis of future earnings, and some went so far as to denounce as an "impertinence" any question as to the right of any corporation to capitalize at any figure it saw fit.[16]

There were many complaints against the railroads besides the matter of freight costs. The outcry of farmers against the elevator monopoly and ineffective shipment of livestock, as recounted in earlier chapters, could be multiplied indefinitely from the contemporary accounts from the West and South. While wheat growers in the Northwest cried that the James J. Hill railroads would haul no grain from elevators of less than 30,000-bushel capacity, North Carolinian vegetable growers had an equal grievance. The rail-

[14] Hicks, *Populist Revolt*, p. 61.
[15] *Ibid.*, pp. 62–63, 64–65.
[16] *Ibid.*, pp. 65–67.

roads so discriminated in favor of Northern-grown truck that the Tar-Heel producers were driven out of competition in their own city markets. Railroad control of elevators was, in effect, a denial of free markets, and the practice of low grading of wheat added further injury to insult. The railroad land monopoly, looked on by the farmers as sheer theft, could not be forgiven. The land rushes into Oklahoma in 1889 and following were an indication that good farms were getting scarce, unless one succumbed to the railroads' terms; and homeseekers were possessed of long memories. Then, too, the railroads dominated the governments of some of the newer states. As Kansas was controlled by the Santa Fé, so was Nebraska by the Union Pacific and the Burlington. The efforts of the corporations to curry favor in high places throughout the nation were shown in the annual pass system for public officials. In the earlier years, when this implication was poorly realized, even persons who later were to become valiant fighters for the Populists clamored for their passes. These included Ignatius Donnelly of Minnesota and Lemuel H. ("Calamity") Weller of Iowa. In 1886, Donnelly was refusing passes, considering them a bribe. When railroads were reorganized after panic failures, and local security holders found their certificates repudiated, there was further cause for bitterness. It was also remembered how local governments had voted huge bond issues as gifts to the railroads (Kansas alone spent nearly $75,000,000 in this way before 1896), and the farmers contended that these sums had been obtained under false pretense.[17]

The hostility to corporations was not limited to railroad companies. Patent monopolies were the bane of farmers, and nowhere more so than in the Middle West, where the bulk of mechanized improvements were used. Earl W. Hayter sums up the difficulty in the following words:

Deluged with circulars from manufacturers and patentees, they [the farmers] were threatened and harassed by royalty collectors on such articles as sliding gates, milk cans, barbed wire, clover hullers, plows, sewing machines, grain binders, and drivewells. In purchasing one of these commodities they were seldom certain that it was properly patented, and when two or more patents had been granted on the same article they did not know which was void and which valid. One western writer summarized the situation when he wrote: "How is a farmer to know to whom to pay the royalty, even if it was legal, with three or

17 *Ibid.*, pp. 67–73, 76–77. See page 175, above, for bond issues.

four applicants swarming around him, all claiming to be the legal patentees, as in the case with both the drive well and barbed wire[?]" In a
number of instances a person was sued upon something that he had
developed himself or had seen in use among his friends and neighbors
before any patent had been granted. Such anxiety arose among the
farmers that general protest was heard against the entire patent system.[18]

The Iowa Farmers' Protective Association, founded in 1881, is a
good example of organized efforts to combat the patent monopolists. This association was created especially to fight out the issue
of rival patents on barbed wire. The farmer who built a fence was
never sure that he was not facing ruin from royalty collectors of
rival patentees, or by lawsuits if the demands were ignored. But it
was not till February 29, 1892, when the United States Supreme
Court upheld the claims of Joseph F. Glidden, that the matter was
settled.[19] The contest of the Grangers with the McCormick harvester company is well known to all students of the Patrons of
Husbandry.[20]

THE SHORTAGE OF CAPITAL

As on all preceding agricultural frontiers, the Western farmers
of the late decades of the nineteenth century were generally poor,
but in this era of commercialized farming they were all the worse
because of this fact. Competition for markets made necessary large
acreages of land and a continuous process of increased mechanization. This called for capital and, therefore, for reliance on Eastern
moneylenders. Interest rates for ventures in new areas were, as
usual, high, and farmers with slender resources could make little
progress without going into debt. Then, in periods of depression,
it was next to impossible to get out of debt again, and in the rare
years of farm prosperity there was always the human impulse to
expand operations as long as new loans could be procured.

For a generation following the Civil War, the indebted Western
farmer inevitably linked his high interest rates, along with low

[18] Earl W. Hayter, "The Western Farmers and the Drivewell Patent Controversy,"
Agricultural History, XVI, No. 1 (January, 1942), 16–17, quotation by permission
of the editor of *Agricultural History*.
[19] Earl W. Hayter, "An Iowa Farmers' Protective Association: A Barbed Wire
Patent Protest Movement," *The Iowa Journal of History and Politics*, XXXVII, No. 4
(October, 1939), 331–362.
[20] For the Grange, see next chapter.

prices and the rest of his troubles, with the monetary situation. Greenback inflation during the Civil War, and its stimulus to farming expansion, only made the reaction worse during the deflationary movement of the next decade. Though Edwin L. Godkin may not have understood the West, he had a good comprehension of money matters. In 1868, he proceeded to set straight on a number of questions a correspondent from Wisconsin who had complained of the shortage of money. Though agricultural loans were hard to get at 10 per cent, while the rate was down to 4 in the East, he noted that the Wisconsin banks were not lending more than 55 per cent of what they were permitted by law. They were holding a million dollars in greenbacks, above what reserves they needed, and against these greenbacks they could have lent four million dollars in national bank notes or other money, thus virtually doubling the amount in circulation. The reason why the loans were so low, and the interest rates so high, was that too much of the demand on the banks was for greenbacks to settle Eastern accounts. But greenbacks were the legal reserves, and every dollar of them withdrawn canceled the power to lend four other dollars. Where loans were made for ordinary business transactions, they went back into the bank as deposits on which to issue further loans. But when the borrowings simply drained the reserves, the banks had to keep an extraordinary volume of greenbacks on hand and restrict the amount of business done. Therefore, the bankers had to charge interest up to the limit of the law, and then be very careful about the loans. The man who wanted money for ordinary business activities had to pay along with the rest. Godkin continued, in his argument, to castigate the Western speculator who created this situation, but overlooked the financial suzerainty of Eastern interest—the mortgage-loan companies, for example—which were getting these Western greenbacks, and not as the fruits of Western speculation either. Yet, the editor was right in contending that Western credit was tight and business dull, though money was plentiful.[21]

Another thing that Godkin might have noted was that he was talking in the present tense about past conditions. The deflationary policies of Hugh McCulloch, Secretary of the Treasury, were al-

---

[21] [Edwin Lawrence Godkin], "Inflation and the West," *The Nation*, VI, No. 140 (March 5, 1868), 187–190.

ready in operation, and Western speculators were rare indeed. The persons needing the bank credit may or may not formerly have engaged in speculation, but indubitably they were now merely in debt and could see no way out. But deflation itself reached alarming proportions ten years after the war. The greenbacks and other forms of currency that had been issued during the war were for the use of the North alone. The downfall of the Confederacy, leaving these states with no specie and with repudiated paper, and the increase in population of the whole country, resulted in only about half as many greenbacks per capita in 1876–1878 as in 1864, and greenbacks were still the only bank reserves.[22] By 1879, when specie payments were resumed, farmers, who no longer could get extensions on loans secured during the war, were faced with paying them in money worth twice that borrowed, or, more likely yet, they would have to endure foreclosure, so as to let the banks absorb a part of the loss. It was this class to whom Godkin contemptuously referred as persons who merely wanted the coinage adulterated for personal gain, and whom the government should ignore.[23] The greenback theorists commanded the attention of some farmers for a few years, but doctrines concerning a managed currency were either too profound for the great majority, or else they doubted the efficacy of such a measure. Furthermore, the Greenback party candidates did not always inspire confidence.

Without doubt, much of the credit difficulty of the West (as well as the rest of its troubles) grew out of the fact that the section had developed too rapidly. The price and profit structure was based on and maintained by the existence of scarcity. The rapid expansion of the West upset this basis in a period when foreign markets were not standing up; and the price of most of the Western products was fixed by the exportable surplus. Yet, the Kansas farmer could not see why he had to accept ten cents or less a bushel for his corn, when the New York dealers were demanding a dollar or more on their market, and getting it.[24]

In fact, the growth of farm acreage in the country hardly kept

[22] Observer (pseud.), "The Value of Money Is Controlled by Its Quality," *Banker's Magazine* (N.Y.), XXXV, No. 11 (May, 1881), 853–859.
[23] [Edwin Lawrence Godkin], "The Debtor Class," *The Nation*, XVIII, No. 460 (April 23, 1874), 262–263.
[24] Hicks, *Populist Revolt*, pp. 2, 59.

pace with the rise of the urban population; but laborers also were frequently in distress and, therefore, could not always absorb the surpluses created by the decline of foreign markets. Free or cheap land in the West, while failing to provide release for Eastern industrial laborers, lured farmers to regions where distress was inescapable. The railroads played a large part in this exodus to the semiarid localities. They broke down the prejudice that Western land was useless, and that the climate made it a desert. The Union Pacific and the Burlington companies each spent nearly a million dollars advertising and selling land in Nebraska alone. "Follow prairie dogs and Mormons," said a Burlington pamphlet, "and you will find good land." The weather also played into the hands of the railroad companies. For eight years before 1887 there was an unusual amount of rainfall in Colorado and in western Kansas and Nebraska,[25] though in 1881 the wheat states to the eastward had the worst drouth "since the inauguration of crop reporting." [26] People were led to believe that tree planting and irrigation had caused this change, and that heavy settlement would bring a permanent change of weather on the Great Plains.[27]

While this propaganda and fiction were holding sway, people flocked in, money was eagerly offered by Eastern investors, banks became numerous, and mortgage companies flourished, especially at St. Paul, Omaha, St. Joseph, Kansas City, and Denver. Local agents of these companies were found everywhere in the farming areas of the frontier. In 1886 and 1887, many agents had so many offers from Eastern lenders that they could not get enough mortgages to cover them, yet the rates of interest remained high (see pages 188–190, above). The Western farmer was tempted to extravagant speculation. This was especially true in Minnesota and from Kansas to North Dakota, where, in 1890, the per capita amount of mortgages ran near the top for the United States. Kansas excelled every other state in the Union except New York. Kansas and North Dakota had a mortgage for every two people, while Nebraska, South Dakota, and Minnesota had one for every three. Many farms must have been mortgaged several times, for there were more mortgages than families in each of the five states. In

[25] *Ibid.*, pp. 6, 15, 18–19.
[26] Hayter, "Iowa Farmers' Protective Association," p. 339.
[27] Hicks, *Populist Revolt*, p. 19.

some counties, three quarters of all owner-operated farms were
mortgaged, and the total debt was three quarters of the value of all
land taxed. In other words, they were mortgaged for all they
were worth.[28]

In a typical block of six counties in the nonspeculative area of
Nebraska, the average price of land doubled to over $17.50 an acre
between 1881 and 1887. In other places speculation ran "hog wild."
Near Abilene, Kansas, a farm worth $6.25 an acre in 1867 sold at
the peak of the mania for $270 an acre. There were many other
boom towns in 1887, including Omaha and Lincoln in Nebraska,
Atchinson, Topeka, and Wichita in Kansas, and the Kansas City on
each side of the border of Missouri. But Wichita was the worst of
all. In the first five months of 1887, forty-two square miles of land
around Wichita were sold as town lots, and $35,000,000 changed
hands in the sales. There were similar booms in many smaller
towns. Cities and towns were seized with a mania for public
buildings and other improvements, selling bonds to construct them.
Fifteen Kansas towns installed streetcar systems. Each boom town
thought it should have at least one railroad, and preferably more.
Promoters throve on the business of getting governmental units
to vote bonds. Railroads were built whether there was any need
for them or not. The promoters got rich and then unloaded the
lines on the "blue-sky" victims. In the 1880's, Kansas railroads increased in mileage from 3,102 to 8,810; Nebraska lines grew in a
similar ratio; and in Dakota Territory the increase was from 399
miles to 4,726. All these railroads were heavily overcapitalized.[29]

And then the pretty bubble was pricked. Ten years of almost
perpetual drouth began at that time, with only two crops in the
decade. Hot winds and chinch bugs (always worst in dry years)
finished what dry weather alone could not accomplish. Early frosts
came in Dakota. In the lower parts of the Plains and bordering
Prairies the drying-out process began even in 1886. Then the disastrous winter of 1886–1887 finished the cattle corporations' paradise
on the higher Plains. In the intermediate area, when crop failure
became evident in the early fall of 1887, the inhabitants became
panicky and began dumping their speculative holdings on the
market. There was a deluge of mortgage foreclosures, extending

[28] *Ibid.*, pp. 21–24.
[29] *Ibid.*, 24–29.

on down through the panic year of 1893, by which time new troubles arose. Often, however, the farmer welcomed foreclosure, for the mortgage was worth more than the land. Half the population of western Kansas moved out between 1888 and 1892, and large portions of the Plains from Kansas to North Dakota were virtually depopulated. As late as 1891, at least eighteen thousand prairie schooners entered Iowa from Nebraska. Many emigrants from Kansas braved it out with signs painted on their wagons such as: "In God we trusted, in Kansas we busted." Twenty towns in western Kansas were reported as totally depopulated. One of them had a $30,000 opera house and a $20,000 school building.[30] Wichita, though not in the western part of the state, suffered an almost total real-estate collapse. For years after 1900, houses, finished as well as partly built and never inhabited, were seen rotting away miles from the city limits on what had once been sold as city lots.[31]

In the central portions of the tier of states from Kansas to North Dakota, the farmers by 1887 were more firmly rooted, and believed they could succeed. They had bigger investments than those of the inhabitants of the western counties. They also were overmortgaged and in danger of foreclosure; nevertheless, enough of them remained solvent, though burdened by interest and the taxes they had voted on themselves for improvements, so that a majority of the population remained on the land. These farmers were the core of the Populist movement in those states. In the eastern counties, the drouth was not so bad (there is a distinct difference in rainfall even between Manhattan, Kansas, and Lawrence, only eighty miles to the eastward), and crops were fairly continuous. Also, the eastern counties were so well settled before 1880 that land became less speculative than in the western areas. The rural population actually increased in the eastern counties during the bad years. But other boom towns than Wichita shrank in numbers. In two years' time Wichita lost 13,000 people and Leavenworth 15,000. Census statistics have to be used for the other states, and they tell only a part of the story. Great numbers of people came into and left the towns and counties between the census years of 1880 and 1890. In the rural areas the authorized count was unreliable, for many of the officials of counties worst hit by the

[30] *Ibid.*, pp. 30–32, 84.
[31] Personal observation.

drouth falsified the figures. Yet, the census shows from a third to half the counties of Kansas, Nebraska, and South Dakota with fewer people in 1900 than in 1890. In the western counties some population was left, but those who remained were the ones best adapted to subsist on a jack-rabbit standard of living, and they were only reasonably dissatisfied. The eastern counties were not a fertile field for radical doctrines. But the struggling holders-on in the middle counties were ready to listen to any argument for a way out of their desperation. On many an earlier frontier farmers had faced conditions as bad as these, but then there was always a promised land to the westward. Now they could not move on when adversity struck: they had either to stay or to turn back. Those who stood at bay also fought.[32]

THE FARMERS' POLITICAL MOVEMENT OF THE 1870'S

As soon as depression began to settle down on the farm, after the Civil War, farmers' clubs began to appear in many states of the Middle West and South. Some of them had existed for many years earlier, but now they multiplied in number and became more political in their aims. Then came the Grange in 1867 (see next chapter), with its elaborate secret ritual and all-round program of social, cultural, and economic uplift for farmers. The constitution of the Grange prohibited political action, but there was no restriction on individual participation in third-party movements. When a local grange adjourned from its regular meeting, it often resumed activities in the same place as a unit of a farmers' political party. Though many kinds of political and economic reforms were agitated, the chief objective of these third-party organizations was railroad regulation. Many farmers resented the secrecy of the Grange as well as its opposition to developing into a political party. So farmers' independent clubs grew up in the same areas as the Grange, and in some ways in opposition to it. Yet, the members all voted together in the Independent, Reform, Anti-Monopoly, and Farmers' parties which were active in eleven states by 1874. In Illinois, Wisconsin, Iowa, and Minnesota the Grangers had a numerical superiority over their rivals, and the Granger name was given to the legislation that ensued. In some other states the inde-

[32] Hicks, *Populist Revolt*, pp. 32–35, 95.

pendent clubs predominated. Occasionally the Democrats lent support as a means of weakening the dominant Republican party.[33]

The Grange itself reached an estimated membership of some 268,000 by the spring of 1874, and it grew to more than 858,000 early in 1875,[34] after which the numbers dropped to about 759,000 by the first of October. At the later date, Missouri had the largest roll,. with more than 80,000, followed in order by Indiana, Ohio, Kentucky, Iowa, Kansas, Texas, Tennessee, Michigan, Mississippi, Illinois, Pennsylvania, Arkansas, Georgia, Alabama, Wisconsin, and Minnesota, the latter having 16,617 members. Seventeen states had to be listed before two of the most prominent of 1873–1874 could be included. But Southern states, such as South Carolina and Mississippi, with 118 and 112 local granges, were high in the list as early as 1873, while Iowa, with 1,507 granges, had slightly more than half the 2,991 of the twelve states of the North Central division. The Grange was far from being an organization peculiar to the states bordering the upper Mississippi River. For that matter, at the height of the movement in 1874, Nebraska and Kansas had the largest ratio of granges to the total farming population, while Indiana, Missouri, Dakota, Kentucky, Tennessee, Arkansas, and six states and territories of the Far West exceeded Wisconsin, and all but three of this list surpassed Illinois.[35] But political power was more equally divided in Illinois, Wisconsin, Iowa, and Minnesota than in the rest of the strong Granger states, while in the West the railroads exerted too much influence to be effectively curbed. Hence, the railroad legislation which somewhat erroneously takes the Granger name was centered in the states on the upper Mississippi River.

Farmers' clubs in Illinois inaugurated a movement for railroad regulation, some years before the Grange became prominent in that state. In 1867, they got a Warehouse Act adopted to compel railroad companies to handle grain from independent elevators. In 1870, they got a constitutional amendment permitting state control of the railroads, and in 1871 the legislature fixed a scale of maximum freight and passenger rates. The carriers refused to abide by these regulations, and ejected passengers who insisted on

[33] Solon Justus Buck, *The Granger Movement . . . , 1870–1880* (Cambridge: Harvard University Press, 1913), pp. 73–74.

[34] Information furnished by the National Grange.

[35] Buck, *Granger Movement*, insert between pp. 58, 59.

paying only the legal fares. In 1873, the state supreme court over-ruled the rate law, after which it was re-enacted along more cautious lines, and remained long in effect. In 1871, Minnesota adopted rate regulation, followed by Iowa and Wisconsin in 1874, but these acts were all repealed a few years later. After fighting such legislation from the political stump to the state courts, the railroads carried appeals to the United States Supreme Court. Meanwhile, they made use of loopholes in the laws to make the acts unpopular with their patrons. For example, the train service in Wisconsin was reduced until the law of that state was repealed. Then in October, 1876, the Supreme Court gave opinions favorable to the farmers' contentions in eight cases originating in laws of the four regulating states. In the fundamental case of Munn vs. Illinois the right to regulate was established, and in succeeding decisions, notably Peik vs. Chicago and Northwestern Railroad, it was declared that a state might regulate rates even for interstate traffic, on shipments entering or leaving the state.[36]

Thus was the first battle won in the efforts at railroad regulation. Though some of the legislation was repealed, though the courts later limited state rate-fixing powers (see page 178, above). at least a precedent was set. Truly effective regulation was not to come till the next century, but, as the table on page 296 shows, drastic downward rates began in the period of Granger agitation, and continued afterward. Perhaps other factors, even more important, affected this change, but the fear of even more rigorous legislation seems to have been ever present. Incidentally, it is now generally held that the Granger laws were eminently fair to the carriers, as well as to the public.[37] The business activities of the Grange, and its decline, are discussed in the following chapter.

THE BEGINNINGS OF THE FARMERS' ALLIANCES

Though the Grange dropped out of sight as a political force after the late 1870's, farmers' clubs continued their activities and tended to coalesce into alliances. In 1874 or 1875, Lampasas, Texas, had an alliance for catching horse thieves, recovering estrays, and buying supplies. It was a secret society which also fought land

[36] *Ibid.*, pp. 123–237.
[37] *Ibid.*, pp. 233–237.

monopolists and the big cattlemen who were inclined to ignore the rights of small competitors. This idea soon spread to other counties and, in 1878, a Grand State Alliance was organized, only to be all but killed by dissensions over greenbackism. Revival was rapid, and in 1880 a new Grand State Alliance was incorporated by the state, as a benevolent society of a secret nature. By 1885, it claimed 1,200 lodges and 50,000 members. It fought against low prices, crop liens, and the oppression of the country merchants. By 1886, it was beginning to demand higher taxes on speculative landholdings, a ban on alien landowning, laws against dealing in futures, higher taxes on railroads, more paper money, and other issues later absorbed by the Populist party. These demands caused threats of further schism; whereupon C. W. Macune stepped forward, saved the Alliance, and started a movement for combination with other groups throughout the South.

The largest of all these rivals started in Arkansas, in 1882, as a debating society, and in 1883 took the name of the Agricultural Wheel. By the processes of absorption and expansion, the Wheel extended into eight states by 1887, and claimed half a million members. The merger of the Alliance and the Wheel was effected in 1889, under the temporary compromise name of the Farmers' and Laborers' Union. Lawyers, merchants and their clerks, and stockholders in banks or stores of other than the cooperative variety were denied membership. By 1890, the enlarged society had a membership of over a million.[38] Working in close sympathy with this alliance were the Farmers' Clubs fostered by Benjamin R. Tillman in South Carolina.[39]

During these same years, the farmers of the Northwest were also active in organization. The National Farmers' Alliance, commonly called the Northwestern Alliance, may have had some generic connection with an alliance of Grangers in New York, uniting for political purposes, in 1877. The latter may have got the idea from a Settlers' Protective Association started in Kansas in 1874, to help squatters in their fight against the railroad land monopolies. Such

[38] Hicks, *Populist Revolt*, pp. 104–113.
[39] Francis Butler Simkins, *The Tillman Movement in South Carolina* (Durham: Duke University Press, 1926), pp. 111–113; H[enry] R[ichardson] Chamberlain, *The Farmers' Alliance: What It Aims to Accomplish* (New York: The Minerva Publishing Company, 1891), p. 28, credits the Alliance with electing Tillman as Governor in 1890.

are the claims, though slightly overwrought. But it was Milton George of Chicago, editor of the *Western Rural*, who in 1880 established the alliance that, within two years, was to claim 2,000 local groups with 100,000 members. This organization followed on the heels of two or three years of hard times in the Prairie states. As conditions improved, in 1883 and 1884, interest lagged. Then, following low wheat prices in 1884–1885, membership picked up in all the wheat states of the Northwest, and by 1887 the Northwestern Alliance was beginning to demand such things as federal competition with railroads and the revival of free coinage of silver. In the Minneapolis convention of that year, there was some tendency to cooperate with the Knights of Labor. By 1890, the Midwest farmers were thoroughly class conscious. Kansas claimed 130,000 alliance members, while Nebraska, the Dakotas, and Minnesota were close rivals. The organization had already spread through fifteen states, and was reaching out for more.[40]

There was ample reason for the great outburst of farmer unrest as exemplified in the rapid growth of the alliances in the late 1880's. In the South, so long as the price of cotton remained at ten cents or more a pound, and in the West, while Eastern capital continued to flow in, the farmers merely grumbled at middlemen, trusts, and the railroads. But after 1881, the price of cotton did not reach a dime a pound for the remainder of the century, and sometimes was hardly half that. After the collapse of the land bubble in the West, in 1887, the mortgage companies clamped down. Where interest rates of 8, 10, or 12 per cent had prevailed, the charge now was from 18 to 24 and sometimes as high as 40. In Kansas there were over 11,000 foreclosures between 1889 and 1893, and nine tenths of the land in some counties changed hands. When land could no longer be mortgaged, money had sometimes been borrowed on chattels. In consequence, during the bad years many families could not leave the Dakotas because their horses and vehicles were mortgaged and could not be removed from the state. In either West or South, the farmer had even less control over the cost of what he had to buy than over the valuation of the goods he sold. Price fixing, trusts, and monopolies were already gaining headway. A Missouri editor noted in 1888 that as soon as the plow trust was organized the price of plows was doubled. There was, at the same

[40] Hicks, *Populist Revolt*, pp. 96–104.

time, a belated realization of the consequences of installment selling by the harvester trust, continual debt being the outcome. Also, it was noted, land taxes of farmers could not be evaded like those on intangible property, but the railroads were lightly assessed. The carriers even escaped the tax on their huge railroad land grants by postponing the taking out of final patents till the land could be sold.

On the tariff issue, there was much division of opinion, and some farmers' representatives had continuously rolled logs in Congressional tariff bargaining. But there were many farm leaders who noted that their kind always sold in a free market while buying in a protected one. Southern farmers, in general, were vociferous against the tariff. In the South, the crop-lien system and bondage to the country merchants, along with the low price of cotton, were causing many yeoman farmers to slide down into the tenant or sharecropper status.[41] The evidence all points to the conclusion that it was this class of small, white farmers, struggling against submergence, that furnished the main support of the Alliance movement and Populism in the South, as it was the debt-ridden or foreclosed classes in the West.[42] The collapse of the cattle boom in the Great Plains area [43] and the complaints of the silver-mining interests must also be taken into consideration.

While demands were pouring upon the farmers for more money for taxes and interest, for installments on their mortgages and farm machinery, and for monopoly-fixed prices on many of their necessities, they could easily feel that an increase in the nation's stock of money was a likely solution of the difficulty. When the most money in hand was needed——in crop-moving time—credit was always scarce. Later, when the crops had been dumped on the market at low prices to meet urgent obligations, credit became plentiful and the speculators reaped the profits. It seemed that money and credit were being manipulated by the creditors for their own further enrichment. Farmers out of debt could stand the money and credit situation. They made very little, but they did not pay out much. In the West and South, however, there were few debt-free farmers, and interest, commissions, and the like seldom

---

[41] *Ibid* , pp. 78–86.
[42] See table of tenancy, 1880–1900, in Appendix, page 418.
[43] See pages 225–226, above.

totaled less than 20 or 25 per cent. It was easy for them to believe that the creditors also had conspired to enact and perpetuate the "Crime of '73," the Resumption Act of 1875, and other measures that restricted the nation's supply of money.

The national banking system came in for its share of attack. Among other grievances, the worst was that national bank notes were always scarcest when needed most, and were plentiful in flush times when their abundance merely led to rash speculation. The national bank notes were secured by deposits of government bonds in the federal treasury. In boom times, nonbanker holders of bonds liked to sell them so as to facilitate speculation in projects promising high returns. This depressed the value of the bonds and made it profitable for the banks to buy them, whereupon the volume of bank notes would be expanded just when some deflation was needed to cool the speculative fever. But when panics and depressions came, the former speculator wanted to sink in the security of government bonds all he managed to save from the crash. This drove up their market price, inducing the national-bank officials to sell at a profit. This automatically reduced the amount of bank notes in circulation, just when some inflation was needed to prime the economic pump. Hence came the demand to abolish national bank notes, and all other kinds of paper money except greenbacks, entirely, and substitute a flexible greenback system that would maintain stable business conditions.[44]

To supplement this cry for greenbacks, strength was gradually added to the demand for a renewal of the free and unlimited coinage of silver at the time-honored ratio of approximately sixteen to one with gold. In 1873, following a tendency already under way in Europe, the American Congress had adopted a law stopping the coinage of silver for domestic circulation, and giving only a limited legal-tender value to silver coins already in existence. At that time, little attention was paid to the law, because for many years the silver in a dollar had been worth more in exchange than the dollar itself, and consequently very little silver was being coined. But at the same time, the stock of silver in America was increasing rapidly. The Western silver mines were multiplying their output, and the tendency of the Western world to drift toward a gold monetary standard was limiting the markets for the disposal of silver. By

[44] Hicks, *Populist Revolt*, pp. 87–95.

1875, the silver in such dollars of full weight as still circulated was worth only 96 cents. It was then that the mining interests started to condemn demonetization as a conspiracy, and to refer to the act as the "Crime of '73." Also, they wasted no opportunity to show the stricken farmers that a revival of free coinage at the old ratio would quickly solve the rural monetary difficulty.

Orthodox economists immediately declared that remonetization would demonstrate Gresham's law. Gold would go out of circulation. The United States would revert to a purely silver basis, absorbing all the cheap silver of the world that did not flow to Asia or Latin America. Nobody can say the economists were wrong, for the plan was never tried. But most of the dire consequences seem imaginary. Had the experiment been tried and proved dangerous, it could have been repealed quickly. But there is another point that should be considered. Down to 1900, even when the ratio of silver to gold would have made a silver dollar worth only 49 cents, the price of silver stayed very close to the curve of general prices. As far as money affected the situation, it was the fact that gold alone was insufficient as a basis for coinage that made general prices so low. This gave great force to the free silverites' claim that a bimetallic standard, or silver alone, would have maintained a stable price level. They were invoking the "immutable" quantity theory of money to offset the "immutable" Gresham's law.[45]

The Bland-Allison Act of 1878, which was offered as a sop and compromise to the silver interests, fell far short of the demands. The Secretary of the Treasury was to buy not less than $2,000,000 and not more than $4,000,000 worth of silver bullion each month and have it coined into dollars of full-legal-tender value. A futile gesture was also made toward an international free-silver congress, which ultimately met and adjourned after doing nothing. The new law did not stabilize the price of silver, and it did not expand the currency enough either to please the inflationists or to alarm the gold-standard advocates. During the twelve years that the act was in force, each of the five Presidents was a gold-standard man, and never more than the minimum amount of silver was bought. Some $378,000,000 were put in circulation from silver that cost the Treasury about $300,000,000, the profit going to the government instead of to the mining companies. But, during these same years,

[45] Dewey, *Financial History of the United States*, pp. 403–405.

$100,000,000 were withheld from circulation as a reserve to protect the value of greenbacks. From a virtually empty Treasury in 1878, the surplus above reserves against paper money grew to over $220,-000,000 in 1890, while the volume of national bank notes declined from nearly $359,000,000 in 1882 to $186,000,000 in 1890. They had stood at $325,000,000 in 1878. Here was nearly $460,000,000 taken out of circulation to offset any additions of silver and gold coin. Had not the stock of gold increased from $213,000,000 to $696,-000,000 there would have been less money to circulate among the people in 1890 than in 1878; and a reversal in trade balances was soon to drain some of this gold out of the country again. By 1893, the stock had dwindled to $598,000,000.[46] There was nothing in the slight gold inflation of the period to gladden the hearts of indebted farmers. The continuing fall in the price of silver, till the dollar in 1889 was worth only 72 cents,[47] showed the silver interests also that the Bland-Allison Act was not enough for them.

THE POPULIST MOVEMENT

Thus, before 1890, the monetary and credit situation became a big thing that the Farmers' Alliances were stressing in their platforms. But it seemed obvious that one big alliance, instead of separate ones for the South and the Northwest, would be more effective in procuring reforms. Also, there ought to be some form of cooperation with the labor movement. Furthermore, there was a Colored Farmers' National Alliance and Cooperative Union, founded at Houston in 1886 and boasting of a membership of one and a quarter millions four years later, which should be brought into the partnership. An effort was made at St. Louis, in 1889, to effect some sort of merger, but the different elements had too many conflicting interests to do more than adopt similar platforms. The Southern Alliance was secret and excluded Negroes; the Northwestern was just the opposite. The Northwestern Alliance wanted to ban substitutes for lard and butter, but this struck at the cottonseed oil of the South. The Southern Alliance wanted a subtreasury system, under which the federal government would make loans at 1 per cent interest up to four fifths of the value of deposited

---

[46] *Ibid.*, pp. 406–408; *Statistical Abstract of the United States*, 1931, pp. 248–249.
[47] *Ibid.*, p. 791.

nonperishable farm goods. Because Northern products were more perishable than cotton, the Northwestern Alliance would not listen to this. Also, the Northwestern Alliance was the smaller and did not want to be submerged. The Knights of Labor fraternized, and exchanged indorsements of policy with the alliances, but that was as far as union went. The American Federation of Labor would take no part at all, because the alliances included employing farmers.[48]

Nevertheless, the two white alliances drew up very similar platforms. Both demanded the abolition of the national banks and the substitution of greenbacks for bank notes, the amount of greenbacks to be regulated according to the needs of business, and all money to be legal tender. Both wanted government ownership and operation of the railroads, and the Southern Alliance included all means of transportation and communication. The Southern Alliance asked for economy in government and for laws to end dealing in futures for farm goods, to prevent alien ownership of land and to recover the land grants from the railroads (land monopolies supplying the grudge), and to authorize free and unlimited coinage of silver. The Northwestern Alliance agreed on economy, insisted on the payment of the debts of the Union and Central Pacific railroads to the government, asked for a graduated income tax, a Lakes-to-Gulf ship canal, and national aid in irrigation experiments, called for the secret ballot, and included a generalized labor plank.[49] Here was much lumber for the later Populist platforms.

The Southern Alliance (now officially the National Farmers' Alliance and Industrial Union) and the Northwestern Alliance continued to go their separate ways, but the alliances in Kansas and the Dakotas soon affiliated with the Southern group. These facts made little difference, for the Populist party was soon to absorb both. Even before political union was achieved, the alliances were strong enough to force Congress to make a further gesture on the silver question. The admission into the Union of six new Western states, in 1889 and 1890, made a free-silver body of the Senate,

[48] Buck, *Agrarian Crusade*, pp. 111–131; Herman Clarence Nixon, "The Cleavage within the Farmers' Alliance Movement," *Mississippi Valley Historical Review*, XV, No. 1 (June, 1928), 22–33; Hallie Farmer, "The Economic Background of Frontier Populism," *ibid.*, X, No. 4 (March, 1924), 406–427; Hicks, *Populist Revolt*, pp. 114–125.

[49] Hicks, *Populist Revolt*, pp. 427–430.

and the House of Representatives was willing to make some con-
cession in order to win Western votes in the Senate for the Mc-
Kinley tariff bill. So the Western farmers tied themselves to a tariff
policy that was to do them untold harm for decades, and in exchange they got a silver act that did not live up to their hopes.
For the time being, at least, the Sherman Silver Purchase Act of
1890 provided for government buying of about the whole output of American mines, and for further inflation than the Bland-
Allison Act as it had been applied. Each month the government was
to buy 4,500,000 ounces of silver, which was to be stored in the
Treasury vaults as bullion. The silver was to be paid for with new
Treasury notes, which might be redeemed in either silver or gold.
Only as much silver should be coined as was necessary to redeem
Treasury notes when silver was asked in exchange. But the wealthy
interests that held the notes almost invariably asked for gold, and
Presidents Harrison and Cleveland both held that the customer
was always right. Consequently, very little silver was coined, and
that which was minted merely replaced Treasury notes.[50]

Before 1892, the price of silver was lower than ever, and was
continuing to drop. This disgruntled the silver interests. The inflationists also had their grievance. The lower the price of silver
fell, the less 4,500,000 ounces cost, and only the cost of the silver
went to swell the money supply. Under the act of 1878, the cheaper
silver became, the more dollars went into circulation, thus providing some of the sort of elasticity that was desired for the currency.
At the time the Sherman Act was passed, the mere discretion of the
President in buying the maximum under the Bland-Allison Act
would have absorbed more silver and put more money into circulation than the Sherman Act did. Before all silver purchases were
stopped in 1893, the liberal application of the Bland-Allison principle would have furnished some real inflation. The inflationists
now realized that the Sherman Act was a positively reactionary
measure. Even before the election of 1890, alliance men were disgusted with the seeming fraud of the plan. Fourteen-cent corn,
five-cent cotton, and interest rarely as low as 10 per cent, combined with the rising cost of living caused by the McKinley Tariff,
however, were the main factors in causing the alliances to join in

[50] Dewey, *Financial History of the United States*, pp. 436–438.

the overthrow of the Republicans in the House of Representatives in that year.

The alliance men were quite active in the campaign, and they had their reward. In the West they formed local parties, while in the South they strove for control of the Democratic machines. In Georgia, the alliance men, led by Thomas E. Watson, won a sweeping victory.[51] In South Carolina, Tillman's farmers' clubs were working in unison as a machine of their own, and overthrew the leadership of the hero of the old guard, Wade Hampton. Tillman himself was elected governor, and Hampton was ousted from the Senate by the newly elected legislature.[52] In the whole country, the alliances and their allies got in control of seven state legislatures, besides having three senators, three governors, and fifty-two federal representatives, most of the gains being in the South. It was in that year that Mary Elizabeth Lease shocked Eastern sensibilities by telling Kansas farmers to "raise less corn and more Hell." It was the doctrine rather than the language that hurt, for Mrs. Lease convinced her hearers. It was in the same state that William A. ("Whiskers") Peffer defeated the veteran John J. Ingalls for the Senate, and "Sockless" Jerry Simpson ousted his "silk-stockinged" opponent James J. Hallowell from the House of Representatives.[53]

Elated by the election of 1890, alliance leaders held various conventions in the next two years, calling in representatives from every reform organization that showed any friendly interest, and by 1892 they had the new People's, or Populist, party in order for a great compaign. At the St. Louis gathering in February, 1892, different associations of farmers and laborers were represented by 860 delegates. The Southern Alliance stood first, with 246; followed by the Colored Alliance, 97; the Knights of Labor, 82; the Patrons of Industry, 75; the Farmers' Mutual Benefit Association, 53; and then the Northwestern Alliance, 49. After this "Washington's Birthday Industrial Congress" came the nominating convention at Omaha on July 4, the dates representing the dominating theme of independence. The platform repeated most of the demands of the preceding three years. The free coinage of silver was added "at the present legal ratio of 16 to 1," and a circulating medium of at least

[51] C[omer] Vann Woodward, *Tom Watson: Agrarian Rebel* (New York: The Macmillan Company, 1938), pp. 146–166.

[52] Simkins, *Tillman Movement*, pp. 103–134, 152–153.

[53] Buck, *Agrarian Crusade*, pp. 134–138.

$50 per capita was stressed as imperative. Next came the demand for a graduated income tax, followed by the usual plea for economy and honesty in government. Postal savings banks and government ownership and operation of all railroads and telegraph and telephone systems came next. And finally, there was the demand for abolition of all landownership "by railroads and other corporations in excess of their actual needs," and the reclamation by the government of all alien landholdings. Some recommendations followed: for better laws against contract labor, for restricted immigration of undesirable persons, for shorter work hours, for the extinction of the Pinkerton system of labor spies, and for indorsement of the Knights of Labor label. A call for the initiative and referendum and for one term only for the President and Vice President rounded out the document. The direct election of senators had been indorsed, and universal suffrage flirted with, in previous conventions.[54]

The presidential candidate, James B. Weaver of Iowa, was known as a leader of lost causes. In spite of all the efforts to win labor votes in the East, the Populist vote in 1892 came mainly from the rural areas of the West and South. Neither then nor later were the Populists strong even in Illinois, where a desperate effort was made at a labor alliance.[55] Yet, by combination with Republicans in the South and the Democrats in the West, the Populists in 1892 cast more than a million votes, or about 9 per cent of all. For a time, the Southern Negro got more political consideration than he had known since Reconstruction days. Both Democrats and Populists sought colored support. Thomas E. Watson of Georgia, who in later years was almost psychopathic in his determination to grind down all Negroes, as well as Jews, was in 1892 the Negroes' champion for political and civil rights.[56] On the other hand, in South Carolina the Tillmanites gave their support to the gold-standard Cleveland,[57] and only about 2,400 Populist votes were cast in the

[54] Nathan Fine, *Labor and Farmer Parties in the United States, 1828–1928* (New York: Rand School of Social Science, c.1928), pp. 77–78; Hicks, *Populist Revolt*, pp. 430–438. For the Patrons of Industry, see Sidney Glazer, "Patrons of Industry in Michigan," *Mississippi Valley Historical Review*, XXIV, No. 2 (September, 1937), 185–194.

[55] Chester McA[rthur] Destler, "Consummation of a Labor-Populist Alliance in Illinois, 1894," *Mississippi Valley Historical Review*, XXVII, No. 4, March, 1941), 589–602.

[56] Woodward, *Tom Watson*, pp. 220–222, 231, 402, 431–450.

[57] Simkins, *Tillman Movement*, p. 172.

state. Though large Populist totals were rolled up in Texas, Alabama, North Carolina, and Georgia, no electoral votes were secured. But in the West, Weaver carried Colorado, Idaho, Kansas, Nevada, and one electoral vote each in North Dakota and Oregon— a total of twenty-two. He lost Nebraska by less than a hundred votes, while his greatest popular vote was the 163,000 of Kansas.[58]

Events in the next two years added greatly to the Populist appeal. Cleveland was returned in 1892. Then came the Panic of 1893. Along with the general social distress following the panic, farming sank deeper in depression year by year till the worst was reached in 1898. The trend toward recovery was only slightly reflected by farm prices in 1899.[59] With the panic there came also a reversal in the balance of international trade, and gold began to leave the country. In order to satisfy their foreign creditors, merchants began presenting greenbacks to the Treasury for gold, thus causing a serious drain on the hypothetical reserve held to redeem such notes. At the same time, the silver purchases were costing about $3,500,000 a month, and most of the Treasury notes thus emitted were presented in like fashion for gold. Cleveland could have ordered payment in silver, but feared this would injure the federal credit. Then his gold-standard principles rose above all his other policies. In 1893, he sacrificed his civil service reforms and his hopes of a sane tariff by surrendering all the federal patronage at his disposal to secure the repeal of the purchase clause of the Sherman Silver Act. The wreckage of his administrative leadership gained little for the gold reserve. The drain caused by the Treasury notes was stopped, but there were still over $346,000,000 in greenbacks that could be presented, redeemed, reissued, and turned in again in an endless chain. The fact that the reserve was not protected was amply revealed by the continuance of raids clear down to the summer of 1896. Four bond sales, amounting to $265,000,000, had to be floated between 1893 and December, 1895, to buy gold to keep up a reserve of $100,000,000. Most of the gold procured by the first two sales of $50,000,000 each was first removed by the bankers, from the Treasury, by the greenback route, thus leaving no more reserves than before. Only the stabilization of trade

---

[58] Fine, *Labor and Farmer Parties*, pp. 79–80.
[59] See tables in *Agricultural Yearbook*, 1899, pp. 759–765; Dewey, *Financial History of the United States*, pp. 444–447, for general economic conditions.

balances, and the fear of bankers, in 1896, that any more gold raids would stampede the country into the adoption of free silver, made the gold reserve finally secure.[60]

It is small wonder that Cleveland's policies added mightily to the free-silver cause, and thereby to Populist strength. In 1894, when jobless men were marching on Washington, Congress appropriated no money to provide them work; but it did continue to sanction bonds to bolster the gold reserve. At the same time that railroad strikers in Chicago were threatened by the standing army, the President vetoed a measure to coin the seigniorage of the stored bullion in the Treasury vaults, thus prolonging the deflationary movement that was partly responsible for unemployment and labor unrest. The outflow of gold was not as serious as was imagined, but nearly sixty million fewer dollars were in circulation in 1895 than in 1894, and between 1892 and 1897 the per capita declined from $24.60 to $22.92. While this was going on, the hard-pressed farmers found a spokesman in William H. Harvey, who published a book called *Coin's Financial School*. It contained in words and pictures all the arguments that the silver men wanted, and in a language they could understand and repeat. In 1894, it was selling in a cheap edition at the rate of a hundred thousand copies a month.[61]

In the election of 1894, the Populists increased their vote by half, yet the Republicans regained control in some Western areas. Western Republicans, like the Democrats, were beginning to talk free-silver doctrine, and the forces were divided. Henry M. Teller, Republican from Colorado, was coming to be one of the most convincing of the free-silver spokesmen.[62] The silver-mining interests of the Mountain states were also putting in effective strokes in shaping the issue. Free silver was coming to occupy a position in Populist doctrine out of all proportion to its importance and relevance. The result was to confuse thought among Populists about the fundamentals of agricultural uplift. But, even in the thick of the fight, some of the cool-headed leaders pounded away at the older issues. At Omaha, in 1892, the railroad plank had got more applause

[60] Dewey, *Financial History of the United States*, pp. 440–455.

[61] Currency figures from *Statistical Abstract of the United States*, 1931, p. 249.

[62] Elmer Ellis, *Henry Moore Teller, Defender of the West* (Caldwell, Idaho: The Caxton Printers, 1941), pp. 184–240 *passim*.

than free silver, and the land plank was given a "regular Baptist camp meeting chorus." [63]

The Democratic party was now in sore straits. In some of the Western states most of its adherents had gone over to the Populists or the Republicans. In the East the Democrats almost outdid the Republicans in their devotion to the single gold standard. Great gains were made by the Populists in the South, wherever the party machinery of the Bourbon element of the Democrats could still be seized by a combination of debtor Democrats and Populists. So strong was the silver issue becoming that in 1895 nothing but the surety of a Presidential veto which could not be overcome prevented Congress from passing a free-silver bill. The Democrats, trying to recover their prestige, were laying extra stress on the expansion of the currency when talking to Western and Southern audiences. Now, everything was staked on the election of 1896.[64]

For the forthcoming battle of the standards, the Populists had plenty of able leaders, but what they needed was one who could sway the masses and break up old party ties. Ignatius Donnelly, Thomas E. Watson, William V. Allen of Nebraska, and others had their followings, but all had serious shortcomings as national leaders. Among the more reactionary element in the East most of the Populist leaders were looked upon as "destitute of personal or political integrity. They are political vagabonds, slanderers and demagogues." [65] The users of such phrases apparently were sincere, but they were becoming hysterical over the outcome of the approaching election. It was only to calm their own fears that the Republicans coined the slogan: "Pay no attention to the Populists." The quandary of the Populists was in no way connected with what confirmed gold-standard men might think of their leaders. Their difficulty was finally solved by the action of the Democratic convention in selecting William Jennings Bryan as candidate for President in 1896, and by its adoption of a clear-cut, free-silver plank. This move was a hearty bid for Populist fusion, but there were

---

[63] Hicks, *Populist Revolt*, pp. 231–232, 413.

[64] Buck, *Agrarian Crusade*, pp. 168–169; Fine, *Labor and Farmer Parties*, p. 81.

[65] John D[onald] Hicks, "The Political Career of Ignatius Donnelly," *Mississippi Valley Historical Review*, VIII, Nos. 1–2 (June–September, 1921), 80–132 *passim;* Alex Mathews Arnett, *The Populist Movement in Georgia* (New York: no publisher, 1922), pp. 197–201. The slanderous statements were those of Frank Basil Tracy, "Rise and Doom of the Populist Party," *The Forum*, XVI, No. 2 (October, 1893), 246.

many Populists who realized that much of their cherished program would be sacrificed by coalition. They were not even sure that free silver was their most important issue. The subtreasury plan, one of the most vital and valid of Populist planks, was one of those dropped in the platform of 1896.

Senator Marion Butler of North Carolina, temporary chairman of the Populist convention that followed, warned against the surrender of party identity. "If the People's party were to go out of existence tomorrow, the next Democratic National Convention would repudiate the platform it recently adopted at Chicago, and Mr. Bryan would stand no more chance four years hence of being nominated by that party than Thomas Jefferson would if he were alive." On the other hand, a Democratic success would achieve an important part of the Populist program, and perhaps the rest could be attained later, so a partial fusion was effected. Bryan was indorsed for President, but the Populists could not stomach the conservative Maine banker, shipbuilder, and railroad president, Arthur Sewall, for Vice President, so they nominated Watson for that place.[66] This created an anomaly that may have had something to do with the losing of the election. Separate electoral slates would mean a division of the vote just as much as if no fusion at all had been achieved. So a device was worked out whereby the Populist electors alone would appear on the ballot in the states where they were strongest, and Democratic electors only in the rest of the states.

It is not known how many adherents of both parties this compromise discouraged from voting at all. In some states each party nominated its own candidates for local offices. In the South, the Populists sought Republican support; in the West, Silver Republican and Democratic. But the confusion in party lines was so great that Illinois had eleven minor parties on the ballot.[67] The political story of the ensuing campaign ought need no retelling here. It was largely a confusion of issues that gave the Republicans, with William McKinley, the victory by a margin of half a million popular and ninety-five electoral votes. Yet Bryan's 6,468,000 ballots were more than any candidate had ever received before, and more

[66] William Jennings Bryan, *The First Battle* (Chicago: W. B. Conkey, c.1896), pp. 297–298, quotation p. 261.
[67] Fine, *Labor and Farmer Parties*, p. 86.

than any Democrat was to get again till twenty years later. It is impossible to measure the Populist strength in 1896. Watson got twenty-seven electoral votes for Vice President, but that means little because of the ambiguous nature of the fusion.[68]

THE CONSERVATIVE TRIUMPH

The victory of McKinley meant, largely, the continuation of the monetary policy of Cleveland; and the new President decided that he had been elected for the primary purpose of getting a higher tariff. But the Senate for a time continued to have a free-silver majority, which in 1898 forced a little silver inflation into a war-revenue act. The Sherman silver was to be coined at the rate of 1,500,000 silver dollars a month till all was used up. This policy was continued under the Gold Standard Act of March 14, 1900. Since the silver would replace far more dollars than its original cost in Treasury notes, this coinage of the seigniorage was at least a little balm to the Populists. By about 1910, all the bullion had gone into circulation, either in "cart wheels" or in silver certificates, and the Treasury notes had been retired.[69]

For a dozen years after 1896, the Populists tried to keep up their party organization, but it was a losing struggle. They fused with the Democrats again in 1898, and completely in 1900, though in that year Bryan made free silver a secondary issue to anti-imperialism. The Middle-of-the-Road Populists then nominated their own candidates, who, with 50,000 votes, came out less than half as well as the Prohibitionists. After two more presidential campaigns, the Populists dissolved permanently.

The reason for the collapse of the Populist revolt was that a number of the chief causes for discontent were removed by a revival of general prosperity. By 1897, the effects of the panic had worn off for business, and farm prosperity came later. As business improved, credit grew more plentiful for farmers as well as for industry, and interest rates no longer were so oppressive. Also, the prices of farm products began to rise, and the hope of clearing off debts was again felt. The steady climb in prices during the next

[68] See Ellis, *Henry Moore Teller*, pp. 265–286 *passim;* Oscar Ameringer, *If You Don't Weaken* (New York: Henry Holt and Company, c.1940), pp. 153–155; Bryan, *The First Battle, passim,* for some of the interesting particulars.

[69] Dewey, *Financial History of the United States*, pp. 468–470.

several years was at least partially connected with the rapid growth in the world's supply of money. The per capita of circulating money increased almost by half between 1897 and 1906 (from $22.92 to $32.77).[70] By 1920, as a result of inflation of various kinds, even the Populist demand of $50 per capita was slightly exceeded, with results not nearly as bad as had once been feared. The story of monetary and credit expansion after 1897 is not for these pages.[71] It is sufficient to note that, as credit improved and prices rose, the farmers began to drift back into the Republican and Democratic lines.

Their leaders had once been absorbed with lofty ideals and sound ideas of reform. Railroad domination of politics was to be broken up by the direct election of senators and by the initiative and referendum. The land monopolists should be made to disgorge their huge holdings in order to make the Homestead Act less of a mockery. The subtreasury scheme would provide short-term and intermediate credit in amounts and at such times as they were most needed, and also would give the right sort of elasticity to the currency. The graduated income tax would shift the burden of governmental expense upon the shoulders of the persons benefiting most from the government. Federal ownership and operation of the railroads, telegraph lines, and telephone systems, managed like the post offices, would eliminate the transportation abuses of preceding decades. In fact, the underlying principle of Populism was that the people, not the corporations and men of wealth alone, should control the government, and that the government should suppress the tendencies of the plutocrats to exploit the poor. Or, as Bryan expressed the issue, "Shall the people rule?"[72] But the mass of the Populist voters brooded over these matters only when their expenses exceeded their incomes. They sought no fundamental social and economic reorganization. They wanted higher prices for their crops, and after 1900 they were getting them.[73] Now that their main grievances were allayed, they were content once more to worship at the old altars. When they felt financially secure again they feared the disturbing effect of any change. The Weavers of Iowa and their one-time followers in Kansas slipped back into the

[70] *Statistical Abstract of the United States*, 1931, p. 249.
[71] See Volume VII, by Harold U. Faulkner, in this series.
[72] Hicks, *Populist Revolt*, p. 406.
[73] *Statistical Abstract of the United States*, 1931, pp. 703–707.

Republican fold, and accepted. the doctrine that the victory of McKinley, the gold standard, and the Dingley tariff were causing them to prosper.

In the South, the race question came back to help in the conservative reaction. When cotton prices fell to five cents and lower, the Negro might be called on for help; but hardly had the upturn begun, when a chilling fear began to run up the backbones of the whites. The hard times had not passed before grandfather clauses and poll-tax requirements for voting were sweeping the cotton belt. Poor white men, in increasing numbers, were disfranchised by the same poll-tax device, and those who could still vote often bowed down again to the gods of the Bourbon Democrats. Demagogues were to arise who would, now and then, win over a sufficient following to bring about some needed reforms, but almost never without singing white domination as their theme song. Class problems were submerged beneath race questions, and great reforms were, therefore, not to be achieved.

In succeeding political administrations, following 1896, much of the Populist platform was put into legislation, not mainly because of the agitation of the Populists, but merely, as of old, because government was catching up with the social and economic needs of the preceding generation. The Populist platforms of the 1890's sounded strangely conservative in the 1940's. The postal savings banks came under the almost reactionary Taft. The national banking system was started on the way toward an expanded currency under the conservative Theodore Roosevelt. The direct election of senators came under Wilson. The initiative and referendum and—not asked for by Populists—the recall were sweeping the states before 1912. Effective railroad regulation, an alternative demand of the Populists, started in 1903, and continued until most of the old abuses were ameliorated. Currency based on deposits of agricultural goods in warehouses has become an established and hardly questioned fact. Inflation came, though not by silver; and by 1917 the farmers were lured into a new era of speculative expansion, thus laying the basis for the next era of farm depression.[74] The development of a deeply rooted class philosophy for the farmers was not to emerge from only a single generation of hard times.

[74] Hicks, *Populist Revolt*, pp. 404–423.

CHAPTER XIV

Farmers' Cooperative Movements

THE GRANGE

THOUGH the nineteenth-century farmers failed to solve their problems by political measures, and though their organization in other respects was never profound or widespread enough to achieve all the objectives sought, yet it would be unfair to leave the subject without showing how the vision and experiences of the few prepared the way for success in some distant future. The experiments of the Grangers furnish a good introduction to the activities of many other groups.

The Patrons of Husbandry was a secret society founded in Washington, D.C., in 1867, by Oliver Hudson Kelley and some other clerks in the Department of Agriculture. Kelley had lived in Boston, in Iowa, and in Minnesota, and in 1866 had studied conditions in the South. The latter mission had confirmed his opinion of farmers all over the country: that what they needed more than anything else was a social life that would give them a broader social vision. Kelley had enough faith in his new organization to resign from his government position, with the expectation of collecting a salary of $2,000 a year from fees paid by the local granges he would charter. But, in the late sixties, the farmers had not yet felt the full pinch of hard times, the result being that by the end of the year 1868 only 10 granges had been established, 6 of them in Minnesota. A year later that state, where most of the effort had been concentrated, had only 37 local lodges. Then, as depression settled on the farm preparatory to the Panic of 1873, 1,105 granges were founded in 1872. This was followed by 8,400 in the panic year and 4,700 in January and February of 1874. Driven to desperation, the farmers were now ready to rush into anything ·that gave a reasonable promise of relief, and they thronged into the Patrons of Husbandry. The initiation fee was three dollars for men and fifty cents for women.[1]

By this time, the original social and educational features of the Grange were taking second place to the attacks on middlemen and railroads. The fundamentals were not ignored, but farmers joined primarily for economic benefits, and they intended to get them. In the annual convention of 1874, the National Grange proposed "working together, buying together, selling together, and generally acting together for . . . mutual protection and advancement. . . ."[2] In order to reduce the difference between what the farmer got for his products and what the consumer paid, or between what goods cost the manufacturer and what the farmer paid, the grangers proposed to eliminate unnecessary middlemen.[3] The procedure was described by a member as follows:

A State agent is appointed whose duty it is to correspond and negotiate with manufacturers and large wholesale dealers, and ascertain upon what terms they will sell their goods direct to the members. If these terms are satisfactory they are communicated to the Subordinate Granges, the members of which make out their orders and forward to the State agent with the amount of purchase money in cash. The State agent forwards them direct to the manufacturer or merchant with instructions for the shipment of the goods direct to the purchaser. In this way it is made the interest of the merchant, farmer, and the manufacturer to dispense almost entirely with middle men. . . .

This system was soon simplified by having an agent in each large purchasing center who would do the buying and ship direct to the consumer.[4] All grangers were supplied with a list of such manu-

---

[1] O[liver] H[udson] Kelley, *Origin and Progress of the Order of the Patrons of Husbandry in the United States . . . , 1866–1873* (Philadelphia: J. A. Wagenseller, 1875), pp. 11–90; Fred E[mory] Haynes, *Third Party Movements Since the Civil War* (Iowa City: State Historical Society of Iowa, 1916), p. 52.

[2] Jonathan Periam, *The Groundswell* (Cincinnati: E. Hannaford & Company, 1874), p. 573.

[3] John R[ogers] Commons and others, eds., *A Documentary History of American Industrial Society* (Cleveland: The Arthur H. Clark Company, 1911), X, 102.

[4] A. B. Smedley, *The Principles and Aims of the Patrons of Husbandry* (Burlington, Iowa: R. T. Root, 1874), pp. 34–35.

facturers as cared to *"deal directly* with State and Subordinate Granges." [5]

Montgomery Ward and Company started business in Chicago, in 1872, with the express purpose of dealing with grangers, and it was not long before local dealers had to effect economies and reduce prices to meet the new competition. Various implement dealers made concessions, and Illinois grangers could buy reapers a hundred dollars below the $275 charged by ordinary middlemen. Many other implements were bought at proportional reductions. The McCormick company was one that would make very few concessions. Some fire insurance was handled directly by the Grange, but only a little success was achieved with life insurance. California was the only state where Grange banking was done. Cooperative selling made the most headway in Iowa, where thirty elevators were operated by the local granges. There were also attempts at the packing of meat and the milling of grain.[6]

It was in the manufacture of farm machinery that the most ambitious and disastrous cooperative efforts were made, and the scene was in Iowa. There, in 1873, the State Grange bought the Werner harvester factory and, in the next year, sold some two hundred and fifty machines at about half the usual price. Three plow factories were also bought, and a few other implement works. This enterprise induced the National Grange to invest a large part of its resources in a like manner. But this experiment died in infancy. The independent competitors were not always fair in their practices, and the management of the granges was too slow in developing efficiency. Furthermore, the policy of price cutting proved a bad one. It provoked price wars in which the older and stronger companies were the better able to endure. Selling too close to cost, the cooperatives had no funds left for improvements, expansion, bad seasons, or law suits. Consequently, the Iowa experiment failed in 1875, and the National Grange's investment was soon swept out of existence. Rather than be sued for their debts, the proprietor granges disbanded, and a general breakup of the order followed. But the dissolution was not complete. With the seeming success of their efforts at railroad regulation and the

---

[5] Kelley, *Patrons of Husbandry*, pp. 385–386.

[6] Buck, *The Granger Movement*, pp. 238–278 *passim;* Nevins, *Emergence of Modern America*, pp. 172–173.

failure of their business enterprises, after 1876 the diminished membership returned to the original principles of the improvement of rural life, and the grangers ultimately became more numerous than they had been in the 1870's.[7] Meanwhile, lessons in cooperation had been learned that others could benefit from, if they would only heed. But the general experience was that each new group had to learn from its own mistakes, and often it did not survive that effort. Whole generations of trial and error had to be endured preparatory to the development of a true cooperative spirit. The early efforts at cooperation were doomed by too much jealousy and suspicion within the organizations, too much insistence on spontaneous miracles, and a too easy disgust at faltering progress.

THE GRAIN ELEVATOR MOVEMENT

It was in the North Central states, where the Grange had flourished especially, that cooperative grain elevators were generally found—these were the first, the most numerous, and the most successful. They both preceded and followed the grangers' efforts. The first of them all, it seems, was founded by the Dane County Farmers' Protective Union in Wisconsin, in 1857. The extortionate charges made by the independent dealers were the reason. In this, as in later ventures, dependence had to be placd on commission men in the larger markets to find an outlet for the grain. Though there were other examples, except for those of the Grange this movement did not seem to make much headway before 1890. Illinois had its first cooperative elevator in 1884, 4 in 1890, and only 16 in 1900. Meanwhile, 3 more had been organized and gone out of business. That the movement was to be a continuous and successful one is shown by the fact that in 1914 there were 254 and that in the preceding thirty years only 17 others had gone out of business.[8]

Some caution has to be used in the study of cooperative ele-

---

[7] Buck, *Agrarian Crusade*, pp. 60–70.

[8] J[ames] W[arren] Cummins, "The Cooperative Marketing of Grain in the United States," Pan American Union, Division of Agricultural Cooperation, *Series on Cooperatives*, No. 7 (Washington: mimeographed, September, 1937), p. 1; J[oseph] M[artin] Mehl, "Cooperative Grain Marketing," U.S. Department of Agriculture, *Department Bulletin* No. 937 (Washington: Government Printing Office, April 9, 1921), p. 2; Lawrence Farlow, *The Farmers Elevator Movement in Illinois* (n.p.: Farmers Grain Dealers Association of Illinois, 1928), pp. 41–42.

vators, for, as in some other enterprises, the word "cooperative" sometimes was put in the name of an independent, merely as a catch for unwary farmers. The elevators hereafter mentioned were all, as far as can be determined, of the truly cooperative sort. A study of their development in Illinois will show most of the problems involved. Apparently the first in Illinois was started at the town of Dakota, in Stevenson County, in 1884. Next was the Sheldon Coöperative Grain Association, begun in Iroquois County in 1887. It was destroyed by fire six years later, but was followed by another. The Goodwine Grain Company was incorporated in the same county in 1889, and outlived its predecessors, thus becoming the oldest of the permanent group. A few others were established before 1896, some permanent and a few enduring only a short span of years. Then a more rapid growth of the movement became imperative. In the previous years, farmers who wanted to deal directly with the central markets simply ordered freight cars and loaded them themselves. But, in 1896, the Illinois Grain Dealers' Association was formed with the purpose of forcing commission men to refuse the "scoop shovel" business of the farmers. The association also induced the railroad companies to cease hauling grain except from elevators. From that time on, the number of farmers' elevators began to grow with accelerated speed, though it was not till 1905 that they numbered more than a hundred. Sometimes, as in McLean County in 1895, the farmers would build an elevator merely to create competition, and lease it to some operator, only to take it over on a cooperative basis later.[9]

The association of the independent dealers remained powerful enough to dictate to a good proportion of the commission merchants in markets such as those at Chicago, Milwaukee, Peoria, and St. Louis. They also attempted to run the cooperatives out of business by rate wars. Then the farmers showed an unusual trait by signing marketing contracts containing a loyalty clause. This was an idea that seems to have developed first among the farmers around Rockwell, Iowa, in 1889. The members agreed to pay a penalty to the cooperative on each bushel of wheat they shipped through an independent. Thus, though they might have gained a temporary advantage by deserting their own elevators, they stuck to their agreements and saved themselves much in later years. By 1901, the

[9] Farlow, *Farmers Elevator Movement in Illinois*, pp. 9–14, 42.

independent dealers were fighting hard to ruin their competitors by a boycott. Commission men in the grain centers who bought from cooperatives were threatened and blacklisted by the Illinois Grain Dealers' Association, and some of them were virtually ruined. But, in 1903, the Illinois Warehouse Commission ended this discrimination, and also ordered the Illinois Central railroad company to furnish cars to all persons requesting them. The cooperative movement continued to prosper, and by 1910 its business was being solicited by nearly all central dealers. If anything, the boycott, by arousing rural indignation, actually stimulated the growth of membership. A state association of farmers' elevators was organized in 1903 to carry on the fight. The movement made little headway in Iowa, Kansas, and Nebraska before 1900, and North Dakota was just considering the idea.[10] For that matter, it was hardly strong anywhere.

Most of the farmers elevators were separate from all others in ownership, the growers in a locality raising the money among themselves to buy or build. As the movement spread in Kansas, though this was mainly after 1900, a county-wide management was developed to bring still further economies. Among the hardest problems in the early years was the procuring of a site for the building. The railroad companies, taking the part of the independents, would not allow any encroachment on their right of ways, nor would they build sidings except in such states as had laws requiring it. Sometimes the elevator had to be built as near the track as land could be procured, and long chutes were used to reach the cars. More often, when the independent found that the elevator was going to be built anyway, he would sell out for fear of being unable to compete.[11]

DAIRY AND LIVESTOCK COOPERATIVES

Among the earliest of producers' cooperatives were a few cheese factories in the 1840's and 1850's, and in 1856 a farmers' creamery began doing business in Orange County, New York. A cheese manufacturing association of 1863 in Montgomery County, New York, was

[10] *Ibid.*, pp. 16–20, 22–25, 27–32, 34; Joseph B[ernard] Kenkel, *The Cooperative Elevator Movement* (Washington: Catholic University of America, 1922), pp. 16, 21–22.

[11] Mehl, "Cooperative Grain Marketing," pp. 15–18.

still in operation sixty-two years later. The first movements of the sort were mainly in New York and New England, but by 1870 the Commissioner of Agriculture noted their expansion into Ohio, Indiana, Illinois, and other Western states. A creamery started in Vermont in 1880 well exemplifies the growth of such enterprises. By 1900, it was utilizing the cream from three thousand cows, making eight or ten tons of butter a day in the busiest season or over three million pounds a year. In 1900, cooperatives were found all over New England, and especially in Massachusetts, where thirty-four of the forty-one creameries under the supervision of state authorities were of that designation. Units at Springfield and Lowell were particularly successful, though the supply of cream was none too plentiful.[12]

In 1872, there was an effort to establish a farmers' milk marketing association of the producers for the metropolitan area of New York, but it was unavailing, and ten years later the producers paid the penalty for their failure, by being confronted with an independent buyers' trust known as the New York Milk Exchange, Ltd. This company was compelled to dissolve in 1895 because of its practices of fixing the price paid to the farmers, but it was immediately reorganized as the Consolidated Milk Exchange, and continued to regulate prices more cautiously. This new subterfuge stampeded the producers of New York, New Jersey, Pennsylvania, Connecticut, and Massachusetts into the formation of the Five States Producers' Association of 1898, the purpose being to combat the trust. Under the guidance of the new organization, local associations set up many creameries, but the contest with the Consolidated Milk Exchange failed, and by 1907 the efforts ceased.[13]

The Illinois and Wisconsin Dairymen's Association of 1867 and the state and sectional organizations following it were accompanied by an expansion of the cooperative movement into the West. Thereafter, the progress was rapid but somewhat spotty. By 1900,

[12] Roland Willey Bartlett, *Cooperation in Marketing Dairy Products* (Springfield, Ill.: Charles C. Thomas, Publisher, c.1931), p. 75; U.S. Commissioner of Agriculture, *Report*, 1870, p. 542; W. S. Harwood, "Coöperation in the West," *The Atlantic Monthly*, LXXXV, No. 510 (April, 1900), 543; Edward W[ebster] Bemis, "Coöperation in New England," Johns Hopkins University *Studies in Historical and Political Science*, VI, Nos. 1–2 (Baltimore: Johns Hopkins University, 1888), 84–85; R[alph] H[enry] Elsworth, "Agricultural Cooperative Associations, Marketing and Purchasing, 1925," U.S. Department of Agriculture, *Technical Bulletin* No. 40 (Washington: Government Printing Office, January, 1928), p. 4.

[13] Bartlett, *Cooperation in Marketing Dairy Products*, pp. 33–34.

about 1,000 of the 1,600 creameries of Wisconsin were cooperative, at least in name. Though there was none in Minnesota in 1890, ten years later 9 out of each 13 of the 650 creameries were operated by farmer groups. In Iowa, despite the prevalence of unsound business practices in the movement, over a third of all the creameries were cooperative by the end of the century. The Dakotas also showed a trend toward the cooperative pattern, but in Nebraska and Kansas the proprietary system was little threatened.[14]

Though the movement did not achieve any great importance before 1900, it should also be noted that livestock-shipping associations were beginning to attract some attention. Evidences of joint action in this field might be found at rather remote periods, but it was not till about 1908 that associations existed for that purpose alone.[15] As far as has been discovered, the first progenitor of this sort of cooperative effort was the Sangamon County Stock and Produce Sale Association, organized in Illinois, in 1874, by some forty farmers. The object was "to bring together the producer and consumer of live stock and other farm-products, and to eliminate, as far as possible, the large profits of middlemen, especially in commissions, expenses of shipment, &c." [16] The Goodlettsville, Tennessee, Lamb Club was another early example, started in 1877 merely as a neighborhood auctioning association. It was of small consequence, for the organized buyers prearranged the bids. The club then tried joint shipments to the markets, whenever prices otherwise were too low.[17]

In 1889, the first known attempt was made to set up cooperative livestock-selling agencies in the terminal markets. This was the American Livestock Commission Company, incorporated under Illinois law with a nominal capital of $100,000, a quarter of which

[14] Harwood, "Coöperation in the West," pp. 540–541; E. E. Miller, "The American Farmer as a Coöperator," The Forum, LII, No. 4 (October 1914), 598.

[15] Edwin G[riswold] Nourse and Joseph G[rant] Knapp, The Co-operative Marketing of Livestock (Washington: The Brookings Institution, 1931), p. 9; John Lee Coulter, "Organization among the Farmers of the United States," Yale Review, XVIII, No. 3 (November, 1909), 296; S. W. Doty, "Cooperative Livestock Shipping Associations," U.S. Department of Agriculture, Farmers' Bulletin No. 718 (Washington: Government Printing Office, April 10, 1916), p. 2.

[16] U.S. Department of Agriculture, Monthly Report, February-March, 1875 (Washington: Government Printing Office, 1875), p. 136.

[17] Nourse and Knapp, Co-operative Marketing of Livestock, p. 12; Duane Howard Doane, "The Coöperative Lamb Club as an Agency for Lower Marketing Costs," American Academy of Political and Social Science, Annals, L (November, 1913), 218–222.

was actually paid in. Commission firms were then put to work in Chicago, Kansas City, St. Louis, and Omaha. Failing to retain membership in the Chicago livestock exchange, the company went out of existence, but others took its place. Really notable success was not attained until after 1916.[18]

FARMERS' STORES

Cooperative buying, as well as selling, went on in the North, contemporary with and after the Granger attempts of the 1870's. In fact, this was a time-honored expedient even before 1860. Most of the efforts of the earlier period, like the union stores of New England (1847–1859), failed or turned capitalistic because of the price cutting by independents, which was invited by the cooperatives' practice of selling below prevailing levels. In 1864, a store was opened in Philadelphia, operating on the Rochdale plan. The underlying principles were the issuance of a limited amount of stock, each holder to have only one vote and receiving a fixed rate of interest on his investment; selling at prevailing prices, so as to encourage outside buying and prevent price wars; and the division of surplus earnings among the members according to the amount of their purchases. The Granger stores received the bulk of attention during the next decade, but most of them failed, like their predecessors, by following the price-cutting system. A few were reorganized on the Rochdale plan, and such of them as were properly managed continued in business for a number of years, but, in 1888, Albert Shaw was no longer able to find evidence of the existence of any. Some, however, had only changed their allegiance or membership. The Farmers' Exchange of Grinnell, Iowa, was in 1873 limited to grangers, but, when the local lodge declined, it admitted others to membership, and continued to do a thriving business at least down to 1890.[19]

The Patrons of Industry, another Northern farmers' organiza-

---

[18] C[ortes] G[ilbert] Randell, "Cooperative Marketing of Livestock in the United States by Terminal Associations," U.S. Department of Agriculture, *Technical Bulletin* No. 57 (Washington: Government Printing Office, February, 1928), pp. 6–9.

[19] Edward W[ebster] Bemis, "Cooperative Distribution," U.S. Department of Labor, *Bulletin* No. 6 (Washington: Government Printing Office, 1896), pp. 613, 615–616; Albert Shaw, "Coöperation in the Northwest," Johns Hopkins University *Studies in Historical and Political Science*, VI, Nos. 4–6 (Baltimore: Johns Hopkins University, 1888), 307; Haynes, *Third Party Movements*, pp. 87–88.

tion operating west of New England, also fostered retail stores through its local associations. In some cases they bought direct from the manufacturers, and in others they secured special contracts through local dealers. According to the Supreme Secretary of the association, the amount of business done was "enormous," but the adjective was not defined. More lucid was the declaration that the members effected savings of not less than 10 per cent on everything they bought.[20] In 1900, the day was still far in the distance when a Farmers' Union store, selling everything from sugar, calico, and machinery to coal, gasoline, and fence posts, was to be found in every fair-sized town in the West. But at that very time the Farmers' Union was beginning to emerge from the Alliances, and the experiences and failures of the nineteenth century were behind it for guidance and a warning.

SOUTHERN COOPERATIVES

The Southern credit system, with its crop-lien drag on agricultural progress, prevented any extensive cooperative enterprises among the common run of farmers, and for reasons that need no further explanation. Yet, there were some places where diversified farming was followed and the workers were not tied down to the new form of bondage. In such places, first the Grange and later the Farmers' Alliance made some headway in cooperation, but there was very little effort outside those two movements. The landowners themselves could engage in joint marketing projects, while denying the benefits of cooperative stores to their tenants. In 1873, the Grange entered Texas and spread rapidly. The Democratic leaders were suspicious that the order might undermine their political power, but this did not prevent the less docile of their followers from joining. The neophytes entered with the understanding that the program of the order would be primarily economic, yet the State Grange proceeded only gingerly toward business undertakings. The Texas Cooperative Association of 1878 was organized by the state body, and the membership was limited to Grangers. This was not long in becoming a leading cotton-marketing agency at Galveston, and, in addition, for a number of years it sold around fifty thousand dollars worth of goods annually at its cooperative

[20] Bemis, "Cooperative Distribution," p. 612.

stores. At the height of its power these retail outlets numbered 155. The wholesale agency was at Galveston. The high point of the project was in 1883. Thereafter the steady encroachment of the Southern rural-credit system limited sales that formerly had been made to outsiders. Also, there was a growth away from true co-operative principles. The whole movement was dormant by 1896. Efforts at cooperative farm machinery manufacturing hardly even got a good start in the 1870's.[21]

In Alabama, Georgia, Mississippi, Louisiana, and Arkansas there were ambitious marketing programs. "Cooperative organizations were established and arrangements made with cotton firms to handle members' cotton." While some of the associations succeeded for a few years, many died quickly, sometimes because they strove for the unattainable, and again because the management was poor. At one time or another, the marketing associations had some members in nearly every farming community in the cotton belt, but they were landlords. No other organization achieved the eminence of the Texas Cooperative Association.[22]

It was at about the time that the last of the grange efforts were flickering out that the Farmers' Alliance grew strong enough to take over the work. By 1885, the alliance was interesting itself in the credit problems of cotton farmers, trying to get better treatment for its members from the local merchants. The next step, before 1890, was the establishment of a sort of commission business of buying and selling between the members, manufacturers, and produce markets, the farmers getting their groceries, dry goods, and other supplies through the same agency that disposed of their crops, eliminating some middlemen's profits in both directions. The Texas Alliance organized county cotton yards that reduced the warehouse and handling charges against its members. Later it fixed special sales days for the disposal of cotton to buyers. This worked for a short time, but there was so much opposition from local merchants and so little interest shown by buyers from the central markets that the project had to be abandoned before many years.

[21] Robert Lee Hunt, A History of Farmer Movements in the Southwest (n.p., n.d.), pp. 7, 20, 22–25; William O. Scroggs, "Economic Experiments in Coöperation since 1865," South in the Building of the Nation, VI, 580–581.

[22] O[mer] W[esley] Herrmann, "Cooperative Cotton Marketing in the United States," Pan American Union, Division of Agricultural Cooperation, Series on Co-operatives, No. 3 (Washington: mimeographed, November, 1936), pp. 1–3.

Small, independent farmers might have profited greatly by the arrangement had not their enemies been too strong for them. Undaunted, the alliance tried out another plan, that of a state exchange at Dallas, for the collection of cotton at county warehouses for direct sales to the mills. This time the unfavorable credit status of the member farmers prevented success. Then, as the amalgamation of the Southern alliances went forward in the late eighties, a state Alliance Exchange was inaugurated in Texas. But, shortly after this, the alliance itself began to break up, as the lure of free silver pulled the members into political action.[23]

One of the most important features of the cotton program was the establishment of cooperatively owned gins. As the old plantation system disintegrated in the South, custom ginning was introduced, and, as new cotton areas were developed, the custom gin became an integral part of the economy. Then, as the commercial value of the seeds was exploited, companies came into control of whole chains of gins so as to get all the seeds possible. The cost of custom ginning was so high in many sections that the farmers were readily attracted by any proposal by which it seemed possible for them to procure and operate their own machines. Probably the first cooperative gin association was founded at Greenville, Texas, in 1887, by alliance men, and on the copartnership basis. Some others were joint-stock companies. Such associations had the further advantage of retaining the seeds for their own sale, thus adding at least a little to the individual income. After 1900, many of the gins passed from the control of the farmers' organizations for lack of restrictions preventing the sale of stock to other than owner-users.[24]

Between 1875 and 1905, several other group ventures were undertaken in the South. Among those particularly interested in procuring the most from the marketing of cotton were the Mississippi Valley Cotton Planters' Association, the Southern Cotton Growers' Association, the Southern Cotton Growers' Protective Association, and the Southern Cotton Association. These were not true cooperatives, and were not concerned with the mechanics of marketing. Instead, they tried to raise prices by one sort or another of mo-

[23] Hunt, *History of Farmer Movements in the Southwest,* pp. 29–34; Herrmann, "Cooperative Cotton Marketing," pp. 3–4; Clarence N. Ousley, "A Lesson in Cooperation," *Popular Science Monthly,* XXXVI, No. 6 (April, 1890), 821–828.

[24] Herrmann, "Cooperative Cotton Marketing," pp. 27–28.

nopoly control, by limitation of acreage, and by partial crop destruction.[25] The recommendations of Herbert Hoover and the accomplishments of F. D. Roosevelt toward the plowing under of cotton were, after all, only old devices revived and made general.

FRUIT GROWERS' PROJECTS

The cooperative marketing of fruits elsewhere in America antedates any of the attempts in California, but the later magnitude of the Western ventures naturally attracts attention first in that direction. The Orange Growers' Protective Union of 1885 was the first enterprise of the kind in California. It was brought about in consequence of a disastrous decline in prices and the loose practices of many commission houses. The vast distances to the larger markets, the big part of the value of the crop taken to pay freight and commissions, the scant knowledge of the growers as to market conditions, and the seasonal glut of some areas coupled with a dearth in others made some sort of organization necessary to the preservation of the industry. The members of the Protective Union had the fruit boxed by commercial packers and turned over to certain dealers for further disposal. This was only a halfway measure, and the organization was never firmly established. From the start, it was bitterly opposed by the intrenched shipping and distributing firms, and after a few seasons it was forced to disband. Revived again in 1890, it lasted only three years and then gave way to a new enterprise. Similar to the Protective Union were at least three other southern California associations that were organized in 1891, and rapidly went out of existence.[26]

During the season of 1892–1893, two strictly cooperative groups were in working order: the Pachappa Orange Growers Association at Riverside, and the Claremont Fruit Growers Association. The Redlands Orange Growers' Association also dated from about the

[25] *Ibid.*, p. 4.

[26] Rahno Mabel MacCurdy, *The History of the California Fruit Growers Exchange* (Los Angeles: no publisher, 1925), pp. 10, 13–14; Ira B[rown] Cross, "Co-operation in California," *American Economic Review*, I, No. 3 (September, 1911), 540; A[ndrew] W[illiam] McKay, "Organization and Development of a Cooperative Citrus-Fruit Marketing Agency," U.S. Department of Agriculture, *Department Bulletin* No. 1,237 (Washington: Government Printing Office, May, 1924), p. 9; John William Lloyd, *Co-operative and Other Organized Methods of Marketing California Horticultural Products* (University of Illinois *Studies in the Social Sciences*, VIII, No. 1, Urbana: University of Illinois, c.1919), p. 52.

same time. The Claremont group, and apparently the rest as well, broke away from the old system, did their own packing and shipping, and carried on their business directly with Eastern brokers. Sometimes they sold at auction, but they also engaged outright in exportation. A series of disastrous seasons from 1890 to 1893 had nearly ruined the growers. Five or six large, independent marketing agencies had just about monopolized the business of the southern part of the state by 1890, and they were looked upon as the major cause of the depression. As business slackened and prices fell, the new type of cooperative seemed to be the only hope of salvation. So, in the summer of 1893, others were founded and they all federated into seven district exchanges. Each district followed a common marketing plan. The exchanges sold independently, but the policies of all were made to conform to the regulations of an executive board that held weekly meetings in Los Angeles while shipping was in progress.[27]

The organization within these exchanges continued to develop as experience showed the way, and in 1895 the Southern California Fruit Exchange was the culmination. This agency set up branches in the more important markets, and, from that time on, the selling of citrus fruit was on a reasonably secure basis. By 1903 the exchange is said to have controlled 47 per cent of the shipments from California.[28] A period of experimentation had ended, and a new era of cooperative monopoly was under way. The account, thus far, deals only with the southern part of California. There it must stop, for organization in the northern part of the state did not begin till after the close of the period under discussion.[29]

The earliest producers' fruit marketing association of known record, in the East, was the Fruit Growers' Union and Coöperative Society, founded at Hammonton, New Jersey, in 1867. It is not definitely known how long this society remained active (probably thirty years), but as late as 1887, after a reorganization three years

[27] McKay, "Cooperative Citrus-Fruit Marketing Agency," pp. 7, 9–10; A[ndrew] W[illiam] McKay and W[ayne] Mackenzie Stevens, "Operating Methods and Expenses of Cooperative Citrus-Fruit Marketing Agencies," U.S. Department of Agriculture, *Department Bulletin* No. 1,261 (Washington: Government Printing Office, July 22, 1924), pp. 1–2.

[28] McKay, "Cooperative Citrus-Fruit Marketing Agency," pp. 10–12; Lloyd, *Marketing California Horticultural Products,* p. 54.

[29] J. L. Nagle, "California Fruit Exchange," Thirty-eighth Fruit Growers' Convention of the State of California, 1910, *Proceedings* (Sacramento: W. W. Shannon, Superintendent of State Printing, 1911), p. 60.

earlier, it had a membership of 233 and net assets of a little more than eight thousand dollars. As its name suggests, the group was not confined purely to the selling of fruit. It was also engaged in the retail merchandise business, handling numerous things such as implements, fertilizer, hay, coal, and the like. The trade, in 1886, amounted to nearly forty-six thousand dollars, from which dividends of 5 per cent were paid to member buyers and half that rate to nonmember customers. The main purpose, however, was fruit marketing, the members being charged a 2 per cent commission to cover the costs. It is also said that the railroads paid a percentage on all fruit they distributed in Eastern markets. This could mean only one thing—rebates. New Jersey also had an association of cranberry growers as early as 1872.[30]

The existence of other such groups can be traced through the literature, out to Colorado and even into Oregon. Sometimes the data are fragmentary, and not always is it clear when a society began or when it dissolved. The likelihood is that many were abortive and others ineffective. The Grand Junction Fruit Growers' Association was the oldest and most prosperous in Colorado before 1907. It originated in 1891, "when a few growers combined and appointed one of their number salesman of their fruit for the season. This arrangement continued with varying degrees of success up to 1897, when it became apparent that the increased business . . . would necessitate employing a manager. . . ." Thereafter, the business increased year by year. Undoubtedly the example was soon copied, for by 1907 there were over thirty organizations in the state for the sale of fruit and other produce. Where there was little fruit to be shipped, the association itself would do the packing; elsewhere, the growers did this work for themselves. In the earlier years, sales were made through commission men at the distributing centers. But reports came back that the fruit was arriving in so damaged a condition that regular market prices could not be paid. Later methods of auctioning, or shipping f.o.b., eliminated this sharp practice. The cooperative handling of apples in the Pacific

[30] A. W. McKay, "Cooperative Marketing of Fruits and Vegetables in the United States," Pan American Union, Division of Agricultural Cooperation, Series on Cooperatives, No. 10 (Washington: mimeographed, April, 1938), p. 2; Edward W[ebster] Bemis, "Coöperation in the Middle States," Johns Hopkins University Studies in Historical and Political Science, VI, Nos. 2–3 (Baltimore: Johns Hopkins University, 1888), 149–150; Elsworth, "Agricultural Cooperative Associations," p. 5.

Northwest came so late that any discussion of it here would be inappropriate.[31]

Usually the pioneer fruit-marketing associations were locally inspired and unconnected with each other. Many were unincorporated. After a time, the neighborhood groups were prone to federate by districts or states in order to procure more uniform and effective action. The first such federation seems to have been among the citrus fruit growers of Florida, about 1886. In a combination of this sort the local units took care of all problems up to the marketing stage. Then the graded, packed, and loaded goods were shipped and sold, and the proceeds were distributed by the federation. Fruit and vegetable growers also introduced the "centralized" association, the first being organized in 1892 in the Chautauqua grape area of New York. This type was a large-scale cooperative covering an entire producing region—sometimes an entire state or parts of two or more adjoining states. The older associations managed to retain a remarkable amount of local autonomy, while surrendering to the central body authority over matters of common interest.[32] Pooling, and other devices to stabilize prices and give equal protection to all members, had not come into existence, or at least were not common, before 1900. The cooperatives, wherever formed, were successful just in proportion as the members observed the rules. Separate cooperative produce exchanges were also in existence, as that at Norfolk in 1870. This one had a continuous existence, and by 1914 had four hundred members. In general their experiences were quite like those of the fruit growers, but to 1900 they were neither as common nor as highly organized.[33]

MISCELLANEOUS ENTERPRISES

Since insurance, in one form or another, played so large a part in most of the farmers' associations, it is only natural that direct insurance also should have been stressed. The Farmers' Mutual In-

[31] "Cooperation in Marketing Fruit and Truck Crops," U.S. Department of Agriculture, *Farmers' Bulletin* No. 309 (Washington: Government Printing Office, September, 1907), pp. 20–23.

[32] McKay, "Cooperative Marketing of Fruits and Vegetables," pp. 13–15; Edwin G[riswold] Nourse, "The Philosophy of Co-operative Marketing," Pan American Union, Division of Agricultural Cooperation, *Series on Cooperatives*, No. 1 (Washington: mimeographed, April, 1936), p. 15.

[33] Miller, "The American Farmer as a Coöperator," pp. 596–597.

surance Company, of Clayton County, Iowa, in business as early as 1866, was possibly the first of the long list for fire protection. This kind of insurance cost all policy holders together very little more than the actual losses, and it was an activity quickly taken up and expanded by the Grange. The companies became especially numerous in the states of the upper Mississippi Valley, and they have had a longer history of uniform success than any other form of farmers' business organization. Nothing like complete data are available for their number at the end of the nineteenth century, but official lists were obtained from thirty-four states in 1913, showing 1,867 companies, ranging from 237 in Pennsylvania, 230 in Illinois, and 203 in Wisconsin, down to 1 each for Oklahoma and Rhode Island. Estimates growing out of investigations by the Department of Agriculture to 1907 showed fire, lightning, hail, and wind insurance companies numbering approximately 2,000; life insurance, 7,500; sickness, funeral, and family relief insurance, 6,000; and livestock insurance, 150.[34]

Farmers' line telephone companies were another striking example of the benefit of cooperative effort. These businesses were developed by having each patron buy his own telephone, and join in the work of building the line by contributing his own labor and materials, or money for materials. Oftentimes the wires were strung along the tops of fence posts, and frequently the farmer's own barbed wire was used. The village storekeeper might be entrusted with the switchboard, but, more often, a private home and the service of one of the women of the house were utilized. The rates were generally no more than half what was charged by private companies, and, though the service was likely to be correspondingly low, the standards were steadily raised. When connections were attempted with larger commercial companies, the charges were often outrageously high, and sometimes no connection would be granted at all unless the farmers' company sold out completely. By 1907, the number of companies was estimated at fifteen thousand.[35]

Toward the very end of the century, a movement was started in

[34] Shaw, "Cooperation in the Northwest," p. 341–344; *Agricultural Yearbook,* 1908, pp. 184, 186; *ibid.,* 1913, p. 243; James B. Morman, "Business Coöperative Organizations in Agriculture," *Cyclopedia of American Agriculture,* IV, 256–257.

[35] Morman, "Business Coöperative Organizations in Agriculture," p. 256; E. K. Eyerly, "Co-operative Movements among Farmers," American Academy of Political and Social Science, *Annals,* XL (March, 1912), p. 62.

the Swedish community of Svea, Minnesota, that showed what might be done by all-round, thoroughgoing cooperation. Perhaps Old World experiences had something to do in guiding the enterprise. Though most of the achievements came in the twentieth century, the fact that the experiment was started in 1896 shows the culmination of a generation of farmers' experiences. These Swedes set out to achieve a complete cooperative existence, even if the idea never should spread beyond their neighborhood. The first step was the starting of their own creamery. Most of the members of the company had been Farmers' Alliance men, and, failing to better themselves by legislation, they decided to try economic means. The creamery, operated on the Rochdale plan, became the basis of their later expansion and prosperity. Next, they took over a telephone system, then an insurance company and a bank. In 1909, they bought out the village store. The town pastor told of the benefits he received from the venture. He bought stock for $100, giving his note in payment. At the end of the year, after subtracting the principal and interest on the note from the rebates on his purchases, he had $44.60 coming to him. From this success, the Svea farmers advanced on the county seat, and acquired their own grain elevator. Before 1914, their experiences were stimulating adjacent communities to copy the example.[36] Interestingly enough, this movement was started and getting under way at the very time that Eugene V. Debs and his wing of the Social Democratic party were abandoning their plans for the establishment of a Western cooperative commonwealth on a state-wide scale.[37]

The Department of Agriculture survey, mentioned above, showed some 85,000 cooperative societies in 1907, with a membership, exclusive of duplications, amounting to above 3,000,000, or half the farmers of America. Besides the insurance and telephone concerns, already enumerated, there were 30,000 irrigation companies, 1,800 grain elevators, 4,000 buying agencies, 1,000 selling associations, 1,500 social, economic, and educational groups, 75 production agencies, 50 communities, colonies, and settlements, and

[36] Clarence [Hamilton] Poe, *How Farmers Co-operate and Double Profits* (New York: Orange Judd Company, 1915), pp. 75–82; Miller, "The American Farmer as a Coöperator," pp. 599–600.

[37] Fine, *Labor and Farmer Parties*, pp. 190-194.

300 of a miscellaneous nature.[38] Surely, the number could not have been disproportionally smaller a decade earlier.

CONCLUSIONS

If half the farming population was engaged, in one way or another, in cooperative activities, the question may well be raised: why did not more good come of it? To this the answers are many, but the most obvious fact is that there was not enough cooperation. Six out of every seven of the enterprises just mentioned were insurance, telephone, or irrigation combinations. Farmers do not prosper by what they save on telephone bills and insurance alone, and the great bulk of the three million families were engaged no further in cooperation than this. They had built their own telephone lines only because private enterprise made no effort to supply them or else made the cost prohibitive. It was either cooperate or do without. As to the irrigation units, they were on the average very small, and again, if the farmers did not throw up dams and dig ditches they did without water, and a different system for each farm was unthinkable. Beyond the distribution of water, there was rarely any cooperation, and there was plenty of hard feeling over who was getting the most water. The net effect of limited cooperation of that sort was about the same as farmers in the more humid regions sharing the same rainfall.

The stores, marketing associations, and elevators comprised about all the rest of the businesses of any economic significance, and these totaled less than seven thousand by 1907, or possibly half as many a decade earlier. It was in these lines that the greatest growth occurred after 1907. If there were a thousand cooperative elevators by the end of the century, they may have benefited a hundred thousand grain growers. But as long as the farmers had no control over the exchanges, and did little if anything to limit their crops to the visible market—as long as the industrial worker was so poorly paid that he could not eat his fill—the saving on marketing costs often was not enough to do more for the farmer than allow him to break even. Much the same might be said for the

[38] Morman, "Business Coöperative Organizations in Agriculture," pp. 256–257; *Agricultural Yearbook*, 1908, p. 186; Eyerly, "Co-operative Movements among Farmers," p. 59.

marketing associations and stores. They were all very nice in their way, but they did not go far enough. Even a perfected Svea organization could only partly have solved the problem as long as it operated in an economic system where all the outside influences were determined by opposing, and often hostile, forces.

But there were faults within the organizations themselves, and most of these grew out of the lack of knowledge and the lack of a true cooperative spirit among the presumed cooperators. As Henry Alvord said, ". . . some of the farmers cannot or will not pull together. . . ."[39] But if individualism was still too strong, the fact of the growth in number and membership of the societies shows that the trait was beginning to crack. Even where the will to submerge the individual in the common good was strongest, this alone was not enough. An enterprise not sufficiently well managed was sure to fail. As a Farmers' Alliance lecturer put it:

The question of failure or success depends upon whether honesty and business methods are combined in the management. Failures have more generally resulted from lack of applying business methods in the conduct of business. Too often have farmers . . . rushed into the formation of a joint company for the purpose of conducting a co-operative store. The company . . . when once organized . . . [is] placed under the direction of a man who has no business experience nor aptitude for business. The result is business failure, and general disorganization of the farmers. In other cases failures are due to farmers failing to patronize their co-operative store. Merchants organize to break down the co-operative effort, and by dividing up among themselves they reduce prices below the cost of profitable handling. . . . Farmers are thus decoyed by a temporary advantage to forsake their own enterprise. And again the result is failure.[40]

[39] As quoted in Harwood, "Coöperation in the West," p. 541.
[40] N. B. Ashby, *The Riddle of the Sphinx* (Chicago: Mercantile Publishing and Advertising Co., 1892), p. 375.

CHAPTER XV

The Farmer and the Nation

AGRICULTURE IN THE NATION'S ECONOMY

JUST as the War for Independence was drawing to a close, Thomas Jefferson expressed the hope that America would always remain an agricultural nation, relying on Europe for manufactures. He feared that the rise of cities, dependent on trade and mechanical industry, would imperil American liberty. But thirty-five years later, at the close of the second war with England, he was advocating the fostering of manufactures as a means of preserving independence from foreign countries. By 1850, the rising industrial structure was beginning to challenge the supremacy of agriculture, and, before 1900, the farmer had taken a secondary position in the nation's economy. The numbers of farms and farmers, the volume and total value of products, and the amount and value of agricultural exports had increased; but the ratio of farm population, production, trade, income, and wealth, to the total for all lines of economic activity had steadily declined. This development had little, if any, connection with the hopes or fears of philosophers, or with any national policy for the creation of self-sufficiency. Even the loudly debated tariff, from 1816 to 1897, did little more than favor one business at the expense of another; it has not been demonstrated that industrialization as a whole was benefited.

The diversification of activity and the near self-sufficiency that was created in America, before 1900, were mainly the outcome of enormous and manifold natural resources scattered over three million square miles of land; of every kind of productive soil found anywhere in the temperate zones of the world; of a great variety of climates; of a restless, polyglot population, constantly on the lookout for material advancement; and of freedom from governmental trade restrictions throughout the entire area. Any growth of precariousness in the prosperity of the individual farmer was in spite, rather than a consequence, of the eclipse of agriculture as a whole. The rise of city markets and the ability of the urban industries to cater to rural needs for manufacturers should have added to the comfort and well-being of the farm families. The failure of large sections of the rural population to benefit from these changes has already been chronicled. Next comes an attempt at analysis of the degree of the secondary role agriculture was falling into.

In this effort, the farm population and the number of persons directly engaged in agricultural occupations must be stated in rough estimates rather than in proved figures. No attempt was made by the census takers of the nineteenth century to enumerate farm population. Their distinction between urban and rural communities, with its earlier 8,000 division point, or even the later 2,500, is clearly useless for this purpose. Since 1920, when farm population was first counted, it is noticeable that the ratio to the total population is fairly close to the ratio of all persons gainfully employed on the farm to those in all lines of activity. If it is assumed that this relation existed also in the latter half of the nineteenth century, then the problem of estimating farm population from 1860 to 1900 becomes a little simpler. Data, after a fashion, were collected on occupations. But, in 1860, only those persons were counted who were above fifteen years of age. In later censuses, the ten-year limit was fixed, thus complicating any comparison with 1860. Again, from decade to decade, the classifications were shuffled so as to include one group or another as agricultural workers one time, and omit it the next. Individuals in personal service were often not differentiated between occupation on or off the farm. Nevertheless, statisticians have made valiant efforts to unscramble the figures, and the results of P. K. Whelpton withstand severely critical tests.[1]

His estimates show an increase in the number of gainfully employed persons, ten years of age and over, between 1860 and 1900,

---

[1] For an analysis of his calculations, see P[ascal] K[idder] Whelpton, "Occupational Groups in the United States, 1820–1920," *Journal of the American Statistical Association*, XXI, No. 155 (September, 1926), 335–343.

from 10,531,000 to 29,073,000, while the number engaged in agriculture grew from 6,287,000 to 10,699,000. This means that, in 1860, some 59.7 per cent of the workers of the country were on the farm, whereas, by 1900, the ratio had diminished to 36.8 per cent (the census showed 35.7). Meanwhile, the numbers employed or engaged in manufacturing and trade, and in transportation, grew from 2,715,000 to 13,298,000, or from 25.79 to 45.74 per cent of the total. As the accompanying graph shows, nearly all the percentage loss of agriculture was absorbed by those next two classifications.

Relative Proportion of the Population, 10 Years of Age and Over, Engaged in Agriculture and in Other Occupations, 1860–1900 [2]

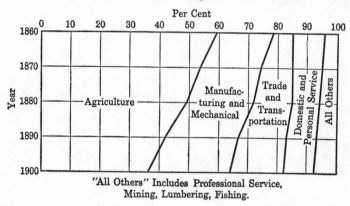

"All Others" Includes Professional Service, Mining, Lumbering, Fishing.

It is a fair estimate, therefore, that about three fifths of the 31,400,000 persons in the United States in 1860, or less than 19,000,000, lived on farms; and that slightly over a third of the nearly 76,000,000 of 1900, or about 28,000,000, were truly a farm population. This is far less than the 45,600,000, or 60 per cent of the total, that were classed as "rural" by the Census of 1900. As a check on the calculation, it may be noted that in 1920, when the first census of farm population was made, the rural contingent was set at 48.6 per cent, but the farm people were only 29.9 per cent.[3] Only three fifths of the rural population actually lived on farms. That proportion of the rural population of 1900 was very close to the 28,000,000 calculated above on the basis of agricultural workers.

[2] *Ibid.*, pp. 339–340.
[3] *Statistical Abstract of the United States*, 1931, pp. 8–9, 637.

Judging from such data as the preceding, it is clear that, from 1870 to 1900, the farm population increased in each of the five major divisions of the country, except New England and the Middle Atlantic states. Whelpton's data were not broken down to show the sectional distribution, so the somewhat different figures from the census had to be used. On the basis of Whelpton's figures, the total farm population at both dates would be about 1,000,000 more than the figures below. The striking growth in the Central states was largely by additions in the trans-Mississippi area. The Western states (Mountain and Pacific) showed a great proportional gain, but numerically they remained fairly insignificant. The estimates for the sections are as follows:

GROWTH OF FARM POPULATION, BY SECTIONS, 1870–1900 [4]

Area	1870		1900	
	Farm Population	Per Cent of Total	Farm Population	Per Cent of Total
United States	19,000,000	100	27,000,000	100
North Atlantic	3,230,000	17	2,700,000	10
South Atlantic	4,180,000	22	5,700,000	20
North Central	6,460,000	34	9,180,000	34
South Central	4,750,000	25	8,640,000	32
Western	380,000	2	1,080,000	4

The basic data for farm income are probably even less dependable than those for population. Farmers, as before stated (page 291), seldom kept books, and few took any reckoning of what they consumed of the goods they produced. Nevertheless, different studies of this problem have arrived at strikingly similar results. Apparently, the agricultural income of 1860 was just about 30 per cent of the national figure, and in 1900 it was just a shade over 20 per cent. The low point was in 1889 and 1890 (as far as the censuses show), one estimate revealing 15.8 per cent in 1889 and another 18.7 per cent in 1890. Whether the ratio would have been still lower in the depression years of the 1890's is uncertain. There were millions of hard-pressed industrial laborers as well as millions of

[4] Based on figures of gainfully employed persons in farm occupations in *Ninth Census: Population and Social Statistics*, p. 671; *Twelfth Census:* Population, II, cxxxv, and calculated on estimates of total farm population given above, in text.

harassed farmers at that time. In general, it would seem, the individual farmer's share of the national income changed hardly at all during the four decades. The ratio of farm to national population declined a third, and the income did likewise. But the total agricultural population was multiplied by 1½, while the income was multiplied by 2½. Thus, the per capita income of the farm dweller, in 1859, was probably about $70, whereas that of 1900 was nearer to $112. It is doubtful whether all the increase represented expanding standards of living. These estimates are based on the following figures:

AGRICULTURE'S SHARE OF NATIONAL INCOME,
BY DECADES, 1859–1899, AND IN 1900 [5]

(*Values in millions*)

Census Year	National Income	Agricultural Income	
		Amount	Per Cent of National
1859	$ 4,098	$1,264	30.8
1869	6,288	1,517	24.1
1879	6,617	1,371	20.7
1889	9,578	1,517	15.8
1899	13,836	2,933	21.2
1900	14,550	3,034	20.9

In their share of the national wealth, the agricultural classes fared hardly as well as in income, though the doubtful value of the income statistics may be the underlying reason for this seeming fact. Land, houses, stock, and equipment were more easily measured than income. Of nearly $20,000,000,000 of wealth in 1860, agricultural people claimed almost $8,000,000,000, or 40 per cent. In 1900, the farmers' $20,000,000,000 was less than a sixth of the nation's $126,000,000,000. Yet, the per capita of farm wealth had increased from approximately $416 to some $755, in current monetary values. By decades, the growth of wealth was as follows:

[5] Robert F[itz-Randolph] Martin, *National Income in the United States, 1799–1938* (National Industrial Conference Board, *Studies*, No. 241, New York: National Industrial Conference Board, Inc., c.1939), pp. 58, 60; cf. *The Agricultural Problem in the United States* (New York: National Industrial Conference Board, Inc., 1926), p. 46.

AGRICULTURE'S SHARE OF NATIONAL WEALTH,
BY DECADES, 1860–1900 [6]

(Values in billions)

Census Year	National Wealth	Agricultural Wealth	
		Amount	Per Cent of National
1860	$ 19.8	$ 7.9	39.9
1870	30.4	8.9	29.3
1880	49.9	12.2	24.4
1890	78.5	16.1	20.5
1900	1≈6 7	20.4	16.1

Among the five major divisions of the country, the greatest percentage gain in agricultural wealth, over the 1860 figure, was in the Pacific and Mountain states. But in absolute gain there was nothing to compare with the North Central states, whose wealth, in 1900, was more than half that of the nation. The North Atlantic states barely held their own. The Southern divisions did not recover their prewar values till 1890, after which the South Central group showed substantial gains, mainly from westward expansion. Approximate figures for the different censuses are next given for comparison.

AGRICULTURAL WEALTH, BY SECTIONS AND DECADES, 1860–1900 [7]

(Values in millions)

Area	1860	1870	1880	1890	1900
United States	$7,980	$8,945	$12,181	$16,082	$20,440
North Atlantic	2,454	2,947	3,197	2,970	2,951
South Atlantic	1,207	741	1,053	1,333	1,454
North Central	2,523	4,109	6,108	8,518	11,505
South Central	1,672	907	1,290	1,891	2,816
Western	123	241	532	1,371	1,715

It is clear from these data that only the North Central and Western farmers approximated the pace of growth of national wealth, and only the North Central states kept the ratio from sinking to insignificance. Had this North Central wealth been owned by the farmers instead of, in so large a measure, by the banks and loan companies, the picture might really have been a pleasing one. The

[6] Robert R[utherford] Doane, *The Measurement of American Wealth . . . from 1860 to 1933* (New York: Harper & Brothers Publishers, 1933), pp. 10–11.

[7] *Twelfth Census: Agriculture*, I, 694.

same is true of the figures for income—too much of it merely went through the workers' hands on the way to these same creditors. Of the national farm wealth of 1860, land, with improvements, accounted for $6,645,000,000; implements and machinery, $246,000,000; and livestock, $1,089,000,000. The corresponding figures for 1900 were $16,615,000,000, $750,000,000, and $3,075,000,000.[8] The average value of the farm declined during the forty years, from $3,904 to $3,574, the Southern situation being responsible. But the average value of an acre rose in the same period from $19.60 to $24.39.[9]

During all the years from 1869 to 1900, the home market absorbed a little over 82 per cent (by value) of the products sold off the farm, and never deviated far from that figure. The high point was 86.1 in 1871, and the lowest was 75.6 in 1879. Foreign trade took the rest.[10] Such items as cotton, tobacco, and wheat and meat products generally depended in a far higher proportion on the foreign market. Over 82 per cent of the income from cotton was from foreign sales in 1869, and a good two thirds of the crop was still sold abroad in 1900. Of tobacco, nearly 79 per cent by value was exported in 1871, and 41 per cent in 1900.[12]

On the other hand, in spite of the enormous growth of exports of manufactured goods, the agricultural competitors managed to maintain almost an even pace, except during the Civil War and after 1893. An average of about 76 per cent of all exports for the forty years were agricultural, and in no year did the amount go lower than 65 per cent, till 1900. The high mark was the year 1880, with 84.3 per cent. This is pictured in the graph on page 356, where the area below the uneven line represents agricultural exports and that above is all others. In the later years of the century, it was meat products that did the most to hold up the agricultural average, at a time when cotton and other vegetable goods were proportionally less in demand.[12]

---

[8] *Ibid.*, pp. 696–700. See note 4, page 128, above.

[9] *Ibid.*, p. 695.

[10] Frederick Strauss, "The Composition of Gross Farm Income Since the Civil War," National Bureau of Economic Research, *Bulletin* No. 78 (New York: April 28, 1940), pp. 14–15.

[11] *Ibid.*, p. 18.

[12] Frank H[arris] Hitchcock, "Agricultural Exports of the United States, 1851–1902," U.S. Department of Agriculture, Division of Foreign Markets, *Bulletin* No. 34 (Washington: Government Printing Office, 1903), pp. 8–9.

Agriculture's Share of Total Exports, by Years, 1860–1900 [13]

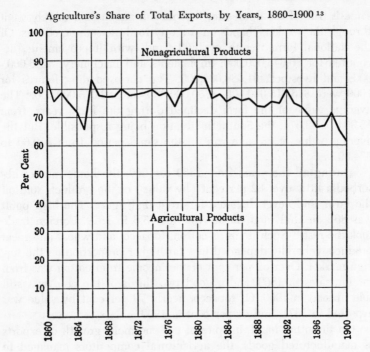

THE CITY AS A SAFETY VALVE FOR RURAL DISCONTENT

The distribution of wealth and income undoubtedly had much
to do with population movements, and the trends support this
conclusion. It is a fact too apparent to require much argument that
the population movement, from 1860 to the end of the century, was
preponderatingly from the farm to the city, rather than the reverse.
Yet, the persistence of a now long-exploded myth that, down to
1890, city toilers flocked to cheap or free land in the West, as a
"safety valve" for labor, seems still to require some further statement on the subject. From 1790 to 1860, during which time the
nation remained predominantly rural, the population of the United
States doubled each twenty-three years, with almost the precision
of geometric progression. During those years the percentage living
in towns and cities of 8,000 inhabitants or more increased from 3.3
to 16.1; the number of such cities from 6 to 141; and their popula-

[13] Constructed from tables *ibid.*, p. 9.

tion from 131,000 to a little over 5,000,000. The great bulk of this urban growth had taken place after 1840, and almost half of it after 1850. Without question, the city was already beginning to draw upon the country for population. But this was only the curtain raiser for the act to follow. In the next four decades the number of such towns and cities was multiplied almost by four, to 547; their inhabitants by five, to 25,000,000; and their percentage of total population by two, to 32.9. These cities had grown more than twice as fast as the nation at large.[14] The same rule applies to all towns and cities of 2,500 and over, their expansion being from a population of 6,500,000 to 30,400,000.[15]

In the same forty years, as already shown, farm population increased barely half, while the total nonfarm population leaped from 12,000,000 to 48,000,000, or by a multiple of four. The cities may have bred pestilence, poverty, crime, and corruption, but there is no evidence that they bred population that rapidly. Immigration cannot explain the phenomenon, for a fair proportion of the aliens settled on the land. If the entire number of 14,000,000 immigrants, after 1860, is subtracted from the nonfarm population of 1900, the remainder still represents twice the rate of growth of farm population. No adequate data seem to exist for those years on the flow of population between town and country, but this other evidence is conclusive in itself. The farms lacked by 18,000,000 of keeping pace with the ratio of population growth of the whole nation, while the nonfarm areas gained 18,000,000 over the same ratio. Whatever data may be discovered in the future, it seems unlikely that it can upset the established rule, previously stated (page 55), that for every city laborer who took up farming, twenty farmers flocked to the city to compete for the vacated job or place in the bread line. This is not the way that safety valves are supposed to operate.

For that matter, outside the cotton belt, the majority of the westward-moving population did not settle on farms. Farmers from farther east took up the Western lands, but they also swarmed to Western cities and towns. When the Eastern city laborer managed to pay his fare or "ride the rods" westward, he also was most likely to establish himself in a mining camp, town, or city, where, as in

[14] *Statistical Abstract of the United States,* 1941, p. 6.

[15] Warren S[impson] Thompson, for the National Resources Committee, "Urban Population Changes," *Population Statistics* (Washington: Government Printing Office, 1937), Pt. III, Sec. I, p. 8.

the Coeur d'Alene region of Idaho, he found that he had exchanged drudgery in an Eastern factory for equally ill-paid drudgery (considering living costs) in a Western factory or mine. The urbanized proportion of the population west of the Mississippi River, where most of the new farms had been created, very nearly kept pace with the national average. In 1900, when nearly half (47.1%) of America's people were living in incorporated towns and cities, the ratio west of the Mississippi River was over three eighths (38.1%). Minnesota exceeded, while Missouri, Iowa, and Nebraska nearly equaled, the national average. The combined eleven Mountain and Pacific states rated even higher than Minnesota, with 50.6 per cent of their population in incorporated places. It was only the Dakotas and the West South Central states that were so overwhelmingly rural as to keep the trans-Mississippi West below the national ratio.[16] On the basis of the gainfully employed (always a better measure), the West showed a still higher proportion of nonfarm population. The census figures for 1870, 1890, and 1900 are used in the following table to illustrate this point.

PERSONS TEN YEARS OF AGE AND OVER GAINFULLY EMPLOYED
IN THE WEST, 1870, 1890, 1900[17]

Area	1870			1890			1900		
	Thousands Employed		Per Cent in Agriculture	Thousands Employed		Per Cent in Agriculture	Thousands Employed		Per Cent in Agriculture
	Total	Agriculture		Total	Agriculture		Total	Agriculture	
United States	12,506	5,922	47.4	22,736	8,466	37.2	29,286	10,438	35.7
Trans-Mississippi West	2,199	1,170	53.2	5,811	2,703	46.5	7,717	3,642	47.1
West North Central	1,157	648	56.0	2,988	1,432	47.9	3,693	1,707	46.2
West South Central	628	417	66.4	1,487	933	62.7	2,322	1,472	63.4
Mountain	134	40	29.9	501	127	25.3	663	192	28.8
Pacific	280	65	23.2	836	212	25.4	1,039	271	26.1

In each decade, the Far Western sections were well below the national ratio of agricultural to town and city labor, and to 1890 they were far below. In 1870, outside the West South Central states

[16] *Twelfth Census: Population*, I, lxii.
[17] Calculated from *Ninth Census: Population and Social Statistics*, pp. 670–671; *Eleventh Census: Population*, II, 306–337; *Twelfth Census: Population*, II, cxxxv.

and Iowa, the figure averaged 44.3 per cent—seventeen Western states thus comparing with 47.4 per cent for the United States. In the next twenty years, when free land was presumed to be the greatest lure of the West, the towns gained on the farms till the latter included only 46.5 per cent of the Western total, in spite of the still preponderatingly rural character of the West South Central division. Then in 1890, according to the legend, the gate to free land flew shut with a bang, and the safety valve for urban labor rusted tight forever. Yet, the increase in agricultural population in the next ten years was nearly a fourth larger than the average for the preceding decades. Whereas the city had been draining labor from the farm before 1890, now that the theoretical safety valve was gone, the Western farm was gaining on the Western city. Good land—free, cheap, or at speculators' prices—undoubtedly was more abundant before 1890 than afterward. Before that date this land, without cavil, had helped keep down *rural* discontent and unrest. Yet, more farmers had sought refuge in the city than on new land. But another release for farmers was also beginning to fail by 1890. The cities were approaching a static condition, and began to lose their attraction for farmers. This condition continued till, between 1930 and 1940, there was virtually no net shift of population between town and country. All this suggests the idea that the time is ripe for somebody to advance a new hypothesis: that the rise of the city in the nineteenth century was a safety valve for rural discontent.[18]

THE FARMER'S "HIRED HAND"

The lack of opportunity for the city laborer to find on the farm a release from his distress is also shown in the gradual descent of established freeholders into share cropping or tenancy, as revealed in preceding chapters, and likewise in the condition of hired agricultural workers. The cost of transforming new land into farms,

[18] *Statistical Abstract of the United States,* 1941, p. 671. A more complete analysis of safety valves for industrial laborers and for farmers is in Fred A[lbert] Shannon, "A Post Mortem on the Labor-Safety-Valve Theory," *Agricultural History,* XIX, No. 1 (January, 1945). Some excerpts from this article have been utilized in the preceding paragraphs with the consent of the editor of *Agricultural History.*

even before 1860, was too great for the resources of the day laborer. Clarence Danhof has shown that, independent of the cost of the land itself, the experienced farm boy with less than a thousand dollars in capital was likely to fail at the effort.[19] The industrial laborer, with his lack of experience, was in a still sorrier plight. After the Civil War, when farming became a more mechanical task, the cost and difficulty of making a start were correspondingly enhanced. Even the cost of equipment for successful tenant farming was more than the price of a quarter section of land at the old government minimum.

Yet, in a period when freeholders were becoming tenants on their own former possessions, some tenants did manage to buy enough land for an independent start, and it cannot be denied that some agricultural wage laborers did likewise. The latter group, however, were most likely to be surplus sons of established farmers, whose work was not needed on the paternal acres. Such lads, generally in the North Central or Western states, worked for several years for other farmers, living as a social equal with the family, and sometimes marrying the employer's daughter. They saved their earnings; then, with some aid from the father or the father-in-law, and probably with a mortgage hanging over them, they were ready to make a start for themselves. According to testimony before the Industrial Commission, this opportunity was much greater before 1880 than in the years following.[20]

In any statistical study of the supply of farm labor after 1860, it is just as well to omit all data for the initial year, because the South, so largely dependent on hired labor (wage and sharecropper) after the war, had very little of it during the existence of slavery. In the later years, the difficulty comes in trying to ascertain from the census reports just how many laborers were agricultural, because of the fact that the enumerators so often listed individuals as "laborers," with no further designation. This may help to explain the seeming discrepancy in the trend of numbers of agricultural laborers as shown in the Census of 1890. The putative figures, derived from the census reports, are as shown in the following table.

[19] Danhof, "Farm-Making Costs and the 'Safety Valve': 1850–1860," pp. 317–359 passim.
[20] [U.S.] Industrial Commission, Report, X, passim.

AGRICULTURAL LABORERS, TEN YEARS OF AGE OR OVER, 1870–1900 [21]

	1870	1880	1890	1900
All persons engaged in agriculture	5,919,993	7,663,043	8,466,363	10,249,651
Agricultural laborers	2,885,996	3,323,876	3,004,061	4,410,877
Laborers' per cent of all engaged in agriculture	48.7	43.4	35.5	43.0
Female laborers' per cent of all engaged in agriculture	12.9	16.1	14.9	15.0

As between the different sections of the country, the South Central had the largest number of farm employees. In 1900, these numbered 35.5 per cent of the total for the United States; the North Central had 27.7 per cent; the South Atlantic, 23.7 per cent; the North Atlantic, 9.4 per cent; and the Far West, between 3 and 4 per cent.[22]

If to these hired laborers there be added the share croppers and tenant farmers, whose economic status was rarely any better, it is seen that, in 1880, three out of each seven persons in agricultural occupations were owners of the enterprises they operated, and in 1900, only three out of each eight or nine. Among the strictly hired workers, generally about a seventh were female. In 1890 and 1900, when the occupations were enumerated by races, just about a third of all agricultural laborers were Negroes, and all but a handful of these were in the South. There were 1,344,000 Negro wage workers in 1900, and 510,000 of these (three eighths) were women and girls. The total of female workers of all races was 663,000, all but 19,000 of them being in the South. Of these, 76.8 per cent were Negroes.[23]

While the South had the bulk of Negro and female workers, the rest of the country had nearly all the foreign element. Alien farm laborers, in 1890, numbered 247,000, or 13.1 per cent of all white laborers; in 1900, they were 258,000, or 8.51 per cent. At the height of their percentage ratio, in 1890, a sixth of all white farm employees in the North Atlantic states, a fifth in the North Central, and over a quarter in the West were of foreign birth. The South

[21] George K[irby] Holmes, "Supply of Farm Labor," U.S. Department of Agriculture, Bureau of Statistics, *Bulletin* No. 94 (Washington: Government Printing Office, 1912), pp. 14–15. See p. 14 for comment on enumeration of 1890.

[22] Calculated from *ibid.*, p. 19.

[23] *Ibid.*, pp. 14–16, 20.

Atlantic states had 1.07 per cent, and the South Central, 3.63.[24] In 1900, about one seventh of the employees were of foreign parentage (father, mother, or both). By section of their residence, and in numerical order of their ancestry, they were as shown in the following table. The excellence of Italians in gardening, and the lack of serious competition in that work, explains the relatively large number of them in the South.

AGRICULTURAL LABORERS OF FOREIGN PARENTAGE, 1900.
SOURCE AND LOCATION [25]

(All figures in thousands)

Section	Total	Germany	Scandinavia	Ireland	Great Britain	English Canada	Austria-Hungary	French Canada	Poland	Italy	Russia	Other Countries	Mixed Foreign Parentage
United States	765.6	263.0	113.7	100.4	67.0	40.1	22.9	16.5	13.2	11.8	10.0	74.5	32.5
North Atlantic	126.1	28.4	4.4	35.5	15.1	11.4	2.0	8.7	5.4	2.8	1.7	6.3	4.6
South Atlantic	8.7	3.7	.1	1.7	1.3	.2	.3	.0	.1	.1	.1	.8	.3
North Central	497.6	201.2	99.8	52.8	35.9	24.1	14.7	6.8	6.8	.4	7.2	26.0	22.0
South Central	56.4	18.9	1.6	3.5	3.2	.8	5.2	.1	.9	4.5	.6	15.6	1.4
Western	76.7	10.9	7.8	6.8	11.6	3.6	.7	.8	.1	4.0	.6	25.7	4.2

The wages paid these workers varied greatly between the sections, and within the sections as well, but the South stood far below all others. In a region where the climate required little clothing and scant attention to housing, a laborer could exist if he got hardly more than his food. In 1899, Professor E. R. Lloyd of the agricultural experiment station of Mississippi wrote to the Industrial Commission: "Our labor is all colored, and is growing more worthless and harder to manage each year." [26] Here, arrogance admitted probably more than was intended. Though many witnesses attested to the general dependability and docility of the Negroes, there were others who sided with Lloyd. No doubt, some of these detractions on the workers were correct, for it is hard to understand how any person could toil efficiently on a diet of corn meal and salted hog fat every day in the year. If the workers were becoming more unmanageable, this showed that some spark of self-respect yet remained in them. But the absence of actual revolt in the next generation would indicate that this spark was effectually kept from spreading.

24 *Ibid.*, pp. 31.
25 *Ibid.*, pp. 32–33.
26 Industrial Commission, *Report,* Vol. XI, Pt. III, p. 95.

It is hard to get an unbiased picture of actual conditions among the laborers, from the thousand and more pages of testimony recorded by the Industrial Commission. Field workers of the Department of Agriculture, lawyers, bankers, politicians, and employers were questioned, but among the 94 witnesses, not one was a hired agricultural laborer. Yet, occasionally, the employer himself supplied some startling information. L. W. Youmans, a farmer-merchant of Fairfax, South Carolina, testified that his plowmen did "5½ days' honest good work each week," for which they got "1 peck of meal and 3 pounds of bacon and salt, 90 cents in trade, to be traded out in the stores at 50 per cent profit, and 20 cents in cash." In addition, each was allowed to work two acres for himself on Saturday afternoons and evenings. This, translated into prevailing values, means 10 or 15 cents' worth of corn meal, 25 or 30 cents for "fatback," 60 cents in trade (independent-store values), and 20 cents in cash: $1.20 and the truck-patch yield, for a week's work. Labor hired by the day fared hardly any better, even when employed. "I pay them 30 cents, one-fourth in cash and three-fourths to be traded out at 50 per cent profit, and yet raising the crops as cheaply as that the proceeds will not meet the expense of raising." In cash value, the day laborer was getting 22½ cents, or $1.35 a week, and did not have to worry with a truck patch. Youmans also said that he paid monthly laborers "$5.20 for 26 days' work" (20 cents a day), and he believed that his men were "about as well paid, as well clothed, and I think the best satisfied labor in that vicinity." At about the same time, James Barrett, a farmer-employer of Augusta, Georgia, stated that the maximum wage he paid was food and $6.00 a month, and the minimum was $2.00. He paid strictly in cash.[27] Slave labor in the 1850's was never as cheap as that.

In 1866, and periodically thereafter, the Bureau of Statistics of the United States Department of Agriculture made a number of studies of average wage payments in each of the states. In 1912, it issued a bulletin, in which the greenback values for 1866 to 1879 were adjusted to gold equivalents. This becomes the most reliable source for general averages. In every category, South Carolina consistently paid the smallest wage, and one or another state in the Far West was the highest. The most considerable number of labor-

[27] *Ibid.*, X, 46, quotation 117–118.

ers were those hired by the year or season, and paid monthly. Without board, in 1866, South Carolina paid such persons $8.45, and Nevada averaged $75.00. With board, the figures were $5.39 and $60.00. Food in South Carolina was reckoned at $3.00 a month, and in Nevada at $15.00. Assuming that other living costs were *five* times as high, at the same time Nevada paid *ten* times South Carolina's wage. In 1880, South Carolina's rates were $10.43 and $7.95;

Average Wage Rates of Outdoor Labor of Men on Farms, by the Month, in Hiring by the Year, without Board, in Selected Years from 1866 to 1899 [28]

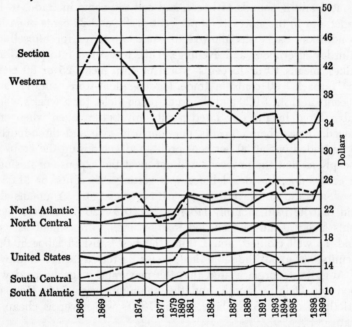

Montana's were $45.00 and $30.50. Nevada paid $35.00 with board, and did not list pay without board. At the depth of the depression in 1895, South Carolina paid $9.91 and $6.93; Nevada, $40.71 and $27.67.[29]

The accompanying graph shows the situation in a rather favorable light, because only the wages of men are given, and these

[28] George K[irby] Holmes, "Wages of Farm Labor," U.S. Department of Agriculture, Bureau of Statistics, *Bulletin* No. 99 (Washington: Government Printing Office, 1912), pp. 29, 32.

[29] *Ibid.*, pp. 29–30, 32–33.

without board. Nevertheless, it fairly represents the trends in good times and in bad. One item not explained by the statistician is the reason why from 1881 to 1884 the national average rises 11 cents while the North Atlantic, North Central, and South Central sections showed drops of 33, 57, and 87 cents, respectively. The rise in the South Atlantic states was only 9 cents, and in the Far West 42 cents, and the West had relatively few wage laborers.

The Industrial Commission tried in various ways to show the brighter tints in the picture. First, it compared American wages with those of other countries: $225 a year, as contrasted with $150 in Great Britain, and on down the line to $30 in India. But the commission offered no evidence that these estimates were made on reliable or comparable statistics, gave no hint as to differing living costs, and for America it omitted the wages of women and children.[30] Again, on one page it presented graphs showing American farm wages with a slight tendency to rise, as contrasted with a fall in the index of farm prices from nearly 150 in 1879 to 70 in 1896.[31] But, as indicated herein, in an earlier chapter, the index of farm prices was not the sole measure of agricultural prosperity. Perhaps in the bad years some laborers saved a little money, while their employers lost, but there are no data for a convincing study of the relationship between farm prosperity and the wages of farm labor. It may be noted, however, that the years of greatest rural unrest among the employers were the years of lowest wages for their hired men.

On the other hand, the great difference in wages between the South and the North accurately represents the difference in standards of living between the sections. The cost of standard items of food and clothing did not vary greatly between North and South, but a continuous diet on the very cheapest of all foods, and an absence of all clothing not absolutely essential, allowed the Southern worker to subsist on less. Neither were rents, for habitations of equal comfort, widely different, North and South. But the Southern wage laborers, like the share croppers, lived in shacks that the better Northern farmers would have hesitated to use for sheltering hogs. Perhaps the Southern economy could furnish no better, but the reasons for this sectional poverty have already been discussed

[30] Industrial Commission, *Report*, Vol. XI, Pt. III, p. 82.
[31] *Ibid.*, facing p. 144.

in another connection. In the Far West, it is true, living costs were far greater than in the Northeast or Southeast, thus helping to explain the higher wage level.

The difference between wages, with and without food, is a good evidence of the standard of living of the workers in the different sections, again with some discount for the Far West. In that section the coming of the railroads (in 1869 and following) greatly reduced the food differential, but, till 1900, the average remained about twice the national figure. Some estimates for the United States and its major divisions follow.

ESTIMATED MONTHLY COST OF FOOD FOR FARM LABORERS,
1866–1899 [32]

Area	1866	High in Year	Low in Year	1899
United States	$ 5.41	$ 6.54 (1891)	$ 5.41 (1866)	$ 6.07
North Atlantic	8.11	9.01 (1893)	7.81 (1879)	8.84
North Central	6.92	7.83 (1881)	6.44 (1889)	7.39
South Atlantic	3.99	4.98 (1891)	3.79 (1877)	4.09
South Central	4.08	5.34 (1881)	4.08 (1866)	4.50
Far West	14.40	17.69 (1869)	10.17 (1898)	10.45

Other things than money wages and board affected the well-being of the worker. For example, the Commissioner of Labor of Michigan reported that in his state, in 1895, about a quarter of the farm laborers got one or more of the following additions: the use of a house, pasture for a cow, a garden plot, or the use of a team. His estimate was that the average worth of such allowances was $6.22 a month, which sounds too high to be convincing. Tables have been prepared showing what perquisites were given certain laborers in various localities of all the states, but they do not inspire confidence. The item of house rent at $2.38 a month in Massachusetts and $2.43 in Georgia or $3.30 in Louisiana just does not make sense.[33] There was not that much good material in some of the Southern hovels, and it was not the policy to grant one worker, in any locality, much more than what was allowed the least fortunate. To do so might breed discontent. Throughout the testimony before the Industrial Commission, there breathed the spirit that

[32] Holmes, "Wages of Farm Labor," pp. 55–56.
[33] *Ibid.*, pp. 49–52.

tractability of the laborer must be preserved at any effort short of increasing his wages.

In general, it may be said that the total income of the farm laborer reflected the condition of workers in the adjacent towns and cities. But the continuous movement from the farm to the city indicated that, for one reason or another, the boy who left the farm rarely cared to return to it. It was noted that farm wages near an industrial or Western mining center were always higher than in more remote places, and because of the competitive conditions. Distant areas had to pay far higher than the prevailing monthly rates to get hands in harvest seasons. In 1880, South Carolina was paying an average of $1.14 a day to cotton pickers, that being the high point for a forty-year period. A year later, Dakota Territory was paying $2.65 a day for wheat harvesters, this also being the top wage before 1900.[34] But migratory labor was not as yet a very considerable part of the total of the farm supply, and the workers who got these occasional high wages needed all they received to spread over their periods of unemployment. The migratory worker belongs mainly to the twentieth century.

The average working day for all laborers was ten hours or more, the South and the Northwest ranging a little higher than the Northeast.[35] Again, reported averages mean little. In busy seasons, laborers milked the cows by lantern light before breakfast, and turned the horses into the barn at dusk. Nine or ten hours in December were balanced by fourteen or fifteen in June. The average for the year was equated by days and part days when weather conditions or physical disability prevented any work. Evidence on this point can still be gathered from persons who lived through the experience. Very little data have been preserved relating to the domestic work of women on the farm, except for the years after 1900. But at least one calumny of early years has been refuted. Farm women in the past decades were no more prone to insanity than their urban sisters. They were too busy to bother much with their solitude, and their drudgery was of a varied sort. Their amusements were few and rare, but when they came there was no satiety to dull the enjoyment.[36]

[34] Ibid., pp. 36–37; Holmes, "Supply of Farm Labor," pp. 38–39.
[35] Industrial Commission, Report, Vol. XI, Pt. III, p. 82.
[36] See Holmes, "Wages of Farm Labor," pp. 71–72.

THE FARM HOME

The living conditions of farm workers would be inadequately described without some attention to the general rural housing problem. The homes of the farmers were as diverse in their architecture, style, comfort, and cost of construction as were the homes of the city dwellers. This is another subject that received little attention from the writers and statistics gatherers of the period. As late as 1932, President Hoover's Conference on Home Building and Home Ownership observed: "Literature on housing in America has almost completely neglected the farm and village except for a few monographs, each decidedly limited in the geographical area covered or in the phase of the subject dealt with." [37] Books abound on old houses, but, like most of the houses themselves, they pertain almost exclusively to that small class of owners who could afford to build enduring structures. Among the relics of the postwar decades there are samples of the log cabins of the Ohio Valley, sod houses and dugouts of the Plains, and ramshackle shanties that have somehow escaped entire collapse, as well as the better houses of the era. Also still in use are some of the colonial mansions of the Atlantic seaboard, the roomy, storybook-style plantation houses of the South, and the Spanish type of house of San Antonio, Santa Fé, and California. In larger number, there are the box-shaped dwellings, with two-gabled roofs, more or less adorned in front with an ample supply of scroll-saw work.

The standard books on American architecture [38] tell of the transition from the prewar Greek Revival to the postwar structures of hybrid design, featuring every country and age in the same structure: Greek columns, Roman domes, Moorish minarets, Gothic buttresses and windows, Romanesque massiveness, mansard roofs, dormer windows, cupolas, battlements, and always an abundance of scroll and iron-trellis work, all or as many as possible cluttered in the same nightmarish heap. But relatively few farmers, except the gentleman variety, could afford such luxury. It was the common saying of the late-nineteenth century that, where the farm home

[37] Bruce L. Melvin, *Farm and Village Housing* (Vol. VII of *Publications of the President's Conference on Home Building and Home Ownership,* John M. Gries and James Ford, general eds., Washington: The Conference, c.1932), x.

[38] Such as [Sidney] Fiske Kimball, *American Architecture* (Indianapolis: The Bobbs-Merrill Company, c.1928).

was more imposing than the barn, "the woman is the boss." More often it was true that, in the struggle for prosperity, first attention had to be paid to such buildings as represented capital investment rather than living comfort. The average farmer hoped sometime to erect a better dwelling house, but there was so often something else that had to come first.

The one-or-two-room clapboarded shanty, with an exterior chimney built of crossed sticks, plastered with mud, remained the typical home of the poorer people of the South. Where danger of flood prevented laying the floor on the ground (or using the dirt itself as a floor), these houses were built on stilts. Apparently, none of them were ever painted. The interior, as poor as the outside, needs hardly be described. The mild winters made it feasible for the more opulent people, also, to save money on foundations, except of the stilt variety. In the 1860's, in the North, frame and occasionally brick houses began to supplant the earlier log buildings, and in much of the Prairie region frame construction was used from the earliest settlement. Sometimes the farmers of northern Illinois lived in tents, while doing their first plowing and awaiting shipments of lumber.[39] Even on the Great Plains, frame houses were more numerous than the famous "soddies," but in the bitter winters and in the summer heat they were declared to be less comfortable.

The frame houses of Illinois, which seem to be typical of much of the country, were of rigidly simple design. The customary pattern called for two rooms downstairs, and two up. In the story-and-a-half houses, the upstairs rooms were partly within the gabled roof. Often, the stairways were on the outside, and, sometimes, outside doors had to be used to get from one room to another. The builder or the carpenter decided on the design, and it depended on individual notions or skills. Usually there were no halls, closets, or any of the other "modern conveniences."[40] The furniture in such homes ranged from splendid antiques, then valued mainly as heirlooms, to the roughest of home-made articles. In the older dwellings, such as the French houses of Illinois, heating, cooking, and a good part of the ventilation were provided by the huge fireplaces,

[39] Russell Howard Anderson, "Agriculture in Illinois during the Civil War Period, 1850–1870" (Manuscript thesis in University of Illinois Library), p. 26.

[40] W. C. Flagg, "The Agriculture of Illinois, 1683–1876," Illinois Department of Agriculture, *Transactions*, 1875 (Springfield: State Journal Book and Stereotype Rooms, 1876), pp. 331–335; Anderson, "Agriculture in Illinois," 27.

some of which have been preserved. But in the newer structures, stoves were used—for wood or coal, depending on which fuel was more prevalent. Sewing machines had become a common fixture by 1860, for such families as could afford them, but there was rarely any other form of mechanical equipment, especially in the frontier areas. Kitchenware (dining rooms were a dispensable luxury) consisted of a few dishes, knives, spoons, a skillet or spider, a pot or kettle, drinking gourds, a coffee pot, a coffee mill, and, where cookstoves were not modernized, a Dutch oven.[41] There were differences of opinion as to whether forks were a necessity. As soon as they could afford it, the settlers bought factory-made furniture of many sorts. The cheap processes of woodworking, developed after 1865, made it relatively inexpensive to gratify this craving, though the products were often not of an enduring quality.[42]

Before 1860, the tallow candle and the smoking fat-pine torch had been supplanted by lamps for home lighting. The lamps burned whale oil, lard oil, any of several different vegetable oils, camphene (a mixture of rosin and turpentine), or spirit gas (camphene mixed with alcohol, dangerous but widely used). Sometimes coal oil—actually distilled from coal—was burned. Later, the same name was applied to kerosene. The development of the petroleum industry, during the Civil War years, produced the fuel that was to illuminate most homes for the remainder of the century, and the majority of farm homes down to the 1940's. Other household conveniences were rare. Kitchen sinks were hardly known. A few homes had wooden bathtubs, lined with zinc, but the lack of a supply of running water made these out of the question for the great majority. The Saturday evening bath was obtained in the kitchen, in the same wooden tub that served for the laundry work. Sometimes a quart of water in the tinned wash basin, set on the dining table, served the necessary purpose. Before 1900, a few houses contained enameled, cast-iron bathtubs, supplied by a tank in the attic, the tank being filled by hand or windmill pumps. In many other ways there was a lack of pleasing adornment and comfort. Pictures and wallpaper, like furniture, were more a response to social demand

[41] Natalia Maree Belting, "Early History of Urbana Champaign to 1871" (Manuscript thesis in University of Illinois Library); Seraphina Gardner Smith, ed., *Recollections of the Pioneers of Lee County* (Dixon, Ill.: 1893), *passim*.

[42] John Leonard Conger and William E. Hull, *History of the Illinois River Valley* (Chicago: The S. J. Clarke Publishing Company, 1932), I, 471.

than beautifying features of the house. The large, inconveniently arranged kitchen required an excessive amount of footwork in the preparation of a meal. Even the kerosene lamps were often so placed as to give more glare than useful light.[43]

After about 1875, distinct improvements were noticeable in architecture, construction, conveniences, and comforts. A large percentage of homes built in those years were still occupied in the 1940's, and need little description. Full-frame construction was the rule, with milled weatherboarding and shingle roofs. There was also a sprinkling of houses built of brick, tile, or stone. Plastering was adequately done, though in the South the ceiling of walls with wainscot was continued, and such walls were easily infested with vermin.[44] In roofs, the hip or gambrel style supplemented the older gables. Ceilings were high, often over ten feet, and, like the walls, were papered. Window-screen wire came late in the century, but mosquito bar served the purpose earlier as well as afterward. Improvements in building began at the bottom, with solid foundations and leak-proof cellars, and proceeded upward. Insulation and better ventilation were supplied. Occasional houses were piped for water, thus making possible the installation of bathtubs, water closets, and kitchen sinks. Heating was still mainly supplied by stoves, but some furnaces were in use. As gasoline stoves became common, the old necessity of cooking in the summer kitchen (detached from the house), in the hot months, passed gradually away. The great majority of families still had no such conveniences, or very few of them, but they knew of them and began to yearn for them.[45]

Whatever may have been the effect of the Sanitary Fairs and the Sanitary Commission of Civil War days, on succeeding life in the cities, it was some years before any results were noticeable in the rural areas. Though kitchen slops were fed to the chickens and hogs, wash, bath, and dish water quite often flew out the kitchen door, with perhaps no dangerous effect. But an astonishingly large number of privies stood entirely too near the well or spring, and on

[43] A. F. Murphy, "The John Murphy Family as Pioneers in Illinois," Illinois State Historical Society, Journal, XVIII, No. 2 (July, 1925), 422–431; Mrs. H. C. Johns, "The Farmer's Home," Illinois State Agricultural Society, Transactions, VI, 1865–1866 (Springfield: Baker, Bailhache & Co., Printers, 1868), pp. 292–299.

[44] Ameringer, If You Don't Weaken, p. 231.

[45] Isaac Phillips Roberts, The Farmstead (New York: The Macmillan Company, 1900), pp. 87–103.

the wrong slope from the water supply. The same was true of the stable and unprotected manure pile.[46] Sometimes privies were dispensed with altogether. This was a factor in the spreading of hookworm in the South, after as well as before 1900.

By 1875, greater attention was being paid to sanitation, and the advance of scientific knowledge gave direction to the new movement. Homes supplied with plumbing and proper drainages benefited most. If the soil pipes were properly laid, and led far enough from the house, the gain was large. When cesspools were used, much depended on where they were located. Often they were of no value for the protection of drinking water. Before 1900, farmers were being urged to drain the pools and swamps near the house to eliminate stagnant water. Even the agronomists' insistence on the proper storage and protection of barynard manure, for its better utilization as fertilizer, had the further virtue of being another safeguard for the homes.[47] The part played by patent medicines and their advertising, the medicine show, folklore herbs, charms, other superstitions, and the country doctor, in guarding or undermining rural health, cannot be told adequately in a limited scope.

THE RURAL SCHOOL AND CHURCH

Next to the home, the rural school and church played the largest part in the farmers' social life, and they should be considered briefly. The country school of 1860 was very much as it had been created in the educational revival of the 1830's and 1840's, and for several years more it underwent very little change. The "loud school," where every pupil studied at the top of his lung power and voice, to convince the master of his industry, was getting out of date by 1865. But even the "quiet school," which succeeded it, was noisy enough. The scratching of slate pencils, snapping of fingers, clattering of cowhide boot heels or copper toeplates, and

[46] Herbert Anthony Keller, ed., *Solon Robinson, Pioneer and Agriculturist* (Vols. XXI, XXII of *Indiana Historical Collections*, Indianapolis: Indiana Historical Bureau, 1936), II, 308; Theobald Smith, "Sewage Disposal on the Farm, and the Protection of Drinking Water," U.S. Department of Agriculture, *Farmers' Bulletin* No. 43 (Washington: Government Printing Office, 1896), pp. 3–5.

[47] William Paul Gerhard, *Sanitation, Water Supply and Sewage Disposal of Country Houses* (New York: D. Van Nostrand Company, 1909), pp. 217–260; Smith, "Sewage Disposal on the Farm," pp. 11–14; Harvey B[rown] Bashore, *The Sanitation of a Country House* (New York: John Wiley & Sons, 1905), pp. 71–83.

the rattling of the dipper in the bucket, as water was passed around the room, prevented silence from becoming too oppressive. The school term was adjusted to fit the needs of youthful labor on the farm. There might be a few weeks in the summer, for children too small to be of any use in the field, and from six weeks to three months in the winter. The length of the term was largely determined on the basis of how much money was available to pay the teacher. Terms as long as four and five months have been mentioned. Such few compulsory-attendance laws as existed were not enforced. But in the winter months, young men and women up to twenty years of age and beyond often attended, opportunities of courtship on the way to school and returning not being overlooked. The South had not been converted to the newfangled idea of education at the expense of taxpayers; and Southerners were so numerous in southern Illinois that, down into the twentieth century, teachers' salaries there were considerably lower than in the northern counties.[48]

Until years after 1900, many of the country schools were ungraded, the pupils going under their own power and progressing as rapidly as they cared or were able. When the first reader was completed, the second was begun; and the sundry stages in writing, spelling, arithmetic, history, and geography were encountered as the time became ripe. The seven or eight, twelve or thirteen, or nineteen or twenty pupils might represent as many different points of progress in each of the books. This lack of system may have had some praiseworthy aspects, but ability to get through the book did not always represent profundity of knowledge. Among the textbooks used, whose fame was enduring, were McGuffey's readers, Ray's arithmetic, Webster's "blue-back speller," Harvey's grammar, and the Eclectic history and geography. The expression "Three R's" is an unjust aspersion on the efforts of that generation. Soon after 1880, physiology was added to the curriculum, at least in some localities. If the student wanted to acquire education beyond

[48] George Cary Eggleston, *Recollections of a Varied Life* (New York: Henry Holt and Company, 1910), pp. 32–45; David D[emaree] Banta, "Loud Schools," *Readings in Indiana History* (Bloomington: Indiana University, 1914), pp. 327–328; Belle Cushman Bohn, "Early Wisconsin School Teachers," *The Wisconsin Magazine of History*, XXIII, No. 1 (September, 1939), 59; Clifton Johnson, *Old-Time Schools and School-Books* (New York: The Macmillan Company, 1904), p. 118; Theodore Calvin Pease, *The Story of Illinois* (Chicago: A. C. McClurg & Co., 1925), pp. 138–140, 288.

the "sixth reader" (approximately equivalent to completion of the eighth year in a graded school), he had to go to the county seat or some other large town to find a high school or academy. But the high schools and the colleges (springing up so prolifically all over the country) were not a part of the rural scene.[49] Before 1900, a beginning was made toward the grading of the country schools. But they remained one-room, one-teacher units, and the teacher heard thirty or forty five-or-ten-minute classes a day. The consolidation movement was unheard of in the greater part of the nation.

The scholastic standard for teachers was not excessive. Any person, whether he had completed the sixth reader or not, might be examined by the county superintendent and, if deemed proficient, was granted a license or certificate to teach. As late as 1918, a county superintendent in the central part of western Indiana was a man who had tired of mental effort while in the seventh grade; so he diverted his attention from learning and became a teacher. George Cary Eggleston awed a pupil of his by showing that the teacher knew the whole arithmetic and higher branches of mathematics as well.[50] Some teachers, it must be admitted, like Edward Eggleston's *Hoosier Schoolmaster,* were far ahead of the age in their locality, in pedagogical wisdom as well as in learning. Oftentimes the main requirement for a teacher was that he be husky, fearsome of demeanor, and always willing to exert his strength on the refractory school bullies. Mild measures of correction or punishment were viewed with scorn—as evidences of weakness of character—by overgrown boys who had been reared on a system of kicks and cuffs. Pete Jones, in talking to old Jack Means, knew his neighbors, even if he underestimated the ability of the schoolmaster, when he insisted that "'lickin' and l'arnin'" were inseparable. But sometimes a burly schoolma'am, as Edgar Lee Masters could attest, could quite outdo her male rivals in beating a boy black and blue.[51] The vogue for normal schools, in the 1870's, laid stress on

---

[49] Johnson, *Old-Time Schools,* pp. 167–381 *passim;* cf. Hamlin Garland, *Boy Life on the Prairie* (New York: Harper & Brothers, 1899), pp. 20–33.

[50] G. C. Eggleston, *Recollections,* pp. 39–40.

[51] Edward Eggleston, *The Hoosier Schoolmaster* (New York: Grossett & Dunlap edtn., 1892), p. 53; *idem, The Hoosier Schoolboy* (New York: Charles Scribner's Sons, 1914), pp. 60–70; G. C. Eggleston, *The First of the Hoosiers* (Philadelphia: Drexel Biddle, c.1903), pp. 38–41; Edgar Lee Masters, *Across Spoon River* (New York: Farrar & Rinehart, Inc., 1936), p. 40.

better teacher preparation, but the effect was not great on the rural schools during the remainder of the century; for advanced education was generally not yet a prerequisite for certification.

Though the teacher was often underprepared, he usually was not overpaid. Women generally taught the summer schools, and got from $18 to $25 a month. Men and the more robust women handled the winter sessions, and sometimes were paid as high as $25, $30, or $35 a month. The total for the year might be $100, which was less than the pay of a Northern farm laborer. Consequently, the teacher often turned laborer himself between terms, instead of going on further with his own schooling. Down to 1900, teachers' wages in Wisconsin and Illinois were close to the $30 average, but the school term had been lengthened to as many as six months. The teacher also served as janitor, save when some of the pupils offered this service. Board could be had at homes in the community for about $1.50 a week—somewhat more for a man who required laundry work. The fare tended largely toward "hog and hominy," with additions of sorghum molasses, known in the Middle West as "long sweetin'," but this was the mainstay of the family as well.[52]

In 1860, many of the schoolhouses were still one-room log buildings, with puncheon or packed-clay floors. Desks were of rough boards, sometimes circling the room and fastened to the walls. Seats were plank benches, occasionally without backs. Some split-log benches, partially smoothed on the upper side, were in use in southern Illinois as late as 1885. But by 1870, the log structures were pretty thoroughly replaced by one-room frame buildings with board floors. Blackboards were exactly that. Planed boards were painted black, and erasing was done with wet cloths or sponges. Just where the "little red school house," of the Central states and westward, was located must be left to the poets who coined the phrase. The actual schoolhouses were generally painted white. Very little paper was used by the pupils in these schools, slates being employed for everything but formal essays and examinations, and sometimes for those as well.[53]

[52] Bohn, "Early Wisconsin School Teachers," p. 59; Johnson, *Old-Time Schools,* pp. 127–128.

[53] Thomas Huston MacBride, *In Cabins and Sod-Houses* (Iowa City: State Historical Society of Iowa, 1928), pp. 7–14; Bohn, "Early Wisconsin School Teachers,"

School was not all drudgery and punishment. There was usually a quarter- or half-holiday on Friday afternoon, which was given over to contests in the schoolroom. Spelling bees, ciphering matches, and geography contests were held, in which the parents and elder brothers and sisters of the pupils were permitted to compete. Sometimes there were interschool matches. In any school the new boy who would not fight was doomed to a life of misery if he remained. If he knocked out his first two or three assailants, he became a hero, and was never bothered except by adulations. If puny or unskilled, and therefore beaten, he was all right just so he arose and returned to the contest till knocked cold. Thereafter, he would be relegated to those of his own class. But if he whimpered or ran, there was no peace left in life for him. Of all the pleasures of school, the Christmas holidays, preceded by a treat from the teacher, and the last day of school in the spring, stood supreme. The idea was never conquered that the pleasantest thing of all about school was the arrival of vacation time.[54]

The school was not the only social center of the community, though the school building might be also the gathering place for the literary society, the spelling school, the singing school, the lyceum course, and the Chautauqua Literary and Scientific Circle. It also often served for a community church. One such Midwestern school was occupied in rotation during the month by the Methodists, Cumberland Presbyterians, Hard-Shell Baptists, and Seventh-Day Baptists.[55] Elsewhere, the church building itself was a community center second only to the school. But the school, not being consecrated, could be used for a greater variety of activities.

A building was not always considered a necessity for church services in the summer. The camp-meeting fervor of the early part of the century persisted till its close; and the activities within the precincts of the congregation, as well as without, continued to be very much as they were so vividly described by Mark Twain.[56] Brush arbors, made of poles and covered with boughs of trees, and

---

p. 58; G. C. Eggleston, *The First of the Hoosiers,* illustration of a superior early school house, facing p. 52.

[54] For some of these points cf. Garland, *Boy Life on the Prairie,* pp. 333–351.

[55] Christiana Holmes Tillson, *A Woman's Story of Pioneer Illinois* (Chicago: R. R. Donnelley & Sons Company, 1919), pp. 78–79; MacBride, *In Cabins and Sod-Houses,* pp. 105–120.

[56] Pease, *Story of Illinois,* pp. 133–138; DeVoto, *Mark Twain's America,* pp. 42–43.

with logs for benches, were also a frequent place for protracted meetings, whenever the weather permitted. But when a congregation became numerous and wealthy enough, it erected its own special church building, in dimensions and splendor just as far beyond its means as it could go. Generally, however, the members could not support a full-time preacher, so they welcomed such as traveled through, or divided the services of a pastor with several other congregations within a radius of a few miles. Preaching might not be heard more than once a month, but then it was not abbreviated. Sometimes two or three preachers would occupy the pulpit in succession, for hours, with intervening recesses for relaxation. If the exhorter was sometimes more noisy and muscular than learned, at least he had a convincing way of pointing out the shortcomings of his listeners. Conviction of sin, among some groups, often brought on wholesale trances—and, sometimes, real ones.[57]

The education of the pastor usually reflected the intellectual perceptions of his flock. The number of preachers was seldom equal to the demand, but the income from the profession was not such as to encourage a plethora of applicants. In circuit-riding communities, local preachers, or exhorters, performed the day-by-day drudgery of the minister, generally without pay. But, whether or not church services were regular, the substantial farmers of the community were stern with their children about attendance. Also, the discipline of the church was administered with severity. Young people were often dropped from membership ("churched") for dancing or playing Sunday baseball. One woman declared that she was ousted from a Methodist congregation for organizing a dramatic society. Sleigh rides, corn huskings, and other seemingly innocent diversions were frowned on—but maybe the church committee understood what was going on.[58]

Statistical data on many topics such as this are so scanty as to be misleading or useless. Yet, any consideration of the rural school and church leaves the conviction that here, as in population and wealth, the country lagged behind the city. This does not mean that the rural poor were in any worse condition than the urban proletariat. In many ways they were better off. But in the farming

[57] Tillson, A Woman's Story of Pioneer Illinois, pp. 79–80.
[58] Mary Austin, Earth Horizon, Autobiography (Boston: Houghton Mifflin Company, c.1932), p. 119; DeVoto, Mark Twain's America, p. 43.

communities there was no concentration of wealth, and its external display, to compenstate for the duller features. One of the most disturbing characteristics was what has been called the "rural attitude": a conscious suspicion of outsiders; a feeling by the farmer that he was looked upon as a "rube"; and a reaction in defense of everything that might be designated as rustic. Puritanism originated among town dwellers, when they were deemed to be different from the "better" classes. In its less complimentary definition, it lingered on the farm, and probably for the same reason. This attitude was still at its height in the days of McKinley, free-silver agitation, and budding imperialism. Some features of it persisted longer. The chief manifestation was resistance to what might be considered outside interference, or anything nonrural in origin.[59]

But there was much justification for this attitude. The life of the farmer had been a hard one. He could, and did, withstand the buffetings of nature, but he resented the outside forces that subjected him to an unfavorable commercial control. Many and rosy had been the promises of outside help. He had voted for county railroad bonds, and been left in the lurch. He had supported tariff protection, and was paying the cost. His father had supported homestead legislation, and had been forestalled by speculators. The rest of the list need not be repeated. Any new scheme must have more than a gilt-edged prospectus to be alluring. Though, at the end of the century, hardly a perceptible dent had been made in the farmer's shell of dependence on his own, individual effort, he was still open to conviction. But the proofs must be substantial. He was still learning, and would continue to do so.

[59] On the rural attitude, see James Mickel Williams, *The Expansion of Rural Life* (New York: Alfred A. Knopf, 1926), pp. 32–37.

CHAPTER XVI

The Literature of the Subject

GUIDES

NO exhaustive treatises of American agricultural history have been written for the period since 1860, like those of Gray on the South and Bidwell and Falconer on the North for the earlier years, but there is a great mass of monographic literature, in addition to an almost inexhaustible supply of documentary material. The most complete guide to this information is Everett E[ugene] Edwards, *A Bibliography of the History of Agriculture in the United States* (U.S. Department of Agriculture, *Miscellaneous Publication* No. 84, Washington: Government Printing Office, 1930). Dr. Edwards has included many additional suggestions in a mimeographed circular entitled *A Guide for Courses in the History of American Agriculture* (U.S. Department of Agriculture Library, *Bibliographical Contribution* No. 35, Washington: September, 1939). A brief but very useful bibliography is Louis Bernard Schmidt, *Topical Studies and References on the Economic History of American Agriculture* (Philadelphia: McKinley Publishing Company, rev. ed., 1923). This also has been supplemented by a short mimeographed list entitled *Topical Studies and References on the History of American Agriculture* (Ames, Iowa: Department of History and Government, Iowa State College, 1937).

The *Agricultural Index* (New York: H. W. Wilson Co., 1916–) includes references to many secondary contributions on the earlier periods. Published monthly, with cumulations, it lists by subject the offerings of a large number of books, bulletins, and agricultural periodicals. For articles contemporary to the years 1860–1900, *Poole's Index to Periodical Literature* (Boston: James R. Osgood & Co., 1882), with its supplementary volumes II–VI (Boston: Houghton Mifflin Company, 1882–1907), remains surprisingly useful. The *Readers' Guide to Periodical Literature* (New York: H. W. Wilson Co., 1900–), together with the *Readers' Guide Supplement* (1907–1919) and the *International Index to Periodicals* (1920–), both published by the same company as the *Readers' Guide*, are useful mainly for the present century, but list articles on earlier periods.

The search for federal public documents published before 1881 is rendered rather painful by the inadequacies of the indexes. In 1885 Ben: Perley Poore got out his *Descriptive Catalogue of the Government Publications of the United States, September 5, 1774–March 4, 1881*, which was published as *Senate Miscellaneous Document* No. 67, 48 Cong., 2 Sess. Its greatest deficiency is the lack of subject entries. This difficulty is partially overcome by the *Tables of and Annotated Index to the Congressional Series of United States Public Documents* (Washington: Government Printing Office, 1902). It includes nothing but the Congressional series. Better done than the work by Poore is John G. Ames, *Comprehensive Index to the Publications of the United States Government, 1881–1893*, two vols. It is *House Document* No. 754, 58 Cong., 2 Sess., and was published in 1905. For the period since 1893 there is a separate index for each Congress. The titles vary, but librarians know what is meant when they are asked for the *Document Catalog*.

The most comprehensive guide for state documents is Adelaide R[osalie] Hasse, *Index of Economic Material in Documents of the States of the United States* (13 vols., Washington: Carnegie Institution of Washington, 1907–1922). The contributions of the numerous state and local historical societies contain many items of importance to agricultural history, and they can be scanned with the aid of Appleton Prentiss Clark Griffin, *Bibliography of American Historical Societies* (Vol. II of American Historical Association, *Annual Report*, 1905, Washington: Government Printing Office, 1907). Additional bibliographical material, relating to the standard guides less devoted to the agricultural theme, may be found in Edwards's *Bibliography*, mentioned above, in Homer Carey Hockett,

Introduction to Research in American History (New York: The Macmillan Company, 1931), and in Edward Channing, Albert Bushnell Hart, and Frederick Jackson Turner, *Guide to the Study and Reading of American History* (Boston: Ginn and Company, c. 1912). *The Harvard Guide to American History* is promised soon, to replace the Channing, Hart, and Turner *Guide,* which has so long needed revision.

GENERAL WORKS

An interesting, though brief and elementary, consideration of American agriculture from the earliest times, and including the period since 1860, is Albert Hart Sanford, *The Story of Agriculture in the United States* (Boston: D. C. Heath & Co., 1916). More recent, but sketchy in its approach, is Joseph Schafer, *The Social History of American Agriculture* (New York: The Macmillan Company, 1936). This, comprised of the lectures given by Dr. Schafer at University College, University of London, in 1936, is, from the nature of its purpose, far from complete. The newest general synthesis of American agriculture, and exceedingly satisfactory in consideration of its brevity, is Everett E[ugene] Edwards, "American Agriculture—The First 300 Years," U.S. Department of Agriculture, *Yearbook,* 1940 (Washington: Government Printing Office, 1941?), pp. 171–276, also listed as *Yearbook Separate,* No. 1730. The most useful substitute for a general textbook in the subject continues to be Louis Bernard Schmidt and Earle Dudley Ross, eds., *Readings in the Economic History of American Agriculture* (New York: The Macmillan Company, 1925). It is compiled mainly from secondary writings and is so assembled as to approximate a history of the subject. L[iberty] H[yde] Bailey, ed., *Cyclopedia of American Agriculture* (4 vols., New York: The Macmillan Company, 1907), while not primarily historical in approach, yet was so generously conceived as to contain articles on almost every phase of agriculture, with a historical approach to many; for the most part, the writers were excellently chosen for their tasks. Various phases of agricultural life may also be traced through Arthur Meier Schlesinger and Dixon Ryan Fox, eds., *A History of American Life* (12 vols., New York: The Macmillan Company, 1927–1944). The volumes pertaining to the last half of the nineteenth century are Arthur Charles Cole, *The Irrepressible Conflict, 1850–1865;* [Joseph] Allan Nevins, *The Emergence of Modern America, 1865–1878;* Ida M[inerva] Tarbell, *The Nationalizing of Business, 1878–1898;* and Arthur Meier Schlesinger, *The Rise of the City, 1878–1898.*

DEPARTMENT OF AGRICULTURE PUBLICATIONS

The most voluminous collection of general documents and articles on the subject is in the innumerable publications of the Department of Agriculture itself, together with the output of the experiment stations. From 1837 to 1862, agricultural statistics and information were included in the Patent Office, *Reports.* Then, from 1862 to 1889, came the annual Commissioner of Agriculture, *Reports;* and, after 1889, the annual Secretary of Agriculture, *Reports,* each being published by the Government Printing Office at Washington. Before 1894, these reports contained many articles of general interest regarding farming practices and agricultural history. Then, in 1894, was begun the practice of issuing an annual *Yearbook* of the Department of Agriculture, and only routine matters were left for the annual *Reports.* The *Yearbook* for 1899 (Washington: Government Printing Office, 1900) is a volume of 880 pages, nearly seven hundred of which are given over to twenty-six articles by department experts on the history of different phases of agriculture from the beginnings of America down to the end of the nineteenth century.

Many bureaus of the department have also issued their annual reports, such as those of the Bureau of Animal Industry. A useful list of the department's publications is R. B. Handy and Minna A. Cannon, comps., "List of Titles of Publications of the United States Department of Agriculture from 1840 to June, 1901, Inclusive," U.S. Department of Agriculture, Bureau of Publications, *Bulletin* No. 6 (Washington: Government Printing Office, 1902). The more important of the *Bulletins* of the agricultural experiment stations are accounted for in the "Bulletins of the Experiment Stations," U.S. Department of Agriculture, *Department Bulletin* No. 1199 (Washington: Government Printing Office, May 26, 1924). Some 12,500 items are included.

PERIODICAL LITERATURE

The only journal devoted solely to the history of agriculture is *Agricultural History*, a quarterly published since 1927 by the Agricultural History Society. It covers the world, and ancient as well as modern times, but it contains quite a bit of secondary material on the United States from 1860 to 1900. The *Journal of Farm Economics*, a quarterly published since June, 1919, by the American Farm Economic Association also contains some articles of historical interest. The regular, well-known monthly and weekly magazines of the period under consideration contain scattered articles, often by eyewitnesses, relating to farming in all its aspects, but they are mainly devoted to other matters. Separate entries will be made in this bibliography for the more important articles that have been used.

The enormous number of farm weeklies, biweeklies, semimonthlies, and monthly magazines of the period can be appreciated by looking through any number of the *Union List of Serials* under the initial words "Farm" and "Farmers" alone. Many of these journals were of an evanescent character, and either went out of business or merged with other journals after a few years' existence. For example, the *American Agriculturist* has absorbed between thirty and forty other magazines. A list of some of the more important of the journals follows, enumerated alphabetically, and including mainly those that started either before 1860 or between 1860 and 1890, and which had a continuous existence past the end of the nineteenth century. The titles have varied from period to period in many instances, as mergers were made or interests expanded. Also, many of them changed about from weeklies to monthlies, or the reverse, and back again. The *Prairie Farmer* went through several of these changes.

The journals include *American Agriculturist*, New York, 1842–; *Breeder's Gazette*, Chicago, 1881–; *California Cultivator and Live Stock and Dairy Journal*, Los Angeles, 1887–; *Country Gentleman*, Albany, Philadelphia, 1853– (from 1866 to 1897 this was the *Cultivator & Country Gentleman*); *Dakota Farmer*, Aberdeen, S.D., 1881–; *Farm and Fireside*, New York, Springfield, Ohio, 1877–; *Farm and Home*, Springfield, Mass., 1880– (Eastern and Western editions); *Farm and Ranch*, Dallas, Texas, 1883–; *Farm Journal*,

Philadelphia, 1877–; *Farmers' Advocate,* Topeka, Vols. 1–31 (absorbed by *Kansas Farmer,* q.v., 1908); *Farmers' Home Journal,* Lexington, Louisville, Ky., 1867–; *Farmers' Review,* Chicago, Vols. 1–50, 1877–1918 (absorbed by *Orange Judd Farmer); Hearth and Home,* New York, Vols. 1–9, 1866-1875; *Iowa Homestead,* Des Moines, 1855–; *Journal of Agriculture,* St. Louis, Vols. 1–62, 1856–1921 (absorbed by *Missouri Ruralist); Kansas Farmer and Mail and Breeze,* Topeka, 1863– (known through many years as *Kansas Farmer); Michigan Farmer and Live Stock Journal,* Detroit, 1843– (goes under numerous variations of title and series of volumes); *Nebraska Farmer,* Lincoln, Omaha, 1877–; *New England Farmer,* Boston, etc., 1822–1847, 1865–1913 (suspended 1847–1865); *New England Homestead,* Springfield, Mass., 1867–; *Orange Judd Farmer,* Chicago, 1884– (since 1924 known as *Orange Judd Illinois Farmer); Pacific Rural Press,* San Francisco, 1871–; *Prairie Farmer,* Chicago, 1841–; *Rural New Yorker,* New York, 1849–; *Southern Cultivator and Dixie Farmer,* Athens, Atlanta, Ga., 1843– (through Vol. 43 known as *Southern Cultivator); Southern Planter,* Richmond, Va., 1841–; *Wisconsin Agriculturist,* Racine, 1877–. This list is an attempt to cover nearly all parts of the country and most kinds of farming.

PHYSICAL BASIS

For the general reader, the most comprehensive synthesis and symposium on the new soil science is the U.S. Department of Agriculture, *Yearbook,* 1938 (Washington: Government Printing Office, 1939?). It bears the special title of *Soils & Men,* is 1,232 pages in length, and contains as a frontispiece a photograph of Curtis Fletcher Marbut, the American pioneer of the new soil science. The original work in the American language on this subject was K[onstantin] D[mitrievich] Glinka, *The Great Soil Groups of the World and Their Development* (translated from the German by C. F. Marbut, Ann Arbor: Edwards Bros., 1927). This appears in mimeographed form. It was first published in German in 1914. Before that time there was no general work in a language known to many scientists of the Western World. Glinka was Director of the Agricultural Institute of Leningrad at the time of the American edition. A further amplification and American adaptation of the work of Glinka and Marbut is a bulletin by Charles E[dwin] Kellogg, "Development and Significance of the Great Soil Groups of the United States," U.S. Department of Agriculture, *Miscellaneous Publication* No. 229 (Washington: Government Printing Office, April, 1936).

The complexity of soil types is best shown in the 791-page work by Curtis F[letcher] Marbut, Hugh H. Bennett, J. E. Lapham, and M. H. Lapham, *Soils of the United States* (U.S. Department of Agriculture, Bureau of Soils, *Bulletin* No. 96, Washington: Government Printing Office, 1913). An older but useful study is E[ugene] W. Hilgard, *Soils: Their Formation, Properties, Composition, and Relations to Climate and Plant Growth in the Humid and Arid Regions* (New York: The Macmillan Company, 1906). Containing more of the modern viewpoint is Gilbert Woodring Robinson, *Soils: Their Origin, Constitution, and Classification* (London: Thomas Murby & Co., 2d ed., 1936). Practical applications of soil knowledge is the theme of E[dward] John Russell, *Soil Conditions and Plant Growth* (London: Longmans, Green and Co., 6th ed., 1932). Milton Whitney, *Soil and Civilization* (New York: D. Van Nostrand Company, 1925), is terribly worded and suffers from long, literary flourishes, but it has valuable spots here and there. It contains an apt analogy of the soil to a living organism. The author was Chief of the Bureau of Soils of the U.S. Department of Agriculture.

An excellent commentary on the newer geographic knowledge of climate is C[harles] Warren Thornthwaite, "The Climates of North America, according to a New Classification," *The Geographical Review*, XXI, No. 4 (October, 1931), 633–655. The *Yearbook of Agriculture* for 1941, entitled *Climate and Man* (Washington: Government Printing Office, 1941), is a vast storehouse of articles of many sorts on the subject. For the entire range of geographic relations to agriculture nothing can approach O[liver] E[dwin] Baker, comp., *Atlas of American Agriculture* (Washington: Government Printing Office, 1936). This atlas was originally published in several parts and later combined. Each section contains a full text of description, exposition, and analysis, in addition to the maps. The separate parts with their dates of publication are as follows: F. J. Marschner, *Land Relief* (1936); J[oseph] B[urton] Kincer, *Climate: Precipitation and Humidity* (1922); Kincer, *Climate: Tem-*

perature, Sunshine, and Wind (1928); William Gardner Reed, *Climate: Frost and the Growing Season* (1918); C[urtis] F[letcher] Marbut, *Soils of the United States* (1935, often referred to as Marbut's *Atlas*); H[omer] L. Shantz, *Natural Vegetation: Grassland and Desert Shrub* (1924); and Raphael Zon, *Natural Vegetation: Forests* (1924). The last two were published together, and may properly be referred to as Shantz and Zon, *Natural Vegetation.*

AGRICULTURAL SETTLEMENT

The standard histories of the West include discussions of settlement and sometimes have references to agriculture, aside from the cattle-herding industry. Among these are Frederic Logan Paxson, *History of the American Frontier, 1763–1893* (Boston: Houghton Mifflin Company, c.1924); Robert E[dgar] Riegel, *America Moves West* (New York: Henry Holt and Company, c.1930); E[dward] Douglas Branch, *Westward: The Romance of the American Frontier* (New York: D. Appleton and Company, 1930); Dan Elbert Clark, *The West in American History* (New York: Thomas Y. Crowell Company, 1937); and LeRoy R. Hafen and Carl Coke Rister, *Western America* (New York: Prentice-Hall, Inc., 1941). Frederic Logan Paxson, *The Last American Frontier* (New York: The Macmillan Company, 1910), has little about the farmer, but is useful for background. Randall Parrish, *The Great Plains* (Chicago: A. C. McClurg & Co., 1907), is a gossipy, popular account, taking the story down only to 1870, but is colorful on many phases of Western life. Cardinal [Leonidas] Goodwin, *The Trans-Mississippi West, 1803–1853* (New York: D. Appleton and Company, 1922), hardly belongs to this list. Aside from being largely a story of the acquisition of the new regions, it is rather early in date, but it gives information as to why settlement happened to be as it was before 1860. Everett [Newfon] Dick, *The Sod-House Frontier, 1854–1890* (New York: D. Appleton-Century Company, 1937), gives more of the actual living conditions on the frontier than do most books on the subject.

Angie Debo, *The Rise and Fall of the Choctaw Republic* (Norman: University of Oklahoma Press, 1934), is most illuminating on the subject of agricultural practices among the civilized Indians of the frontier. James F. Willard and Colin B. Goodykoontz, eds.,

The Trans-Mississippi West (Boulder: University of Colorado, 1930), is a collection of articles by specialists on different phases of the history of the region. Certain of the articles will be mentioned individually later. The part played by railroads in the distribution of settlement is well illustrated in James Blaine Hedges, *Henry Villard and the Railways of the Northwest* (New Haven: Yale University Press, 1930); and Richard C[leghorn] Overton, *Burlington West: A Colonization History of the Burlington Railroad* (Cambridge: Harvard University Press, 1941).

General treatises on population movements, that have a bearing on the problem in America, include Robert R[ené] Kuczynski, *Population Movements* (Oxford, Eng.; The Clarendon Press, 1936); Warren S[impson] Thompson and P[ascal] K[idder] Whelpton, *Population Trends in the United States* (New York: McGraw-Hill Book Company, Inc., 1933); Otis Tufton Mason, "Migration and the Food Quest: A Study in the Peopling of America," Smithsonian Institution, *Annual Report,* 1894 (Washington: Government Printing Office, 1896), pp. 523–539, somewhat rhetorical and Latiny, and devoted mainly to Indian movements, as far as America is concerned; Corrado Gini, Shiroshi Nasu, Robert R[ené] Kuczynski, and Oliver E[dwin] Baker, *Population* (Chicago: The University of Chicago Press, c.1930), mainly useful for the period since 1900; and James W[illiam] Robertson, *Movement of Population* (Ottawa, Ontario: C. H. Parmelee, 1912), nineteen pages of testimony before a Canadian Senate Committee on population movement, including some matters relating to conditions in the United States. Highly useful are the graphic maps in C[harles] Warren Thornthwaite and Helen I. Slentz, *Internal Migration in the United States* (Philadelphia: University of Pennsylvania Press, 1934). The essence of Thornthwaite's work, as well as other valuable material, is also in Carter [Lyman] Goodrich and others, *Migration and Economic Opportunity* (Philadelphia: University of Pennsylvania Press, 1936).

Among the standard works on immigration after 1860 are George M[alcolm] Stephenson, *A History of American Immigration, 1820–1924* (Boston: Ginn and Company, c.1926), and Carl [Frederick] Wittke, *We Who Built America: The Saga of the Immigrant* (New York: Prentice-Hall, Inc., 1939). The posthumous works on immigration by Marcus Lee Hansen pertain to the period before 1860, except for his *The Mingling of the Canadian and American*

Peoples (completed by John Bartlett Brebner, New Haven: Yale University Press, 1940). This is the most thorough item on the subject.

THE PUBLIC LANDS

The newest treatise on the public lands is Roy M[arvin] Robbins, *Our Landed Heritage: The Public Domain, 1776–1936* (Princeton: Princeton University Press, c.1942). This may be supplemented by Benjamin Horace Hibbard, *A History of the Public Land Policies* (New York: The Macmillan Company, 1924). The greatest compendium of undigested information for the period covered is the 1,343 pages of Thomas Donaldson, *The Public Domain* (Washington: Government Printing Office, 1884). More intelligent comment than is to be found elsewhere on land policies since 1860 is contained in a number of scattered articles by Paul Wallace Gates. These include "Federal Land Policy in the South, 1866–1888," *The Journal of Southern History*, VI, No. 3 (August, 1940), 303–330; "Recent Land Policies of the Federal Government," *Certain Aspects of Land Problems and Government Land Policies* (Part VII of the *Supplementary Report of the Land Planning Committee to the National Resources Board*, Washington: Government Printing Office, 1935), 60–85; and "The Homestead Act in an Incongruous Land System," *American Historical Review*, XLI, No. 4 (July, 1936), 652–681. Accompanying the latter article is Fred A[lbert] Shannon, "The Homestead Act and the Labor Surplus," *American Historical Review*, XLI, No. 4 (July, 1936), 637–651, which includes, among other things, further information about the diversion of lands from actual settlers.

Among the larger federal government reports on the lands are the Public Lands Commission, *Report*, 1880 (*House Executive Document* No. 46, 46 Cong., 2 Sess.); and the Public Lands Commission, *Report*, 1905 (*Senate Document* No. 189, 58 Cong., 3 Sess.). Both these documents contain voluminous testimony as well as reasoned summaries. The different land laws are best searched out in the U.S. *Statutes at Large*, but a handy compilation of the most important and permanent acts is John W. Keener, comp., *Public Land Statutes of the United States*, 1916 (*Senate Document* No. 547, 64 Cong., 1 Sess.). It also includes many of the repealed statutes. The efforts of the Land Office to encourage homesteading can be seen in Willis Drummond, *Brief Description of the Public Lands of the United States of America, Prepared by the Commissioner of the General Land-Office for the Information of Foreigners Seeking a Home in the United States* (Washington: Government Printing Office, 1873), and in the *Circular from the General Land-Office Showing the Manner of Proceeding to Obtain Title to Public Lands under the Homestead, Desert Land, and Other Laws* (Washington: Government Printing Office, 1899). Individual efforts in the same direction are illustrated in Henry N[orris] Copp, *The American Settler's Guide: A Popular Exposition of the Public Land System of the United States of America* (Washington: Published by the editor, 2d ed., 1882).

Some of the better results of the Timber Culture Act are shown in Royal S[haw] Kellogg, "Forest Belts of Western Kansas and Nebraska," U.S. Department of Agriculture, Forest Service, *Bulletin No. 66* (Washington: Government Printing Office, 1905). The scandals connected with the disposal of forest lands are ably exposed in John Ise, *The United States Forest Policy* (New Haven: Yale University Press, 1920), and again, by one of the looters himself, in S[tephen] A[rnold] D[ouglas] Puter and Horace Stevens, *Looters of the Public Domain* (Portland, Ore.: The Portland Printing House, 1908). One of the earliest and most intelligent critics of the land policy was George W. Julian, and his articles are scattered through much of the periodical literature of the time, but the most incisive, and generally accurate, indictment was Henry George, *Our Land and Land Policy* (New York: Doubleday and McClure Company, 1901). The first edition of this work was copyrighted by the author in 1871, and its strictures on land policy are still unrefuted. A later, fairly reliable addition to Henry George's indictment is J[ames] D[avenport] Whelpley, "The Nation as a Land Owner," *Senate Document* No. 183, 57 Cong., 1 Sess. (1902). This was reprinted from *Harper's Weekly* in the issues of November 30, December 7, and December 14, 1901.

The most satisfactory accounting for the amounts of land actually received by the railroads is "Aids to Railroads," Federal Coordinator of Transportation, Section of Research, *Public Aids to Transportation* (Washington: Government Printing Office, 1938), II, Pt. 1. John Bell Sanborn, *Congressional Grants of Land in Aid of Railways* (University of Wisconsin, *Bulletin* No. 30, *Economics, Political Science and History Series,* Vol. III, No. 2, Madison: 1899), is pretty thin in content and covers little more than a review of congressional measures. Lewis H[enry] Haney, *A Congressional History of Railways, 1850–1887* (University of Wisconsin, *Bulletin* No. 342, *Economic and Political Science Series,* Vol. VI, No. 1, Madison: 1910), is somewhat more thorough, but it also evades most of the deeper implications. The numerous Land Office reports and other government documents remain a more fruitful source of information. An example of the nature of revelations thus available, though in another branch of the land question, is Binger Hermann and E[than] A[llen] Hitchcock, "Commuted Homestead, etc., Entries Attacked on Grounds of Fraudulent Intent," *Senate Document* No. 130, 57 Cong., 2 Sess. (1903).

Some idea of the mismanagement of state lands can be secured from William Albert Hartman, "State Land-Settlement Problems and Policies in the United States," U.S. Department of Agriculture, *Technical Bulletin* No. 357 (Washington: Government Printing Office, 1933); but a more illuminating account is in D. M. Richards, "Management of Our School Lands," University of New Mexico, *Bulletin* No. 42, *Educational Series,* Vol. I, Art. 2 (Albuquerque: The University, 1906).

SOUTHERN PROBLEMS

Several books on the South came out in the years immediately after the Civil War. Among those containing valuable information for later students are Sidney Andrews, *The South Since the War* (Boston: Ticknor and Fields, 1866); Robert Somers, *The Southern States Since the War, 1870–1* (London: Macmillan and Co., 1871); and Edward King, *The Great South* (Hartford: American Publishing Company, 1875). Purely on the economic side is James Curtis Ballagh, ed., *Economic History, 1865–1909* (Vol. VI of *The South in the Building of the Nation,* Richmond: Southern Publication Society, 1909). Some of the articles from this volume will be listed separately under the names of the authors. Written from the Southern-white, and rather aristocratic, point of view, but valuable for its abundance of detailed information, is Philip Alexander Bruce, *The Rise of the New South* (Vol. XVII of *The History of North*

America, Guy Carleton Lee, ed., Philadelphia: George Barrie & Sons, c.1905). A more recent work, valuable in places in spite of some adverse reviews, is Emory Q[uinter] Hawk, *Economic History of the South* (New York: Prentice-Hall, Inc., 1934). The most successful effort, to date, to write a comprehensive short history of the South is William B[est] Hesseltine, *A History of the South, 1607–1936* (New York: Prentice-Hall, Inc., 1936). The most scholarly treatise on the postwar period, in all its social ramifications, is Paul H[erman] Buck, *The Road to Reunion, 1865–1900* (Boston: Little, Brown and Company, 1937). An analysis of the exploitation of the South, as well as of the West, by Eastern financial interests is Walter Prescott Webb, *Divided We Stand* (New York: Farrar & Rinehart, Inc., 1937).

The beginnings of the share-cropper system in the South are most ably presented in Oscar Zeichner, "The Transition from Slave to Free Agricultural Labor in the Southern States," *Agricultural History*, XIII, No. 1 (January, 1939), 22–33. Further development of the practice, and other problems of land and labor, are vividly described in Holland Thompson, *The New South* (Vol. XLII of *Chronicles of America Series*, Allen Johnson, ed., New Haven: Yale University Press, c.1919). The system after it was well developed is exposed in George K[irby] Holmes, "Peons of the South," American Academy of Political and Social Science, *Annals*, IV, No. 2 (September, 1893), 265–274. A still later view of the growth of the new form of slavery is one of the themes of Robert Preston Brooks, *The Agrarian Revolution in Georgia* (University of Wisconsin, *History Series, Bulletin*, III, No. 3, Madison: University of Wisconsin, 1914). One phase of the subject is also developed in Carl Kelsey, *The Negro Farmer* (Chicago: Jennings & Pye, 1903). The enlightened, modern Southern viewpoint is revealed by Rupert B[ayless] Vance in *Human Factors in Cotton Culture* and in *Human Geography of the South* (Chapel Hill: University of North Carolina Press, 1929 and 1932). The older view of the incompetence of the freedmen can be gleaned from Walter L[ynwood] Fleming, *Civil War and Reconstruction in Alabama* (Cleveland: The Arthur H. Clark Company, 1911). The class stratification for a representative Southern state is ably expounded by Roger W[allace] Shugg, *Origins of Class Struggle in Louisiana: A Social History of White*

Farmers and Laborers during Slavery and After, 1840–1875 (University, La.: Louisiana State University Press, 1939).

The part played by transportation in the marketing of Southern crops, and in the general agricultural development of the section, is revealed in many places. It is touched on by J. A. Latcha in "Cheap Transportation in the United States," *North American Review,* CLXIV, No. 486 (May, 1897), 592–608. The country highways are considered in N[athaniel] S[outhgate] Shaler, "The Common Road," *Scribner's Magazine,* VI, No. 4 (October, 1889), 473–483; Martin Dodge, "The Government and Good Roads," *The Forum,* XXXII, No. 3 (November, 1901), 292–297. The part played by the steamboat is more vitally exposed than is revealed by the title in Charles Henry Ambler, *History of Transportation in the Ohio Valley* (Glendale, Cal.: The Arthur H. Clark Company, 1932). A brief but illuminating story of the railroad's part is Ulrich B[onnell] Phillips, "Railway Transportation in the South," *The South in the Building of the Nation,* VI, 305–316. Other accounts are W[illiam] W[ilson] Finley, "Southern Railroads and Industrial Development," American Academy of Political and Social Science, *Annals,* XXXV, No. 1 (January, 1910), 99–104; W[illiam] M[ason] Grosvenor, "The Railroads and the Farms," *Atlantic Monthly,* XXXII, No. 193 (November, 1873), 591–610; and H[arry] T[urner] Newcomb, "The Present Railway Situation," *North American Review,* CLXV, No. 492 (November, 1897), 591–599. General marketing problems are discussed in textbook style in James E[rnest] Boyle, *Marketing of Agricultural Products* (New York: McGraw-Hill Book Company, Inc., 1925).

In the following works on the leading Southern crops, treatments on production and marketing are lumped together. M[atthew] B[rown] Hammond, *The Cotton Industry* (New York: The Macmillan Company, 1897), considers many phases of the subject. A second volume was projected but never appeared. Hammond also wrote "Cotton Production in the South," for *The South in the Building of the Nation,* VI, 87–104, and "The Southern Farmer and the Cotton Question," *Political Science Quarterly,* XII, No. 3 (September, 1897), 450–475. Another quite comprehensive treatment is Charles William Burkett and Clarence Hamilton Poe, *Cotton, Its Cultivation, Marketing, Manufacture, and the Problems of the Cotton World* (New York: Doubleday, Page & Company, c.1906).

Thoroughly statistical in its content is Alfred B. Shepperson, *Cotton Facts* (New York: A. B. Shepperson, 1895). The data are all from the Census of 1890. Financial angles are considered in Samuel T. Hubbard, "The Cotton Situation," *Banker's Magazine* [U.S.], L, No. 2 (January, 1895), 175–182. The problems of marketing are well considered in Robert Hargrove Montgomery, *The Coöperative Pattern in Cotton* (New York: The Macmillan Company, 1929). World marketing conditions are the theme of James A[ugustin] B[rown] Scherer, *Cotton as a World Power* (New York: Frederick A. Stokes Company, c.1916).

The most thorough discussion for tobacco is Meyer Jacobstein, *The Tobacco Industry in the United States* (Vol. XXVI, No. 3, of Columbia University *Studies in History, Economics and Public Law*, New York: The Columbia University Press, 1907). His article, "The Conditions of Tobacco Culture in the South," in *The South in the Building of the Nation*, VI, 66–72, is a good short cut to the problem. The same volume contains brief sketches of other Southern crops. These include William C. Stubbs, "Sugar Products in the South," pp. 78–86; Patrick Hues Mell, "The Conditions of Rice Culture in the South since 1865," pp. 72–78; Thomas F. Hunt, "Cereal Farming in the South," pp. 104–117; and Andrew M. Soule, "Vegetables, Fruit, and Nursery Products and Truck Farming in the South," pp. 127–135.

FARM MACHINERY

A book wholly devoted to this subject is R[obert] L. Ardrey, *American Agricultural Implements: A Review of Invention and Development in the Agricultural Implement Industry of the United States* (Chicago: the author, c. 1894). A Department of Agriculture publication on the same subject is Edward H[enry] Knight, *Agricultural Implements* (*House Executive Document* No. 42, pt. 5, 46 Cong., 3 Sess., a report of the Commissioner of Agriculture on the Paris Exposition of 1878). Edward Wright Byrn, *Progress of Invention in the Nineteenth Century* (New York: Munn & Co., Publishers, 1900), contains information on agricultural implements, along with other inventions. General articles of value on the subject include Eldridge M. Fowler, "Agricultural Machinery and Implements," *1795–1895, One Hundred Years of American Commerce*

(Chauncey M[itchell] DePew, ed., New York: D. O. Haynes & Co., 1895), II, 352–356; Charles L. Flint, "Agriculture in the United States," *One Hundred Years' Progress of the United States* (no editor listed, Hartford: L. Stebbins, 1870), pp. 19–102; C. J. Zintheo, "Machinery in Relation to Farming," *Cyclopedia of American Agriculture*, I, 208–217; B[everly] T[homas] Galloway, "Intensive Farming," *The Making of America* (Robert Marion LaFollette, ed. in chief, 10 vols., Philadelphia: John D. Morris and Company, c.1905), V, 332–342; M. C. Horine, "Farming by Machine," *A Popular History of American Invention* (Waldemar [Bernhard] Kaempffert, ed., 2 vols., New York: Charles Scribner's Sons, 1924), II, 246–309; and Frank N. G. Kranich, "Growth of Farm Machinery," *The Field Illustrated*, XXVIII, No. 3 (March, 1918), 147–149.

Some of the consequences of the new machinery are considered in Leo Rogin, *The Introduction of Farm Machinery in Its Relation to the Productivity of Labor in the Agriculture of the United States during the Nineteenth Century* (Vol. IX of University of California *Publications in Economics*, Berkeley: University of California Press, 1931); H[adley] W. Quaintance, "The Influence of Machinery on the Economic and Social Conditions of the Agricultural People," *Cyclopedia of American Agriculture*, IV, 108–113; Willet M[artin] Hays and Edward C. Parker, "The Cost of Producing Farm Products," U.S. Department of Agriculture, Bureau of Statistics, *Bulletin* No. 48 (Washington: Government Printing Office, 1906); and W. B. Thornton, "The Revolution by Farm Machinery," *World's Work*, VI, No. 4 (August, 1903), 3766–3779.

A manufacturer-inspired history of some phases of plow making is Neil M[cCullough] Clark, *John Deere: He Gave to the World the Steel Plow* (Moline, Ill.; privately printed, 1937?). Russell Howard Anderson, "Grain Drills through Thirty-Nine Centuries," *Agricultural History*, X, No. 4 (October, 1936), 157–205, contains some information on developments in the United States. The second volume of William T[homas] Hutchinson, *Cyrus Hall McCormick* (New York: D. Appleton-Century Company, 1935), is the most exhaustive study of postwar developments in the harvester industry. Reuben Gold Thwaites, "Cyrus Hall McCormick and the Reaper," State Historical Society of Wisconsin, *Proceedings,* 1908 (Madison: The Society, 1909), pp. 234–259, also contains interesting materials. Two other works on the subject are Herbert N[ewton] Casson, *The*

Romance of the Reaper (New York: Doubleday, Page & Company, 1908), a popular account; and the Deering Harvester Company, *Official Retrospective Exhibition of the Development of Harvesting Machinery for the Paris Exposition of 1900* (Paris: 1900?). Items covering the early use of the combine are C. C. Johnson, "Combines Long Known in Washington," *The American Thresherman*, XXXIII, No. 1 (May, 1930), 26; A. E. Starch and R. M. Merrill, "The Combined Harvester-Thresher in Montana," University of Montana, Agricultural Experiment Station, *Bulletin* No. 230 (Bozeman: 1930); and Edwin S. Holmes, "Wheat Growing and General Agricultural Conditions in the Pacific Coast Region of the United States," U.S. Department of Agriculture, Division of Statistics, *Miscellaneous Series, Bulletin* No. 20 (Washington: Government Printing Office, 1901). The treatments on power-driven machinery include L[ynn] W[ebster] Ellis and Edward A. Rumely, *Power and the Plow* (Garden City: Doubleday, Page & Company, 1911); John C. Merriam, "Steam," *One Hundred Years' Progress of the United States*, pp. 227–273; and P. S. Rose, "Farm Motors," *Cyclopedia of American Agriculture*, I, 217–231.

THE PRAIRIES

The conditions of life among pioneers on the western Prairies are ably related by Dick, *The Sod-House Frontier*, and in John Ise, *Sod and Stubble: The Story of a Kansas Homestead* (New York: Wilson-Erickson, Incorporated, 1936). There is also more of this than in the usual history of the West in Branch, *Westward*. But one of the earliest detailed accounts, written for scholars, was Arthur Fisher Bentley, "The Condition of the Western Farmer as Illustrated by the Economic History of a Nebraska Township," Johns Hopkins University *Studies in Historical and Political Science*, XI, Nos. 7–8 (Baltimore: The Johns Hopkins Press, 1893), 285–370.

An excellent account of the effect of monopolization of land is William Godwin Moody, *Land and Labor in the United States* (New York: Charles Scribner's Sons, 1883). An effective substantiation of Moody's charges is "Ownership of Real Estate in the Territories," *House Report* No. 3455, 49 Cong., 1 Sess. (1886). Paul Wallace Gates, "Large-Scale Farming in Illinois, 1850–1870," *Agricultural History*, VI, No. 1 (January, 1932), 14–25, contains numerous examples of huge holdings, as does also Arthur Charles Cole, *The Era of the Civil War, 1848–1870* (Vol. III of *The Centennial History of Illinois,* Clarence Walworth Alvord, ed. in chief, Springfield: Illinois Centennial Commission, 1919). Further information is given in A. J. Desmond, "America's Land Question," *The North American Review,* CXLII, No. 351 (February, 1886), 153–158, and in W. B. Hazen, "The Great Middle Region of the United States, and Its Limited Space of Arable Land," *The North American Review,* CXX, No. 246 (January, 1875), 1–34.

An early anonymous account of the bonanza farms, which exemplify so much of the agricultural practices that were being developed in the Prairies, is "The Bonanza Farms of the West," *Atlantic Monthly,* XLV, No. 267 (January, 1880), 33–44. Other treatments, listed according to the dates of their publication, are George N. Lamphere, "History of Wheat Raising in the Red River Valley," Minnesota Historical Society, *Collections,* X, Pt. 1 (St. Paul: Minnesota Historical Society, 1905), 1–33; John Lee Coulter, "Industrial History of the Valley of the Red River of the North," State Historical Society of North Dakota, *Collections,* III (Bismarck: Tribune State Printers and Binders, 1910), 529–672; Edward Van Dyke Robinson, *Early Economic Conditions and the Development of Agriculture in Minnesota* (University of Minnesota *Studies in the Social Sciences,* No. 3, Minneapolis: *Bulletin* of the University of Minnesota, 1915); Alvah H. Benton, "Large Land Holdings in North Dakota," *The Journal of Land & Public Utility Economics,* I, No. 4 (October, 1925), 405–431; and Harold E. Briggs, "Early Bonanza Farming in the Red River Valley of the North," *Agricultural History,* VI, No. 1 (January, 1932), 26–37. Other big-scale farming enterprises are noted in Charles B. Spahr, "America's Working People," *The Outlook,* LXIII, No. 10 (November 4, 1899), 558–569, and in William Allen White, "The Business of a Wheat Farmer," *Scribner's Magazine,* XXII, No. 5 (November, 1897), 531–548.

A proper introduction to the transportation problems of the farmers of the Prairies and westward is given in Robert Edgar Riegel, *The Story of the Western Railroads* (New York: The Macmillan Company, 1926). William Z[ebina] Ripley, *Railroads: Rates and Regulation* (New York: Longmans, Green and Co., 1912), is standard on company practices. Much of value can still be obtained from Arthur Twining Hadley, *Railroad Transportation, Its History and Its Laws* (New York: G. P. Putnam's Sons, c.1885). Contemporaneous with Hadley's publication was the report of the Select Committee on Interstate Commerce, which is *Senate Report* No. 46, 49 Cong., 1 Sess., Vol. I, with its revelations showing the need of regulation. William Larrabee, *The Railroad Question* (Chicago: The Schulte Publishing Company, 1893), was the work of an Iowa governor, at the height of the movement for more effective curbs on the transportation agencies. Further information and warnings are in James F[airchild] Hudson, *The Railways and the Republic* (New York: Harper & Brothers, 3d ed., 1889). Haney's *Congressional History of Railways, 1850–1887* adds something to the discussion. The conservative Eastern horror at state regulation is shown by an editorial of Edwin Lawrence Godkin, "The Latest Device for Fixing Rates of Transportation," *The Nation,* XVII, No. 420 (July 17, 1873), 36–37. Organized efforts to lower rates are revealed in *The National Convention of the American Cheap Transportation Association* (Troy, N.Y.: Whig Publishing Company, 1874).

Contemporary views of agricultural indebtedness are exemplified in W. F. Mappin, "Farm Mortgages and the Small Farmer," *Political Science Quarterly,* IV, No. 3 (September, 1889), 433–451; and in Daniel R[eaves] Goodloe, "Western Farm Mortgages," *The Forum,* X, No. 3 (November, 1890), 346–355. An official defense of the packers against the accusations of the farmers is J[onathan] Ogden Armour, *The Packers, the Private Car Lines, and the People* (Philadelphia: Henry Altemus Company, 1906). An opposite view is that of Charles Edward Russell, *The Greatest Trust in the World* (New York: The Ridgway-Thayer Company, Publishers, 1905). Improvements in the transportation of animals are noted in "Meat Animals and Packing-House Products," U.S. Department of Agriculture, Bureau of Statistics, *Bulletin* No. 40 (Washington: Government Printing Office, 1906). Financial considerations are the theme of Charles H. Cochrane, "Past, Present and Future of American Meats," *Moody's Magazine,* V, No. 1 (December, 1907), 37–39.

Contemporary views of the relations of farmers with the grain dealers include D. C. Cloud, *Monopolies and the People* (Davenport, Iowa: Day, Egbert, & Fidlar; Muscatine, Iowa: Allen Broomhall, 4th ed., 1873); an anonymous article entitled "Mr. Leiter's 'Corner' in Wheat," *The Spectator* [London], LXXX, No. 3,651

(June 18, 1898), 854–855; and Lewis Walker, "Abuses in the Grain Trade of the Northwest," American Academy of Political and Social Science, *Annals*, XVIII, No. 3 (November, 1901), 488–490. A useful pamphlet on wheat prices is James E[rnest] Boyle, *Chicago Wheat Prices for Eighty-One Years* (Ithaca?: 1922). Further problems of the marketing of wheat are discussed in *House Executive Document* No. 46, Pt. 2, 44 Cong., 2 Sess. (1880). The carelessness of the farmer in his use of the soil is shown in Edward Atkinson and L. G. Powers, "Farm Ownership and Tenancy in the United States," American Statistical Association, *Quarterly Publications*, V, No. 40, n.s. (Boston: J. P. Shults, Printer, 1897), 329–344; and in Eugene W. Hilgard, "Progress in Agriculture by Education and Government Aid," *The Atlantic Monthly*, XLIX, No. 294 (April, 1882), 531–541.

THE GREAT PLAINS AND WESTWARD

The standard histories of the West, listed in this bibliography under "Agricultural Settlement," tell a great deal about the geographic conditions, and contain occasional information about farming, but, as far as general agriculture is concerned, they naturally dwell mainly on its most prominent phase, herding. The physical basis is amply told in Nevin M[elancthon] Fenneman, *Physiography of Western United States* (New York: McGraw-Hill Book Company, Inc., 1931), and the agricultural applications are indicated in Oliver E[dwin] Baker, "Agricultural Regions of North America, Part 10—The Grazing and Irrigated Crop Region," *Economic Geography*, VII, No. 4 (October, 1931), 325–364. A pioneer effort to correlate the geographic conditions with the development of institutions is Walter Prescott Webb, *The Great Plains: A Study in Institutions and Environment* (Boston: Ginn and Company, c. 1931). An analysis of Webb's work is in Fred A[lbert] Shannon and others, *Critiques of Research in the Social Sciences: III* (New York: Social Science Research Council, 1940). A somewhat romantic consideration of the routes of travel is William Curry Holden, *Alkali Trails* (Dallas: The Southwest Press, c.1930). Briefer, and to the point, is Louis Pelzer, "Trails of the Trans-Mississippi Cattle Frontier," *The Trans-Mississippi West*, Willard and Goodykoontz, eds., pp. 139–161.

The range cattle industry got its first lengthy treatment of enduring importance from the early cattle buyer Joseph G[eiting] McCoy, in his book *Historic Sketches of the Cattle Trade of the West and Southwest* (Washington: The Rare Bookshop, new ed., 1932). The original edition of 1874 is now very rare, but the one listed is a facsimile reproduction in full. Other early accounts by cattlemen are James S[anks] Brisbin, *The Beef Bonanza: Or How to Get Rich on the Plains* (Philadelphia: J. B. Lippincott and Co., 1885), a rather overly roseate story, and Walter Baron Von Richthofen, *Cattle Raising on the Plains of North America* (New York: D. Appleton and Company, 1885). The standard recent treatises are Ernest Staples Osgood, *The Day of the Cattleman* (Minneapolis: The University of Minnesota Press, 1929); Edward Everett Dale, *The Range Cattle Industry* (Norman: University of Oklahoma Press, 1930); and Louis Pelzer, *The Cattlemen's Frontier* (Glendale, Cal.: The Arthur H. Clark Company, 1936). A brief but very enlightening pamphlet is Will[iam] C[roft] Barnes, *The Story of the Range* (Washington: Government Printing Office, 1926). A popular account is Edward Everett Dale, *Cow Country* (Norman: University of Oklahoma Press, 1942). The Eastern origins of the industry are best presented in James Westfall Thompson, *A History of Livestock Raising in the United States, 1607–1860* (U.S. Department of Agriculture, *Agricultural History Series*, No. 5, mimeographed, 1942). A good unit study of ranching is William Curry Holden, *The Spur Ranch* (Boston: The Christopher Publishing House, c.1934). The transition to modern phases of herding is told in Randall R. Howard, "The Passing of the Cattle King," *The Outlook*, XCVIII, No. 4 (May 27, 1911), 195–204. The best and most convincing story of the cowboy, told by one of the breed, is Philip Ashton Rollins, *The Cowboy* (New York: Charles Scribner's Sons, 1922). A thoughtful analysis of cowboy literature is [Edward] Douglas Branch, *The Cowboy and His Interpreters* (New York: D. Appleton and Company, 1926).

Although Western sheep herding has received only a fraction as much thoughtful attention from scholars as the cattle business, the information on the subject is abundant. Some of the best material is in federal government publications, which include H[ubert] A. Heath, "Condition of the Sheep Industry West of the Mississippi River," U.S. Department of Agriculture, Bureau of Animal Industry, *Sixth and Seventh Annual Reports* (Washington: Government Printing Office, 1891), pp. 247–320; Ezra A[yers] Carman, H[ubert] A. Heath, and John Minto, *The History and Present Condition of the Sheep Industry in the United States* (U.S. Department of Agriculture, Bureau of Animal Industry, *Special Report*, Washington: Government Printing Office, 1892); Jacob Richards Dodge, "Sheep and Wool: A Review of the Progress of American Sheep Husbandry," U.S. Department of Agriculture, *Report* No. 66 (Washington: Government Printing Office, 1900); and E. V. Wilcox, "Sheep Ranching in the Western States," U.S. Department of Agriculture, Bureau of Animal Industry, *Nineteenth Annual Report* (Washington: Government Printing Office, 1903), pp. 79–98. A historian's synthesis of some of the material is L[ouis] G[eorge] Connor, "A Brief History of the Sheep Industry in the United States," American Historical Association, *Annual Report*, 1918 (Washington: Government Printing Office, 1921), pp. 93–197. There is also something of the historical background in Fred[eric] S[amuel] Hultz and John A[rthur] Hill, *Range Sheep and Wool in the Seventeen Western States* (New York: John Wiley & Sons, Inc., 1931). Studies of the effect of protective legislation include William Draper Lewis, *Our Sheep and the Tariff* (Vol. II of *Political Economy and Public Law Series*, Philadelphia: University of Pa. Press Co., 1890); and Chester Whitney Wright, *Wool-Growing and the Tariff* (Boston: Houghton Mifflin Company, 1910).

Among the accounts of observers of Western sheep herding are E. C. Reynolds, "On a Texas Sheep Ranch," *Lippincott's Magazine*, XXXVI, o.s., No. 4 (October, 1885), 321–334; Charles Stedman Newhall, "Sheep and the Forest Reserves," *The Forum*, XXX, No. 6 (February, 1901), 710–716; Charles Moreau Harger, "Sheep and Shepherds of the West," *The Outlook*, LXXII, No. 12 (November 22, 1902), 689–693; Edwin L. Sabin, "On the Western Sheep Range," *Appleton's Booklovers Magazine*, VI, No. 5 (November, 1905), 541–546; and Randall R. Howard, "The Sheep-Herder," *The Outlook*, XCVI, No. 17 (December 24, 1910), 943–950. The contests between the herders of cattle and sheep are told in Charles Michelson, "The War for the Range," *Munsey's Magazine*, XXVIII, No. 3 (December, 1902), 380–382; E. P. Snow, "Sheepmen and Cattlemen," *The Outlook*, LXXIII, No. 14 (April 4, 1903), 839–840; Henry F. Cope, "Sheep-Herder vs. Cow-Puncher," *The World Today*, VII, No. 2 (August, 1904), 1037–1045; and A. W. North,

"The Warfare on the Ranges," *Harper's Weekly*, LIII, No. 2,742 (July 10, 1909), 11–12.

The vicissitudes of Plains farmers in adjusting themselves to the locality are well revealed in James C[laude] Malin, "The Adaptation of the Agricultural System to Sub-Humid Environment," *Agricultural History*, X, No. 3 (July, 1936), 118–141. Other studies by Malin on adaptation of the Western farmer include "The Turnover of Farm Population in Kansas," *The Kansas Historical Quarterly*, IV, No. 4 (November, 1935), 339–372; "Beginnings of Winter Wheat Production in the Upper Kansas and Lower Smoky Hill River Valleys," *ibid.*, X, No. 3 (August, 1941), 227–259; and "An Introduction to the History of the Bluestem Pasture Region of Kansas," *ibid.*, XI, No. 1 (February, 1942), 3–28. Malin's contributions on this subject were combined and completed in *Winter Wheat in the Golden Belt of Kansas* (Lawrence: University of Kansas Press, 1944). The problems of the farmers, in contests with the cattlemen, are shown in a number of federal government publications, prominent among which are Public Lands Commission, *Report*, 1880; *Senate Executive Document* No. 127, 48 Cong., 1 Sess. (1883); *House Report* No. 1325, 48 Cong., 1 Sess. (1883); *House Report* No. 1809, 47 Cong., 1 Sess. (1881); and *House Miscellaneous Document* No. 45, 47 Cong., 2 Sess. (1882), Vols. I-III.

Financial problems on the range are the central topic of Louis Pelzer, "Financial Management of the Cattle Ranges," *Journal of Economic and Business History*, II, No. 4 (August, 1930), 723–741; Charles I[seard] Bray, "Financing the Western Cattleman," Colorado Experiment Station, *Bulletin* No. 338 (Fort Collins: Colorado Agricultural College, December, 1928); T[roy] J[esse] Cauley, "Early Business Methods in the Texas Cattle Industry," *Journal of Economic and Business History*, IV, No. 3 (May, 1932), 461–486; and Edward Everett Dale, "The Cow Country in Transition," *Mississippi Valley Historical Review*, XXIV, No. 1 (June, 1937), 3–20. Rudolph Alexander Clemen, *The American Livestock and Meat Industry* (New York: The Ronald Press Company, 1923), considers these problems, among other things, as do also many of the other items in the list above.

Aside from the works by McCoy and others, before mentioned, much can be learned about the special transportation problems of the Far West from Charles S[umner] Plumb, *Marketing of Farm*

Animals (Boston: Ginn and Company, c. 1927); Ora Brooks Peake, *The Colorado Range Cattle Industry* (Glendale, Cal.: The Arthur H. Clark Company, 1937); Frederic Logan Paxson, "The Cow Country," *American Historical Review*, XXII, No. 1 (October, 1916), 65–82; Clara M. Love, "History of the Cattle Industry in the Southwest," *The Southwestern Historical Quarterly*, XIX, No. 4 (April, 1916), 370–399, cont.; and Josiah Bushnell Grinnell, "The Cattle Industries of the United States," *Agricultural Review and Journal of the American Agricultural Association*, II, No. 2 (May, 1882), 7–74. This is also a central theme in George G. Vest, chm., "The Transportation and Sale of Meat Products," *Senate Report* No. 829, 51 Cong., 1 Sess. (1889), 611 pp.; James E. Downing, "Pioneer Transportation for Livestock," *Breeder's Gazette*, LXXX, No. 8 (August 25, 1921), 249–250; J[acob] R[ichards] Dodge, ed., "The Texas Cattle Trade," U.S. Commissioner of Agriculture, *Report*, 1870 (Washington: Government Printing Office, 1871), pp. 346–352.

Other marketing problems, and relations with the meat packers, are considered by Edward W. Perry, "Live Stock and Meat Traffic of Chicago," U.S. Department of Agriculture, Bureau of Animal Industry, *First Annual Report*, 1884 (Washington: Government Printing Office, 1885), pp. 245–269; Joseph Nimmo, "Range and Ranch Cattle Traffic," *House Executive Document* No. 267, 48 Cong., 2 Sess. (1885); John T. McNeeley, "The Cattle Industry of Colorado, Wyoming, and Nevada, and the Sheep Industry of Colorado in 1897," U.S. Department of Agriculture, Bureau of Animal Industry, *Fifteenth Annual Report*, 1898 (Washington: Government Printing Office, 1899), pp. 377–381; and Louis F[ranklin] Swift and Arthur Van Vlissingen, *The Yankee of the Yards: The Biography of Gustavus Franklin Swift* (Chicago: A. W. Shaw Company, 1927). Information on the subject is also in John Clay, *My Life on the Range* (Chicago: privately printed, c. 1924); Frank S[tewart] Hastings, *A Ranchman's Recollections* (Chicago: The Breeder's Gazette, 1921); and Dan W. Greenburg, *Sixty Years, . . . The Cattle Industry in Wyoming* . . . . (Cheyenne: Wyoming Stock Growers Association, 1932). The special marketing problems of sheep herders are considered in Arthur Harrison Cole, *The American Wool Manufacture* (2 vols., Cambridge: Harvard University Press, 1926).

Various matters of public policy can be best gleaned, though painfully, from the state laws, many of which are listed in the footnotes herein. The histories of the range country also are studded with information on the subject. The following, in addition to many entries above, are useful on this phase of Western economic life: National Stock Growers' Convention, *Proceedings*, Vol. I (Denver: News Job Printing Company, 1898); Frank Wilkeson, "Cattle-Raising on the Plains," *Harper's New Monthly Magazine*, LXXII, No. 431 (April, 1886), 788–795; W. E. Guthrie, "The Open Range Cattle Business in Wyoming," *Annals of Wyoming*, V, No. 1 (July, 1927), 26–31; and William E. Smythe, "The Struggle for Water in the West," *Atlantic Monthly*, LXXXVI, No. 517 (November, 1900), 646–654.

EASTERN AND PACIFIC COAST SPECIALIZATION

The evidences of the effect of Western competition on farming in the East are well presented in Frederick I[rving] Anderson, *The Farmer of Tomorrow* (New York: The Macmillan Company, 1913); Philip Morgan and Alvan F. Sanborn, "The Problems of Rural New England," *The Atlantic Monthly*, LXXIX, No. 475 (May, 1897), 577–598; and William H. Brewer, "The Past and Future of Connecticut Agriculture," Secretary of the Connecticut Board of Agriculture, *Twenty-Fourth Annual Report*, 1890 (Hartford: The Case, Lockwood & Brainard Company, 1891) pp. 153–175. Abandoned farms, as a consequence of this competition, are the subject of William Henry Bishop, "Hunting an Abandoned Farm in Connecticut," *The Century*, XLVII, o.s., No. 6 (April, 1894), 915–924; Charles C. Nott, "A Good Farm for Nothing," *The Nation*, XLIX, No. 1,273 (November 21, 1889), 406–408; Clifton Johnson, "The Deserted Homes of New England," *The Cosmopolitan*, XV, No. 2 (June, 1893), pp. 215–222; J[ames] Madison Gathany, "What's the Matter with the Eastern Farmer?", *The Outlook*, CXXVI, No. 3 (September 15, 1920), 105–109, cont.; and Frederick H. Fowler, "Abandoned Farms," *Cyclopedia of American Agriculture*, IV, 102–107. C. N. Hall, "Some Features of Old Connecticut Farming," *New England Magazine*, XXII, n.s., No. 5 (July, 1900), 549–557, deals with all the foregoing problems of this section. Joseph B. Walker, "The Progress of New England Agriculture during the Last Thirty Years," *New Englander and Yale Review*, XLVII, No.

211 (October, 1887), 233–245, discusses the new farming methods of the East, as do also parts of T[heodore] S[edgwick] Gold, *Handbook of Connecticut Agriculture* (Hartford: The Case, Lockwood & Brainard Co., 1901). A phase of Eastern adjustment, as well as of specialization, in many parts of the country is the theme of Clarence H[enry] Eckles, *Dairy Cattle and Milk Production* (New York: The Macmillan Company, 3d ed., 1939). Aside from the *Yearbooks* and *Reports* of the Department of Agriculture, and the voluminous information in the various census reports, Lee Cleveland Corbett, *Garden Farming* (Boston: Ginn and Company, c. 1913), is also useful on his subject.

Early notes on conditions in the Pacific coast region are contained in Samuel Bowles, *Across the Continent* (New York: Samuel Bowles & Company, 1869). Another early account, written in true California style, is R[olander] Guy McClellan, *The Golden State* (Philadelphia: William Flint & Company, ed. of 1876). Some information is also contained in Albert S[idney] Bolles, *Industrial History of the United States* (Norwich, Conn.: The Henry Bill Publishing Company, 1879). William L. Merry, "Commercial Future of the Pacific States," *The Forum,* XII (November, 1891), 410–417, is hopeful in tone. J. R. Caldwell, "The First Fruits of the Land," *Oregon Historical Quarterly,* VII, No. 1 (March, 1906), 28–38, is an account of early Oregon. E[dward] J[ames] Wickson, *California Nurserymen and the Plant Industry, 1850–1910* (Los Angeles: The California Association of Nurserymen, 1921), is a full-length account of the fruit industry, but the biennial reports of the California, Oregon, and Washington boards of horticulture are more comforting in their completeness.

GOVERNMENTAL ACTIVITIES

The part played by the states in fostering agriculture is one of the many things considered in Edward Wiest, *Agricultural Organization in the United States* (Vol. II of University of Kentucky *Studies in Economics and Sociology,* Lexington: University of Kentucky, 1923). William L[awrence] Wanlass, *The United States Department of Agriculture* (Johns Hopkins University *Studies in Historical and Political Science,* XXXVIII, No. 1, Baltimore: The Johns Hopkins Press, 1920), is a satisfactory discussion of the rise of the

federal agency. Other writings include M[ilton] S[tover] Eisen-
hower and A[rthur] P[ercy] Chew, "The United States Department
of Agriculture," U.S. Department of Agriculture, *Miscellaneous
Publication* No. 88 (Washington: Government Printing Office,
1934); Charles H[oward] Greathouse, *Historical Sketch of the
United States Department of Agriculture* (U.S. Department of
Agriculture, Division of Publications, *Bulletin* No. 3, Washington:
Government Printing Office, 2d rev., 1907); and W[illet] M[artin]
Hays, "The United States Department of Agriculture," *The Outlook*,
LXXX, No. 14 (August 5, 1905), 863–867. The substance of Alfred
Charles True's several articles on education, in the *Yearbooks* of
the United States Department of Agriculture, is contained in *A
History of Agricultural Education in the United States, 1785–1925*
(U.S. Department of Agriculture, *Miscellaneous Publication* No. 36,
Washington: Government Printing Office, 1929). The most thor-
ough work on the origin of the state agricultural colleges is Earle
D[udley] Ross, *Democracy's College: The Land-Grant Movement
in the Formative Stages* (Ames: Iowa State College Press, 1942).
He gives, perhaps, too little credit to Jonathan B. Turner, but this
can be offset by Eugene Davenport, *History of Collegiate Edu-
cation in Agriculture* (Urbana: University of Illinois, 1907), a brief
but pointed discussion. A good case study is Ronald J[ames] Slay,
The Development of the Teaching of Agriculture in Mississippi
(New York: Columbia University, Bureau of Publications, Teachers College, 1928). Broad phases of the subject are developed in
Whitney H[art] Shepardson, *Agricultural Education in the United
States* (New York: The Macmillan Company, 1929).

Several of the preceding list contain material on the experiment
stations. The best on this subject is Alfred Charles True, *A History
of Agricultural Experimentation and Research in the United States,
1607–1925, Including a History of the United States Department of
Agriculture* (U. S. Department of Agriculture, *Miscellaneous Publication* No. 251, Washington: Government Printing Office, 1937).
Also, with V. A. Clark, he published a history and an account of the
work of the various stations, *Agricultural Experiment Stations in the
United States* (U. S. Department of Agriculture, Office of Experiment Stations, *Bulletin* No. 80, Washington: Government Printing
Office, 1900). It is well to supplement these with Eugene Davenport, *The Relations between the Federal Department of Agriculture*

and the Agricultural Colleges and Experiment Stations (Urbana: University of Illinois, 1913), in which an agricultural college dean speaks from long experience of some things other than pleasant relations. Some of the intricacies of the work are shown in W[ilbur] O[lin] Atwater, "Organization of the Agricultural Experiment Stations in the United States, . . . 1889," U.S. Department of Agriculture, Office of Experiment Stations, *Experiment Station Bulletin* No. 1 (Washington: Government Printing Office, 1889).

The amazing amount of work carried on directly or otherwise by the United States Department of Agriculture is well revealed by a series of articles in its *Yearbook* for 1899. These include, aside from several of the contributions of A. C. True, the following: F. H. Bigelow, "Work of the Meteorologist for the Benefit of Agriculture, Commerce, and Navigation," pp. 71–92; D. E. Salmon. "Some Examples of the Development of Knowledge Concerning Animal Diseases," pp. 93–134; L. O. Howard, "Progress in Economic Entomology in the United States," pp. 135–156; B. T. Galloway, "Progress in the Treatment of Plant Diseases in the United States," pp. 191–200; Harvey W. Wiley, "The Relation of Chemistry to the Progress of Agriculture," pp. 201–258; T. S. Palmer, "A Review of Economic Ornithology in the United States," pp. 259–292; Gifford Pinchot, "Progress of Forestry in the United States," pp. 293–306; George K. Holmes, "Progress of Agriculture in the United States," pp. 307–334; Milton Whitney, "Soil Investigations in the United States," pp. 335–346; F. Lamson-Scribner, "Progress of Economic and Scientific Agrostology," pp. 347–366; Maurice O. Eldridge, "Progress of Road Building in the United States," pp. 367–380; Henry E. Alvord, "Dairy Development in the United States," pp. 381–402; A. C. True and R. D. Milner, "Development of the Nutrition Investigations of the Department of Agriculture," pp. 403–414; George F. Thompson, "Administrative Work of the Federal Government in Relation to the Animal Industry," pp. 441–464; Herbert J. Webber and Ernst A. Bessey, "Progress of Plant Breeding in the United States," pp. 465–490; and Charles H. Greathouse, "Development of Agricultural Libraries," pp. 491–512. These articles are in addition to several others of a historical nature, but not directly connected with the activities of the Department of Agriculture. Extension work of the Department is best presented in Alfred Charles True, *A History of Agricultural Extension Work in the United States, 1785–1923* (U. S. Department of Agriculture, *Miscellaneous Publication* No. 15, Washington: Government Printing Office, 1928).

AGRARIAN DISCONTENT

A good brief discussion of this subject is Solon Justus Buck, *The Agrarian Crusade* (Vol. XLV of *Chronicles of America Series*, New Haven: Yale University Press, 1921). Because of the close connection of grangerism with the cooperative movement, works on the Patrons· of Husbandry appear in the next section. The fiscal problems of the time are sufficiently well summarized in Davis Rich Dewey, *Financial History of the United States* (New York: Longmans, Green and Co., 8th ed., 1922). The [United States] Industrial Commission, *Report* (Washington: Government Printing Office, 1900–1902), especially Vol. XIX, contains much information on general economic conditions. An excellent analysis of the underlying conditions of farmer discontent is in John D[onald] Hicks, *The Populist Revolt* (Minneapolis: The University of Minnesota Press, c. 1931). Special phases of the background are also contained in, or can be deduced from, George F[rederick] Warren, "Prices of Farm Products in the United States," U.S. Department of Agriculture, *Department Bulletin* No. 999 (Washington: Government Printing Office, 1921); and H[arry] T[urner] Newcomb· and Edward G. Ward, "Changes in the Rates of Charge for Railway and Other Transportation Services," U.S. Department of Agriculture, Division of Statistics, *Miscellaneous Series, Bulletin* No. 15, Revised (Washington: Government Printing Office, 1901). Quite specific are John D. Barnhart, "Rainfall and the Populist Party in Nebraska," *American Political Science Review*, XIX, No. 3 (August, 1925), 527–540; Hallie Farmer, "The Economic Background of Frontier Populism," *Mississippi Valley Historical Review*, X, No. 4 (March, 1924), 406–427; Earl W. Hayter, "The Western Farmers and the Drivewell Patent Controversy," *Agricultural History*, XVI, No. 1 (January, 1942), 16–28; and Hayter, "An Iowa Farmers' Protective Association: A Barbed Wire Patent Protest Movement," *The Iowa Journal of History and Politics*, XXXVII, No. 4 (October, 1939), 331–362. Two articles showing the usual Eastern misunderstanding of Western conditions are [Edwin Lawrence Godkin], "Inflation and the

West," *The Nation*, VI, No. 140 (March 5, 1868), 187–190; and [Godkin], "The Debtor Class," *ibid.*, XVIII, No. 460 (April 23, 1874), 262–263.

Because of its scant effect on the farmers' uprising, the greenback movement is only casually mentioned in this work, and the material in Dewey's *Financial History*, together with that in Nathan Fine, *Labor and Farmer Parties in the United States, 1828–1928* (New York: Rand School of Social Science, c. 1928); and in Fred E[mory] Haynes, *Third Party Movements since the Civil War, with Special Reference to Iowa: A Study in Social Politics* (Iowa City: State Historical Society of Iowa, 1916), is deemed sufficient.

A rather unsympathetic early treatment of the Populists was published for the American Economic Association and written by Frank LeRond McVey, *The Populist Movement* (New York: The Macmillan Company, 1896). The most complete and authoritative work to date is Hicks, *The Populist Revolt* (mentioned above). Accounts of the Farmers' Alliances and Populism, or related movements, for the different states include Francis Butler Simkins, *The Tillman Movement in South Carolina* (Durham: Duke University Press, 1926); C[omer] Vann Woodward, *Tom Watson: Agrarian Rebel* (New York: The Macmillan Company, 1938); J. D. Hicks, "The Political Career of Ignatius Donnelly," *Mississippi Valley Historical Review*, VIII, Nos. 1–2 (June–September, 1921), 80–132; Alex Mathews Arnett, *The Populist Movement in Georgia* (New York: n.p., 1922); Herman Clarence Nixon, "The Economic Basis of the Populist Movement in Iowa," *Iowa Journal of History and Politics*, XXI, No. 3 (July, 1923), 373–396; Nixon, "The Populist Movement in Iowa," *ibid.*, XXIV, No. 1 (January, 1926), 3–107; William DuBose Sheldon, *Populism in the Old Dominion: Virginia Farm Politics, 1885–1900* (Princeton: Princeton University Press, 1935); Leon W. Fuller, "Colorado's Revolt against Capitalism," *Mississippi Valley Historical Review*, XXI, No. 3 (December, 1934), 343–360; Daniel M. Robinson, "Tennessee Politics and the Agrarian Revolt, 1886–1896," *ibid.*, XX, No. 3 (December, 1933), 365–380; Chester McA[rthur] Destler, "Consummation of a Labor-Populist Alliance in Illinois, 1894," *ibid.*, XXVII, No. 4 (March, 1941), 589–602; Sidney Glazer, "Patrons of Industry in Michigan," *ibid.*, XXIV, No. 2 (September, 1937), 185–194; and Harvey Wish, "John P. Altgeld and the Background of the Campaign of 1896," *ibid.*, XXIV,

No. 4 (March, 1938), 503–518. Some dissensions within the movement are shown in H. C. Nixon, "The Cleavage within the Farmers' Alliance Movement," *ibid.*, XV, No. 1 (June, 1928), 22–33. One of the most vicious attacks on the movement was Frank Basil Tracy, "Rise and Doom of the Populist Party," *The Forum*, XVI, No. 2 (October, 1893), 241–250. The best account of the campaign of 1896 is still William Jennings Bryan, *The First Battle* (Chicago: W. B. Conkey, c. 1896). The work of the silver Republicans is well told by Elmer Ellis, *Henry Moore Teller, Defender of the West* (Caldwell, Idaho: The Caxton Printers, 1941).

COOPERATIVES

That the zeal for cooperation far outdistanced the results is revealed in part by the voluminous literature on the subject. The purpose here is merely to present a few of the general works and special treatments of different phases of the movement. A good comprehensive survey is Herman Steen, *Coöperative Marketing* (Garden City: Doubleday, Page & Company, 1923), but production and buying agencies are not considered. E[dwin] G[riswold] Nourse, *The Philosophy of Co-operative Marketing* (Pan American Union, Division of Agricultural Cooperation, *Series on Cooperatives*, No. 1, Washington: mimeographed, April, 1936), is a small item with the same limitations. Eward W[ebster] Bemis, "Coöperation in New England," Johns Hopkins University *Studies in Historical and Political Science*, VI, Nos. 1–2 (Baltimore: Johns Hopkins University, 1888), is a part of a symposium on the subject, valuable for the period covered. Clarence N. Ousley, "A Lesson in Co-operation," *The Popular Science Monthly*, XXXVI, No. 6 (April, 1890), 821–828, is a good microscopic example. Edward W. Bemis, "Cooperative Distribution," U.S. Department of Labor, *Bulletin* No. 6 (Washington: Government Printing Office, 1896), 610–644, helps balance the story. General articles on farmers' cooperatives include John Lee Coulter, "Organization among the Farmers of the United States," *Yale Review*, XVIII, No. 3 (November, 1909), 273–298; James B. Morman, "Business Coöperative Organizations in Agriculture," *Cyclopedia of American Agriculture*, IV, 255–264; E. K. Eyerly, "Co-operative Movements among Farmers," American Academy of Political and Social Science, *Annals*, XL (March, 1912),

58–68; E. E. Miller, "The American Farmer as a Coöperator," *The Forum*, LII, No. 4 (October, 1914), 595–602. Clarence [Hamilton] Poe, *How Farmers Co-operate and Double Profits* (New York: Orange Judd Company, 1915), is a book of 244 pages on the subject. N. B. Ashby, *The Riddle of the Sphinx* (Chicago: Mercantile Publishing and Advertising Co., 1892), is the work of a Farmers' Alliance man.

The standard reference on the Patrons of Husbandry is Solon Justus Buck, *The Granger Movement, . . . 1870–1880* (Vol. XIX of *Harvard Historical Studies,* Cambridge: Harvard University Press, 1913). The story of the rise of the movement, written by the founder, is O[liver] H[udson] Kelley, *Origin and Progress of the Order of the Patrons of Husbandry in the United States from 1866 to 1873* (Philadelphia: J. A. Wagenseller, 1875). Still earlier accounts by participants in the movement are Jonathan Periam, *The Groundswell* (Cincinnati: E. Hannaford & Company, 1874), and A. B. Smedley, *The Principles and Aims of the Patrons of Husbandry* (Burlington, Iowa: R. T. Root, 1874). Much documentary material is contained in John R[ogers] Commons and others, eds., *A Documentary History of American Industrial Society,* Vol. X (Cleveland: The Arthur H. Clark Company, 1911).

Special Southern problems are considered in William O. Scroggs, "Economic Experiments in Coöperation since 1865," *The South in the Building of the Nation,* VI, 580–583; and O[mer] W[esley] Herrmann, *Cooperative Cotton Marketing in the United States* (Pan American Union, Division of Agricultural Cooperation, *Series on Cooperatives,* No. 3, Washington: mimeographed, November, 1936).

The farmers' grain elevator activity is described in Lawrence Farlow, *The Farmers Elevator Movement in Illinois* (Farmers Grain Dealers Association of Illinois, 1928); Joseph B[ernard] Kenkel, *The Cooperative Elevator Movement* (Washington: Catholic University of America, 1922); J[oseph] M[artin] Mehl, "Cooperative Grain Marketing," U.S. Department of Agriculture, *Department Bulletin* No. 937 (Washington: Government Printing Office, April 9, 1921); and J[ames] W[arren] Cummins, *The Cooperative Marketing of Grain in the United States* (Pan American Union, Division of Agricultural Cooperation, *Series on Cooperatives,* No. 7, Washington: mimeographed, September, 1937). On this and other sub-

jects is R[alph] H[enry] Elsworth, "Agricultural Cooperative Associations, Marketing and Purchasing, 1925," U.S. Department of
Agriculture, *Technical Bulletin* No. 40 (Washington: Government
Printing Office, January, 1928). Another activity of the grain belt is
discussed by Roland Willey Bartlett, *Cooperation in Marketing
Dairy Products* (Springfield, Ill.: Charles C. Thomas, Publisher,
1931).

The marketing of livestock is the central theme of Robert Lee
Hunt, *A History of Farmer Movements in the Southwest* (n.p.,
n.d.); W. S. Harwood, "Coöperation in the West," *The Atlantic
Monthly,* LXXXV, No. 510 (April, 1900), 539–546; Edwin G[ris-
wold] Nourse and Joseph G[rant] Knapp, *The Co-operative Market-
ing of Livestock* (Washington: The Brookings Institution, 1931);
S. W. Doty, "Cooperative Livestock Shipping Associations," U.S.
Department of Agriculture, *Farmers' Bulletin* No. 718 (Washington:
Government Printing Office, April 10, 1916); U.S. Department of
Agriculture, *Monthly Report,* February and March, 1875 (Washing-
ton: Government Printing Office, 1875); Duane Howard Doane,
"The Coöperative Lamb Club as an Agency for Lower Marketing
Costs," American Academy of Political and Social Science, *Annals,*
L (November, 1913), 216–222; and C[ortes] G[ilbert] Randell,
"Cooperative Marketing of Livestock in the United States by Ter-
minal Associations," U.S. Department of Agriculture, *Technical
Bulletin* No. 57 (Washington: Government Printing Office, Febru-
ary, 1928).

The special problems of Pacific coast fruit shippers are handled
by Rahno Mabel MacCurdy, *The History of the California Fruit
Growers Exchange* (Los Angeles: 1925); John William Lloyd,
*Co-operative and Other Organized Methods of Marketing Cali-
fornia Horticultural Products* (University of Illinois *Studies in the
Social Sciences,* VIII, No. 1, Urbana: University of Illinois, c. 1919);
Ira B[rown] Cross, "Co-operation in California," *American Eco-
nomic Review,* I, No. 3 (September, 1911), 535–544; A[ndrew]
W[illiam] McKay, "Organization and Development of a Coopera-
tive Citrus-Fruit Marketing Agency," U.S. Department of Agricul-
ture, *Department Bulletin* No. 1,237 (Washington: Government
Printing Office, May, 1924); A. W. McKay and W[ayne] Mackenzie
Stevens, "Operating Methods and Expenses of Cooperative Citrus-
Fruit Marketing Agencies," U.S. Department of Agriculture, *De-*

partment Bulletin No. 1261 (Washington: Government Printing Office, July 22, 1924); J. L. Nagle, "California Fruit Exchange," Thirty-Eighth Fruit Growers' Convention of the State of California, 1910, *Proceedings* (Sacramento: W. W. Shannon, Superintendent of State Printing, 1911), pp. 60–62; and A. W. McKay, *Cooperative Marketing of Fruits and Vegetables in the United States* (Pan American Union, Division of Agricultural Cooperation, *Series on Cooperatives,* No. 10, Washington: mimeographed, April, 1938).

THE FARMER AND THE NATION

Source materials, and especially the census reports, are the main reliance for data on population, wealth, income, and farming classes. In determining what part of rural population lived on the farm P[ascal] K[idder] Whelpton, "Occupational Groups in the United States, 1820–1920," *Journal of the American Statistical Association,* XXI, No. 155 (September, 1926), 335–343, is useful. Carefully compiled materials on wealth and income are in Robert F[itz-Randolph] Martin, *National Income in the United States, 1799–1938* (National Industrial Conference Board, *Studies,* No. 241, New York: National Industrial Conference Board, Inc., c. 1939); *The Agricultural Problem in the United States* (New York: National Industrial Conference Board, Inc., 1926); and Robert R[utherford] Doane, *The Measurement of American Wealth . . . from 1860 to 1933* (New York: Harper & Brothers Publishers, 1933). For exports see Frank H[arris] Hitchcock, "Agricultural Exports of the United States, 1851–1902," U.S. Department of Agriculture, Division of Foreign Markets, *Bulletin* No. 34 (Washington: Government Printing Office, 1903); and Frederick Strauss, "The Composition of Gross Farm Income since the Civil War," National Bureau of Economic Research, *Bulletin* No. 78 (New York: April 28, 1940). Testimony and an analysis of farm labor are in the Industrial Commission, *Report,* Vol. X, and Vol. XI, Pt. 3. A better understanding of the matter is in George K[irby] Holmes, "Supply of Farm Labor," U.S. Department of Agriculture, Bureau of Statistics, *Bulletin* No. 94 (Washington: Government Printing Office, 1912); and the same author's "Wages of Farm Labor," *ibid.,* No. 99 (1912). Further statistical aid is in the National Resources Committee study. Warren S[impson] Thompson, "Urban Population Changes," *Popu-*

lation Statistics (Washington: Government Printing Office, 1937), Pt. 3, Sec. 1, pp. 1–31. For theories regarding safety valves see Fred A[lbert] Shannon, "A Post Mortem on the Labor-Safety-Valve Theory," *Agricultural History*, XIX, No. 1 (January, 1945), pp. 31–37.

The housing situation is treated somewhat in retrospect in Bruce L. Melvin, *Farm and Village Housing* (Vol. VII of *Publications of the President's Conference on Home Building and Home Ownership,* John M. Gries and James Ford, general eds., Washington: The Conference, c. 1932). Contemporary writings, reminiscences, and recollections touch incidentally on the subject of the whole family life. Such include W. C. Flagg, "The Agriculture of Illinois, 1683–1876," Illinois Department of Agriculture, *Transactions,* 1875 (Springfield: State Journal Book and Stereotype Rooms, 1876), pp. 286–346; Seraphina Gardner Smith, ed., *Recollections of the Pioneers of Lee County* (Dixon, Ill.: 1893); A. F. Murphy, "The John Murphy Family as Pioneers in Illinois," Illinois State Historical Society, *Journal,* XVIII, No. 2 (July, 1925), 422–431; Charles Wesley Marsh, *Recollections, 1837–1910* (Chicago: Farm Implement News Company, 1910); and Isaac Phillips Roberts, *The Farmstead* (New York: The Macmillan Company, 1900). Some idea of efforts at improved sanitation can be gained from William Paul Gerhard, *Sanitation, Water Supply and Sewage Disposal of Country Houses* (New York: D. Van Nostrand Company, 1909); Theobald Smith, "Sewage Disposal on the Farm, and the Protection of Drinking Water," U.S. Department of Agriculture, *Farmers' Bulletin* No. 43 (Washington: Government Printing Office, 1896); and Harvey B[rown] Bashore, *The Sanitation of a Country House* (New York: John Wiley & Sons, 1905).

Rural schools are discussed in George Cary Eggleston, *Recollections of a Varied Life* (New York: Henry Holt and Company, 1910); *idem, The First of the Hoosiers* (Philadelphia: Drexel Biddle, c. 1903); and are the main theme of Edward Eggleston, *The Hoosier Schoolmaster* (New York: Grossett & Dunlap edn., 1892); *idem, The Hoosier Schoolboy* (New York: Charles Scribner's Sons, 1914); and Belle Cushman Bohn, "Early Wisconsin School Teachers," *Wisconsin Magazine of History*, XXIII, No. 1 (September, 1939), 58–61. Material on church and school, as well as other phases of farm life are in Thomas Huston MacBride, *In Cabins and Sod-Houses* (Iowa City: State Historical Society of Iowa, 1928); Hamlin Garland, *Boy Life on the Prairie* (New York: Harper & Brothers Publishers, 1899); Christiana Holmes Tillson, *A Woman's Story of Pioneer Illinois* (Chicago: R. R. Donnelley & Sons Company, 1919); and Mary Austin, *Earth Horizon, Autobiography* (Boston: Houghton Mifflin Company, c. 1932).

Appendix

ACREAGE, PRODUCTION, VALUE, PRICES, AND EXPORTS OF COTTON
IN THE UNITED STATES, 1866 TO 1898, INCLUSIVE

Year	Area	Average yield of an acre	Production	Average farm price of a pound, Dec. 1	Value	Domestic exports, fiscal years beginning July 1
	(Acres)	(Bales)	(Bales)	(Cents)	(Dollars)	(Bales of 500 pounds)
1866	6,300,000 a	.33	2,097,254		204,561,896	1,322,947
1867	7,000,000	.36	2,519,554		199,583,510	1,569,527
1868	7,000,000	.34	2,366,467		226,794,168	1,288,655
1869	7,750,000	.40	3,122,551	16.5	261,067,037	1,917,117
1870	8,680,000	.50	4,352,317	12.1	292,703,086	2,925,856
1871	7,378,000	.40	2,974,351	17.9	242,672,804	1,867,074
1872	8,500,000	.46	3,930,508	16.5	280,552,629	2,400,127
1873	9,350,000	.45	4,170,388	14.1	289,853,486	2,717,204
1874	10,982,000	.35	3,832,991	13.0	228,113,080	2,520,837
1875	10,803,030	.43	4,632,313	11.1	233,109,945	2,982,801
1876	11,677,250	.38	4,474,069	9.9	211,655,041	2,890,738
1877	12,600,000	.38	4,773,865	10.5	235,721,194	3,215,067
1878	12,266,800	.41	5,074,155	8.2	193,467,706	3,256,745
1879	12,595,500	.46	5,761,252	10.2	242,140,987	3,644,122
1880	15,475,300	.43	6,605,750	9.8	280,266,242	4,381,857
1881	16,710,730	.33	5,456,048	10.0	294,135,547	3,479,951
1882	16,791,557	.41	6,949,756	9.9	309,696,500	4,576,150
1883	16,777,993	.34	5,713,200	9.0	250,594,750	3,725,145
1884	17,439,612	.33	5,706,165	9.2	253,993,385	3,783,318
1885	18,300,865	.36	6,575,691	8.5	269,989,812	4,116,074
1886	18,454,603	.35	6,505,087	8.1	309,381,938	4,338,914
1887	18,641,067	.38	7,046,833	8.5	337,972,453	4,528,241
1888	19,058,591	.36	6,938,290	8.5	354,454,340	4,769,633
1889	20,171,896	.36	7,311,322	8.3	402,951,814	4,943,599
1890	20,809,053	.42	8,652,597	8.6	369,568,858	5,814,717
1891	20,714,937	.44	9,035,379	7.3	326,513,298	5,870,439
1892	18,067,924	.37	6,700,365	8.4	262,252,286	4,424,230
1893	19,525,000	.39	7,549,817	7.0	274,479,637	5,366,564
1894	23,687,950	.42	9,901,251	4.6	287,120,818	7,034,866
1895	20,184,808	.36	7,161,094	7.6	260,338,096	4,670,452
1896	23,273,209	.37	8,532,705	6.6	291,811,564	6,207,509
1897	24,319,584	.45	10,897,857	6.6	319,491,412	7,700,528
1898	24,967,295	.45	11,189,205	5.7	305,467,041	7,546,820

a estimated.
Source: *Agricultural Yearbook*, 1899, pp. 764–765. These figures do not correspond at all points with those in the *Statistical Abstract of the United States* for 1909, p. 587, but either set is adequate for illustration of trends.

LABOR IN THE PRODUCTION OF TWENTY BUSHELS (1 ACRE) OF WHEAT

Hand Method, 1829–1830

Four different persons and two oxen worked ten hours a day to produce the 200 bushels used as a basis for this estimate.

Work done	Machine, implement, or tool used	Motive power	Persons necessary on one machine	Men and animals at work			
				Total number	Time for work, h. m.	Pay per diem, dollars	Labor cost, dollars
Breaking ground	Plow	Ox	1 man	1 man	6–40	.50	.3333
				2 oxen	13–20	.12½	.1667
Sowing seed	Sack	Hand	1 man	1 man	1–15	.50	.0625
Pulverizing top soil and covering seed	Brush	Ox	1 man	1 man	2–30	.50	.1250
				2 oxen	5	.12½	.0625
Reaping, binding, shocking	Sickles	Hand	1 man	2 men	20	.75	1.5000
Hauling sheaves to barn	Wagon	Ox	2 men	2 men	4	.50	.2000
				2 oxen	4	.12½	.0500
Threshing, stacking straw	Flail, Pitchfork	Hand	1 man	4 men	13–20	.50	.6667
Winnowing	Shovel, measure, sheet on rods	Hand	3 men	3 men	10	.50	.5000
Gathering up and sacking	Shovel, measure, needle	Hand	1 man	1 man	3–20	.50	.1667
Total labor cost							3.8334
Average labor cost for one bushel							.1917
Ratio of labor cost of one bushel to common laborer's daily pay							38.34%

Machine Method, 1895–1896

Six different persons and 36 horses worked ten hours a day to produce the 20,000 bushels used as a basis for this estimate.

Work done	Machine, implement, or tool used	Motive power	Persons necessary on one machine	Men and animals at work			
				Total number	Time for work, h. m.	Pay per diem, dollars	Labor cost, dollars
Breaking ground	Disc gang plow	Horse	1 man 12 h.	3 men 36 h.	1 12	1.50 .50	.1500 .6000
Sowing seed	Broadcast seeder	Horse	2 men 2 h.	2 men 2 h.	15 15	1.50 .50	.0375 .0125
Pulverizing topsoil and covering seed	Five-section harrow	Horse	1 man 8 h.	2 men 16 h.	12 1–36	1.50 .50	.0300 .0800
Reaping, threshing, sacking	Combine	Horse	4 men	Separator tender	15	4.50	.1125
				Header tender	15	3.00	.0750
				Sack sewer	15	2.50	.0625
				Driver	15	2.50	.0625
			26 h.	26 h.	6–30	.50	.3250
Hauling to granary	Wagons and tenders	Horse	1 man 8 h.	2 men 16 h.	52 6–58	1.50 .50	.1305 .3480
Total labor cost							2.0260
Average labor cost for one bushel.							.1013
Ratio of labor cost of one bushel to common laborer's daily pay							6.75%

Tables are given in the same source for production with steam tractor power, showing just a little over half the cost for each bushel. But, since the daily rental value of the tractor and cost of fuel are not included the data are useless for comparison.

Source: U.S. Commissioner of Labor, *Thirteenth Annual Report*, 1898: *Hand and Machine Labor* (Washington: Government Printing Office, 1899), II, 470–473.

WHEAT STATISTICS, 1866–1898

Year	Area (Acres)	Average yield of an acre (Bushels)	Production (Bushels)	Average farm price of a bushel Dec. 1 (Cents)	Farm value December 1 (Dollars)	Domestic exports including flour, fiscal years beginning July 1 (Bushels)	Export price based on wheat alone without flour (Cents)	Wheat alone exported (Mil. bu.)
1866	15,424,496	9.9	151,999,906	152.7	232,109,630	12,646,941	141	6
1867	18,321,561	11.6	212,441,400	145.2	308,387,146	25,284,803	127	6
1868	18,460,132	12.1	224,036,600	108.5	243,032,746	29,717,201	190	16
1869	19,181,004	13.6	260,146,900	76.5	199,024,996	53,900,780	139	18
1870	18,992,591	12.4	235,884,700	94.4	222,766,969	52,580,111	129	37
1871	19,943,893	11.6	230,722,400	114.5	264,075,851	38,995,755	132	34
1872	20,858,359	11.9	249,997,100	111.4	278,522,068	52,014,715	147	26
1873	22,171,676	12.7	281,264,700	106.9	300,669,533	91,510,398	131	39
1874	24,967,027	12.3	308,102,700	86.3	265,881,167	72,912,817	143	71
1875	26,381,512	11.1	292,136,000	89.5	261,396,926	74,750,682	112	53
1876	27,627,021	10.4	289,356,500	96.3	278,697,238	57,043,936	124	55
1877	26,277,546	13.9	364,194,146	105.7	385,089,444	92,071,726	117	40
1878	32,108,560	13.1	420,122,400	77.6	325,814,119	150,502,506	134	72
1879	32,545,950	13.8	448,756,630	110.8	497,030,142	180,304,180	107	122
1880	37,986,717	13.1	498,549,868	95.1	474,201,850	186,321,514	125	153
1881	37,709,020	10.2	383,280,090	119.2	456,880,427	121,892,389	111	151
1882	37,067,194	13.6	504,185,470	88.2	445,602,125	147,811,316	119	95
1883	36,455,593	11.6	421,086,160	91.1	383,649,272	111,534,182	113	106
1884	39,475,885	13.0	512,765,000	64.5	330,862,260	132,570,366	107	70
1885	34,189,246	10.4	357,112,000	77.1	275,320,390	94,565,793	86	85
1886	36,806,184	12.4	457,218,000	68.7	314,226,020	153,804,969	87	58
1887	37,641,783	12.1	456,329,000	68.1	310,612,960	119,624,344	89	102
1888	37,336,138	11.1	415,868,000	92.6	385,248,030	88,600,742	85	66
1889	38,123,859	12.9	490,560,000	69.8	342,491,707	109,430,467	90	46
1890	36,087,154	11.1	399,262,000	83.8	334,773,678	106,181,316	83	54
1891	39,916,897	15.3	611,780,000	83.9	513,472,711	225,665,812	93	55
1892	38,554,430	13.4	515,949,000	62.4	322,111,881	191,912,635	103	157
1893	34,629,418	11.4	396,131,725	53.8	213,171,381	164,283,129	80	117
1894	34,882,436	13.2	460,267,416	49.1	225,902,025	144,812,718	67	88
1895	34,047,332	13.7	467,102,947	50.9	237,938,998	126,443,968	57	76
1896	34,618,646	12.4	427,684,346	72.6	310,602,539	145,124,972	65	61
1897	39,465,066	13.4	530,149,168	80.8	428,547,121	217,306,005	75	80
1898	44,055,278	15.3	675,148,705	58.2	392,770,320	222,694,920	98	148

Source: *Agricultural Yearbook*, 1899, p. 760; Guetter and McKinley, *Statistical Tables*, p. 26; next to last column calculated from *ibid*.

PERCENTAGES OF CROPPERS AND TENANTS TO ALL FARMERS,
1880–1900

Area	Cash Tenants			Share Croppers and Tenants			All Croppers and Tenants			Increase in 20 years
	1880	1890	1900	1880	1890	1900	1880	1890	1900	
United States	8.0	10.0	13.1	17.5	18.4	22.2	25.5	28.4	35.3	9.8
North Atlantic	7.0	7.9	9.8	9.0	10.5	11.0	16.0	18.4	20.8	4.8
South Atlantic	11.6	12.8	17.9	24.5	25.7	26.3	36.1	38.5	44.2	8.1
North Central	5.2	7.7	9.5	15.3	15.7	18.4	20.5	23.4	27.9	7.4
South Central	11.8	14.0	17.3	24.4	24.5	31.3	36.2	38.5	48.6	12.4
West	5.5	5.0	7.7	8.5	7.1	8.9	14.0	12.1	16.6	2.6
Alabama	16.8	24.7	33.3	30.0	23.9	24.4	46.8	48.6	57.7	10.9
Arizona	5.5	3.6	5.2	7.7	4.3	3.2	13.2	7.9	8.4	−4.8
Arkansas	10.5	13.2	15.3	20.4	18.9	30.1	30.9	32.1	45.4	14.5
California	8.9	8.7	12.5	10.9	9.1	10.6	19.8	17.8	23.1	3.3
Colorado	3.7	3.6	9.0	9.3	7.7	13.6	13.0	11.3	22.6	9.6
Connecticut	6.3	8.0	10.3	3.9	3.5	2.6	10.2	11.5	12.9	2.7
Delaware	5.8	6.7	7.8	36.6	40.2	42.5	42.4	46.9	50.3	7.9
Dist. of Columbia	34.5	34.3	42.0	3.7	2.4	1.1	38.2	36.7	43.1	4.9
Florida	15.1	11.5	19.3	15.8	12.1	7.2	30.9	23.6	26.5	−4.4
Georgia	13.4	17.2	26.2	31.5	36.4	33.7	44.9	53.6	59.9	15.0
Idaho	1.7	1.1	2.3	3.0	3.6	6.4	4.7	4.7	8.7	4.0
Illinois	8.1	12.1	14.5	23.3	21.9	24.8	31.4	34.0	39.3	7.9
Indiana	4.4	5.5	5.8	19.3	19.9	22.8	23.7	25.4	28.6	4.9
Indian Territory	....	....	19.5	....	....	55.4	....	....	74.9	74.9[a]
Iowa	4.5	12.4	19.5	19.3	15.7	15.4	23.8	28.1	34.9	11.1
Kansas	3.2	6.0	10.3	13.1	22.2	24.9	16.3	28.2	35.2	18.9
Kentucky	10.1	8.1	7.1	16.3	16.9	25.7	26.4	25.0	32.8	6.4
Louisiana	13.8	17.0	25.0	21.4	27.4	33.0	35.2	44.4	58.0	22.8
Maine	2.5	3.2	3.4	1.8	2.2	1.3	4.3	5.4	4.7	0.4
Maryland	9.6	8.0	8.8	21.4	23.0	24.8	31.0	31.0	33.6	2.6
Massachusetts	6.0	6.7	8.3	2.2	2.6	1.3	8.2	9.3	9.6	1.4
Michigan	3.3	4.8	4.8	6.8	9.2	11.1	10.1	14.0	15.9	5.8
Minnesota	1.4	2.9	3.3	7.8	10.0	14.0	9.2	12.9	17.3	8.1
Mississippi	17.1	21.0	32.0	26.7	31.8	30.4	43.8	52.8	62.4	18.6
Missouri	9.2	9.9	11.0	18.1	16.9	19.5	27.3	26.8	30.5	3.2
Montana	1.1	2.2	4.7	4.2	2.6	4.5	5.3	4.8	9.2	3.9
Nebraska	3.1	7.9	9.6	14.9	16.8	17.3	18.0	24.7	26.9	8.9
Nevada	4.5	3.9	7.4	5.2	3.6	4.0	9.7	7.5	11.4	1.7
New Hampshire	3.8	4.5	5.6	4.3	3.5	1.9	8.1	8.0	7.5	−0.6
New Jersey	10.5	11.2	15.3	14.1	16.0	14.6	24.6	27.2	29.9	5.3
New Mexico	0.4	0.7	2.2	7.7	3.8	7.2	8.1	4.5	9.4	1.3
New York	7.5	8.7	10.7	9.0	11.5	13.2	16.5	20.2	23.9	7.4
North Carolina	5.5	5.9	8.9	28.0	28.2	32.5	33.5	34.1	41.4	7.9
North Dakota	....	2.0	1.3	....	5.0	7.2	....	7.0	8.5	8.5[a]
Ohio	6.0	7.5	8.7	13.3	15.4	18.7	19.3	22.9	27.4	8.1
Oklahoma	....	0.1	8.0	....	0.6	13.0	....	0.7	21.0	21.0[a]
Oregon	4.6	4.2	7.4	9.5	8.3	10.4	14.1	12.5	17.8	3.7
Pennsylvania	8.0	8.5	10.6	13.2	14.8	15.4	21.2	23.3	26.0	4.8
Rhode Island	15.9	16.6	19.0	4.0	2.1	1.1	19.9	18.7	20.1	0.2
South Carolina	23.4	27.8	36.7	26.9	27.5	24 4	50.3	55.3	61.1	10.8
South Dakota	....	2.6	3.4	....	10.6	18.4	....	13.2	21.8	21.8[a]
Tennessee	11.6	11.3	12.6	22.9	19.5	28.0	34.5	30.8	40.6	6.1
Texas	6.9	8.8	7.3	30.7	33.1	42.4	37.6	41.9	49.7	12.1
Utah	0.6	1.2	2.6	4.0	4.0	6 2	4.6	5.2	8.8	4.2
Vermont	6.1	7.1	7.3	7.3	7.5	7.2	13.4	14.6	14.5	1.1
Virginia	11.3	9.4	9.9	18.2	17.5	20.8	29.5	26.9	30.7	1.2
Washington	3.2	3.0	7.1	4.0	5.5	2.3	7.2	8.5	9.4	2.2
West Virginia	6.9	5.9	8.1	12.3	11.9	13.7	19.2	17 8	21.8	2.6
Wisconsin	2.8	4.9	6.0	6.3	6.5	7.5	9.1	11.4	13.5	4.4
Wyoming	1.1	1.9	3.8	1.8	2.3	3.8	2.9	4.2	7.6	4.7

[a] Total increase given because of lack of data for 1880.

Source: *Twelfth Census: Agriculture*, I, 688–689.

Index

INDEX

427